Telling Facts:
History and Narration in Psychoanalysis

Psychiatry and the Humanities, Volume 13

*Assistant Editor*
Gloria H. Parloff

Published under the auspices of the
Forum on Psychiatry and the Humanities,
The Washington School of Psychiatry

# Telling Facts

## History and Narration in Psychoanalysis

Joseph H. Smith, M.D., *Editor*
Humphrey Morris, M.D.,
*Associate Editor*

The Johns Hopkins University Press
Baltimore and London

The Johns Hopkins University Press, 701 West 40th Street
Baltimore, Maryland 21211-2190
The Johns Hopkins Press Ltd., London

The paper used in this book meets the minimum
requirements of American National Standard for
Information Sciences—Permanence of Paper for Printed
Library Materials, ANSI Z39.48–1984.

Library of Congress Cataloging-in-Publication Data

Telling facts : history and narration in psychoanalysis /
Joseph H. Smith, editor ; Humphrey Morris, associate
editor.
    p.    cm.—(Psychiatry and the humanities ; v. 13 )
  Includes bibliographical references and index.
  ISBN 0-8018-4305-7 (alk. paper )
  1. Psychoanalysis.  2. Psychology—Biographical
methods.  3. History—Psychological aspects.
4. Discourse analysis, Narrative.  I. Smith, Joseph H.,
1927–  .  II. Morris, Humphrey.  III. Series.
RC321.P943  vol. 13 [RC506]
616.89 s—dc20 [616.89'17]          91-31044

## Contributors

*Rachel B. Blass*
Doctoral candidate, Department of Psychology, Hebrew University of Jerusalem; Smolen Fellow, Sigmund Freud Center for Psychoanalytic Study and Research, Hebrew University of Jerusalem

*Cynthia Chase*
Associate Professor, Department of English, Cornell University

*Dorrit Cohn*
Professor of German and Comparative Literature, Harvard University

*Barbara Johnson*
Professor of English and Comparative Literature; Chair, Afro-American Studies Department, Harvard University

*Richard H. King*
Reader in American Studies, University of Nottingham

*Thelma Z. Lavine*
Clarence J. Robinson Professor of Philosophy and American Culture, George Mason University

*Humphrey Morris*
Faculty, Psychosocial Program, McLean Hospital, and Boston Psychoanalytic Institute

*Roy Schafer*
Training and Supervising Analyst, Columbia University Center for Psychoanalytic Training and Research; private practice in New York City

*Bennett Simon*
Clinical Associate Professor of Psychiatry, Harvard Medical School, at the Cambridge Hospital; Training and Supervising Analyst, Boston Psychoanalytic Society and Institute; Sigmund Freud Professor of Psychoanalysis, Hebrew University of Jerusalem, 1989–90

*Joseph H. Smith*
Chairman, Forum on Psychiatry and the Humanitites, Washington School of Psychiatry; Supervising and Training Analyst, Washington Psychoanalytic Institute; Clinical Professor, Uniformed Services University of the Health Sciences

*Sherry Turkle*
Professor, Program in Sciences, Technology, and Society, Massachusetts Institute of Technology

*Hayden White*
University Professor of Historical Studies, University of California, Santa Cruz

*Robert Winer*
Chair, Psychoanalytic Object Relations Family and Couples Therapy Training Program, Washington School of Psychiatry; faculty, Washington Psychoanalytic Institute

# Contents

Introduction   ix
*Humphrey Morris*

1   Reading Freud's Legacies   1
*Roy Schafer*

2   Freud's Case Histories and the Question of Fictionality   21
*Dorrit Cohn*

3   Translating Transmission: Representation and Enactment in
Freud's Construction of History   48
*Humphrey Morris*

4   Translating the Transference: Psychoanalysis and the
Construction of History   103
*Cynthia Chase*

5   Mourning, Art, and Human Historicity   127
*Joseph H. Smith*

6   Echoes of the Wolf Men: Reverberations of Psychic
Reality   140
*Robert Winer*

7   Freud on His Own Mistake(s): The Role of Seduction in the
Etiology of Neurosis   160
*Rachel B. Blass and Bennett Simon*

8   The Quicksands of the Self: Nella Larsen and Heinz
     Kohut   184
     *Barbara Johnson*

9   Transformations: Psychoanalytical and Political   200
     *Richard H. King*

10  Psychoanalytic Culture: Jacques Lacan and the Social
     Appropriation of Psychoanalysis   220
     *Sherry Turkle*

11  Ricoeur, Freud, and the Conflict of Interpretations   264
     *Thelma Z. Lavine*

12  Historiography as Narration   284
     *Hayden White*

     Index   301

# Introduction

## *Humphrey Morris*

W hat is the truth of history in psychoanalysis? The difficulty of the question might be expressed in the ambiguities opened up by constructing a related question around a play on words: If history lies on the couch, what truth does it tell? The psychoanalysis of history has had its own history, beginning with the first "applied psychoanalysis," going through "psychohistory," and proliferating now in a burst of psychoanalytic-historical endeavors that range from "Freud studies" to political theory. Among historians and analysts the reception has been mixed; to many, these psychoanalytic pursuits of history have often seemed lacking in intellectual responsibility. The seemingly self-evident conjunction of history and psychoanalysis—the "and"—calls for closer questioning.

One might begin by asking about the order of the terms, the two directions of inquiry: history and psychoanalysis, psychoanalysis and history. "History and psychoanalysis" could include everything from the story of Freud and his followers, a story newly available archives are making it possible to retell, to an analysis of the evolution of psychoanalytic theory. "Psychoanalysis and history" could range from particular questions of motivation, as they are suggested by historical accounts of different sorts, to general questions of method, as they are raised by the way historians and other historically minded critics seem sometimes to have accorded superior authority to psychoanalytic imports. Yet orderings of the terms, and distinctions between the two directions of inquiry, seem unstable. History "and" psychoanalysis tends toward history "in" psychoanalysis, and vice versa; the vantage point becomes one of the things looked at. Exploration of the relationship between the fields ends up having to speak to the particular trouble each has had knowing where its boundaries lie, and where to turn for a standard of authoritative discourse.

While the essays here cover different areas of this large domain, a number of them express a focal and recurrent concern with the particular ways, not always self-evident, history can be said to be "in" psychoanalysis. "History," speaking broadly, is both the always changing aggregate of past "events" and presumed "causes," and the enterprise of presenting those events and causes, usually in the form of an explanatory narrative—both the facts that are telling, and the telling of facts. In the first sense, "history in psychoanalysis" would include the determining contingency of a variously buried, distorted, and constructed past; the reality, however inaccessible, of our temporal predicament; and the transmission of hypothesized structures through time. In the second sense, not rigorously separable from the first, "history in psychoanalysis" would be a set of narrative conventions for telling the past, conventions that historicize theoretical, atemporal structures and drives (or more contemporary replacements for drives) through the narration of their evolution and transmission. The place accorded developmental theory in psychoanalysis speaks to the power of these historicizing narrative conventions. History would be "in" psychoanalysis in the distinctive ways psychoanalysis historicizes its object, or its subjects, and that conferral of historicity would be fraught with historical motivations of all kinds, including the contradictory motivation to deny the power of history as a determining contingency in psychoanalytic theory and practice.

One effect of history in, or on, "psychoanalysis" has been to multiply and scatter the meanings of that term. "In order to assess properly each and every version of psychoanalysis," Roy Schafer writes here, "one must read it as a document situated in a personal context that in turn is linguistically situated in a historical and ideological context of dialogue .... We must accept the idea that psychoanalysis is not property: it belongs to no one in particular .... We cannot afford to neglect the transformations that take place in the dialogues that transmit psychoanalysis from one generation to the next." As it runs through the volume, this theme of transmission registers the impact of history in and on psychoanalysis. The history lesson would seem to be that there are at this point not only many psychoanalytic theories, but many psychoanalytic practices. However difficult that may make it to establish and maintain the distinctions between theories and practices, the professionally diverse authors gathered here also suggest that the distinctions matter. The various current practices of "the psychoanalysis of psychoanalysis," for all their refinements, can end up putting psychoanalysis of Freud's text on a level with Freud's psychoanalysis of his patients and with the psychoanalysis of Freud. In this they would drift back toward what they repudiate, the old psychobiographical approach to fiction that lumps the empirical author and the narrator together on the couch. It is a premise of this volume that to acknowledge the historicity of "psychoanalysis" is to start by drawing the distinctions among its varieties—among, for example, the psychoanalysis of a historical figure, the psychoanalysis of a fictional character, and the clinical psychoanalysis of a real person, and among the various "texts" that convey these different "lives."

The theoretical conjunctions and different practices of psychoanalyst Roy Schafer and historian Hayden White serve here to open the question of history in psychoanalysis. Schafer and White both approach the problem of historical reconstruction by asserting the centrality of narrative processes to the discovery and presentation of what count as facts. Each points to the necessity for any author of any history to establish, as a precondition of speaking or writing, figurative presences—and absences—as a narrator. This narrative necessity would affect every analysand, and every analyst. As Schafer puts it:

> We are forever telling stories about ourselves. In telling these self-stories *to others* we may, for most purposes, be said to be performing straightforward narrative actions. In saying that we also tell them *to ourselves*, however, we are enclosing one story within another. This is the story that there is a self to tell something to, a someone else serving as audience who is oneself or one's self. When the stories we tell others about ourselves concern these other selves of ours, when we say, for example, "I am not the master of myself," we are again enclosing one story within another. On this view, the self is a telling. From time to time and from person to person, this telling varies in the degree to which it is unified, stable, and acceptable to informed observers as reliable and valid. [1983, 218–19]

Schafer's interest in the narrative dimension of history in psychoanalysis shows in his framing of the psychoanalytic dialogue as first of all an intralinguistic event. Giving one's history, locating one's self-story in the historical past, is a present narrative action, a narration. The "traditional transference narration," in Schafer's reading, "tells of life history as static, archival, linear, reversible, and literally retrievable" (220). In his alternative telling, transference, "far from being a time machine by which one may travel back to see what one has been made out of, is a clarification of certain constituents of one's present psychoanalytic actions" (220). Most radically for psychoanalysis as a historical discipline, he asserts: "The time is always the present. The event is always an ongoing dialogue" (239). Is this simply to reject Freud's model of history and its founding "archaeological metaphor"? Or is it to raise, among others, the question taken up in different ways by several of the essays here: How do Freud's historical narratives function rhetorically in *his* telling of psychoanalytic theory and practice?

White's conception of the historian's work raises questions that are similarly disruptive. White grants to tradition that history has a "communicative function," that it can be "conceived to be a 'message' about a 'referent' (the past, historical events, and so on) the content of which is both 'information' (the 'facts') and an 'explanation' (the 'narrative' account)" (1987, 40). But for him history is also to be thought within a "performance model": "From the perspective provided by this model, a discourse is regarded as an apparatus for the production of meaning rather than as only a vehicle for the transmission of information about an extrinsic referent .... In historical discourse, the narrative serves to transform into a story a list of historical events that would otherwise be only a chronicle .... On this level of encodation, the historical discourse directs the reader's attention to a secondary referent, different in kind from the events that make up the primary referent, namely, the plot structures of the various story types cultivated in a given culture" (42–43). These plot structures, or the meanings they convey, are the truth of the past that only narrative can reveal: "Thus envisaged, the narrative figurates the body of events that serves as its primary referent and transforms these events into imitations of patterns of meaning that any literal representation of them as facts could never produce .... The 'truth' of narrative form can display itself only indirectly, that is to say, by means of *allegoresis*. What else could be involved in the representation of a set of real events as, for example, a tragedy, comedy, or farce?" (45–46).

Schafer brings similar ideas about historical narrative directly to bear on psychoanalysis:

> In saying there is no single knowable reality as a final test of truth, one establishes a basis for characterizing psychoanalysis as a narrative method for constructing a second reality. This second reality is organized largely in the terms of what Freud called unconscious mental processes ....
> this reality is as real as any other reality. Although this second reality sometimes overlaps the ordinary, conscious, rational, or pragmatic reality of everyday life, it need not do so, and in crucial respects it does not do so. In many ways, the second reality of psychoanalysis is more

akin to the reality constructed in poetry, story, visual arts, and myth.
[1983, 256]

Both Schafer and White acknowledge the heritage in their inno-
vations of Northrop Frye's (1957) archetypal criticism, which turns
on a "theory of myths." But such an approach could easily be called
into the service of the most reductive kind of psychoanalytic-historical
thinking. What is to prevent that? Schafer, when he associates the
historicizing "second reality" of psychoanalysis with myth, emphasizes
its aspect of narrative *construction* and rejects the "time machine"
tradition for which psychic reality would be more like a mythical
meaning waiting to be retrieved. That tradition, in and out of the
office, does depend methodologically on a less mediated form of
psychoanalytic-historical reduction, and can tend toward intellectual
imperialism as psychoanalysis itself becomes the historical "meaning"
it finds in everything else. Voices from fields that have been in this
way colonized by psychoanalysis speak to the loss behind the apparent
gain. To quote from the introduction to *The Trial(s) of Psychoanalysis*, an excellent recent collection of essays by nonpsychoanalyst
scholars: "Psychoanalysis has infiltrated such diverse areas as literature
(to which it owes its myths), linguistics, philosophy, anthropology,
history, feminism, psychology, archeology, neurology, to name some.
And it is in the notion of 'some,' perhaps, that lies the crux of the
problem. For there is in psychoanalysis an overt conviction that it
exists as the ultimate totality, of which everything else is a part" (Meltzer
1987, 216).

In clinical culture, the history of the "time machine" tradition's
treatment of the "historical" meanings it has claimed to retrieve is
given voice by analysands—many of them become analysts. They
describe their experience of what can now begin to be discussed as
an implicitly authoritarian ideology of a "neutral" analyst. This ideology
is often laid at Freud's door, and traced to what is taken to be the
historical literalism of his "archeological model." But the analyst is
hardly hidden, and hardly neutral, in Freud's case histories. The figure
of the neutral analyst appears, or rather disappears, as the absent
narrator of the psychoanalytic literature of the thirties and forties. As
a historical figure, this anonymous-analyst narrator, with its associated
conventions of retrieval of meaning, may say less about Freud than
about the import/export transferences attending upon the transmission of psychoanalysis by emigré analysts functioning as psychoanalytic
colonizers.

To admit that "psychoanalysis" itself does not stand outside the forms of history it has found in individual analysands or in culture, to admit to the historicity not only of its conventions of practice but of its most formalized theoretical statements about psychic structure, might be to begin to take account, in psychoanalysis, of the second historical reality pointed to by Schafer and White. This historicized psychoanalytic reality might now present itself as something less comprehensive and totalizing, something more particular to circumstance, something more narratively fragmented, than what we would wish for. Historian Dominick LaCapra suggests that the "problem of articulating history and psychoanalysis" springs from the distorting power of wishes for "a totality that never existed": "An obvious question is the extent to which the ideal of providing comprehensive accounts or global theories that 'bring order to chaos' entails phantasmatic investments—notably when this ideal prompts questionable methodological solutions, for example, in the form of classical narratives and noncommital analyses of situations in which one is transferentially implicated" (1987, 242). The question of "history and psychoanalysis" would on this view have especially to do with the ways psychoanalytic theory and practice are marked by their own historicity, and by defenses against it.

LaCapra emphasizes the Freudian point that any historian's relationship with the past, and through it with the present, is a transference relationship, and that in this transference repetition and denial come more easily than working through and mourning. Not only would the analysand and the analyst, as clinical historians, be caught in these pulls, but the theoretician, the theory, and the institution itself of psychoanalysis. History would be "in" psychoanalysis as a task of mourning not just particular lost objects, but wishfully invested ideals of "comprehensive accounts and global theories." If the construction of the narrative history of the transference *is* for Schafer the psychoanalytic way of mourning, for both Schafer and LaCapra the ideal of *a* narrative history, of one comprehensive telling, is what is principally, and most difficultly, to be mourned. Whatever sense psychoanalysis helps make of the past, facing the "second reality" of psychoanalysis, and of the past, would now mean tolerating not only greater complexity, but confusion, chaos, and non-sense. The temptation simply to equate the construction of history in psychoanalysis with the finding of meaning would be among the wishes to be analyzed by both parties to the transference. As analysts with many histories of training and many varieties of technique, the authors in this volume seem to me united in that task.

## References

Frye, Northrop. *Anatomy of Criticism*. Princeton: Princeton University Press, 1957.

LaCapra, Dominick. "History and Psychoanalysis." In *The Trial(s) of Psychoanalysis*, edited by Françoise Meltzer. *Critical Inquiry* 13, no. 2 (1987): 222–51.

Meltzer, Françoise, editor. *The Trial(s) of Psychoanalysis. Critical Inquiry* 13, no. 2 (1987): 222–51.

Schafer, Roy. *The Analytic Attitude*. New York: Basic Books, 1983.

White, Hayden. *The Content of the Form: Narrative Discourse and Historical Representation*. Baltimore: Johns Hopkins University Press, 1987.

Telling Facts:
History and Narration in Psychoanalysis

# 1    Reading Freud's Legacies

## Roy Schafer

*I*

I feel especially honored to have been invited to deliver a lecture dedicated to Dr. Edith Weigert. For many years I have felt a deep sense of kinship with the humanist-existentialist thrust of her contributions to psychoanalytic thought and practice. She illuminated the importance that psychoanalysis accords to the ways in which people define themselves, both for themselves and for others; this they do through their choices of action and the unconscious, if not conscious, recognition of the responsibility they bear for their actions. In these ways, they accept that they are in and of this world, whatever the formative influences to which they have been subject, however differently they may experience this world consciously, however they may impinge upon it. They feel that they are agents, and they present themselves in analysis as human beings, even if as human beings who are trying to shed or transcend their humanness or else trying to safeguard that humanness by leading manifestly inert, untrusting, and lonely existences.

As evidence of my affinity to Dr. Weigert's approach (Weigert 1970), I remind you that in my 1970 paper, "The Psychoanalytic Vision of Reality," I presented a version of the humanistic existentialism intrinsic to psychoanalysis; there I emphasized the analyst's phenomenological focus on modes of experience and especially the analyst's recognition of the tragic knots in human lives and in analysis itself. In my later work on action language and narration (1976, 1978, 1981, 1983), I

1

have been attempting, among other things, to develop further certain aspects of this humanistic existentialism. Thus, for me as for her, people appear neither as test tubes in an experiment, nor as mechanical or electrical mental apparatuses, nor as embryos simply undergoing genetically programmed development. Rather they appear as persons; they are persons in our consulting rooms who should be so represented in our theories as well. I shall return to these propositions later on when I detail the view I take of Freud's contributions and some of the conceptualizations I consider interesting, desirable, and perhaps even necessary if we are to recast his legacy in modern terms.

## II

To give a reading of Freud's contributions and their development up to the present is to face the future as well as the past. Ostensibly, those who write or speak on Freud direct attention to the recent and remote past in order to develop an objective account of a legacy and perhaps to suggest what has been done with it. In this effort, however, they cannot hope to be simply descriptive: like it or not, they are prescriptive at the same time, for, inevitably, they chart a future for psychoanalysis. I say so because I believe that all accounts of psychoanalytic history, however conventionalized they may be, are bound to place certain matters in the foreground, relegate others to the background, and ignore still others. On this understanding, historical accounts have to be imbued with their authors' value judgments. The narratives indicate what the authors hold dear, and it is through this implementation of values that they prescribe a future. In effect, the historian says, "This is what psychoanalysis should be," and in the same breath, two related prescriptions as well: "This is the best way to talk about psychoanalysis," and "This is the way to be or become a psychoanalyst."

If this much is accepted, then it can be added that the mode of telling prescribes allegiance to a particular discourse. A discourse is constituted in part by interlocking modes of establishing values and formulating and challenging truth claims and in part by the practices that, it is believed, legitimize this discourse and are in turn legitimized by it. Therefore, to say that a discussion of Freud's legacy expresses one's aspirations for psychoanalysis is also to argue on behalf of specific values, truth claims, and practices. This, then, must be true of the reading of Freud's legacy that I present. Although my reading obviously owes a lot to familiar discursive traditions in our field, it also draws heavily upon what may be called twentieth-century Enlightenment.[1]

I present this account because I want to convey my version of how we might try to situate Freud in the discourse of contemporary intellectuality. Intellectually, Freud was a child of the Enlightenment that dates roughly from the late seventeenth century, and we would, I think, all agree that it was in the context of the development of that Enlightenment that he tried to be up to date. In this "official" aspect of his effort, he provided a rationalistic, empiricist, objectivist account of his methods, the findings based on them, and his conclusions. He presented himself as working within the prevailing axioms and conventions of discourse of the natural sciences of his time. He also drew heavily on the content of what was, for him, contemporary psychology, anthropology, philosophy, archeology, philology, and other disciplines, all of which were cast from the same epistemological and methodological mold.

In this discourse, language is taken unreflectively as a transparent medium of communication. It is not regarded as bound to person, time, place, culture, or specific conventions. Consequently, Freud did not regard the version of it he used to report his psychoanalytic work as having evolved in such a way as to express and serve primarily the interests of the white, male bourgeoisie of the Western world. Freud viewed language as a transparent and sufficient medium that is, however challenging its content may be, in harmony with the established order of things and what he called its "self-evident" morality.

But the terms of modern critical thought are not the terms of this earlier and still widely endorsed Enlightenment. In the newer context, language occupies center stage in theoretical thinking and research. Language is seen as that which makes the world that it tells about. Moreover, it makes this world through implicit as well as explicit dialogue; that is to say, it functions and has functioned always in a social context. Language now is a variable and not a constant; it is a message in the guise of a medium, a set of perspectives rather than a clear glass window on the world, an ideological process rather than an essence, a specific cultural net rather than a universal mode of exchange. Additionally, it is an instrument of power to be wielded for good, as in therapy, or for bad, as in racism and sexism. In my reading of Freud's legacy, therefore, I think it appropriate to try to situate him for our time, that is, amid the multiple perspectives that characterize this linguistic turn. Although my effort here is incomplete, sketchy, and highly contestable, it conveys my allegiance to the idea of psychoanalysis as a discipline with an ongoing life.

To focus on the language of psychoanalysis requires paying particularly close attention to its dialogic nature. Equally important is the recognition that the practice of psychoanalysis is rooted in dialogue between analyst and analysand, between analytic teacher and student, and between colleagues. So much being a matter of interchange, we may say that through dialogue psychoanalysis keeps coming into being. All the more reason to establish a dialogic context for this presentation.

To develop this context, let us consider first dialogue in relation to the general history of ideas. Progress in any discipline has always depended on continuing dialogue. Continuing dialogue over conflicting aspirations and truth claims helps refine one's notions of importance, one's methods, samples, and arrangements of data, one's logical tools, one's conclusions, and always the rhetoric one relies on to make a case persuasively. Through dialogue, one also learns better how the opposition makes its case. Learning that, one then tries to find common ground, and, failing that, one begins to develop more persuasive arguments for one's point of view. In the process, once the questions asked are modified, the answers are framed differently, and even the subject of inquiry may be changed to whatever now seems to be more urgent or more fruitful than its predecessors. Goals are never set with finality. And taking into account all those contemporary dialogues aimed at connecting as well as contrasting the different perspectives associated with race, gender, and social class can only add further to the sense that the history of ideas, of theory and practice, is always in flux.

Turning next to the history of psychoanalysis, I suggest that, from what has already been said, it follows that history should be written, read, and taught from this dialogic point of view. To give one example of the movement of dialogue: in reaction to changing times and interests, based in part on extensive philosophy-of-science debates over the problems of traditional metapsychology and in part on the widening scope of analytic perception and practice, which has been increasing the influence of Kleinian object-relational thought, we have been witness in the course of one generation to a spectacular change: specifically, most psychoanalysts have shifted their discussions away from refined elaborations and critiques of the theory of psychic energy and the energic underpinnings of psychic structure; further, they have even been moving away from rigorous debates over the idea of structure itself and the explanatory value of structural concepts. As I make it out, the present trend is to use the term *structure* descriptively. *Structure* used descriptively merely refers to whatever the observer pieces together into stable patterns of motives or modes of experience and overt conduct that are relevant to the thesis being developed. Unlike Freud, one does not regard structure as a fixed essence of things to be discovered and does not ponder the question of how it is ever possible for structure to come into existence, develop, and remain stable, all as though structure were an essence found in nature.

Instead, increasing numbers of analysts seem to find it more engaging and worthwhile to join dialogues that feature object relations and self-experience and corresponding refinements in theoretical and technical conceptions of early development as it is reflected in the experience of transference and countertransference. In these dialogues they weigh a variety of approaches to understanding and modifying psychopathology of every sort, and they emphasize particularly the development and the disruption of their empathy with archaic motives, fantasies, anxieties, and defensive shifts of orientation and experience.

Earlier, I mentioned the need for persuasive rhetoric, and because rhetorical issues figure prominently in what follows, I should explain now what I meant. If all cases are made through implicit or explicit dialogue, each such case can be developed adequately only if its insecure or assailable aspects are recognized, explicitly confronted, and either persuasively justified or artfully dodged. In any event, the success of one's argument depends to a noteworthy extent on rhetorical adroitness. Rhetoric is, however, not something one chooses to use; every way of speaking or writing is subject to rhetorical analysis, and every way may be used more or less adroitly. Emphasizing and exploring how this is so is a conspicuous part of the linguistic turn in the recent history of ideas.

I shall take a moment here to illustrate this rhetorical perspective on psychoanalytic language. My example is the drab style of much of the psychoanalytic literature. I suggest that this style is a specialized and conventionalized rhetorical attempt to be persuasive. It attempts to be persuasive by creating an image of the writer as a reliable member of the Old Enlightenment: a neutral, value-free, countertransference-free, well-trained scientific observer; a genderless, raceless, classless expert delivering a monologue that gives all the appearance of having been stripped of rhetorical ploys. In part, this image is designed to instill a false sense of security in the reader. "Trust me," it says. And unquestioning trust is badly needed in many cases because it serves to blind the reader to two obvious difficulties that arise in connection with the detailed deterministic explanations usually featured in psychoanalytic publications. The first difficulty is that those deterministic explanations cannot stand up to the simplest of *traditional* scientific tests, if indeed any such test can even be formulated, because the testing of psychoanalytic propositions calls for a quite different approach to corroboration. The second difficulty is that the deterministic accounts do not satisfy the fictitious standard of perfect authorial disinterestedness, for usually it is easy to show that their author is trying hard to win readers over to the conclusions drawn by more than the content and logic of the "findings" reported. That *more* is a self-conscious rhetorical effort to be persuasive, and it is felt to be required because others working in the same area have already presented persuasive arguments for other conclusions or else soon will.

I want to add an interpretation of defense to this account of the drabness of much psychoanalytic rhetoric. I suggest that this conventionlized drabness is an attempt to deny that there is much about Freud's creation of psychoanalysis, and thus of his legacy to us, that may be characterized as a triumph of vivid and masterful rhetoric. Freud wrote psychoanalysis: he wrote it in the teeth of powerful scientific opponents, and he wrote it persuasively. Consequently, in reading him, one cannot separate his content from what is widely acknowledged to be his powerful and beguiling, and sometimes even beautiful, style. Freud's winning language is now known, however, to have covered a multitude of shortcomings in his arguments. One may say so now in this more enlightened and permissive period of psychoanalytic history without being thought to deny the least aspect of Freud's creative genius. Other writers on psychoanalysis, even those most closely identified with Freud, use their own rhetoric and so create more or less different versions of the discipline.

My general point is that there is no absolutely specific and static Freudian essence. Nothing lies beyond any one writer's rhetoric and thus beyond the realm of implicit and explicit dialogue. Consequently, in order to assess properly each and every version of psychoanalysis, one must read it as a document situated in a personal context that, in turn, is linguistically situated in a historical and ideological context of dialogue.

*III*

All this said, how shall we begin to approach more directly the large topic of Freud's legacy? I shall begin by proposing that we give up the idea that there is just one legacy to sum up. For in a world forever constituted anew through continuing dialogue, there can never be only one theoretical or technical legacy. There can only be lega*cies*, linguistic legacies, legacies that are theoretical through and through.

Freud's texts will remain open forever to alternative readings and writings: scientific, literary, and cultural. The absolutist writings and readings on theory and technique, with which we are so familiar and which still are published in official analytic journals, will with time become a thing of the past; already they come across to some of us as narrowly doctrinaire if not old-fashioned bravura performances. In the perspective of the modern Enlightenment, it will be Freud's readers and Freudian writers who will continuously co-create Freud's legacy. This they will do by how they read his texts and by how and what they write. As the readers and writers change—and they do change— Freudian psychoanalysis changes.

Further support for this elevation of reading and writing can be mustered by any survey of single topics in the analytic literature, for it requires no strain to read each such segment of our literature as a battlefield of competing, incompatible, and newly triumphant claims as to what Freud said, meant, intended, or laid the groundwork for. One example is the ongoing dispute over Freud's general orientation to psychoanalysis that is based on the assumption that there is a single best or correct way to translate Freud from one language to another: Was he scientific or humanistic? Does *Ich* mean "ego" or "self" or both? Another example is the often repeated, authoritarian recommendation on how to settle disagreements: "Back to Freud!" When that recommendation is made as a simple absolute rather than as a prod to keep up one's reading of Freud, it suggests wrongly that one could hope to read Freud in an absolutely selfless, value-free, culture-free, nondialogic way and thereby reach not only the right answer for the moment but the one and only true Freud. "Back to Freud!" is perhaps the greatest rhetorical ploy of all. The adviser is saying, "Back to *my* Freud; repress the rest."

What is the basis of these interpretative wars? It is not only that Freud was not always perfectly consistent or explicit in his creative work; nor is it just that the rhetoric through which he created and conveyed his contributions ranged from the highly tentative, uncertain, apologetic, and ingratiating all the way to the virtually dictatorial, and ranged as well from the rigorously and mechanistically scientific all the way to the free-flowing and evocatively humanistic; nor yet are these interpretive wars based solely on what is commonly recognized to be the influence of personality, training, and experience on the way readers read Freud and new writers write Freud. There is more to add to this list of undeniably important factors.

Here, I shall discuss only one additional set of factors: those related to power. The adversarial readings and writings I have referred to have been based to a significant extent on both the *general* history of changing organizational conditions within the psychoanalytic movement and the *specific* history of official policy regarding the programming of meetings, the publication of articles in the analytic journals, the making of referrals to colleagues, and the selection of candidates. In these respects, it seems as though, in any one period of time, power has played a major role in deciding the truth about Freud's legacy. I refer to power that has not always been attained and maintained through intellectual and clinical accomplishment and consensus.

It should come as no surprise that the play of power within organizations of analysts has figured importantly in the intellectual and professional history of psychoanalysis: the exercise of power is always with us. Psychoanalysis is no exception to this general principle, and the principle need not stimulate despair. What is not only hopeful but interesting in this regard is that, necessarily, shifts do occur in the conditions of power and in the modes of its employment. These shifts are the result of dialogue that cannot be silenced. And correlated with these shifts are shifts in the intensity of the surveillance, discipline, and punishment of those who oppose or disregard the doctrines that the powerful try to enforce. It is these shifts that enable changes to be established in what has been taken to be important and true. Consequently, one may say that changes in power will always play an important role in the flux that characterizes the truths and the values of psychoanalysis. Consideration of Freud's legacy cannot be split off from the history of power.

Witness, for example, the relatively recent growth of interest in the preoedipal period, that period that was once not to be made too much of. With this growth of interest has come progressive articulation of the concepts of mothering, parenting, and selfhood; an ever more insistent emphasis on understanding early aggression and early stages of guilt in treating extreme cases; and also special attention to preestablished adaptation, the acquisition of language, and early modes of cognition. Another example is found in the many competing and as yet unstable but terribly important modifications of what has been represented as the psychoanalytic truths about women and the importance of those truths for the general theory of psychoanalysis. Not one of these changes has taken place outside the arena of power; each has had to be fought for, and some are still being fought for and often fought over as well.

Power in new hands; power diffused and wielded differently; surveillance relaxed; professional discipline and punishment themselves under extreme suspicion, not to speak of their curtailment by actual or potential intramural strifes and even lawsuits: these changes have allowed and fostered an altered set of facts of life in contemporary psychoanalysis. One new feature of today's freer psychoanalytic life is the tolerance, both genuine and feigned, of multiple and competing claims about what psychoanalysis is. Another feature is that, far from being monolithic, each contemporary school of psychoanalytic thought may be heard more accurately as a din of voices in argument over readings. No longer is it possible to claim legitimately to be presenting an exclusive, purportedly final or unarguable account of Freud's legacy.

I suggest that this pluralistic view of Freud's legacy, this view that there can only be legacies that are forever subject to change, is itself one of Freud's legacies. Although it is my impression that Freud always wanted to be in control of the development of psychoanalysis, I believe that he also wanted his discipline to be open to challenge and improvement through revision. Even if he often seemed to want to be the absolute judge of proposed change, if not the prime originator of it, in his role as dedicated scientist he presented psychoanalysis with the correct recognition that, for it to qualify as a science, its propositions should be forever on trial. Certainly, he continually reviewed his own formulations and changed them. But in his wanting to have the last word, he revealed that he did not always live up to his own ideals, for it is one consequence of the open-minded scientific attitude that he espoused so well in other respects that there never can be a last word; no one ever can have the last word, because no investigator or writer can control history. Certainly, no one can ever end it. No one can stop the ongoing dialogue. Any one language has its limits. Power and prestige have their limits. Closure will elude us forever.

No one can even dictate how a name is to be used. Freud, contrary to his wish, could not even own the word *psychoanalysis* for long. Although one may regret, as I do, the extreme diffusion of meaning of *psychoanalysis* in today's world, one cannot hope to halt or reverse it. Diffusion has already gone so far that, whenever *psychoanalysis* is used, one must wonder just what it refers to. In my view, the history of psychoanalysis has reached a point where it has become futile to argue whether this or that and nothing else is the true or real psychoanalysis. At this point, it makes more sense to argue that only this or that specific idea or practice conforms to the version of psychoanalysis to which one is committed, or to the version that a certain group of respected peers consider to have the longest and strongest tradition behind it or the greatest heuristic power. Today, one must always be prepared to argue the merits of one's chosen position.

It was not always so, or so plainly a matter of choice of what to value and wish to transmit to the future. We must accept the idea that psychoanalysis is not property: it belongs to no one in particular. On this view, much controversy in psychoanalysis can be seen to be no more than pointless and history-blind debate over ownership.

*IV*

We cannot afford to neglect the transformations that take place in the dialogues that transmit psychoanalysis from one generation to the next. This consideration alone could compel us to regard Freud's legacies as ongoing processes. One may say that these legacies continuously come into being; they are constantly in transition; they do not remain identical to themselves. Or one may say that for every generation, Freud is always here and now, never there and then.

I suggested earlier that transmission of ideas occurs through a process that may be called a dialogue between Freud and his readers and writers, and I want now to add that, phenomenologically speaking, in this dialogue Freud may be said to be constantly talking back to his readers. I have in mind the Freud who is always here and now. His constant presence is felt by those who keep restudying his texts without being locked into an infantile transference to him or to their teachers: they find that the texts are so rich that they continuously correct and supplement their earlier readings; the texts even provide reminders of how Freud paved the way toward analytic ideas that keep on being put forward as new, as truly modern, even as revolutionary and superior alternatives to his ideas. In saying this I am not implying that Freud knew it all, nor that he could have known all that he did know in the same way a modern analyst knows it, nor yet that he would approve of much that is now commonly accepted by those who called themselves classical Freudian analysts. Amazingly, however, there is a Freud who, for serious students, can be felt to be holding up his end of a lively and invariably refocusing conversation.

This inexhaustible and zestful readiness for continuing dialogue with his changing readers is another of Freud's legacies. That there is a Freud who can be always present to us is attributable to his having written in a way that steadily invites the continuation of dialogue. In his welcoming aspect, he stands above many of his influential follow-ers—specifically, those whose tone suggests that we are being told what's what rather than being prompted to consider what's next. It is only in this processive and dialogical sense that the admonition, "Back to Freud!" can have a nonauthoritarian, modern meaning, the meaning that it is in the nature of the work never to be done.

## V

Engaging as this contribution to dialogue may be, Freud made a far more fundamental one. I venture to claim that out of Freud's genius issued an altogether new form of dialogue. He made it possible for therapists and patients to engage in consequential forms of transformational dialogue that had never existed before. He showed therapists how to do things with words to help revise radically their patients' hitherto fixed, unconsciously directed constructions of both subjective experience and action in the world: to use words to change lives in a thought-through, insightful manner. No one before him had done anything as profound, comprehensible, skillful, basically rational, and effective. Of the many possible ways to describe this monumental achievement, I submit the following. Freud's clinical dialogue alters in crucial ways the analysand's consciously narrated presentation of the self and its history among people by destabilizing, deconstructing, and defamiliarizing it. I note before proceeding further that it is arbitrary to discuss the processes of destabilization, deconstruction, and defamiliarization in sequence, as though they were logically and temporally distinguished; however, my account will, I think, be clearer if I describe each of these processes somewhat differently and invoke each in a somewhat different context. Think of it as using different windows to look into the same room and never seeing things quite the same way. I also note that although much communication goes on nonverbally, it is conventionally accepted that a *psychoanalytic* therapy requires bringing significant issues into verbal dialogue; psychoanalysis is the "talking cure."

To achieve the destabilization, deconstruction, and defamiliarization of the patient's narratives, the classical psychoanalytic dialogue uses the free association method; frequent sessions for continuity; and sessions that last for most or all of an hour so that time is available for each day's dialogue to develop, double back on itself, seemingly cancel itself out, or otherwise enter into the larger treatment process. The classical psychoanalytic dialogue also features the interpretation of defenses against full expression and felt interaction; and with the help of the mixture of the "regressive" and "progressive" phenomena it elicits, it reconstructs the way in which the history of these defenses and their motives is grounded in the typical subjective danger situations of early childhood.

Because the life narratives with which the analysand has come for treatment are more or less stabilized by these defenses, the invaluable analysis of defense, insofar as it is effective, necessarily *destabilizes* them. The process destabilizes both the established stories of guilt, trauma, neglect, misunderstanding, and blissful, unambivalent love, and the stories that seem to have been put together spontaneously in the thick of the ongoing analysis. The patient develops a new slant on lives that have been lived and that are yet to be lived; at the least, the versions of lives that gain importance are far more complex, less rigid and one-sided, and more tragically and ironically constructed.

What now of *deconstruction*? The analysand's narratives are deconstructed through the analyst's steadily focusing on (1) their internal contradictions, their being founded on displacements, condensations, and marginalizations, and their erasures of expectable, emotion-laden, crucial life experience; and (2) the hidden hierarchies of value in taken-for-granted polarities such as male-female, active-passive, and dominant-submissive. Psychoanalytic deconstruction brings out particularly the contradictory or otherwise incoherent types of overt and fantasized relationship that the analysand tries to develop with the relatively neutral and relatively opaque figure of the analyst. This deconstructive handling of transference clarifies the complex, unstable, and conflictual nature of the analysand's enduring attempts at self-definition and relationship. The analyst also takes up many paradoxical reasons for repetitious enactments of these often quite painful transferences. In principle, though for practical reasons not always in practice, nothing is taken for granted about any version of self, relationship, or reality in general.

Contrary to popular prejudice, however, deconstruction is not a lofty name for destructiveness and disillusionment; psychoanalytic deconstruction makes possible new and sounder construction, in particular the construction of more fulfilling narratives of lives in progress. The analyst uses the analytically defined elements of narrative incoherence to begin to *retell* the analysand's presentations and to bring the analysand into the process of retelling, now in the terms of unconsciously developed and maintained conflict and taken-for-granted or well-rationalized compromise formation. At the same time, the analyst and analysand together construct *a* history for what Freud called the analysand's "conditions for loving," to which phrase many of us today would want to add "conditions for hating" and "conditions for playing dead or empty." Among the virtues of the new constructions will be their being both more confident and more provisional than those they have replaced. (It is to take account of variation among analysts that I say *a* history, not *the* history.)

Certainly, any dedicated deconstructionist would approach even these new and provisional analytic narratives with an eye to their incoherent and contradictory elements; being the kind of method it is, deconstruction accepts no self-exclusionary limits on its application; it recognizes that to develop its position it must use the very language whose basic coherence it regularly challenges. But here the therapeutic goals of the analytic dyad intervene: a judgment, based on shared health values, is made by analyst and analysand that any attempt at further change at this time might create more problems than benefits or might just lack adequate momentum, and it may also be judged that the patient is in a more or less adequate position to continue the work of analysis independently, as the need arises and to the extent necessary. At this point, the joint work of deconstruction and new construction comes to an end.

There is more, however—specifically, the *defamiliarization* accomplished by the analytic dialogue. In the therapeutic interaction, the analyst begins to retell insightfully, roundedly, and empathically much that the analysand initially has told and is telling naively, abjectly, seductively, or aggressively and, in any case, defensively. By introducing new or revised or unexpectedly interdependent story lines as major amendments to the analysand's narratives or as supplements to them, the analyst begins the process of defamiliarizing them and here, too, engages the analysand in the process. The nature of life history changes; its variables and its conceptions of time and place, of process and progress, and of relevance continue to change. As the patient's sense of the "timeless unconscious" develops, established accounts of present circumstances and future prospects also become less familiar. Secretly or obviously, the analysand always approaches with great trepidation these new ways of making history and the new versions that result from them; consequently, much working through always remains to be done, both during the analysis and after its conclusion. Insightful mastery is achieved through the kind of repeated defamiliarization and working through that psychoanalysis alone is capable of effecting. With the sense of real life as an ongoing process, the patient is prepared to accept the fruits of these labors as always open to further modification.

In the foreground of these retellings is the figure of the analysand as an active party to the bringing about of much that initially is or was experienced in passive, frequently victimized terms. In this respect, the dialogue helps the analysand shift toward some form of assertive and responsible psychosexual and psychosocial maturity. In other respects, however, as in the case of hitherto denied or minimized trauma or abuse, the analysand remains no longer defensively omni-potent, being better able to accept that in many respects she or he has been, is, and will be more or less passive, helpless, needful, or yielding. In the latter respects, one often observes a beneficial reduc-tion of grandiose inflations of self-esteem, guilt, independence, and imperviousness.

Freud taught us to see the action in apparent inaction and accident, but he taught us, too, how much of our sense of power and control is illusory, is compensatory fantasy that denies and reverses the pow-erful and sometimes dire necessities of the body. He showed us that we share with others in our world a great amount of helplessness over our life cycles. In this, as in the entirety of his psychology, which is a psychology of unconscious conflict and necessary ambiguities and paradoxes that pervade human experience and action, he introduced into our conceptions of tragedy and irony a modern tone (Schafer 1970); the understandings and narratives of human existence could never be the same. We may add this legacy to all the others.[2]

## VI

One outstanding feature of the analytic dialogue is its showing by interpretation that, both in the past and in the present, dialogic ex-perience is never limited to two people present to one another physically. Far from it. The analysis brings it about that the analysand is able to develop and tolerate accounts of the dialogue that no longer feature predominantly abstract tendencies, general patterns, habits, socially defined traits, and social existence defined only in the con-ventional terms of behavioral social interaction. Instead, the crucial analytic versions tell of a multitude of voices rising from his or her own imagined inner world as well as a multitude of inner-world voices that, by perception or projection or both, the analysand locates in the analyst or others in the surround. Ideally, analysis brings it about that this concordant and discordant chorus of voices is no longer obliter-ated or muted by repression and other defenses and no longer mis-located by projection. Once it can be heard clearly, it is accessible to sorting out; each influential voice may then become clear enough to be traced back to early experience in real or imagined relations with others; at least, its power is reduced because it is recognized for what it is. Thus far I have spoken only of voices, but of course other powerful

sensory images of the inner multitude, some of them purely kines-
thetic, are often presented eloquently.

Particularly significant for the analytic narrative are all those fantastic, libidinal and aggressive, body-centered, emotion-laden elaborations and misunderstandings that young children regularly introduce
into their experience of their relationships and then elaborate further
over time. The sorting out of these features and sources is rendered
especially difficult and time consuming by the interplay of introjective
and projective processes that, according to the analytic retelling,
characterizes the analysand's unconsciously carried-out construction
of experience both in the past and in the here-and-now of the
analytic relationship. In other words, the interpenetration of inner
and outer worlds and past and present worlds is extensive, often
subtle, and regularly fluid, and its analysis can never totally eliminate
ambiguity.

*VII*

These inner-world phenomena make up a large part of another of
Freud's great legacies—specifically, his idea of psychic reality. That
idea embraces much more than what is conventionally meant by subjectivity and its individual variations. In psychoanalysis, psychic reality
begins with that conventional notion; in addition, however, it goes on
to include the analytically essential idea of unconscious fantasies that
include all those twists and turns that are encountered in dreams and
their interpretation.

Psychic reality refers to still more than that. It refers as well to
individually different and persisting wishful but conflictual and com-
promised modes of *constructing* new experiences on all levels of
development. It refers to how, unconsciously, people make and remake
their own subjective experience, how they do so continuously, that
is, when awake as well as asleep, and how, at later stages of development, they may have to exaggerate the weight and impact of their
preserved accounts of early experience. Thus it is that they may be
said to live in a second reality.

This second reality lies beyond conventional reality. In it, space and
time and identity are in constant flux and disarray, so that then and
now, there and then, no and yes, disturbing and insignificant, I and
thou, all co-exist, mingle, or change places; all may be reversed or
fragmented or otherwise isolated from conventional rationality. Freud's
dialogue centers more and more on this powerfully influential second
reality. The dialogic chorus of voices is heard mostly in this reality.

The multitude of images resides there. The transference and defenses live in it. Dreams and screen memories portray it.

The "first" reality, by which is meant not one that necessarily originated earlier in time but one that is conscious, rationally organized, impersonal, and adapted to convention—that reality is not dismissed as irrelevant or altogether inconsequential. For clinical purposes, however, it provides only a shrunken account of the analysand's mental activity and so is limited in its therapeutic usefulness. It is the largely unconscious second reality that emerges as the chief locale or scene of effective psychoanalysis.

## VIII

Freud's new dialogue may be characterized in yet another way; it is a supplementary way in that this characterization implies all that has come before it. One may say that Freud developed a therapeutically consequential dialogue that, to a very large extent, is about itself. Basically, it is self-reflexive. However much the dialogue refers to other matters, such as past life history or current problems in work, love, and self-esteem, again and again it takes a self-referential turn. The focus necessarily and productively shifts to what was said or left unsaid in the analytic relationship and how it was or was not recounted, and when, why, and on what understanding. The focus also shifts to how each development is encased in a set of hopeful and fearful fantasies. Further, it shifts to the ways in which the formal features of the verbal and nonverbal dialogue may be construed either as attempts to remember and communicate with the analyst through enactment much material that has been deeply repressed or, if not that, as attempts to introduce new material in order to refute or confirm interpretations already in play in the analysis. These formal features may even be construed in both ways: repeating the old *and* introducing the new. In any case, these communications are made mostly unconsciously.

There are, however, many ways in which a dialogue could be about itself; it is the *psychoanalytic* way that Freud devised and developed to a considerable degree, the way that I have been reviewing, that seems to me to be essential to the dialogue's therapeutic and transformational potential.

## IX

It remains to take up briefly what I consider to be another of Freud's great legacies: his contribution to the further development of feminism. If we are to situate Freud in contemporary intellectual life, then we must take him up in relation to the profoundly influential, relatively recent revolution in critical theory that has been sparked by feminism.

I claim Freud for feminism even though it is now plain that he shared and implicitly endorsed much of the bourgeois sexism of his time. Among other things, he was dismissive of feminism itself. On the other hand, however, he was at least able to begin to transcend his biases in his more specifically psychoanalytic propositions. His curiosity and creativity did not stop at the borders of the mentality of the men he studied. However imperfectly and even woundingly he did it, by attempting to present women as fully human, by reversing the tendency to marginalize them, he participated relatively early in the historical process of restoring to them aspects of worth and dignity equal to those of men. This he did not only through the very fact of his studying women in their psychological development, dilemmas, and psychological ailments, but also through his clarifying the anxiety-ridden, conflictual basis of male sexuality, including the anxiety and aggression toward women that men express in their simultaneous fear, idealization, and degradation of them. This psychoanalytic "humbling" of men could not but elevate women to the level of fellow creatures. Freud did all this for women in the same way that he laid the basis for a deeper understanding of the prejudices against, and the mistreatment of, children, Jews, people of color, foreigners, the sexually unorthodox, and all the others included in the list of suspects usually rounded up for discriminatory treatment by the traditional white male community, whose world this Western one pretty much still is. A wonderful legacy, indeed! It is a legacy of liberating and humane ideas and a legacy of incredible boldness of vision and persistence.

## X

I should like to return in conclusion to my introductory comment on the humanist-existentialist aspect of Freud's creation. It must be said first that Freud could not have been prepared to consider that aspect suitable for theoretical purposes. Instead, he simply took it for granted as a component of both clinical empathy and his novelistic feel for the language of clinical work. For theory he turned to the scientific models of his day: Newton, Helmholtz, Darwin, and others in their line. These were men who had concerned themselves with the grand concepts of force, energy, structure, and mechanism, and also with biological survival, adaptation, and evolution. They had taken for granted the account of the scientific observer as a totally detached, objective figure. In their tradition, Freud tried to construct the grand meta-psychology that would establish psychoanalysis as a respectable empirical science.

Historically and psychohistorically understandable, Freud's effort has been said, by a number of eminent commentators, to have manifested misunderstanding of his own creation. Neither as a therapy nor as a method of investigation, nor as a theory of the human mind, did psychoanalysis follow the established models. It can even be claimed that Freud misunderstood the place of psychoanalysis in the roster of disciplines, for although it was, as he claimed, a psychology, psychoanalysis required a conceptual and methodological framework that did not then exist within psychology and is still kept in the margins of academic psychology. There were no frameworks anchored in relativistic, contextualistic epistemologies. Existential and structuralist or poststructuralist hermeneutic turns in the history of social thought had not yet been taken. Analytic and phenomenological philosophies were not available to help map out the linguistic and experiential realms in which psychoanalysis travels. Unavailable or unknown to Freud were modern explorations of the narrative and dialogic nature of human communication and its role in the coming into being of differentiated self-object relations. In sum, the language of Freud's creation had to wait for the development of twentieth-century thought. It is true that he could have brought to bear the teachings of Nietzsche and thereby have developed a more modern understanding of his work as deconstructive and narrative and so on, but he did not do so and later disclaimed any knowledge of them—somewhat disingenuously, it seems, according to modern scholarship. But it has taken generations of modern thought to see clearly just what Nietzsche was setting forth, so that it is, I think, going too far to require Freud to have been on the cutting edge of the philosophical thought of his time.

Ahead of his time in so many respects, Freud tried to be of his time—what else could he do?—and so he misunderstood himself. But in being ahead of his time, he facilitated some of those developments he would have needed to understand himself better, to be adequately understood by others, and yet to remain clearly open to continuing revision of those understandings.

That it is acceptable for more than one legitimate and arguable reading of Freud's achievement to exist was itself virtually unforeseeable and unthinkable in his time. Today, we are better prepared to tolerate, if not accept, the pluralism that is the ground for my claim that we can speak of Freud's having provided more than just one legacy. By the same token, we are readier—at least intellectually readier—to accept the idea that our present readings of him will be superseded in time. We can, however, maintain some confidence that newer readings will not be modeled on the laboratory sciences or on simple evolutionism and organicism. The nineteenth-century versions of empiricism and naturalism are no longer dominant at the frontiers of the human disciplines. Doctrinaire adherence to the last century's narrow discourse and restrictive methods of proof no longer reigns supreme in psychoanalysis.

In conclusion, we may say that Freud invented a new discipline. Its roots and its branches extend into many realms of knowledge, and experts in every one of these realms—psychology, biology, history, anthropology, literature, among others—may legitimately develop for their own purposes specialized perspectives on psychoanalysis, specialized applications of it, and specialized critiques of it. Nevertheless, psychoanalysis seems destined to withstand total appropriation by any one discipline. In this sense it will always belong only to itself. Fundamentally, it answers only to itself. Although Freud could not fully appreciate the gigantic magnitude and the special requirements of the texts he left for our perusal, he gave us tools and values that have helped us to appreciate those texts more than he ever could or did. It was not for him but for us to attempt to specify just what he bequeathed us.

## Notes

This essay was the Fourteenth Edith Weigert Lecture, sponsored by the Forum on Psychiatry and the Humanities, Washington School of Psychiatry, 19 October 1990.

1. For this essay, I have drawn on so many sources of ideas and inspiration that it would be both tediously pedantic and misleading to try to provide a list of references. I must, however, mention my special indebtedness to the contributions of the following theorists and to works in their background or stimulated by them: Mikhail Bakhtin, Wayne Booth, Jacques Derrida, Stanley Fish, Michel Foucault, Jürgen Habermas, Frank Kermode, Paul Ricoeur, Gilbert Ryle, Hayden White, and Ludwig Wittgenstein.

2. I thank Drs. Humphrey Morris and Joseph H. Smith for encouraging me to include in this context some of my earlier (1970) emphasis on necessity, helplessness, and the modern sense of the tragic and ironic.

## References

Schafer, Roy. "The Psychoanalytic Vision of Reality." *International Journal of Psycho-Analysis* 51 (1970): 279–97.

———. *A New Language for Psychoanalysis.* New Haven: Yale University Press, 1976.

———. *Language and Insight: The Sigmund Freud Memorial Lectures, University College London, 1975–1976.* New Haven: Yale University Press, 1978.

———. *Narrative Actions in Psychoanalysis: Narratives of Space and Narratives of Time.* Worcester, Mass.: Clark University Press, 1981.

———. *The Analytic Attitude.* New York: Basic Books, 1983.

———. "Discussion of Panel Presentations on Psychic Structure." *Journal of the American Psychoanalytic Association* 36 Supplement (1988): 295–314.

Weigert, Edith. *The Courage to Love: Selected Papers of Edith Weigert, M.D.* New Haven: Yale University Press, 1970.

# 2 Freud's Case Histories and the Question of Fictionality

## Dorrit Cohn

Among literary critics and their readers, Freud's stature as a novelist is growing rapidly. Already he has been compared with Dickens, Dostoevsky, Henry James, Conan Doyle, Joseph Conrad, Proust, Mann, Joyce, Faulkner, Virginia Woolf, Nabokov, Borges, and several other masters of fictional Realism and Modernism. This reputation rests largely on the three texts nicknamed "Dora," "Rat Man," and "Wolf Man," notwithstanding the rather less literary sound of their full names: "Fragment of an Analysis of a Case of Hysteria" (*Bruchstück einer Hysterie-Analyse*), "From the History of an Infantile Neurosis" (*Aus der Geschichte einer infantilen Neurose*), and "Notes upon a Case of Obsessional Neurosis" (*Bemerkungen über einen Fall von Zwangs-neurose*). By now it no longer surprises us to find these works featured in critical, historical, and theoretical studies on fiction. In *Reading for the Plot* (1984), Peter Brooks sandwiches his "Fictions of the Wolf Man" between chapters on *Heart of Darkness* and *Absalom, Absalom!* In *Representations* (1975), Steven Marcus's influential essay, "Freud and Dora," concludes a series of studies on assorted nineteenth- and twentieth-century novels and novelists. In *Aufschreibsysteme 1800/1900* (1987), Friedrich Kittler aligns the "psychoanalytic case novels [*Fall-romane*]" of the "novelist [*Romanschreiber*] Freud" with Rilke's *Malte Laurids Brigge* and other turn-of-the-century novels to define a literary period code. In "The Freudian Novel" (1981), Michel de Certeau places Freud's case histories at a turning point of literary history, proposing that they dismantled the fictional norms of the nineteenth century in the manner *Don Quixote* deconstructed the Spanish *Hidalguia* three centuries earlier. Many further instances could be cited

21

to show that among literary critics—regardless of their general admiration for or hostility to the *chose freudienne*—these texts are well
on their way to becoming canonical works of modern fiction.

Remembering Freud's image of the polar bear and the whale—who
don't engage in warfare because nature confines them to their respective habitats (*S.E.* 17:48)—it is perhaps natural that dissenting
voices should begin to arise, not from within the professional species
that treats patients and records their histories on a daily basis, but
from within the one that habitually concerns itself with the nature of
literature, fiction, and the novel. My own motivation, at any rate, in
engaging a critical examination of the generic assignation highlighted
above, is my uneasiness with the general trend to ignore distinctions
between different textual categories—creative and critical, literary
and scientific, fictional and historical—and more specifically my ongoing concern with retracing the vanishing boundaries between fictional and nonfictional narrative.[1] Using the generic reception recently
accorded Freud's case histories as a case of my own, I propose the
following argumentative moves: (1) to uncover the vagarious concept
of fiction that has prompted it; (2) to look to narrative poetics for
stabilizing distinctions that may counter it; (3) to confront the fictional
reception of Freud's case-historical writings with his own overt intention; (4) to examine these writings themselves for objective grounds
to dispel this reception; (5) to close by an opening to Freud's conception of historiography in the narration of individual lives.

*I*

As the philosopher Hans Vaihinger remarked several decades ago, "the
word 'fiction' is subject to confused and perverse usages; even logi-
cians employ it in different meanings, without taking pains to define
them or to distinguish among them" (1918, 140, my translation). The
semantic conundrum is further compounded when the term is not
confined to a philosophical context—as it is in Vaihinger's work and
was until quite recently in general German usage—but, as it is in
English, is likewise applied to the genre of literary narrative, that is,
(most commonly) the novel. The scope and slipperiness of this word's
referential field accordingly enable imperceptible glides that account
for the ease—if not for the eagerness—with which the generic borderline between fictional and factual texts has been erased. This semantic instability, as well as the confusions and misapprehensions that
ensue, can easily be detected by a critical look at recent writings on
Freud's case histories.

I will pass quickly over the derogatory everyday use of the term *fiction* to designate an untrue statement, both in the sense of a lie uttered with intent to deceive and an account based on erroneous data. Only a reader who has never reflected that "the poet nothing affirms and therefore never lieth" would mistake a purportedly factual text for a literary fiction on account of its containing mis- or disinformation. And although Freud's case histories are known to contain certain factual inaccuracies—if only because, for reasons of discretion, he variously altered the circumstances of his patients' lives—the claim that Freud is a fiction writer is usually based on more sophisticated connotations attending the term. I would nonetheless suggest that this meaning of factual inadequacy willy-nilly contaminates the word *fiction* with a degree of negativity or frivolity when it is applied to nonliterary discourse and that this implication is not entirely absent from *any* of its applications in discussions of Freud's case histories.

I will also note only in passing another meaning of *fiction* that, so long as it is used in its strict sense, remains semantically segregated from the generic literary term: the specific and complex concept of "theoretical (scientific) fiction," the subject of Vaihinger's *Philosophie des Als Ob*.[2] But the application of *fiction* (unmodified) to mental abstractions has lately grown far beyond Vaihinger's rigorous bounds, with inevitably destabilizing effects on generic discrimination.

In modern critical language it has become quite the norm to label as "fictions" all verbal accounts that superimpose a general significance, a meaningful interpretation, on events after the fact. "Any human verbalizing," says a theorist of autobiography, "is a process that by its very nature fictionalizes experience" (Olney 1980, 53). In this meaning the word *fiction* is now commonly used to "deconstruct" all those essential concepts formerly taken for granted in biographical writing: such notions as self, subject, person, identity, memory, even "life" itself (see, for example, Olney 1980, 22). By this token Freud, given the quantity of conceptual abstractions he introduces into the telling of his patients' lives, can easily qualify as the supreme "fiction" writer. But it is far less plausible to assert on this basis "the fictionality of case history as a literary genre" (Mahony 1984, 99). Likewise one may readily agree with Peter Brooks when à propos of the Wolf Man he uses *fiction* in the sense just described: "Biography, even in the form of the case history, appears to be intimate with fiction: it is a hypothetical construction" (1984, 279); one may even want to replace "even" by "especially." But this idea by no means coincides or coheres with the principal argument of "Fictions of the Wolf Man," where *fiction* (as the titular ambiguity suggests) signifies both the literary works that haunt the mind of the patient and those that haunt the psychoanalyst's narrative text (i.e., the novels of the Modernist canon).

Closely related to the above meaning of *fiction*, and at least equally pervasive in the present-day critical idiom, is the more specific attribution of fictionality to all texts that are narrative in structure. The novelist E. L. Doctorow insists that "there is no fiction or nonfiction as we commonly understand the distinction: there is only narrative" (1977, 231); Northrop Frye calls fiction "any work of literary art in a radically continuous form," including especially autobiography (1967, 303, 307). This meaning dominates the influential work of Hayden White, for whom historical texts are no less "verbal fictions" than their purely imaginary counterparts in literature (1978, 82). White's conflating move is clearly dictated by the common denominator he discerns in both, which he labels "emplotment" (83): the teller's imposition of a coherent, consequential temporal order on a succession of events, with a view to structuring it into a unified plot with beginning, middle, and end. This turns out to be the principal meaning most Freud critics have in mind most of the time when they call his case histories "fictions." Steven Marcus, for example, quite cogently explains that in the "Dora" case Freud wants to arrive at "a connected and coherent story, with all the details in explanatory place, and with everything . . . accounted for, in its proper causal or other sequence" (1975, 277). But before long he adds: "It [the case history] is a story, or a fiction," explaining that this is so "not only because it has a narrative structure but also because the narrative account has been rendered in language, in conscious speech, and no longer exists in the deformed language of symptoms." His summary conclusion to this argument reads as follows: "What we end with, then, is a fictional construction which is at the same time satisfactory to us in the form of the truth, and as the form of the truth" (278).

I have quoted at length from the Marcus essay not only because he so tellingly identifies the process of telling itself with the fashioning of a fiction, but also because of what happens in the paragraph immediately following the one I have cited. For here we can observe how easefully one can skid around the semantic field of fiction: how one can glide quite inadvertently from calling a narrative "fiction" in the sense of emplotment to calling that same narrative "fiction" in the sense now of the literary genre we habitually identify with the novel. It is, we are presently told, "the great bourgeois novels of the nineteenth century" that furnished the model for Freud's case history of Dora. "Indeed, we must see Freud's writings—and method—as themselves part of this culmination, and at the same moment, along with the great modernist novels of the first half of the twentieth century, as the beginning of the end of that tradition and its authority" (278–79). One of the ways Marcus tries to substantiate this claim in the course of his essay is by pointing up parallels between Dora's family history (as told by Freud) and the plots and characters of "late-Victorian romance" (256)—as well as Ibsen's dramas (264)—without ever asking himself whether it would not be possible (and rather more plausible) to explain these parallels by the fact that novels and dramas by Freud's contemporaries reflect the same psychologically damaging domestic situations that Freud knew at first hand from the real confessions of his real patients.[3]

Be that as it may. The fact remains that it is one thing to say that novels and case histories are both emplotted life stories and quite another to say that case histories are novels (or, for that matter, that novels are case histories). So long as the term *fiction* clearly designates only features that all narrative texts hold in common, the attribution of fictionality to Freud's three published studies of individual patients is harmless, if rather self-evident. But when the term is semantically narrowed to the *generic* meaning of *fiction*, its association with these Freud texts becomes far more problematical. For it now carries one or both of the following implications: that Freud intended his case histories as imaginative literature, and that he unintentionally lapsed into discursive modes reserved for the representation of imaginary beings. It implies, in short, that Freud's case histories are nonreferential texts.[4]

## II

Unlike the three usages of the term previously described—(1) to mean "untruth," (2) "theoretical construct," and (3) to mean "plotted narrative"—*fiction* in the restricted sense just alluded to, the sense of *nonreferentiality*, allows one to discriminate between two different *kinds* of narratives, according to whether they deal with real or imaginary events and persons. Narratives of the first kind include historiographic works, journalistic reports, biographies, and autobiographies; narratives of the second kind include novels, novellas, short stories, ballads, and epics. The binary opposition between these two kinds is most simply expressed by saying that the first is subject to judgments of truth and falsity, whereas the second is immune to such judgments. Or, to put this a different way, we might say that referential (and in this sense nonfictional) texts are verifiable and incomplete, whereas nonreferential (and in this sense fictional) texts are unverifiable and complete: we can check on the accuracy of a Thomas Mann biography, point out factual errors, and write a new one, perhaps based on newly discovered evidence; but no competent novel reader would be inclined to check on the accuracy of Hans Castorp's life as told in *The Magic Mountain* or consult the archives to find out whether he was killed on the battlefield where his fictional life ends.

Let me say at this point that this restricted meaning of *fiction* as nonreferential narrative seems to me the only functionally *meaningful* way of using the term in the discourse of literary criticism. Short of campaigning for lexical reform, I try to stick to this meaning in my own critical practice and do so in the continuation of this chapter.[5] I am aware, of course, that the criterium of referentiality is controversial in itself: indeed, it has been the principal bone of contention between theorists who deny and those who affirm a distinction between factual and fictional discourse.[6] But even modern theorists who agree that the emancipation from referentiality is the be-all and end-all of fiction (notably speech-act theorists) have tended to locate its distinctiveness solely in circumstantial evidence extrinsic to the texts themselves—in the communicative conventions, for example, that make us read a story in a volume entitled *Fantastic Tales* in a different key from an article in the *Chicago Tribune*.

Granting the importance of extra- and paratextual signals for the recognition of an author's generic intention, I would nonetheless maintain that the full separatist case can only be made by drawing attention to differences that the speech-act theorists overlook or deny on principle[7]: to distinctive markers inscribed within the fictional text itself and stemming directly from its unique potential to represent those imaginary beings we customarily call "characters." These textual markers can be shown to stamp fictional characters as citizens of an artfully created world, a world that, no matter how close the resemblance, is never identical to the one inhabited by the author who has invented it and by his readers.

I have found that the clearest way to bring this deviance of fiction into view is to compare novels that center on a single character's life in third- or first-person form with their corresponding historiographic genres, biography and autobiography, respectively.[8]

Take the case of third-person novels first: say, *A Portrait of the Artist* or *Tonio Kröger*. The narrators of such novels have cognitive powers that are normally denied to historical biographers, notably the entirely *un*natural ability to penetrate the psyches of their protagonists and to focalize the world that surrounds them through their eyes. Biographers, by contrast, are severely constrained when they come to presenting their subject's inner life. They can do no more than speculate, conjecture, or infer what their historical subjects may, might, or must have thought or felt or perceived at certain junctures of their lives. In short, where inside views are concerned, the gap between the discursive codes of historical and fictional biography is as wide as it is deep: to one side the unreal transparency of fictional characters, to the other the opacity of real persons as we know them in everyday life. This "magic" profoundly affects the structure and style of fictional, as compared to historical, lives.

The case of first-person novels is clearly different. A fictional work that presents itself in the form of a self-narrated story normally imitates its nonfictional counterpart, historical autobiography, in every respect, including its introspective optics. Such fictional autobiographies, as they are often called—*David Copperfield*, for example, or *The Confessions of Felix Krull*—look exactly like accounts that real persons bearing their narrators' names might give of their lives, not excepting their mental lives. If we nonetheless know that these narrators are *not* real persons, it is because their imaginary status is signaled by the names they bear—more precisely, by the fact that they don't bear the same names as their authors. Whether they stamp this mark of fictionality on their title pages—as do Dickens and Mann—or inscribe it only within the pages of their texts—as Hesse does in *Steppenwolf*—authors who want their readers to recognize the nonreferential, novelistic status of a fictional autobiography always sooner or later reveal the nonidentity between the narrator-protagonist and their own person.

We have yet to consider a third type of life story, a combinatory type that bears no standard name but that I call witness biography. Boswell's *Life of Johnson* is a well-known example, as is Max Brod's Kafka biography or Stanislav Joyce's *My Brother's Keeper*. Since biographers of this type have known their subjects personally, they may have privileged information concerning them, stemming from intimate conversations, for example. But they are generally even more acutely aware than standard biographers that direct access to the inner life of the other, the biographed person, is severely barred to them. These historical witness biographies, with their strong component of autobiography, have often been imitated in fiction: in Mann's *Doctor Faustus*, as indicated by its subtitle, *The Life of the German Composer Adrian Leverkühn As Told by a Friend*, and in Scott Fitzgerald's *The Great Gatsby*, Conrad's Marlow novels, Nabokov's *The Real Life of Sebastian Knight*, and Günther Grass's *Cat and Mouse*. Like the narrators of fictional autobiographies, the narrators of fictional witness biographies are fictional characters: Zeitblom, Marlow, and Pilenz are, as their names indicate, every bit as imaginary as Leverkühn, Kurtz, and Mahlke. And these narrating characters, unlike the omniscient tellers of third-person novels, simulate the natural (referential) discourse of their real-life counterparts, including the cognitive constraints that apply to the other whose life they relate.

With this third narrative mode for telling lives—which, as we will see, has special relevance for Freud's case histories—my generic borderline is essentially staked out. Much more, needless to say, could be said about the norms I have used to trace it, and especially about texts that infringe or ambiguate these norms: such as biographies that give us "illicit" inside views of their subjects; or, conversely, novels that never allow us to read their protagonists' minds; or first-person narratives whose tellers remain nameless. In narratology, as elsewhere, norms have a way of remaining uninteresting, and often even invisible, until and unless we find that they have been broken—or want to show that they have *not* been broken. Which brings me at long last to Freud's case histories.

## III

I take for my starting point a passage from one of Freud's earliest case histories, "Fräulein Elisabeth von R.," in *Studies on Hysteria* (1893–95):

> I have not always been a psychotherapist. Like other neuropathologists, I was trained to employ local diagnoses and electro-prognosis, and it still strikes me myself as strange that the case histories I write should read like short stories [*Novellen*] and that, as one might say, they lack the serious stamp of science. I must console myself with the reflection that the nature of the subject is evidently responsible for this, rather than any preference of my own. The fact is that local diagnosis and electrical reactions lead nowhere in the study of hysteria, whereas a detailed description of mental processes such as we are accustomed to find in the works of imaginative writers [*von Dichtern*] enables me, with the use of a few psychological formulas, to obtain at least some kind of insight into the course of that affection. Case histories of this kind are intended to be judged like psychiatric ones; they have, however, one advantage over the latter, namely an intimate connection between the story of the patient's sufferings [*Leidensgeschichte*] and the symptoms of his illness—a connection for which we still search in vain in the biographies of other psychoses. [*S.E.* 2:160–61; *G.W.* 1:227]

This passage has been quoted time and again to legitimate a fictional

reading of Freud's later case histories.[9] Steven Marcus calls it Freud's
"disarming admission" that he regards himself as a "genuine creative
writer" (1975, 273), while Michel de Certeau comments: "This [the
realization that his case histories read like fiction] happens to him as
would a sickness. His manner of treating hysteria transforms his manner of writing. It is a metamorphosis of discourse, ... displacement
toward the poetic or novelistic genre. Psychoanalytic conversion is a
conversion to literature" (1981, 123). For me this same passage opens
a different, indeed a diametrically opposed, perspective[10]: I understand
it as the germinating moment of Freud's enduring concern with the
ways analytic investigation of the human psyche differs from fictional
creation and, as well, of his continuing effort to distance his case
histories from their spurious resemblance with "short stories" (*Novellen*).

Note that Freud pinpoints the fictionlikeness of "Fräulein Elisabeth
von R." quite specifically: "a detailed description of mental processes
such as we are accustomed to find in the works of imaginative writers"
(*eine eingehende Darstellung der seelischen Vorgänge, wie man sie
von Dichtern zu erhalten gewohnt ist*). He clearly refers here to the
horizon of expectation of his own contemporaries, expectations that
have long since ceased to apply in our own age: the age of psychobiography and psychohistory, when we as readers have become fully
"accustomed" to close-paced analytic accounts of individual psychology outside the domain of fiction. In the pre-Freudian days of *Studies
on Hysteria*, however, Freud quite correctly perceived that his case
histories, on the face of it, resembled fictional narratives far more
closely than nonfictional texts of any sort. What they resembled least
of all were the case reports of contemporaneous neuropathologists.
These professional works, for the most part, recorded their clinical
findings in nonnarrative form: by way of static descriptions of observable symptoms and syndromes that aimed at diagnostic classifi-
cations of the various mental illnesses. Writings on hysteria were no
exception. Freud's predecessor and mentor Charcot, for example, charted
the visual fields, the affected body parts, and of course the *grandes
attaques* of his hysterical patients in meticulous detail, without—even
for his prima donna Blanche Wittman—reporting on their lives prior
to hospitalization.[11] The case studies of hysterics written by Freud's
principal rival, Pierre Janet, are likewise very largely synchronic: biographical data are limited to the traumatic episode (the so-called
*accident initial*) that triggered the pathological crisis.[12]

It is not at all surprising, then, that Freud himself, emerging from
these clinical surroundings, should have been acutely aware that his

narrative presentation of mental life broke the code of scientific discourse; nor that he should have anticipated the charge that his case histories were unserious and unscientific—"that, as one might say, they lack the serious stamp of science" (*dass sie sozusagen des ernsten Gepräges der Wissenschaft entbehren*). In this perspective the preemptively defensive rhetoric in the quoted passage can hardly be taken as a "disarming admission" that he was in fact infringing on the fictional preserve, much less as a symptom of his "conversion to literature." He is, much rather, asking *his readers* to convert: to a different scientific code, a code in which texts that "read *like* novellas"— *Krankengeschichten, die ... wie Novellen zu lesen sind*—are not read *as* novellas, but as bona fide scientific contributions: "Case histories of this kind are intended to be judged like psychiatric ones" (*solche Krankengeschichten wollen beurteilt werden wie psychiatrische*). And with Freud's syntax here underlining the immediacy of the advance—an effect that is largely lost in the English translation— the same sentence now goes on to claim for narrative a unique cognitive and curative power: to understand the dynamics of a mental illness that can only be treated by tracing it back to its origin. Which is as much as to say that stories—biographical stories—are his medium because they are his message.

In his later writings, even as he continued to point up the affinity between psychoanalytic and fictional narratives, and indeed came to regard creative writers as pioneers of his own principal discoveries (see *S.E.* 9:9, 44, 53–54; 1960, 251, 340), he nonetheless increasingly stressed the essential differences that separate psychoanalysts from novelists. Indeed, he tended to draw attention to these differences most insistently when the thematic analogies between their writings struck him most deeply: in his analysis of Jensen's novel *Gradiva*, in his letters to his "double" (*Doppelgänger*) Arthur Schnitzler, and in the preface to "Contributions to the Psychology of Love."

It is well known that Freud attributes the novelist's knowledge of the psyche to sources different from those to which he attributes his: whereas he acquired his knowledge by conscious, systematic study of abnormal behavior in his patients, novelists acquire theirs by subliminal apprehension of unconscious desires in others and in themselves (*S.E.* 9:92, 11:166; 1960, 340). But the difference that stems from the aesthetic aim of creative writers and its effect on their productive process, as Freud conceived it, has even more immediate bearing on the case of his case histories: the belief that the writer's principal allegiance is to the pleasure principle, an allegiance he shares with— and inherits from—the child at play (*S.E.* 9:144, 152). In this respect it is important to note that pleasure and play in Freud's language have a common antonym, namely reality: as in the contrastive pair, pleasure principle/reality principle (*Lustprinzip/Realitätsprinzip*) and in the statement, "The opposite of play is not what is serious but what is real" (*der Gegensatz zu Spiel ist nicht Ernst, sondern—Wirklichkeit*) (*S.E.* 9:144; *G.W.* 7:214). On this basis it becomes clear that his binary opposition between novelistic and psychoanalytic narratives is drawn along lines that essentially correspond to the criterium of referentiality. It is the nonreferentiality of fiction—"the unreality of the writer's imaginative world" (*die Unwirklichkeit der dichterischen Welt*) (*S.E.* 9:144; *G.W.* 7:214)—that grants the creative writer his freedom to alter life as he knows it, to fashion it into appealingly persuasive stories inhabited by characters whose motivations are far more consistent than those of real persons and real patients. After describing this "poetic license," as he himself calls it, Freud adds, in "Contributions to the Psychology of Love":

> In consequence it becomes inevitable that science should concern herself with the same materials whose treatment by artists [*deren dichterische Bearbeitung*] has given enjoyment to mankind for thousands of years, though her touch must be clumsier and the yield of pleasure less. These observations will, it may be hoped, serve to justify us in extending a strictly scientific treatment to the field of human love. Science is, after all, the most complete renunciation of the pleasure principle of which our mental activity is capable. [*Die Wissenschaft ist eben die vollkommenste Lossagung vom Lustprinzip, die unserer psychischen Arbeit möglich ist.*] [*S.E.* 11:165; *G.W.* 8:66][13]

That Freud conceived of his case histories quite self-consciously as scientific works in the sense of "the most complete renunciation of the pleasure principle" is confirmed by his inclusion of a passage in "Dora" that addresses the same question almost a decade earlier. At the point of introducing the subject of his patient's homoerotic attachment to Frau K., her father's mistress, he tells us:

> I must now turn to consider a further complication to which I should certainly give no space if I were a man of letters engaged upon the creation of a mental state like this for a short story, instead of being a medical man engaged upon its dissection [*sollte ich als Dichter einen derartigen Seelenzustand für eine Novelle erfinden, anstatt ihn als Arzt zu zergliedern*]. The element to which I must now allude . . . would rightly fall a sacrifice to the censorship of a writer [*des Dichters*]. . . . But in the world of reality [*in der Wirklichkeit*], which I am trying to depict here, a complication of motives . . . is the rule. [*S.E.* 7:59–60; *G.W.* 5:220]

One would think that this passage might have given pause to critics who argue that Freud designed this case history as a work of fiction. But this would be to underestimate the powerful effect that preconceived generic assumptions have on a reader's understanding of every textual moment. Thus Steven Marcus, after reminding us that "nothing is more literary—and more modern—than the disavowal of all literary intentions," quotes this very passage to catch Freud at "another of his crafty maneuverings with the reader," "an elaborate obfuscation ... truly representing how a genuine creative writer writes" (1975, 272–73). If one carried this reasoning to its logical conclusion, one would have to attribute "crafty maneuverings" to Freud's every claim of scientific intent, making his theoretical no less than his clinical publications into the works of a "genuine creative writer": a novelist who plays at being a psychiatrist.

A rather more plausible and responsible case can, I think, be made for Freud as a repressed novelist, who severely (perhaps over-severely, i.e., compulsively) censored his inclinations to express himself creatively. It is to an inhibition of this sort that Peter Henninger (1980, 175–81) attributes what at times may appear as overstatements on Freud's part when he distances himself from creative writers: as when, in the essay on *Gradiva* or in the letters to Schnitzler, he fails to acknowledge that introspection and intuition played a similarly crucial role in his own discovery of the unconscious as in its discovery by the novelists he admires. One might also agree with Peter Gay, when he writes in his recent Freud biography: "At times, Freud's comments on poets read like the revenge of the scientist on the artist. The tortoise maligning the hare" (1988, 317–18). But although Gay, too, believes that Freud had "certain artistic ambitions," he concludes that "with all his affections for literature Freud was all his life more interested in truth than in poetry" (323).[14]

In sum, what we know of Freud's conscious intentions in no way entitles us to read his case histories as fiction. We have yet to examine whether, and by what means, Freud succeeded in implementing his intentions in practice.


*IV*


That the problems of narrative form were on Freud's mind during the composition of all three of his major case histories is documented by numerous comments, both within these works themselves and in contemporaneous letters. While preparing a first version of the "Rat Man" case for a psychoanalytic congress, he wrote to Jung: "I am having great difficulty with my paper, because a real, complete case cannot be narrated but only described" (1974, 141). And over a year later, as he was revising the same case for publication: "It [Freud's paper about the Rat Man] is almost beyond my powers of presentation. How bungled our reproductions are, how wretchedly we dissect the great art works of psychic nature" (1974, 238). Is he implying here—in a rare show of his Romantic affinities—that nature, the supreme artist, can be emulated only by artists? Perhaps. As a scientist, at any rate, he despaired of finding a fully convincing manner to convey the matter he experienced in his consulting room. "It is well known," he tells us near the beginning of the "Wolf Man," "that no means has been found of in any way introducing into the reproduction of an analysis the sense of conviction which results from the analysis itself" (*S.E.* 17:13). Nonetheless, he was intent on finding a way, and the one he chose deliberately renounced from the start the principal privilege of the creative writer: to present the psyche of his subjects "omnisciently," in the manner of the narrator of a third-person novel.

In order to understand that this amounted to a genuine choice, we must remember that Freud would have been theoretically, at least on the grounds of his own theory, in a privileged position for narrating in this novelistic manner. As he said himself, toward the end of the treatment, "We have before us an intelligible, consistent, and unbroken case history" (*eine in sich konsequente, verständliche und lückenlose Krankengeschichte*) (*S.E.* 7:18; *G.W.* 5:175). Had he chosen to tell his patients' lives from the vantage point of this "end," he would have known (or could have created the impression that he knew) all there was to know—could have told all, once and for all, in chronological order. What he chose to do instead, of course, was to tell not only the story he had learned from his patients in the course of the treatment but the story of the treatment itself, not only what he knew but how he got to know it. Introducing the "Wolf Man" case, he describes his intention to "write a history neither of the treatment nor of the illness [*weder eine Behandlungs- noch eine Krankengeschichte*], but ... to combine the two methods of presentation" (*S.E.* 17:13). The result (as a number of critics have shown in detail[15]) is not only a text that is formidably entangled in its temporal structure, but also one that includes Freud himself, the narrator, as a figure in the past time and space of the story he tells: the therapeutic hours patient and doctor shared in the consulting room.

Now it must be granted that by avoiding a pseudo-omniscient narrative stance, Freud's case histories do not escape fictionlikeness altogether. In fact, they correspond structurally to at least two novel types: to mystery novels by way of their anachronic temporal arrangement, with Freud himself cast in the role of detective; and to fictional witness biographies by way of their narrative situation, with Freud in the position of Marlow, Zeitblom, and other witness narrators in the works of this type mentioned earlier. But the decisive point is that neither of these novelistic genres conforms to structures that are distinctive of *fictional* narratives. The anachrony of who-done-it stories, where the body is found at the beginning and doer and deed are not revealed till the end, replicates the natural order of journalistic reports and court records; or—somewhat closer to Freud's texts in subject matter—think of Berton Roueché's "Annals of Medicine" pieces in the *New Yorker*, where the discovery of the mysterious symptom regularly precedes the discovery of its cause. The anachronic "detective" structure of the case histories therefore in no sense lends support to the thesis that Freud wrote like a novelist.[16]

The same is true for the analogy with fictional witness biographies, a novelistic genre that, as I have shown earlier, is itself characterized by its simulation of a referential, historical genre. To declare the author of the "Dora," "Wolf Man," and "Rat Man" cases to be a novelist on the grounds of this homology, one would have to find evidence that he conceived his case-historical narrator as a fictional character: a psychoanalyst whose resemblance to Dr. Sigmund Freud is purely coincidental. Meanwhile the fact that the witness structure has been favored—for reasons that do not concern me here—by twentieth-century novelists hardly allows one to assign Freud to their ranks.[17] On this basis his status as a modernist writer would at best be reduced to a tautology: he produced biographical texts that look like novels that mimic (and therefore look like) biographical texts of the type he produced.

I will not go so far as to maintain that Freud opted for his intricate narrative presentation solely, or even mainly, to distance his case histories from novels that take on fiction-specific forms. He himself insists that an elegantly fashioned sequential story—the "smooth [*glatten*] and precise histories" he attributes to some of his colleagues—cannot begin to convey the problematics of mental illness and its analytic treatment: "If I were to begin by giving a full and consistent case history [*eine lückenlose und abgerundete Krankengeschichte*], it would place the reader in a very different situation from that of the medical observer" (*S.E.* 7:16; *G.W.* 5:173). Here Freud's didactic aim is clearly in evidence: by telling his patient's story in the incoherent, fragmented way in which it was revealed to him, he means to ensure the reader's belief in the historicity of his discourse no less than to persuade the reader of its psychological validity.

That Freud's rejection of the pseudo-omniscient and pseudo-objective mode of telling is deeply grounded in the nature of psychoanalytic theory itself has been confirmed by Roy Schafer, who vigorously argues against the "implausibly tidy" accounts of mental illness that have become the professional norm. Recommending Freud's own case histories as formal models to his fellow therapists, he describes them as follows: "In the main each is a narrative of the analysis itself. Or perhaps, taking Freud's accompanying theoretical and methodological remarks into account as well, one should say that each case report is . . . a narrative of Freud's continuing creation of psychoanalysis." And he adds: "I think that the widely recognized literary power of these case studies stems from their artful and brilliant telling of how arduously, and often uncertainly, Freud was creating psychoanalysis" (1981, 44–45).[18] Schafer's views here provide an essential and salutory corrective to those critics who identify narrativity with fictionality: even as he acknowledges the importance and complexity of Freud's narrative practice in the case histories, including their "artful" autobiographical component, he insists on its theoretical and heuristic functionality.

We have yet to observe how, and to what degree, Freud avoided distinctively fictional techniques in presenting his patients' psychic processes, both in the history of the treatment (*Behandlungsgeschichte*)—which covers the only epoch of their lives when he actually "witnessed" them—and in the history of the illness (*Leidensgeschichte*)—which deals with a past he could only get to know indirectly, by way of the patients' own gradually emerging memories, if he could get to know it at all.

Despite the uncommon means Freud employed to get to know what was in his patients' minds as they lay in his consulting room— means that are hardly comparable to those available to the garden-variety witness biographer—he never lost sight of the categorical impossibility of looking inside another mind. The barrier that bars access is nowhere so graphically thematized as in the early "Fräulein Elisabeth von R.," the very case where Freud expressed his apprehension of novella-likeness that I quoted earlier. Since this patient refused to respond to hypnosis (still Freud's preferred technique at the time), he resorted to applying physical pressure—"the device of applying pressure to the head" (*jenen Kunstgriff des Drückens auf den Kopf*)—which he accompanied with the instruction to say the first thing that popped into her mind (*S.E.* 2:145; *G.W.* 1:208). Though less dramatic than this crude manipulation for overcoming Fräulein Elisabeth's hard-headed opacity, the technique of free association that was soon to take its place is no less clearly limited to behavioral clues for what remains forever hidden. It seems to me that Freud's awareness of his cognitive constraint also underlies a passage in "Dora" that Marcus takes as a "fantas[y] of omniscience" on Freud's part (1975, 302): in that passage he stresses the facility he eventually acquired in interpreting what he calls "symptomatic actions" (*Symptomhandlungen*), such as Dora's suspect fiddling with her genitalia-shaped pocket book, and adds: "He that has eyes to see and ears to hear may convince himself that no mortal can keep a secret. If his lips are silent, he chatters with his finger-tips; betrayal oozes out of him at every pore. And thus the task of making conscious the most hidden recesses of the mind [*das verborgenste Seelische bewusst zu machen*] is one which it is quite possible to accomplish [*sehr wohl lösbar*]" (*S.E.* 7:77–78; *G.W.* 5:240). Freud's self-confidence here may touch on braggadocio, but it implies a world of difference between the analyst's power to interpret verbal and gestural symptoms and the novelist's power to create transparent minds. Had he wanted his readers to forget this difference, he would have had nothing to brag about. Nor, we might add, would he have left his readers the possibility of interpreting Dora's words and gestures in his consulting room differently from the way he interpreted them himself: in the manner, say, in which Neil Hertz (1985) reinterprets them by attributing countertransferential motives to Freud's own interpretations.

The relationship of the narrator to his protagonist is different when the hard-headed physical presence of the patient in the story of the treatment (*Behandlungsgeschichte*) fades into the more or less distant past of the story of the illness (*Leidensgeschichte*), where the temptation to take on an omniscient narrative stance is potentially much greater. Freud avoids it precisely by the previously mentioned entwinement of the two stories. This essentially takes the form of his telling us what the patient told him about the past. Sometimes he renders this autobiographical discourse directly, as at the beginning of the "Rat Man" case, where several lengthy paragraphs quote the patient's own voice. More often these memories are presented in the form of indirect discourse or paraphrase, with their inception always clearly marked by an *inquit* phrase: "She [Dora] told me that one day she had met Herr K. in the street" (*S.E.* 7:59); "Dora told me [*machte mir... Mitteilung*] of an earlier episode with Herr K." (*S.E.* 7:27; *G.W.* 5:186); "Thus he [the Wolf Man] could recollect [*weiss also zu erzählen*] how he had suffered from a fear" (*S.E.* 17:15–16; *G.W.* 12:39–

40); "He had preserved a memory of how, during one of these scenes" (*S.E.* 17:28); and so forth. These emphatic introductions clearly ensure that the episodes, though now cast in third-person form and freely referring to the patient's past thoughts and feelings, are not mistaken for omnisciently narrated fictional scenes, in which Freud (the narrator) has adopted the patient's perspective.[19]

Conversely, when Freud gives us his own, now properly biographical and interpretive account of the past, he sets it off explicitly from the patient's autobiographical discourse. His version of the scene, originally quoted in Dora's own words, where Herr K. embraces the fourteen-year-old girl—the version where her revulsion is explained by the supposition that she felt Herr K.'s erect member—is introduced as follows: "In accordance with certain rules of symptom-formation which I have come to know, and at the same time taking into account certain other of the patient's peculiarities, which were otherwise inexplicable, . . . I have formed in my own mind the following reconstruction of the scene. I believe that during the man's passionate embrace she felt not merely his kiss upon her lips" (*S.E.* 7, 29–30). "I believe . . . she felt" (*Ich denke, sie verspürte*; *G.W.* 5:188): modalizing and conjectural phrases of this type abound in all three case histories, indicating that Freud, no matter how certain he was of his inferences, took care to adhere to the narrative code of historical biography.

In this regard it is especially instructive to observe the way Freud presents the most daring and (in)famous of all his biographical conjectures. I mean of course the primal scene (*Urszene*) of parental intercourse observed by the infant Wolf Man. It occurs at a point of the case history where Freud has been adhering to the story of the treatment for several pages, first quoting the Wolf Man's narration of his recurring childhood nightmare about the seven (or six, or five) wolves perched on a tree, then recounting his patient's first associations with this dream and his own first interpretive reactions. With the primal scene itself the narration clearly changes over to the other, the story of the illness: it is the earliest and most crucial moment of his patient's biography that Freud will attempt to recount. He introduces it as follows: "I have now reached the point at which I must abandon the support I have hitherto had from the course of the analysis. I am afraid it will also be the point at which the reader's belief will abandon me" (*S.E.* 17:36). After the conclusion of the primal scene Freud once again anticipates his readers' "doubts as to its probability [*Bedenken der Unwahrscheinlichkeit*]," adding: "Later on I shall carefully examine these and other doubts [*Bedenken*]; but I can assure the reader that I am no less critically inclined than he towards an acceptance [*Annahme*] of this observation of the child's, and I will only ask him to join me in adopting a *provisional* belief in the reality of the scene" (*S.E.* 17:38–39; *G.W.* 12:65–66; Freud's emphasis). Whereupon he returns to the story of the treatment, focusing on the effects his bold interpretation had on its remaining course.

In my perspective, the reader-addressing rhetoric that brackets the primal scene is nothing more nor less than a highly emphatic version of the discursive pattern that characterizes the narration of psychic events in historical biography: the inferential "must have" construction writ large, as surely befits the enormity of the occasion. Having hedged it in this fashion, Freud allows the intervening passage—where he describes the "constructed primal scene" itself—to lapse, though only for the length of one single sentence, into the focalized mode: to show it—as its nature demands—through the eyes (though clearly not through the language) of the observing child: "When he woke up, he witnessed a coitus *a tergo* [from behind], three times repeated; he was able to see his mother's genitals as well as his father's organ; and he understood the process as well as its significance" (*S.E.* 17:37). One should perhaps grant that, read in isolation, this past indicative sentence might be mistaken for an excerpt from a rather bizarre pornographic novel. But this impression would be instantly dispelled by the framing context, which so explicitly subordinates the focalized perception of the infant to the self-consciously daring hypothesis of the psychoanalyst.

V

The nonomniscience signified by Freud's emphatically conjectural narration of the primal scene itself is further compounded in its aftermath: the addition to the case history, some four years after its original composition, of the two passages where he qualifies his own belief in "the reality of this scene." These insertions open to the final question I try to clarify in this chapter: Freud's understanding of what constitutes historicity in the psychoanalytic life narrative. It is an understanding that has, in my view, been gravely misunderstood by deconstructively oriented critics bent on attributing to Freud a vision that obliterates the distinction between fictional and nonfictional narrative. In what follows, I address only one (highly influential) essay that moves along these lines: Peter Brooks's previously mentioned "Fictions of the Wolf Man," where, precisely, Freud's revision figures as key evidence.[20]

The first of Freud's passages (*S.E.* 17:57–60), inserted at the conclusion of extensive arguments that speak *for* the "reality" of the constructed scene, in effect constructs an alternative scenario for the events that preceded and inspired the wolf dream and the infantile neurosis: the child, having watched animals copulating, fashioned a fantasy that superimposed these observations onto a "harmless" scene he had witnessed in the parental bedroom. This fantasy version, Freud concedes, is more plausible than the originally constructed primal scene, but he nonetheless defers the option between actual scene and fantasy to a later moment. That moment comes in the second insertion (*S.E.* 17:95–97), where Freud now provides renewed evidence for the *original* version. But ultimately he once again stops short of a final decision. We are left to share his dissatisfaction at the unanswered question in this individual case—"I should myself be glad to know whether the primal scene in my present patient's case was a phantasy or a real experience"—even as we are told that "taking other similar cases into account, . . . the answer to this question is not in fact a matter of very great importance" (*es sei eigentlich nicht sehr wichtig, dies zu entscheiden*) (97; *G.W.* 12:131).

Peter Brooks describes the first of these revisionary additions, some-what hyperbolically, as "one of the most daring moments in Freud's thought, and one of his most heroic moments as a writer" (1984, 277). He explains that Freud here "perilously destabilizes belief in explan-atory histories" (277); that he makes biography into an "uncontrol-lable" genre, assigning it "to an unspecifiable network of event, fiction, and interpretation" (278); that he signifies that "language itself . . . is in a state of displacement and fictionality" (279). And, to clinch the point that Freud is behaving like a Modernist novelist at this juncture, we are further told that his protagonist "should perhaps be considered less a character from Mann or Proust than a Virginia Woolfman" (278). Without doing Brooks the injustice of taking his pun too literally, I cannot pass it without recalling that Woolf's characters are invariably given life by a narrator who knows them in magically intimate ways—ways in which no real person can ever know another; so that no greater contrast could well be imagined than the one pertaining be-tween her hyperomniscient novelistic discourse—commonly referred to as stream-of-consciousness—and the nescient discourse of Freud at the moment when he most openly avows his uncertainties in telling his patient's mental history.

A less biased reader would, I think, be led to admire Freud's revi-sionary move on account of its kinship with theoretically informed (and reformed) modern historians (rather than with modern exper-imental novelists): those who problematize the relationship between the historical past and its representation in a historiographic account, renouncing the claim that the latter mirrors the former directly, accurately, and with absolute finality. Robert Berkhofer has described this new historiographic mode as "demystification of normal history" (1988, 448), explaining that it "frees the historian to tell many different kinds of 'stories' from various viewpoints, with many voices, emplotted diversely, according to many principles of synthesis" (449), without thereby in any sense spelling "the death of history doing itself" (450). In this light, Freud's self-critical supplementation to the "Wolf Man" case takes on the meaning of enlightened—demystified—historiography applied to the biographical genre: the move of a life historian who refuses to identify referential discourse with the production of a single, irrevocable story. If anything, Freud's decision to add an alternative construction to the one he initially proposed enhances the referential status of the "Wolf Man" case, rather than displacing it toward "fictionality."

Brooks, however, if I understand him correctly, imputes the fictionalizing impact of Freud's revision not solely (or mainly) to its ultimate inclusion in the case history, but also to its content: to Freud's admission that the primal scene may be a fantasy. Now it is true that Freud himself at times described his patients' fantasies in terms that pointedly allude to narrative fiction—as *Dichtung*, even as *Roman*;[21] and we know from such writings as "Creative Writers and Day-Dreaming" ["Der Dichter und das Phantasieren"] how closely he affiliated fantasies in general with literary creation. But the crucial point is of course that the "Wolf Man" revision casts not the analyst but the *patient* (the infant Wolf Man) as the creator of a "fictional" fantasy. The case historian Freud merely offers yet another biographical hypothesis to account for his patient's illness. Accordingly, when he ultimately declares that it remains undecidable whether the Wolf Man's infantile neurosis originated in a real experience or in a fantasy, this undecidability in no sense affects the generic status of his case history: the analyst's discourse is no more fictional—no less referential—when it traces the origin of the patient's neurosis back to infantile fantasies (or "fictions") than when it traces it back to a verifiable biographical event.

That this understanding corresponds to Freud's own is confirmed in a work published shortly before the revisionary "Wolf Man" supplements and to which he himself refers the "Wolf Man" reader (*S.E.* 17:97): lecture 23 of the *Introductory Lectures on Psycho-Analysis*. Most readers seem to have understood this cross-reference to concern merely the possibility of phylogenetic causation for primal fantasies (the matter to which Freud turns next in the inserted passage). But there is an at least equally relevant link with an earlier passage in lecture 23 that clarifies Freud's rationale for declaring that the choice between primal scene and primal fantasy "is not in fact a matter of very great importance." It reads as follows:

> When he [the patient in treatment] brings up the material which leads from behind his symptoms to the wishful situations modelled on his infantile experiences, we are in doubt to begin with whether we are dealing with reality or phantasies. ... It will be a long time before he can take in our proposal that we should equate [*gleichzustellen*] phantasy and reality. ... Yet this is clearly the only correct attitude to adopt towards these mental productions. They too possess a reality of a sort [*eine Art Realität*]. It remains a fact [*eine Tatsache*] that the patient has created these phantasies for himself, and this fact is of scarcely less importance for his neurosis than if he had really experienced what the phantasies contain. The phantasies possess *psychical* as contrasted with *material* reality, and we gradually learn to understand that *in the world of the neuroses it is psychical reality which is the decisive kind* [*dass ... die psychische Realität die massgebende ist*]. [*S.E.* 16, 368; *G.W.* 11:383; Freud's emphases]

As Paul Ricoeur has pointed out (1977, 839–40), from the vantage point of common sense and observational science this conception of infantile fantasies as "a kind of reality" is paradoxical; its epistemological consequences profoundly alter the criteria of scientific truth and verification that apply to psychoanalytic writings.

I would argue that the "psychical reality" concept has an equally profound impact on the criterion of historicity that applies to Freud's case histories. For it imposes the idea that in psychoanalytic telling of individual lives, a nonfactual phenomenon must be regarded as a historical "fact" [*Tatsache*], in the sense of a biographical given, a past actuality that predates the case-historical discourse on the same basis as all other events in the patient's life.[22] No matter how paradoxical the notion of "psychical reality" may appear in other respects, it unequivocally reinforces the frame of referentiality that encloses the psychoanalytic life narrative, enabling it to accommodate "fictional" scenes without thereby transmuting it generically into a case fiction. In this respect, too, Freud's medium is his message, and no matter what we may ultimately think of it, we misread his message when we mistake his medium.

*Notes*

1. I can only note in passing that the tendency to efface generic borderlines has affected not merely the reading of Freud's case histories but likewise the reading of his more purely theoretical texts. See for example Derrida (1975, 38f.), where Freud's analytic commentary on the fairy tale "The Emperor's New Clothes" in *The Interpretation of Dreams* is diagnosed as "belong[ing] no more clearly to the tradition of scientific discourse than to a specific genre of fiction." This and other instances of the deconstructive reading of Freud's oeuvre—sometimes called "French Freud"—are only just beginning to be questioned by literary scholars. See in particular Corngold (1986, 181–95).

2. The concept "theoretical fiction" is clearly relevant to Freud's systematic thought. Its (to my knowledge) only appearance in his writings—toward the end of *The Interpretation of Dreams* (*S.E.* 5:603)—has been searchingly probed by Humphrey Morris (1980, 317–27). But the more general subject still awaits investigation. That Freud knew *Die Philosophie des Als Ob* is attested in *The Future of an Illusion*, which at one point refers to religious beliefs as "fictions" [*Fiktionen*], with a footnote explaining that the word is used in the sense of Vaihinger's concept, "practical fiction" [*praktische Fiktion*] (*S.E.* 21:28–29).

3. The same overestimation of the role literary models played for Freud also pervades Marcus's analysis of the "Rat Man" case (1984). Here the emphasis is not on the imitation of novelistic plots, since the story line is found to be "less traditionally satisfying and adequate" than in Freud's other case histories (96); instead the "Rat Man" is read as a novelistic "character portrait" in the manner of Dickens and Dostoevsky (134, 146).

4. It should be noted that a number of major Freud critics have highlighted the importance of narrative structures in his writings without ever introducing the ambiguous term *fiction*. Among those particularly concerned with the narrative form of the case histories are Sherwood (1969, 190–91), Habermas (1973, 315–21), Ricoeur (1977, 843–44), Schafer (1980, 51–53; 1981, 44–45), Nägele (1987, 177–89).

5. My model for limiting the range of the word's meaning in this fashion is Paul Ricoeur; see Ricoeur (1984, 64) for his justification of this terminological decision.

6. See, for example, Stanley Fish's insistence that news reports and novels cannot be "differentiated on a scale of reality" (1980, 239), as compared to John Searle's distinction between the "serious" (i.e., referential) discourse of news reports and the "fictional" discourse of novels (1975, 325).

7. Searle, for example, maintains that there is "no textual property, syntactic or semantic, that will identify a text as a work of fiction" (1975, 325). Statements of this type reflect (and result from) the speech-art theorists' conception that all fictional discourse is an imitation or representation of referential discourse. See also Barbara Herrnstein Smith (1978, 29–30).

8. For a more extensive development of the generic distinctions between

historical and fictional life stories outlined below, see Cohn (1989).

9. In addition to the critics quoted below, see Muschg (1956, 307), Rey (1977, 327), Worbs (1983, 86).

10. Though I base it on a somewhat different understanding of its details, my reading of this passage agrees with those of Schönau (1968, 11), Nägele (1987, 14), and Yerushalmi (1989, 388).

11. Freud himself pronounced critically on Charcot's shortcircuiting of the biographical dimension as early as 1893, attributing it to an overevaluation of hereditary predisposition (*S.E.* 3:21).

12. The contrast, in this regard, between Freud's case histories and the established norms of psychiatric literature is stressed by Chertok and Saussure (1979, see especially 181–84) and by de Certeau (1981, 124, 130). The case-historical practices of Charcot, Janet, and other contemporaneous psychiatrists are described in Ellenberger (1970). But I have not been able to find any specialized work that probes the historical evolution of the case history as a "genre."

13. The qualified formulation here ("the most complete renunciation of the pleasure principle of which our mental activity is capable") should serve to remind us that for Freud this renunciation can never *be* complete—if only because scientific research, no less than artistic creation, is biographically rooted in the sexual "research" of the child (see Humphrey Morris's chapter in this volume for a discussion of this affiliation in such papers as "The Sexual Theories of Children"). In this perspective, the opposition between the pleasure principle and the reality principle—and concomitantly between art and science—can be seen to be relative rather than absolute.

14. Freud's lifelong stance of distancing his works from those of novelists is forcefully demonstrated in a recent article by Yerushalmi (1989) à propos of the (previously unpublished) preface to *Moses and Monotheism.* Yerushalmi convincingly argues that the initially intended (and later discarded) subtitle, "A Historical Novel," was "certainly idiosyncratic, perhaps even ironic" (379), a "strategy of defense" meant to "disarm potential critics" who might object to the paucity of documented evidence for his historical thesis (390). This defensive gesture—in some respects analogous to the one Freud made forty years earlier when he called attention to the spurious fictionlikeness of "Fräulein Elisabeth von R."—must not, in Yerushalmi's view, detract from the serious historiographic intent and meaning of the Moses study.

15. For the anachronic structure of the "Wolf Man," see Brooks (1984, 272–73), Nägele (1987, 178), and Mahony (1984, 95).

16. Brooks (1984), Marcus (1975, 263–64), and Mahony (1984, 95) are among the critics who stress the affinities between the case histories and fiction on this basis.

17. Janet Malcolm makes this same point in an essay—the only one to date—that takes issue with readers who place the case histories in the context of literary modernism. Addressing in particular Marcus's idea that "Dora" is provided with a "Nabokovian frame," she comments astutely: "In back of every

unreliable narrator of modernist fiction stands a reliably artful author. In Dora, however, the Freud who is writing the case history and the Freud who is narrating it are one and the same person. If 'Pale Fire' had been *written* by the madman Charles Kimbote as well as narrated by him, there would be an analogy between Nabokov's novel and Freud's case history" (1987, 89). It should be pointed out, however, that this argument cannot dispel the Freud-the-novelist thesis when it is based on the axiom that autobiography is a fictional genre; for critics who hold to this axiom, the autobiographical component of Freud's case histories will willy-nilly stamp them as novels: this is the argument, for example, of de Certeau (1981, 124–25).

18. See also Schafer (1980, 51–53). Note that I am not concerned here with Schafer's controversial narrative model for the psychoanalytic treatment itself—to which most of his publications are devoted—but only with the narrative structure he recommends for case histories fashioned in retrospect.

19. That they have nonetheless been so mistaken seems to me due to a willful misreading. I cannot, at any rate, agree with critics who have sensed a fictionlike fusion, or confusion, of voices (or perspectives) between analyst and patient in these works. See, for example, Mahony on the "Rat Man" case: "Freud's prose is truly one of *rapprochement*—interpersonally between author, reader and patient" (1986, 206); likewise Kittler: "which of the two [doctor or patient] is speaking at any moment remains undecidable" (1987, 294; my translation).

20. In the wake of Brooks's reading, another leading critic, Jonathan Culler, discusses these Freudian passages in *The Pursuit of Signs: Semiotics, Literature and Deconstruction* (1981). Taking up the concepts of "Story and Discourse in the Analysis of Narrative," he argues that the axiomatic priority of story over discourse (which he takes—I think erroneously—to be fundamental to narratological poetics) must give way to the recognition of a "double logic" operative in all narrative texts: discourse can always be understood to "cause" the events of a story, in referential no less than in fictional narratives; the "Wolf Man" revision exemplifies the possibility of creating "a fictional or tropological event" out of "discursive requirements" (180) in an ostensibly nonfictional text. I disagree with Culler's understanding of these Freudian passages both on textual grounds (as suggested below) and on theoretical grounds (see Cohn 1990).

21. At one point (though not in relation to the primal scene) Freud calls the Wolf Man's own fantasy life "imaginative composition" (*Dichtung*) (*S.E.* 17:20; *G.W.* 12:43). The terms "tales of the individual's prehistoric past" (*Dichtungen über die Urzeit*) and "imaginative production of a positively epic character" (*episch zu nennende Dichtung*) are applied to the Rat Man's childhood fantasies (*S.E.* 10:207 n; *G.W.* 7:427). Another patient's fleeting fantasy is tagged a "romance" (*Roman*) (*S.E.* 9:160; *G.W.* 7:193), and the latter term is of course enshrined in the special type of childhood fantasy Freud called "family romance" (*Familienroman*). So far as I can see, the only instance— but it is a highly significant one—where Freud uses "fiction" (German *Fiktion*) to refer to imaginary past experiences is the letter informing Fliess of

his growing conviction that his patients' early memories of sexual traumas may have no basis in reality (1985, 264).

22. In this connection it is interesting to note that the distinction between psychical and material reality first appears (though in a rather more tentative formulation) in a passage that Freud added to the concluding section of *The Interpretation of Dreams* in 1914, the year when he began to write up the "Wolf Man" case: "Whether we are to attribute *reality* to unconscious wishes, I cannot say. . . . If we look at unconscious wishes reduced to their most fundamental and truest shape, we shall have to conclude, no doubt, that *psychical* reality is a particular form of existence not to be confused with *material* reality" (*S.E.* 5:620; Freud's emphases). The concept of psychical reality is discussed at some length by Laplanche and Pontalis (1964, 1836–38; see also 1973, 315).

## References

Berkhofer, Robert F., Jr. "The Challenge of Poetics to (Normal) Historical Practice." *Poetics Today* 9 (1988): 435–52.

Brooks, Peter. *Reading for the Plot: Design and Intention in Narrative*. New York: Alfred A. Knopf, 1984.

Chertok, Leon, and de Saussure, Raymond. *The Therapeutic Revolution from Mesmer to Freud*. Translated by R. H. Ahrenfeldt. New York: Brunner and Mazel, 1979.

Cohn, Dorrit. "Fictional versus Historical Lives: Borderlines and Borderline Cases." *Journal of Narrative Technique* 19 (1989): 3–24.

———. "Signposts of Fictionality: A Narratological Perspective." *Poetics Today* 11 (1990): 775–804.

Corngold, Stanley. "Freud as Literature?" In *The Fate of the Self: German Writers and French Theory*. New York: Columbia University Press, 1986.

Culler, Jonathan. "Story and Discourse in the Analysis of Narrative." In *The Pursuit of Signs: Semiotics, Literature, Deconstruction*. Ithaca: Cornell University Press, 1981.

de Certeau, Michel. "The Freudian Novel: History and Literature." *Humanities in Society* 4 (1981): 121–44.

Derrida, Jacques. "The Purveyor of Truth." *Yale French Studies* 52 (1975): 31–113.

Doctorow, E. L. "False Documents." *American Review* 26 (1977): 215–32.

Ellenberger, Henri F. *The Discovery of the Unconscious: The History and Evolution of Dynamic Psychiatry*. New York: Basic Books, 1970.

Fish, Stanley. *Is There a Text in This Class? The Authority of Interpretive Communities*. Cambridge: Harvard University Press, 1980.

Freud, Sigmund. *Gesammelte Werke*. Edited by Anna Freud, E. Bibring, W. Hoffer, E. Kris, and O. Isakower. 18 vols. London: Imago, 1952.

———. *The Standard Edition of the Complete Psychological Works of Sig-*

*mund Freud.* Edited and translated by James Strachey. 24 vols. London: Hogarth, 1953–74.

"Charcot" (1893), vol. 3.

*Studies on Hysteria* (1893–95), vol. 2.

*The Interpretation of Dreams* (1900–1901), vols. 4, 5.

"Fragment of an Analysis of a Case of Hysteria" (1905), vol. 7.

*Delusion and Dream in Jensen's "Gradiva"* (1907), vol. 9.

"Hysterical Phantasies and their Relationship to Bisexuality" (1908), vol. 9.

"Creative Writers and Day-Dreaming" (1908), vol. 9.

"Notes upon a Case of Obsessional Neurosis" (1909), vol. 10.

"Contributions to the Psychology of Love I" (1910), vol. 11.

*Introductory Lectures on Psycho-Analysis* (1916–17), vols. 15–16.

"From the History of an Infantile Neurosis" (1918), vol. 17.

*The Future of an Illusion* (1927), vol. 21.

————. *Letters of Sigmund Freud.* Selected and edited by Ernst L. Freud. Translated by Tania and James Stern. New York: Basic Books, 1960.

————. *The Freud/Jung Letters: The Correspondence between Sigmund Freud and C. G. Jung.* Edited by William McGuire. Translated by Ralph Manheim and R. F. C. Hull. Princeton: Princeton University Press, 1974.

————. *The Complete Letters of Sigmund Freud to Wilhelm Fliess, 1887–1904.* Translated and edited by Jeffrey Mousaieff Masson. Cambridge: Harvard University Press, 1985.

Frye, Northrop. *The Anatomy of Criticism: Four Essays.* New York: Atheneum, 1967.

Gay, Peter. *Freud: A Life for Our Time.* New York: Norton, 1988.

Habermas, Jürgen. *Erkenntnis und Interesse.* Frankfurt: Suhrkamp, 1973.

Henninger, Peter. *Der Buchstabe und der Geist: Unbewusste Determinierung im Schreiben Robert Musils.* Frankfurt: P. D. Lang, 1980.

Hertz, Neil. "Dora's Secrets, Freud's Techniques." In *In Dora's Case: Freud—Hysteria—Feminism.* Edited by Charles Bernheimer and Claire Kahane. New York: Columbia University Press, 1985.

Kittler, Friedrich. *Aufschreibsysteme 1800/1900.* Munich: Fink, 1987.

Laplanche, Jean, and Pontalis, J. B. "Fantasme originaire, fantasmes des origines, origine du fantasme." *Les Temps modernes* 19 (1964): 1833–68.

————. *The Language of Psycho-Analysis.* Translated by Donald Nicholson-Smith. New York: Norton, 1973.

Mahony, Patrick. *Cries of the Wolf Man.* New York: International Universities Press, 1984.

————. *Freud and the Rat Man.* New Haven: Yale University Press, 1986.

Malcolm, Janet. "Reflections: J'appelle un chat un chat." *New Yorker,* 20 April, 1987, 84–102.

Marcus, Steven. "Freud and Dora: Story, History, Case History." In *Representations: Essays on Literature and Society.* New York: Random House, 1975.

————. "Freud and the Rat Man." In *Freud and the Culture of Psychoanalysis:*

*Studies in the Transition from Victorian Humanism to Modernity*. Boston: G. Allen and Unwin, 1984.

Morris, Humphrey. "The Need to Connect: Representations of Freud's Psychical Apparatus." In *The Literary Freud: Mechanisms of Defense and the Poetic Will*, edited by Joseph H. Smith. Psychiatry and the Humanities, vol. 4. New Haven: Yale University Press, 1980.

Muschg, Walter. "Freud als Schriftsteller." In *Die Zerstörung der Literatur*. Bern: Francke, 1956.

Nägele, Rainer. *Reading after Freud*. New York: Columbia University Press, 1987.

Olney, James. *Autobiography: Essays Theoretical and Critical*. Edited by James Olney. Princeton: Princeton University Press, 1980.

Rey, Jean-Michel. "Freud's Writing on Writing." *Yale French Studies* 55/56 (1977): 301–28.

Ricoeur, Paul. "The Question of Proof in Psychoanalysis." *Journal of the American Psychoanalytic Association* 25 (1977): 835–71.

———. *Time and Narrative*, vol. 1. Translated by Kathleen McLaughlin and David Pellauer. Chicago: University of Chicago Press, 1984.

Schafer, Roy. "Narration in the Psychoanalytic Dialogue." *Critical Inquiry* 7 (Autumn 1980): 29–53.

———. *Narrative Actions in Psychoanalysis: Narratives of Space and Narratives of Time*. Worcester, Mass.: Clark University Press, 1981.

Schönau, Walter. *Sigmund Freuds Prosa: Literarische Elemente seines Stils*. Stuttgart: Metzler, 1968.

Searle, John. "The Logical Status of Fictional Discourse." *New Literary History* 6 (1975): 319–32.

Sherwood, Michael. *The Logic of Explanation in Psychoanalysis*. New York: Academic Press, 1969.

Smith, Barbara Herrnstein. *On the Margins of Discourse: The Relation of Literature and Language*. Chicago: University of Chicago Press, 1978.

Vaihinger, Hans. *Die Philosophie des Als Ob*. Leipzig: Felix Meiner, 1918.

White, Hayden. *Tropics of Discourse: Essays in Cultural Criticism*. Baltimore: Johns Hopkins University Press, 1978.

Worbs, Michael. *Nervenkunst: Literatur und Psychoanalyse im Wien der Jahrhundertwende*. Frankfurt: Europäische Verlagsanstalt, 1983.

Yerushalmi, Yosef Hayim. "Freud on the 'Historical Novel': From the Manuscript Draft (1934) of *Moses and Monotheism*." *International Journal of Psycho-Analysis* 70 (1989): 375–95.

# 3 Translating Transmission: Representation and Enactment in Freud's Construction of History

## *Humphrey Morris*

*Words are a plastic material with which one can do all kinds of things.*—Freud (*S.E.* 8:34)

Histtory is inscribed in psychoanalysis. From the palimpsest of *The Interpretation of Dreams* to the biblical texts of *Moses and Monotheism*, the practice of the analyst is figured in reference to marks left behind—inscriptions to be deciphered, memory traces to be detected. From the beginning, historical process is built into Freud's theory as transmission by stratification of these traces, traces in which biological registrations are conceptualized through the analogon of writing: "As you know," he writes to Fliess in 1896, "I am working on the assumption that our psychic mechanism has come into being by a process of stratification: the material present in the form of memory traces being subjected from time to time to a *rearrangement* in accordance with fresh circumstances—to a *retranscription*. Thus what is essentially new about my theory is the thesis that memory is present not once but several times over, that it is laid down in various kinds of indications [*verschiedenen Arten von Zeichen*]" (letter of 6 December 1896; Freud 1985, 207 [English]; 1986, 217 [German]; emphasis Freud's here and in all quotations unless noted otherwise). Like inherited biological traces, these written traces seem to have the power to transmit themselves—according to Freud's theory, but also within his own writing practice: "In its implications the distortion of a text resembles a murder: the difficulty is not in perpetrating the deed, but in getting rid of its traces" (*S.E.* 23:43). This aside about biblical texts in *Moses and Monotheism*, some forty years after the letter to Fliess, not only relies on the same figurative resonances of the "trace" to thematize transmission of psychic material, but predicts an enactment

of this theme in the text at hand, where sixty pages later the historicizing traces return in reference to *Moses* itself: "I found myself
unable to wipe out the traces of the history of the work's origin, which
was in any case unusual. . . . I determined to give it up; but it tormented
me like an unlaid ghost" (*S.E.* 23:103).

Freud taught us to be attentive to the traces of history in such
symptomatic repetitions, and here we could set off on an interpretive
path from *Moses* to murder to (textual) traces to parricide to the
Oedipus complex to Freud's wish to replace his father, or to be his
own father. I mention the possibility of this kind of psychoanalytic
reading not to engage in it, but as a way of beginning to think about
the relationship of psychoanalysis and history, or, to limit that question,
as a way of asking how psychoanalysis thinks historically, and what
happens when it does. To say that "psychoanalysis" thinks historically
is, of course, to personify psychoanalysis and to suggest the beginnings
of an allegorical story line; there might perhaps seem to be less rhetorical obfuscation and more precision in asking how "psychoanalysts"
think historically. Either way, though, one is conceptualizing, and already with *that* figurative displacement the question about history
becomes implicated in the question about rhetoric; to think historically one must certainly conceptualize, and perhaps also allegorize
and tell stories.

My point in tracing a possible path of psychoanalytic interpretation
from the symptomatic repetitions of Freud's *Moses* to Freud's parricidal
and self-engendering wishes is to suggest that allegory is inextricable
from the way psychoanalysis thinks historically about its evidence, the
traces it finds.[1] The privileged example of psychoanalytic-historical
allegory would be the psychoanalyst's use of the oedipal story line to
arrange, or as Hayden White (1973, 7–11) would say to emplot, the
facts of the analysand's relationships. Allegory meets an expository
need by playing out along a historicizing, narrative line of temporal
succession the tensions inherent in intrapsychic or intralinguistic
structures, by transforming synchrony into diachrony. Freud often
makes note of this need, but in a passing way that tends to minimize
any epistemological implications: "Elements in this complicated whole
[*Zusammenhang*] which are in fact simultaneous can only be represented successively in my description of them" (*S.E.* 5:588; *G.W.*
2/3:593). Starting from inferred oedipal structure—a "complex"—he
constructs the oedipal allegory that historicizes this structure in the
life of the individual; then he sets up, most overtly in *Totem and
Taboo* and in *Moses*, a theory about intergenerational historical transmission in the form of an allegory of the first allegory.[2] Allegorically,

the individual is doubly inscribed in time, and in theory too: psychoanalytic *theory*, in the sense of a discourse about structure and
function that is not itself temporally structured, theorizes the inevitability of its own transformation into the temporalizing mode of narrative. The principles of this transformation of theory into allegorical
narrative determine for Freud not only the retranscription of past
collective experience as present individual experience, but the historicizing "translation," as he calls it in the same 1896 letter to Fliess,
between the "successive epochs of life," the translation of individual
experience into individual life history.[3] The Wolf Man, particularly,
calls for a formal statement of the assumption by the individual of
theoretical oedipal structure as tragic historicity:

> I have now come to the end of what I had to say about this case. There
> remain two problems, of the many that it raises, which seem to me to
> deserve special emphasis. The first relates to the phylogenetically in-
> herited schemata, which, like the categories of philosophy, are con-
> cerned with the business of 'placing' the impressions derived from actual
> experience. I am inclined to take the view that they are precipitates
> from the history of human civilization. The Oedipus complex, which
> comprises a child's relation to his parents, is one of them—is, in fact,
> the best known member of the class. Whatever experiences fail to fit
> in with the hereditary schema, they become remodelled in the imagi-
> nation—a process which might very profitably be followed out in detail.
> It is precisely such cases that are calculated to convince us of the
> independent existence of the schema. We are often able to see the
> schema triumphing over the experience of the individual. [*S.E.* 17:119]

Taking this passage as a frame for our historical question, we would
want to know more about the internal workings of psychoanalytic
theory as allegory. Freud's suggestion that we follow out in detail the
encounter of experience and schema, the remodeling of experience
"in the imagination," would pull for very different responses from
different sectors of today's psychoanalytic community, however that
was defined. Some would dismiss the whole business as a bad Lamarckian joke—on Freud. But that would be to overlook the analogy
Freud makes between inherited schemata, in particular the Oedipus
complex, and the "categories of philosophy," which again links historical transmission to linguistic transmission. Read from the perspectives opened by Roy Schafer and Hayden White, the passage could
send us to some version of the "archetypal" criticism of their common
intellectual ancestor, Northrop Frye.[4] Schafer's "The Psychoanalytic
Vision of Reality" (1976) and White's introduction to *Metahistory*
(1973) both begin in Frye and inaugurate projects devoted to asking

how schemata like the categories of philosophy or like literary modes are transmitted, and how experience is allegorically remodeled in the imagination to fit in with them. In this way both Schafer and White engage the general question I have started from here, a question that runs through Freud as a nagging but always circumscribed and disavowed concern: Where is figurative language to be situated in relation to the theoretical enterprise that—to put it figuratively, and is there an alternative?—"employs" it?[5] Schafer and White give particular attention to the question of the narrator, to what they both take to be the inevitability of establishing a fiction, a rhetorical figure, of the narrator in psychoanalytic and historical discourse. This would include theoretical discourse, where the narrator's apparent absence in no way eliminates the question. However manifestly present or absent, the narrator is the mediating principle in the encounter of experience and schema. For White, it is through a narrative transformation into one of Frye's modes, understood as "modes of emplotment"—romance, tragedy, comedy, satire—that the chronicle and other archival forms come to qualify as "history"; for Schafer, the same categories determine the transformations that structure the analysand's construction of a life history.[6]

Freud's suggestion might be taken seriously as an invitation to other kinds of interdisciplinary work as well, using other critical systems that address the historicizing relation of experience and schema. By way of continuing in the general direction pointed by Schafer and White while using a method different from theirs, I will draw particularly on approaches that in various ways depend on rhetorical analysis of narrative structure and process. In this, I risk being seen as having taken sides in a current debate in psychoanalysis and of having given up on the pursuit of the "historical truth" in favor of "narrative truth." I mean instead to get perspective on that debate by considering one of its underlying problems, the tension between process and structure in the experience/schema relation, from a rhetorical point of view. To this end I will state the question of the narrator in terms suggested by Benveniste and Barthes as the question of the encounter between a schema, language-as-system, and given individual "users," whose purposes could include the practice and theory of psychoanalysis and history.[7] To put it in this simplified way is to pass over important distinctions made by narratologists in the interest of staying with Freud's historical question about the relation of experience and schema.[8] The analogy of that relation with the relations speech/language, practice/theory, and chronicle/history suggests an approach to the internal workings of historicopsychoanalytic allegories through the

question of the remodeling transformations—the historicizing translations—in these pairs. I will pursue these translations here through
two texts in which Freud asks himself about the relation of the patient's
"history" and the analyst's historical theorizing, texts in dialogue across
almost the entire span of Freud's own psychoanalytic history: "Fragment of an Analysis of a Case of Hysteria" (written 1901, published
1905) and "Constructions in Analysis" (1937).

My approach is interdisciplinary, and therefore uneasy, by dint of
drawing on both psychoanalysis and literary criticism (broadly defined
to include "literary theory"), enterprises that I do not find to have as
much in common as their active import/export market might suggest,
and within each of which the practice/theory relation is these days
particularly uneasy. But to note this is also to introduce another aspect
of the topic: the inevitability of anxiety accompanying the inevitability
of assuming a narrative stance, particularly when the narrative is an
attempt at reconstructing a history—not only one's own, but another's, or others'. Anxiety and often nostalgia seem to attend upon all
translations from the more unformed first term—experience, speech,
chronicle, practice—to the more formalized second—schema, language, history, theory. Through these affective accompaniments of
historical reconstruction we are brought to the recognition of the
inevitable loss that attends upon our inevitable formalizations, our
allegorizings. My interdisciplinary narrative will try to bring together
a psychoanalytic convention—centering on the words "castration"
and "separation"—of narrating that loss as loss of (fantasies of) emotional access to a primary love object, and a (roughly speaking) lin-
guistic/literary critical convention of narrating it as loss of (fantasies
of) intuitive, perceptual access to the linguistic referent. To that end,
the selective reading of Freud I propose here emphasizes the question
of reference as a way of stating, and staying with, the problem of the
historical truth of loss: how language functions to point to, name, or
represent things, and how it doesn't. I test out on psychoanalysis
certain ideas about reference that some literary critics would endorse,
and others would dismiss, as "deconstruction": that reference is a
function of language, not an intuition, and that allegory both thematizes
and enacts the problem of referential loss, and its attendant nostalgia.[9]
This brings me to the textual relationship between two distinct kinds
of defense against loss, repression and denial, which I associate,
respectively, with the poles of representation and enactment. I choose
to depend, methodologically, on Freud—that is, on textual analysis of
the *Standard Edition* and the *Gesammelte Werke*. Whatever the transferential motives of this dependence, it allows me to develop my

interdisciplinary discourse in relation to an object of both psychoanalytic and literary interest whose public and historical status permits me to engage with professionally various readers and writers. Within this methodological choice, I am a psychoanalyst, and I make my argument about representation and enactment of history in Freud with a view to raising questions about these aspects of psychoanalytic clinical process as well.

## From Metaphor to Allegory in Dora

### ACTS OF NARRATION

"Fragment of an Analysis of a Case of Hysteria," written in 1901, stands as a theoretical statement between *The Interpretation of Dreams* (1900) and *Three Essays on the Theory of Sexuality* (1905). The opening paragraphs of its second section, "The Clinical Picture," manifestly take up the task of connecting the theory of dreams to a theory of symptoms. The discussion soon comes to center on history, in the form of the question how the psychoanalyst can arrive at an "intelligible, consistent, and unbroken case history" (*S.E.* 7:18). Freud begins by reminding the reader that in *The Interpretation of Dreams*, "I showed that dreams in general can be interpreted, and that after the work of interpretation [*Deutungsarbeit*] has been completed they can be replaced by perfectly correctly constructed thoughts [*sich durch tadellos gebildete ... Gedanken ersetzen lassen*] which can be assigned a recognizable position in the chain of mental events [*seelischen Zusammenhang*]" (*S.E.* 7:15; *G.W.* 5:172). The process of replacement—thoughts for dreams—returns later in the paragraph as the metaphor of translation: "At that time I learnt how to translate the language of dreams into the forms of expression of our own thought-language, which can be understood without further help [*Ich erlernte damals, wie mann aus der Sprache des Traumes in die ohne weitere Nachhilfe verständliche Ausdrucksweise unserer Denksprache übersetzen muss*]" (*S.E.* 7:15; *G.W.* 5:172). In the 6 December 1896 letter to Fliess, Freud had noted the relation between translation and defense: "A failure of translation—this is what is known clinically as 'repression'" (1985, 208). Here, translation—*Übersetzung*—from dream-language to thought-language is explicitly the metaphor for establishing understanding by lifting repression. The import of this choice emerges through another term for "translation" in German, *Übertragung*, which also means "transference" and "metaphor."

Figures for translation bring together the intrapsychic and intralinguistic aspects of psychoanalytic understanding; in "The Uncon-

scious" (1915), Freud will make more explicit the connection between lifting repression and translating unconscious "thing-presentations" into preconscious "word-presentations" (*S.E.* 14:201–2). Such
understanding through translation, as he presents it in "Dora," is not
simply a theoretical process, but one emotionally invested and practical: "The following fragment from the history of the treatment of a
hysterical girl is intended to show the way in which the interpretation
of dreams plays a part in the work of analysis. It will at the same time
give me a first opportunity of publishing at sufficient length to prevent
further *misunderstanding* some of my views upon the psychical processes of hysteria and upon its organic determinants" (*S.E.* 7:15; emphasis mine). The translation Freud proposes to perform in "Dora" is
not just from dreams to thoughts, but from theory to practice, and
the understanding he seeks is not just his own understanding of symptoms, but the reader's understanding of the psychoanalytic method of
constructing a "history."

The "Dora" text dramatizes the tension between misunderstanding
and understanding as it occurs in the patient, in the clinician, and
between the patient and the clinician, but also in the reader, in the
narrator, and between the reader and the narrator. The core distinction
made by narratologists between "story" and "discourse" comes to
mind: "Narratives are communications ... from author to audience.
... What is communicated is *story*, the formal content element of
narrative; and it is communicated by *discourse*, the formal expression
element" (Chatman 1978, 31). Freud's text would be more or less,
depending on how one categorized its theoretical portions, a narrative
"discourse" of the "story" told him by the adolescent girl he presents
to his audience under the name "Dora." That discourse would have
two general aspects: it would present the treatment, the translation
of Dora's irrational symptoms into rational thoughts, and it would
present an address on the subject of psychoanalytic theory, with a
manifest agenda of persuasion. Between "story" and "discourse" would
lie the narrative, linguistic *act* of transforming the one into the other.
This act is designated by the French critic Genette as "narration"
(1972, 72, 76); I will use his term as a way of referring to the processes
of transformation between, and within, practice and theory that concern me here.[10]

What are the acts—pun intended—of narration in "Dora"? In what
ways does that actor, the "narrator," through whom Freud figures
linguistically in the text, enact translations between story and discourse, practice and theory? The "Dora" discourse—the text, roughly
speaking, of the story of Dora—is one in which Dora herself, it is

often pointed out, is repeatedly overlooked.[11] In her place, we find a story about psychoanalytic storytelling, about the translation not of psychoanalytic practice into theory but of psychoanalytic theory into practice. The narrator's investment in *that* story is evident in the opening paragraphs of "The Clinical Picture": "The patients' inability to give an ordered history of their life is so far as it coincides with the history of their illness [*geordneten Darstellung ihrer Lebensges- chichte, soweit sie mit der Krankheitsgeschichte zusammenfällt*] is not merely characteristic of the neurosis. It also possesses great the- oretical significance" (*S.E.* 7:16–17; *G.W.* 5:174). Freud makes ref- erence here to his, and the patient's, acts of narrating when he draws the distinction, hidden in the English translation, between the narra- tive, the *Darstellung* ("representation" or, notably, "performance"), and the *Lebens-* or *Krankheitsgeschichte* ("life-" or "illness-" "history" or "story") it conveys.[12] "It is only towards the end of the treatment," he writes in the next paragraph, "that we have before us an intelligible, consistent, and unbroken case history [*konsequente, verständliche und lückenlose Krankengeschichte*]. Whereas the practical aim of the treatment is to remove all possible symptoms and to replace [*ersetzen*] them by conscious thoughts, we may regard it as a second and the- oretical aim to repair [*heilen*] all the damages to the patient's memory. These two aims are coincident [*fallen zusammen*]. When one is reached, so is the other; and the same path leads to them both [*der nämliche Weg führt zu beiden*]" (*S.E.* 7:18; *G.W.* 5:175).

The narrative frame for Freud's verbal portrait of Dora is at the same time the theoretical model for the psychoanalytic case history. In his "Prefatory Remarks" to the case, Freud compares himself to a "conscientious archaeologist" who has brought "to the light of day after their long burial the priceless though mutilated relics of antiquity [*die unschätzbaren wenn auch verstümmelten Reste des Altertums aus langer Begrabenheit an den Tag zu bringen*]" (*S.E.* 7:12; *G.W.* 5:169). He writes that "repression," the term he uses at this time to designate all defenses, has "damaged" Dora's memory (16–18) and— through the archeological analogy—implies that it has "mutilated" the text of her story. He will directly evoke the image of the muti- lated—*verstümmelt*—text in discussions of defense long after "Dora," in *Moses* (*S.E.* 23:43; *G.W.* 16:143) and "Analysis Terminable and In- terminable" (*S.E.* 23:236; *G.W.* 16:81). In those instances, signifi- cantly, he is explicit in associating textual mutilation with mechanisms of defense such as disavowal (*S.E.* 23:43), which he says are to be "sharply differentiated" (*S.E.* 23:236) from repression. It is also rele- vant to the question of defending against anxiety aroused by reconstructive work, and perhaps to the question of Freud's attempt to write about Dora, to note another occurrence in his work of the image of mutilation. In "Some Psychical Consequences of the Anatomical Distinction between the Sexes" (1925), the young boy engages in a research effort to understand sexual difference. Having observed the girl's genitals, he first disavows what he sees, but later is beset by castration anxiety and experiences "two reactions, which may become fixed and will in that case, whether separately or together or in conjunction with other factors, permanently determine the boy's relations to women: horror of the mutilated creature [*Abscheu vor dem verstümmelten Geschöpf*] or triumphant contempt for her" (*S.E.* 19:252; *G.W.* 14:24). In "Dora," the researcher proposes a model of combined reconstruction and construction aimed at the restoration of wholeness—narrative wholeness. Fragments of life history and illness history will be brought to "coincide"—literally, to fall together, *zusammenfallen*—and "the same path [*der nämliche Weg*]" will lead to the "practical aim" and the "theoretical aim" of the treatment. The "mutilated" object will be restored when theory and practice—"replacement" of symptoms and "repair" of memory—coincide, when the translation is transparent. This narrative process is reflexively figured by the text as the ascendancy of "our own [*unserer*] thought-language, which can be understood without further help" (*S.E.* 7:15), over dream-language, *der Sprache des Traumes*, which is in some way not our own, not understandable.

*The Roundabout Path: Narrative Origins of Theory*

It is Freud's very acts of narrative persuasion in these paragraphs, or to be more exact the tropes inseparable from these acts, that end up casting doubt upon the possibility of ever securely establishing such understanding—questions of disavowed anxiety, for the moment, aside. Freud deftly lays out the several reasons for which patients are unable to give "an ordered history of their life insofar as it coincides with the history of their illness," but we are left still wondering about the pitfalls that lie along the path he tries to take from a theory of translation to the practice of psychoanalysis. The term "path" itself provides a way into the problem, for the argument that ends up claiming that the "same path," *der nämliche Weg*, neatly leads to both the "practical aim" and the "theoretical aim" of the treatment begins by implicating that metaphor in the uncertainties of the practice/theory relation.

The metaphorical path that runs through "The Clinical Picture" appears first as the figure for Freud's own mental process: "The problem [of dreams] crossed my path [*Ich fand sie auf meinem Wege*] as I was endeavoring to cure psychoneuroses by means of a particular psychotherapeutic method" (*S.E.* 7:15; *G.W.* 5:172). The metaphor returns a few lines later in the discussion of the dream-language/thought-language translation model, but with a difference that complicates things. The dream, Freud elaborates, "is one of the roads [*Wege*] along which consciousness can be reached by the psychical material"; then he specifies in the next sentence, with emphasis: "The dream, in short, is one of the *détours* [*Umwege*] *by which repression can be evaded*" (15). The *Weg* of the dream has shifted to an *Umweg*. While a path, *Weg*, could at the same time be a detour, *Umweg*—it is a question of its function—the complication arises when, as Freud has invited us to, we read "Dora" in the context of *The Interpretation of Dreams*. There, he carefully distinguished between the "activity of thought," which "constitutes a roundabout path [*Umweg*] to wish-fulfillment which has been made necessary by experience," and "dreams, which fulfil their wishes along the short path of regression [*Der Traum, der seine Wünsche auf kurzem regredienten Wege erfüllt*]" (*S.E.* 5:567; *G.W.* 2/3:572). Freud's wording in this opening section of "Dora" would seem to blur that formal distinction. Within the terms of psychoanalytic theory, it might be said that this terminological inconsistency simply signals the dream's status as compromise formation between wish and defense: it is both a short path to wish fulfillment in the unconscious and a roundabout path along which the unconscious wish, in the disguises of the dream work, enters consciousness. Or it might be pointed out that the dream as *Umweg* circumvents repressions of internal reality, while, in the formulation of chapter 7, the activity of thought as *Umweg* circumvents denials of external reality. But the referential slippage of the metaphors *Weg* and *Umweg* both within this paragraph of "The Clinical Picture," and between chapter 7 of *The Interpretation of Dreams* and "Dora," is also an event at the surface of the text that is not done away with by these clarifications. For a rhetorical analysis of the way Freud stages the relation between practice and theory in "Dora" it raises the question of the referential functioning of his narration. After "Dora," the metaphor *Umweg* will slide in Freud's texts along a line increasingly allegorical. In *Beyond the Pleasure Principle*, the living entity is "striving to return by the circuitous paths [*Umwege*] along which its development leads" to "an *old* state of things, an initial state" (*S.E.* 18:38; *G.W.* 13:40); in the 1935 "Postscript" to *An Autobiographical Study*, the return is Freud's own, as his personified "interest" now takes the path first traced in the psychical apparatus of *The Interpretation of Dreams*: "My interest, after making a lifelong *détour* [*Umweg*] through the natural sciences, medicine and psychotherapy, returned to the cultural problems which had fascinated me long before, when I was a youth scarcely old enough for thinking" (*S.E.* 20:72; *G.W.* 16:32).

*Weg* and *Umweg* are conventional figures through which Freud's narration informally refers to itself, and at the same time terms that come to be invested with specifically psychoanalytic meaning through their occurrence in formal theoretical contexts. With this formal investment of its figures of narration—of self-reference—Freud's narrative mode in *The Interpretation of Dreams* and "Dora" has already begun to depart from the conventional path, *Weg*, of allegorical narration on which it started out,[13] and to move onto a more roundabout, recursive, and specifically psychoanalytic allegorical path, the *Umweg*. In chapter 7 of *The Interpretation of Dreams*, *Weg* and *Umweg* are implicated in the functioning of a formalized, theoretical "psychical apparatus" and, through that, in the rhetorical functioning of psychoanalytic narrative. The theory has directly to do with reference, for it turns on the question of reality testing: how does the apparatus distinguish between a present perception of an external object and an internal reactivation that, passing through the "mnemic image" of the perception, can bring about, in the *absence* of that external object, the hallucinatory repetition of the perception itself? It is a question of establishing the fundamental referential distinctions between inside and outside, present and past. The verbal representation of the corresponding, properly *psychoanalytic* distinction, between the "primary" and the "secondary" "processes," is, to quote again the remark with which Freud introduces the section on that topic in chapter 7, a daunting expository task: "I have set myself a hard task, and one to which my powers of exposition [*Darstellungskunst*] are scarcely equal. Elements in this complicated whole which are in fact simultaneous can only be represented successively in my description of them" (*S.E.* 5:588; *G.W.* 2/3:593).

Freud chooses to present a formal theory, the theory of the relation between primary and secondary process, as a temporally sequential (beginning-middle-end) narrative. This choice is a response to the difficulty of presenting *psychoanalytically* the relation between schema and experience. The particular expository task he has set himself in chapter 7 is to stage that relation by using his formal "schematic picture" of a "psychical apparatus" (*S.E.* 5:536–44) as the basis for the narration of a paradigmatic "experience of satisfaction" (*S.E.* 5:565–67). This "experience" then serves as the starting point for an allegory of psychic development. Evolutionary and individual history are not clearly distinguished; through the allegorized "experience of satisfaction," Freud is taking up the question of origin: how does the apparatus come to be "psychical" in the first place? He employs the historicizing narrative device of postulating a developmentally "earlier stage" of the psychical apparatus in which its "functioning capacity" was limited to a "first psychical activity" (565–66) that he designates (601) as "primary process." Subsequently, in the terms of this "theoretical fiction" (603), "The bitter experience of life must have changed this primitive thought-activity into a more expedient secondary one" (566). In the historicizing narrative, *Weg* is associated with primary process and hallucination, *Umweg* with secondary process and reality testing. Thematically, a theory about psychic origins is played out through a hypothetical "hungry baby" beset by its "major somatic needs" (565). Structurally, this narrative is allegorical both in the sense of dealing, in one set of sequentially ordered and more personified terms, with the relations between another set of simultaneous and more abstract terms (primary and secondary process), and also in the sense of presenting, through the baby as a psychoanalytic Everyperson, a highly abstracted version of the life history of each of us.

The development of the baby's referential function is traced in a series of moments on the allegorical time line. In the first moment, the "experience of satisfaction," a somatic "internal stimulus" is put to an end when the hungry baby receives nourishment through "outside help" (565). This experience establishes a representational structure in the baby: "An essential component of this experience of satisfaction is a particular perception (that of nourishment, in our example) the mnemic image [*Erinnerungsbild*] of which remains associated thenceforward with the memory trace [*Gedächtnisspur*] of the excitation produced by the need" (565; *G.W.* 571). A referential connection or, in Freud's words, an associative "link" (*Verknüpfung*), is established; schematically, the resulting complex if primitive representational structure joins two nonpsychical referents, the nourishment object and the somatic need, through a series of intermediate terms: nourishment object/perception of nourishment object/mnemic image of perception : memory trace of excitation/excitation produced by need/somatic need. The "link" (which I have indicated with a colon) is the basis for what Freud designates as the "first *psychical* activity" (566; emphasis mine): the "next time" the *somatic* need arises, "a *psychical* impulse will at once emerge which will seek to re-cathect the mnemic image of the perception and to re-evoke the perception itself, that is to say, to re-establish the situation of the original satisfaction" (565–66; emphasis mine). But this psychical impulse, or "wish," takes the referential "shortest path" (*kürzeste Weg*) by moving through the associative link between memory trace and mnemic image and on to the perception itself, without obtaining (through motor activity) the real-world referent of the perception— the nourishment: "the shortest path to the fulfilment of the wish is a path leading direct from the excitation produced by the need to a complete cathexis of the perception" (566; *G.W.* 571). Freud terms this hallucinatory re-evocation of the perception, split off from its referent, a "perceptual identity" (566).

Secondary psychical activity, in Freud's developmental narrative, arises because the establishment of perceptual identity "along the short path of regression" does nothing to satisfy the baby's somatic need, which "persists" (566). It is "necessary to bring the regression to a halt before it becomes complete, so that it does not proceed beyond the mnemic image"; now the apparatus "is able to seek out other paths [*Wege*] which lead eventually to the desired perceptual identity being established from the direction of the external world" (566; *G.W.* 572). As Freud says in a 1919 footnote: "In other words, it becomes evident that there must be a means of 'reality-testing'" (566, n. 2). This brings him to *Umweg*, a term he puts in bold print in the German as he describes the apparatus's achievement of what he will call "thought identity" (602) with an ironic touch that anticipates *Beyond the Pleasure Principle*: "But all the complicated thought-activity which is spun out from the mnemic image to the moment at which the perceptual identity is established by the external world—all this activity of thought merely [*nur*] constitutes a roundabout path [*Umweg*] to wish-fulfilment which has been made necessary by experience. Thought is after all nothing but a substitute [*Ersatz*] for a hallucinatory wish" (566–67; *G.W.* 572).

In the interest of staying with the question of Freud's acts of narration in "Dora," I will pass over here the complex further evolution of this primary theoretical model. It is itself the subject of repeated returns throughout his writing, returns that make increasingly problematic the "reality" to be tested; the list of its occurrences would begin with the "Project" (1895), and include "Formulations on the Two Principles of Mental Functioning" (1911), "Instincts and Their Vicissitudes" (1915), "A Metapsychological Supplement to the Theory of Dreams" (1917), *Beyond the Pleasure Principle* (1920), "A Note upon the 'Mystic Writing Pad'" (1925), "Negation" (1925), *Civilization and Its Discontents* (1930), and *An Outline of Psycho-Analysis* (1938). Any analysis of these various statements of the model, even one conducted in the technical terms of psychoanalytic metapsychology, would come up against a question about the structure of the narrative: Why does Freud postulate a primitive apparatus functioning *only* along the short path of primary process? As he himself says in chapter 7, "It is true that, so far as we know, no psychical apparatus exists which possesses a primary process only and that such an apparatus is to that extent a theoretical fiction" (*S.E.* 5:603).[14] Why not construct a theoretical model in which there are from the beginning two processes in shifting states of relative balance? Of course there is no one way to answer this, and no short way, but one approach to an answer would begin from the observation that the fiction of a pure primary process seems to answer certain narrative needs. At the time of *The Interpretation of Dreams* and "Dora," Freud is seeking to establish, through the analogy with archeology, his fundamental claim that primitive, primal relics are preserved and recoverable in the psyche. He is also seeking to establish that his practice can be brought together with his theory. In *The Interpretation of Dreams* he argues that dreams have "preserved for us . . . a sample of the psychical apparatus's primary method of working" (*S.E.* 5:567). In "Dora," he invokes dreams as *representatives* of primary process—given the dream work, they cannot be direct exemplifications—to mediate between practice and theory. In practice, as *Umweg*, the dream would make possible archeological recovery; in the narration of theory, as *kürzeste Weg*, it would itself be the recovered primal relic—a pure form of primitive mental activity that still takes the shortest and historically oldest path postulated by theory, and whose primitive "language" Freud proposes to "translate" for the reader into "our own thought-language," and put to "practical application" (*S.E.* 7:15).

A theoretically deeper expository need for the fiction of a pure primary process lies in a fundamental and destabilizing distinction Freud makes in chapter 7 as background for his understanding of our neurotic failures to take "reality" into account. In his "schematic picture" of a psychical apparatus made up of "$\psi$-systems" and to which "we shall ascribe a sensory and a motor end" (537), a "first differentiation" (538) sets up the sensory-end functions of perception and memory as radically distinct: "We shall suppose that a system at the very front of the apparatus receives the perceptual stimuli but retains no trace of them and thus has no memory, while behind it there lies a second system which transforms the momentary excitations of the first system into permanent traces" (538). This makes for problems of translation that gain in import when Freud goes on to associate perception with consciousness:

It is the *Pcpt.* system, which is without the capacity to retain modifications and is thus without memory, that provides our consciousness with the whole multiplicity of sensory qualities. On the other hand, our memories—not excepting those which are most deeply stamped in our minds—and in themselves unconscious. They can be made conscious; but there can be no doubt that they can produce all their effects while in an unconscious condition. What we describe as our 'character' is based on the memory-traces of our impressions; and, moreover, the impressions which have had the greatest effect on us—those of our earliest youth—are precisely the ones which scarcely ever become conscious. But if memories become conscious once more, they exhibit no sensory quality or a very slight one in comparison with perceptions. A most promising light would be thrown on the conditions governing the excitation of neurones if it could be confirmed that *in the ψ-systems memory and the quality that characterizes consciousness are mutually exclusive.* [*S.E.* 5:539–40]

In a 1919 footnote Freud writes that "*Pcpt.* = *Cs.*" (541, n. 1), but this schematization elides his linguistic figuration. It is, as he says later in chapter 7, a matter of metaphorical substitution, of an "*analogy* [*Analogie*] between our *Cs.* system and the perceptual systems" (616; *G.W.* 2/3:621; emphasis mine). This metaphor is the basis for Freud's account of the conditions under which we pursue our own psychical histories: "But what part is there left to be played in our scheme by consciousness, which was once so omnipotent and hid all else from view? *Only that of a sense-organ for the perception of psychical qualities.* ... The psychical apparatus, which is turned towards the external world with its sense-organ of the *Pcpt.* systems, is itself the external world in relation to the sense-organ of the *Cs.*, whose teleological justification resides in this circumstance" (615–16). In "The Unconscious" (1915) he elaborates:

Just as Kant warned us not to overlook the fact that our perceptions are subjectively conditioned and must not be regarded as identical with what is perceived though unknowable, so psycho-analysis warns us not to equate perceptions by means of consciousness with the unconscious mental processes which are their object. Like the physical, the psychical is not necessarily in reality what it appears to us to be. We shall be glad to learn, however, that the correction of internal perception will turn out not to offer such great difficulties as the correction of external perception—that internal objects are less unknowable than the external world. [*S.E.* 14:171]

The relatively optimistic conclusion of this passage could be read as an effort at narrative containment—containment of theoretical diffi-

culties opened up for psychoanalysis by the basic metaphorical substitution of perception for consciousness. But Freud will also continue
to explore these difficulties—even while continuing to assert the
relative knowability of internal reality—as late in his work as "Constructions in Analysis" (1937).

In the reading I am proposing of the theoretically originating passage from *The Interpretation of Dreams*, difficulties of establishing
"reality" are played out allegorically in, and as, the relation between
the theory and the narrative—categories I take, for my expository
purposes, to be "theoretically" separable. In the theory, it is in the
separation between the metaphorically linked "sensory" systems of
perception and consciousness on one side, and the "associative" (539)
systems of memory on the other, and in the consequent need for
translations, that Freud locates the vulnerability of his apparatus to
referential errors—not just the gross errors of hallucination, but more
subtle errors of transference. The fiction of a pure primary process,
which invokes the formal model of the dream as *kürzeste Weg*, carries
the burden of establishing a *narrative* origin for this theory. In Freud's
terms, that origin lies in the original "link" established by the "experience of satisfaction," and traversed by the primary process, between perception and memory. All psychical functioning would now
be precariously grounded, according to the argument of the narrative,
in the wish to return, by a detour through thought, "to the moment
at which the perceptual identity is established by the external world"
(566–67); all thought, in this way, would refer back to a primary
"primitive thought-activity" (566) in which reality was denied.

The narrative serving as origin for psychoanalytic theory would
seem to evoke, as its starting point and referential standard, a notion
of perception that its own argument, and Freud's explicitly Kantian
theoretical position, would challenge. A "real perception [*reale Wahr-
nehmung*] of the object of satisfaction" (599; *G.W.* 2/3:604), occurring
in the theoretical fiction before the first moment of psychical functioning, is the referential basis not only for the allegorical baby's "experience of satisfaction," its experience of the nourishment referent,
but through that experience, the referential basis for the allegorically
subsequent development of all psychical activity, primary and
secondary. The effect of the allegory is strongly to suggest that in any
apparatus that could be termed "psychical," not just perception-as-
consciousness but even "real perception" can never make present the
"real." The link between the mnemic image of a perception and the
memory trace of an excitation, which allegorically fixes a representational, re-presentational origin for the psychical, also brings any "per-

ception" of any "reality" under the sway of wishful impulses.[15] Yet as a narrative moment, "real perception" is a necessary designation of an origin antecedent to (the theorization of) distinctions between past and present, inside and outside, fantasy and reality. The predicament is suggested in Freud's well-known remark in the closing paragraphs of this closing chapter of *The Interpretation of Dreams*, that "*psychical* reality is a particular form of existence not to be confused with *material* reality" (620). The radical separations made in theory between perception and memory and between the material and the psychical, and the theoretically consequent errors of "reality-testing," signal the difficulty of establishing a referential basis for the narration of that theory.

It is as though Freud as narrator must try to get around the split he has introduced between perception and thought, and around the denial of the referent that his theory of psychical functioning starts from: as though he must deny in the *Umweg* of narration the inevitable implication, for his writing, of his own theory of the inevitability of referential error. The tendency toward solipsism in the psychical apparatus is mirrored in the language of theory, which establishes an epistemological starting point for its own referential function in an allegorical fiction in which the origin recedes in a series of distorting repetitions and substitutions. The dream as theoretical shortest path, as primal relic, is in practice always an *Umweg*: a dream "text," in Freud's words, that is a derivative, narrated version of the hypothetical dream−as−"perceptual identity." The first psychical representation of the external, "real" world is based upon the enactment of a primitive denial—denial of the difference between perception and memory. For the narration of psychoanalytic theory, the mixed gesture of positing and attempting to get around the radical difference between perception and memory, thought, or language would be its only way of grounding itself, giving itself a referential origin. The narration of theory would begin from a kind of necessary denial to the extent that it treated linguistic reference as a matter of "coincidences" grounded intuitively in perception, rather than as a variably successful function of language.[16] Representation, as theoretical origin for psychical process and as linguistic origin for Freud's theorizing process, would depend precariously on maintaining its connection to referents both material and psychical through the metaphorical equation of consciousness with perception. In the argument of the narrative, perception is antecedent to the psychical, and it is from perception that all memory and associative thought are originarily split off. Words themselves could be among the elusive referents of the theoretical narrative:

as Freud abundantly demonstrates in both *The Interpretation of Dreams* and *Jokes and Their Relation to the Unconscious* (1905)—close temporal neighbors of "Dora"—linguistic signifiers are themselves also objects of sensory perception tenuously attached to the meanings thought-activity assigns them. It is not only Freud's psychical apparatus that has trouble taking "reality" into account. Psychoanalytic narration, directing its *Umweg* toward the formal coincidence of practice and theory, predicts its own failures of translation: "Our thinking always remains exposed to falsification by interference from the unpleasure principle" (*S.E.* 5:603).[17]

In "Dora," Freud is testing his new theory against the reality that crosses his path in the form of Dora's symptoms, Dora's resistance. Much of the clinical dialogue will turn on a struggle about reference: Dora's denials of Freud's interpretations, and Freud's denials of these denials. The question of the relation between practice and theory, treatment and text, in this way makes manifest the question of the relation between Freud's acts of narration and the representational structure of the discourse they produce. It is in this relation between language as act and language as representation that the tensions of reference, of the text's way of going about being *about* something, reside. The text, the narration/discourse of "Dora," is not just about the patient's story, and not just about the encounter between Freud and Dora, an encounter forming part of Freud's practice, but also about Freud's attempt to write psychoanalytic theory. As an attempt at persuasion, the narration/discourse proposes to demonstrate the generative principles of a properly psychoanalytic narrative (story/narration/discourse), a complete case history. Such a narrative, according to Freud's paradigm plot, would be made up of many sets of oppositions, layerings, which in the end are revealed to be the effects of the primary opposition between conscious and unconscious, as it is mediated by repression. Everything would seem to be under good narrative control. Psychoanalytic treatment, by lifting repression, would in practice "remove" the symptoms and "replace them by conscious thoughts" and, in theory, "repair all the damages to the patient's memory" (*S.E.* 7:18). The narrative would be restored to an undistorted, complete reflection of the patient's story, of the "events themselves" (17). But the subplot figuring a different and perhaps less easily interpreted mediation, denial, has already been introduced through Freud's acts of language.

In the light of chapter 7, we might now reread Freud's assertion that the practical and theoretical aims of the treatment "are coincident," and that "the same path leads to them both," as an indication of his wishful search for a narrative moment of recovery at the end of the *Umweg* of the psychoanalytic life history, a moment that would stand as a "substitute" for an originary if only allegorical moment at which reference, like perception, was first "established by the external world" (*S.E.* 5:566–67). The very metaphors Freud chooses in "Dora" to set his narration going—*Weg* and *Umweg*—theorize the problem of desire in narrative, the desire of narrative to bypass the problem of referring to "reality" and to take a shorter path to understanding. As he confidently "interprets" Dora's "repressions" and elaborates his theory, Freud also raises indirectly, through his account of her denials, practical and theoretical questions about the limits of interpretive recovery and understanding, questions he will return to and more directly take up in "Constructions in Analysis."

The tension between Freud's repression theory and Dora's denials runs through "Dora," as does the tension between repression and denial as translational principles in narrative. While Freud did not make the theoretical distinction between the two defenses in "Dora," he was already having his doubts about the repression-mediated model of historical and narrative reconstruction. He raised these doubts in connection with "the factor of 'transference'" (13), just after making the "conscientious archaeologist" analogy, and in the 1899 paper, "Screen Memories," he had recently expressed them in a way that would threaten reconstructive work on more purely cognitive grounds as well: "It may indeed be questioned whether we have any memories at all *from* our childhood: memories *relating to* our childhood may be all that we possess" (*S.E.* 3:322). Still, all his manifest doubts concerned the relationships between the patient's story, narration, and discourse; for the doctor, he continued to hold out the ideal of the "intelligible [*verständliche*; literally, "understandable"], consistent, and unbroken case history" (17), a mirror of the patient's true—in the psychoanalytic sense—story.

Freud did not make it explicit in "Dora" that two defensive systems are involved, the doctor's as well as the patient's, and two story/narration/discourse systems. This aspect of the case is often discussed in terms of his repression of his countertransference. By way of getting to the question of the kind of denial enacted by narration, I will put it in other terms, terms suggested by the work of literary critic Dorrit Cohn, and say that Freud glossed over the implications of his "translation" of the patient's first-person narrative into a third-person narrative—a case history—*about* that narrative. This might be seen as the expression of a narrative wish. As Cohn points out, what separates the biographer from the author of a fictional third-person narrative is that the biographer must do without direct access to the reality of the subject's mental process.[18] Freud's allegory of the hungry baby theorizes the possibility that the psychoanalytic biographer's particular hunger for this referent might particularly incline him to enact wishful denials of its perceptual unavailability. By instructing the patient to free associate, it is after all not just to the patient that Freud the narrator of real lives would be hoping to open the unconscious. We remember his early protestation that "it still strikes me myself as strange that the case histories I write should read like short stories" (*S.E.* 2:160) and his many ambivalent remarks about creative writers. The wish? Not to *be* a creative writer, or rather, not to be that only, but to be able, *as a scientist,* to stand in the narrative position of the creative writer—to be both. Freud's ambivalent identification with writers of fiction might be among other things the expression of a wish for their narrative prerogatives.

THE UNNAVIGABLE RIVER: THE PATIENT'S FIRST ACCOUNT, THE ANALYST'S
LAST WORD

In "The Clinical Picture" Freud not only thematizes the mirroring, specular relation of the patient's practical and the doctor's theoretical narrative aims through the claim that "the same path leads to them both." He also, in the manner of a writer of fiction, installs his theme structurally in the text, in the form of a metaphor (conveyed as an analogy) that explicitly refers to the narrative process of the clinical encounter. The patient's "first account" is mirrored, substituted for, by a river: "This first account may be compared to an unnavigable river whose stream is at one moment choked by masses of rock and at another divided and lost among shallows and sandbanks. [*Diese erste Erzählung ist einem nicht schiffbaren Strom vergleichbar, dessen Bett bald durch Felsmassen verlegt, bald durch Sandbänke zerteilt und untief gemacht wird*]" (*S.E.* 7:16; *G.W.* 5:173). Neither analyst nor patient is able to navigate, to travel along this river, which participates in the series of images in the text having to do with the representation of mental and narrative connections by geographical metaphors: path or road (both translations of *Weg*); *détour* (*Umweg*); seeing one's way about (*Orientierung*). Freud uses the same word, *Zusammenhang* (literally, "hanging together"), to designate both mental and narrative connections, and as though to mark the importance to him of having these processes "coincide," *zusammenfallen,* he uses it six times in his two opening paragraphs (it is translated variously as "chain," "thread of connections," "coherent" [from the adjective], and "connection"). The burden of this specular, and also speculative, task of connecting mental and narrative processes is carried by the metaphor of the river, and Freud installs it with a self-conscious rhetorical gesture: "may be compared [*ist . . . vergleichbar*]." As it runs through "Dora" and on into *Three Essays*, this river will turn out to be one of the psychoanalytic archeologist's most ambitious theoretical "constructions."[19]

On one view, a view Freud as narrator often encourages his reader to take, such a metaphor is a rhetorical device to be replaced by more exact language when psychoanalytic knowledge is further advanced. In chapter 7 of *The Interpretation of Dreams*, for example, he contends that he sees no need to "apologize" for his use of analogies—in this case comparing the psychical apparatus to an optical apparatus: "Analogies of this kind are only intended to assist us in our attempt to make the complications of mental functioning intelligible [*verständlich*]. . . . We are justified, in my view, in giving free rein to our speculations so long as we retain the coolness of our judgement and do not mistake the scaffolding for the building. . . . All that we need is the assistance of provisional ideas [*Hilfsvorstellungen*]" (*S.E.* 5:536; *G.W.* 2/3:541). Freud's defensiveness is a reminder that not just speculations about history but analogies too are constructions he wishes to fit in, like the archeologist, with the more "authentic" parts of his work.

How does the metaphor, the watery mirror, of the river function referentially in the "Dora" text? To begin with, it reflects imagistically the patient's impeded narrative flow and locates it as a perceptually available natural object. Repression, an abstraction that according to the theory has produced the distortions and gaps in this narrative, is implicitly naturalized as well, as the "choking" of the river by masses of rock, its "division" and "loss" among sandbanks and shallows. (Strachey's translation participates in this naturalization through the choice of the verb "to choke" for *verlegen*—literally "to obstruct" or "to shift"—which reinforces the coincidence of "account" and "river" through the notion of voice.) The interaction between the patient's narrative process and her underlying psychic structures is even neatly suggested, in the German, by the distinction made between the river itself (*Strom*) and its bed (*Bett*), the latter being the location of the various distorting alterations. Read this way, the metaphor is evidence of Freud's control as a writer, and participates in his rhetoric of persuasion; its suggested possibilities of depth serve to deepen our conviction of the correctness of the argument. All the more authoritative for its literary conventionality, the river metaphor depends on a Romantic comparison of human inner states with the natural surround. Linguistic time is assimilated to natural time through the link the metaphor suggests between the patient's account and the conventional allegory of time's stream. Moreover, space and time are linked in a natural, intuitive way, through the adverbial structure *bald ... bald*—literally "soon ... soon" ("at one moment choked ... at another divided"). As representation and persuasion, the river metaphor would seem in a well-controlled way to support an allegorical process in the text through which theory and practice, the writing of a case history and the treatment of a patient, will move toward mirroring coincidence along a narrative path through space and time. In this allegory of theory—both an allegory representing psychoanalytic theory and a theory about psychoanalytic allegory—figurative language would be the *Umweg* along which theory achieves a truer representation of reality.

This way of reading the river metaphor, a rhetorical construction of Freud's, might itself be thought of as construction; it helps the reader to deepen and hold together an understanding of Freud's argument about the relation of practice and theory. Another way of reading the metaphor opens up tensions within that constructed understanding. This reading could begin simply as a continuation of the attention to thematic implication that grounds the constructionist reading. We note that in the metaphor, the blocked and diverted river does not occur in a state wholly pure, natural, and primary; through the specification "unnavigable" (*nicht schiffbaren*), it is already shifted—*verlegt*—into the secondary context of real-world human commerce. As a ship, and presumably dredging equipment, are introduced into the natural scene, we are reminded that what Freud is trying to refer to is not just the patient's first account in isolation, but his own reception of it. The metaphor stages the relation of analyst to patient, and of Freud's theory to his practice of that theory. The thematization of the difference between man and nature, a difference that in the case of unnavigable rivers can become an antagonism, works against the notion of a mirroring coincidence between a narrated account—*Erzählung*—and the stream of a river, or between practice and theory. The suggestion of man's effort to dominate nature reverberates in the text as Freud's effort to dominate Dora and theory's effort to dominate practice.

Thematic reading could in this way verge not only on a constructionist analysis of the representational structure of "Dora," but on a deconstructionist analysis of its enactments, its acts of narration. The shared approach of various deconstructive readings—and this would include Freud's way of reading psychic conflict—is to question the enactment of hierarchical power relationships implied in the conventional dichotomies around which a text is structured, without suggesting that the terms whose relation this analysis has now altered, or the qualities they refer to, can simply be replaced.[20] Applied to the limited question of the river metaphor, that approach would bring attention first to the language/nature dichotomy implied in the comparison of "account" (*Erzählung*) and "river" (*Strom*). This hardly seems on the face of it to be a power relationship, but the allegory of disencumberment of the river as therapeutic opening up, through derepression, of the patient's life history, takes us back to Freud's claims for the power of psychoanalytic theory and for his authority as Dora's analyst. Whatever the representational, persuasive power of the metaphor of the river as an element in the text's allegory of theory, it can be read also as a moment in another, more extended allegorical-theoretical process in Freud's texts that starts before "Dora" and goes well beyond it. On this reading, the river serves as indication of a series of acts of narration that do not so much support Freud's claims for authority as assert them.

The figurative sources of what will evolve into an entire allegorical-theoretical river system lie in the theoretical sources of "Dora." If the practical goal of "Dora" is to demonstrate the clinical application of *The Interpretation of Dreams*, its theoretical goal is to develop and modify the argument of *Studies on Hysteria*. In discussing Dora's experience with Herr K., Freud early on makes reference to the trauma theory of *Studies*: "The experience with Herr K.—his making love to her and the insult to her honour which was involved—seems to provide in Dora's case the psychical trauma which Breuer and I declared long ago to be the indispensable prerequisite for the production of a hysterical disorder. But this new case also presents all the difficulties which have since led me to go beyond that theory" (*S.E.* 7:26–27). Freud points out, among other things, that "some of these [Dora's] symptoms (the cough and the loss of voice) had been produced by the patient years before the time of the trauma." He concludes: "If, therefore, the trauma theory is not to be abandoned, we must go back to her childhood and look about there for any influences or impressions which might have had an effect analogous to that of a trauma [*um dort nach Einflüssen oder Eindrücken zu suchen, welche analog einem Trauma wirken konnen*]" (27; *G.W.* 5:185–86). In a footnote, Freud asserts directly that he has "not abandoned" the trauma theory: "I do not to-day consider the [trauma] theory incorrect, but incomplete" (27, n. 1). He will complete his theory, just as he will complete Dora's account of her traumatic experience with Herr K., by adding to it the element of repressed childhood sexual fantasy. Trauma itself, the referent of the theory, is proving more elusive than he first thought;

it must be approached, like the psychical apparatus of chapter 7, by historicizing analogy—through childhood influences or impressions "analogous" in their workings to a trauma.

The metaphor of the river, *Strom*, will be integral to this extension and completion of trauma theory in "Dora" and beyond. At its sources in Freud's earlier work it sits, like the concept of trauma, at the boundary between the psychical and the physiological. In conclusion to the 1894 paper "The Neuro-Psychoses of Defence," Freud brings in the "working hypothesis [*Hilfsvorstellung*] ... that in mental functions something is to be distinguished—a quota of affect or sum of excitation—which possesses all the characteristics of a quantity ... and which is spread over the memory-traces of ideas somewhat as an electric charge is spread over the surface of a body." He goes on to argue, using the adjective derived from the verb *strömen*, "to flow," that this hypothesis "can be applied in the same sense as physicists apply the hypothesis of a flow of electric fluid [*strömenden elektrischen Fluidums*]" (*S.E.* 3:60–61; *G.W.* 1:74). Throughout the 1895 "Project," he uses the verb *strömen* and the noun *Strömung* to designate the "flow" of physiological "current" in neurones. At least once in the "Project" he also uses the noun *Strom*, and in a way that anticipates the sentence in "Dora," for the *Strom* is divided—*verteilt*. This occurs in the inhibitory organization he calls, in quotes, the "ego": "A $Q_\eta$ which breaks into a neurone from anywhere will proceed in the direction of the contact-barrier with the largest facilitation and will set up a current [*Strömung*] in that direction. To put this more accurately: the $Q_\eta$ current will divide up [*es wird sich der Strom Quantität... verteilen*] in the direction of the various contact-barriers in inverse ratio to their resistance" (*S.E.* 1:323; *Aus den Anfängen der Psychoanalyse* [1950]:407). In all these occurrences Freud's choice of words follows common metaphorical usage in German: *Strom* can mean electrical "power," and *Strömung* can mean a "current" of electricity as well as the current in a river. In the 1899 paper "Screen Memories," *Strömung* shifts somewhat in Freud's usage toward psychological reference: "The sensual current in my mind [*die sinnliche Strömung in mir den Gedanken*] took hold of the thought" (*S.E.* 3:317; *G.W.* 1:548). After this, for example in *The Interpretation of Dreams*, *Strömung* points in both directions, designating flows of neuronal energy, or thought, or feeling.

In "Screen Memories" Freud uses *Strom* as well as *Strömung*, and in a sense that is now unambiguously psychological: "It is not, I believe, until my sixth or seventh year that the stream of my memories [*Strom der Erinnerung*] becomes continuous" (*S.E.* 3:309; *G.W.* 1:539). Only a major river is called a *Strom*, and here, before "Dora," the figure comes to designate that major feature in the emerging landscape of psychoanalysis, the *discontinuous* memory we have for our first years. An earlier possible source for this specifically psychoanalytic *Strom* can be found in Freud's discussion of "defense hysteria" in the case of Elizabeth von R. (in *Studies*), in a word that becomes "stream of thought" in the translation: "The incompatible idea, which, together with its concomitants, is later excluded and forms a separate psychical group, must originally have been in communication with the main stream of thought [*im Denkverkehre gestanden sein*]. Otherwise the conflict which led to their exclusion could not have taken place. It is these moments, then, that are to be described as 'traumatic': it is at these moments that conversion takes place, of which the results are the splitting of consciousness and the hysterical symptom" (*S.E.* 2:167; *G.W.* 1:234). *Verkehr* usually refers to traffic, exchange, or (sexual) intercourse, and one can use it with the verb *fliessen* ("to flow"). But *Denkverkehr* is not common usage; Freud seems to be searching for a figurative term to fit the theoretical context of thought process split by trauma. Further evidence of this search is to be found in the contemporaneous "Project," where he uses the term *Denkströmung* in a discussion of psychopathology that introduces a clinical example of the deferred action of trauma in hysteria: "We have already, indeed, assumed the existence of a *primary defence* which consists in the current of thought [*Denkströmung*] being reversed as soon as it comes up against a neurone the cathecting of which releases unpleasure" (*S.E.* 1:350; *Aus den Anfängen der Psychoanalyse* [1950]:430). In *The Psychopathology of Everyday Life*, the writing of which he interrupted to work on "Dora" (Strachey's introduction, *S.E.* 6:xii), he borrows from Wundt the metaphor of a stream — a *Fluss*, which is smaller than a *Strom* — of associations, and writes of the coming "into action," in slips, of the "uninhibited stream of associations [*ungehemmte Fluss der Associationen*]" (*S.E.* 6:61; *G.W.* 4:69).

The choked and divided *Strom* of the patient's first account in "Dora" carries the representational task of bringing into language these source hypotheses of psychoanalysis about memory and defenses against it, and, notably, about thought process and language *as action*. The *Strom* reappears in "Dora" later in "The Clinical Picture," at the end of a long paragraph on the perversions. The topic is again action, or the distinction between different kinds of action:

> All psychoneurotics are persons with strongly marked perverse tendencies, which have been repressed in the course of their development

and have become unconscious. Consequently their unconscious *phan-tasies* show precisely the same content as the documentarily recorded *actions* of perverts. . . . Psychoneuroses are, so to speak, the *negative* of perversions. In neurotics their sexual constitution, under which the effects of heredity are included, operates in combination with any ac-cidental influences in their life which may disturb the development of normal sexuality [*Sexualität*]. A stream of water [*Gewässer*] which meets with an obstacle in the river-bed [*Strombett*] is dammed up and flows back into old channels [*Stromläufe*] which had formerly seemed fated to run dry. [*S.E.* 7:50–51; *G.W.* 5:210–11]

Freud has now engaged the figure of the river in deconstructing two fundamental dichotomies his theory continues to depend upon: neurosis/perversion, fantasy/action. The dammed-up river that flows back into old channels would represent the unconscious perverse fantasies of neurotics, which, Freud emphasizes, are equivalent in content to the *actions* of perverts. Closer attention to the structure of the text suggests that another fundamental dichotomy, psy-chology/physiology, is also implicated, for it seems that the antecedent of the "stream of water" is in fact not unconscious fantasy, but "normal sexuality," which is "dammed up" by the "accidental influences" of life. The river that a few pages before in "Dora" stood for a patient's narrative process seems now—or once again, to go back to the texts of the 1890s—to stand for physiological process. What is this act of narration, through which the flow of this "sexuality," substituting for the flow of the patient's account, seems to return us to the flow of Freud's earlier, more physiological currents?

When the stream appears next, in *Three Essays*, both the designation of sexuality as "libido" and the direction taken by Freud's argument suggest that the river's psychological and narrative referents have not been abandoned:

> Most psychoneurotics only fall ill after the age of puberty as a result of the demands made upon them by normal sexual life. . . . Or else illnesses of this kind set in later, when the libido fails to obtain satisfaction along normal lines [*Wege*]. In both these cases the libido behaves like a stream whose main bed has become blocked. It proceeds to fill up collateral channels which may hitherto have been empty [*verhält sich die Libido wie ein Strom, dessen Hauptbett verlegt wird; sie füllt die kollaterale Wege aus*]. . . . In the same way, what appears to be the strong tendency (though, it is true, a negative one) of psychoneurotics to perversion may be collaterally determined. [*S.E.* 7:170; *G.W.* 5:69–70]

Through a comparison—"in the same way"—Freud reasserts the con-nection made by the river between the flow of sexuality and a "tendency ... to perversion" in the internal narratives, the fantasies, of neurotics. The act of naming this sexuality with the ancient and culturally invested term *Libido* also shifts the statement's referential emphasis away from physiological and toward psychological and narrative process. As an act of narration, the detour back through physiology served to locate the *Strom* in an evolving allegorical system in which the kind of psychological conflict evident in the patient's "first account" will be played out between reified theoretical entities like *Libido*. This narrative may seem to have greater referential authority, to give a closer and more scientific depiction of reality, than would a more direct discussion of the original problem of the patient's narrative distortions. But the apparent gain in referential authority depends upon the insertion of an untranslated Latin term into the German text. The authority of *Libido* lies only in its linguistic primariness—its status as a relic of linguistic archeology—and in its evocation of a past tradition of scientific discourse.

In this allegorizing restatement, the *Libido-Strom* that now carries forward and refines theory is no longer mimetic in the same way as the metaphorical river of the patient's first account, although the phrasing is in some places identical (*ein Strom, desen Hauptbett verlegt wird*). Gone are the visually evocative terms of the "Dora" sentence (*nicht schiffbaren, Felsmassen, Sandbänke*); the statement is more conceptually abstract. The antecedent of "it" in the phrase, "It proceeds to fill up the collateral channels," which is ambiguous in the English translation—either the stream or the libido—is in the German unambiguously the libido (*sie* refers back to *die Libido*, not *der Strom*). Across the divide of a semicolon (in the original), *Libido* goes from being said to behave *like* a *Strom* to being said to *be* a *Strom* whose vicissitudes now play out the hypotheses of psychoanalysis, with "collateral channels," for example, taking the place of the "separate psychical group" of *Studies*. The same allegorical synthesis—in which reified abstract concepts like *Libido* metaphorically take the place of concrete natural entities like the river, which themselves metaphorically took the place of abstractions like the flow of mental or narrative process— is continued in the "Summary" section of *Three Essays*. There Freud describes the "preponderance of perverse tendencies in psychoneurotics" as a "collateral filling of subsidiary channels when the main current of the instinctual stream has been blocked by 'repression' [*kollaterale Füllung von Nebenbahnen bei Verlegung des Hauptstrombettes durch die 'Verdrängung'*]" (*S.E.* 7:232; *G.W.* 5:133). The masses of rock that represented repression in the "Dora" river are now in turn replaced by the word "repression" itself, but this "repression," through the metaphorization of the first metaphor, is rhetorically displaced. A reifying otherness from itself, indicated by Freud's quotation marks, signals the assimilation of the word "repression" into an allegory. In a related move, the by now familiar river is not even qualified as "instinctual" in the German; within the allegory, that can be taken for granted.

The river of "Dora," a metaphor that represented the effects of repression, now instead, as allegory, would seem more directly to perform those effects. In the allegory, the gap between theoretical language and its referent, between the psychical apparatus and traumatic forces external to it, like *Libido*, would seem to close. Whatever the uncertainties of the sense organs of perception-consciousness, referential coincidence is suggested between mental representation and the external world of bodily process. But if the allegory seems to perform the fulfillment of this narrative wish, it also comments on and deconstructs that performance. Freud's quotation marks around "repression," where it replaces masses of rock in the stream, indicate the linguistic "nature" of this natural object. The principle of transformation that generates the allegory is translation as intralinguistic transfer, and not, as it may seem, translation as achieved connection between language and nature. In the first river metaphor in "Dora," "river," as signifier, stands for a signified, the concept of the patient's narrated "account"—*Erzählung*. The elusive *referent* of that metaphor would be not the concept of the account but the patient's "account" itself, the thing. In the allegorizing restatement of the metaphor, this referent is replaced by "sexuality," which, through the metaphor and under the name *Libido*, would seem to be brought directly together with the signifier *Strom*. With this, the wish to close the gap between the linguistic sign (signifier/signified) and its referent would be played out through the apparent elimination of the signified. The concept of sexuality is given realism as it is subsumed in a preserved word from an ancient language that intimates the proximity of the referent itself.

Barthes associates similar acts of narration with the production of what he calls the "reality effect" of "historical discourse": "In other words, in 'objective' history, the 'real' is never anything but an unformulated signified, sheltered behind the apparent omnipotence of the referent. This situation defines what we might call the *reality effect*. The extrusion of the signified outside the 'objective' discourse, letting the 'real' and its expression apparently confront each other, does not fail to produce a new meaning, so true is it, once more, that within a system any absence of an element is itself a signification" (1986, 139).

The list Barthes gives of contemporary genres relying on such an effect could be the inventory of Freud's practical and theoretical *topoi*, from the patient's account to archeology to the perceptually immediate image: "the realistic novel, the private diary, documentary literature, the news item [*fait divers*], the historical museum, the exhibition of ancient objects, and, above all, the massive development of photography, whose sole pertinent feature (in relation to drawing) is precisely to signify that the event represented has *really* taken place" (1986, 139). While Barthes might be read as suggesting that historical reference is only illusory, I take him instead to be pointing to the way a *desire* for "history"—in the sense of a complete "account" of the reality of the past, and through it of the reality of the present—may express itself in conflations of the referent and the signifier. To say that with the allegorical river Freud is striving for an "effect" of reality is not to ignore or diminish the referential status of his discourse about psychic history. Through what are often devalued as the intellectualizing mechanisms of allegory, Freud would be seeking to refer to a strange new kind of reality—the reality of the psychoanalytic unconscious—by conferring its "effect" upon the concrete details of the diarylike narratives of his patients.

As rhetoric, the allegory of the river can be read as a cognition about the problem of psychoanalytic reference. It plays out the impossibility of attaining an actual coincidence of the signifier and the referent, or of theory and practice, as it establishes such coincidences only in the linguistic equivalent of the "perverse" actions the allegory analyzes as a primary-process shortcut. As Freud uses the river allegory to deconstruct the neat oppositions neurosis/perversion and fantasy/action, and to show that the "higher" form is always latently shaped by the "lower," his acts of narration undo the neat conventional opposition between metaphor as evocative representation and allegory as dry language play. The theory of trauma—to go back to the sources of the river, and of "Dora"—is a theory of transmission that must sustain itself without being able to establish what, exactly, is its traumatic starting point, its referent. As allegory, the evolution of psychoanalytic theory away from a trauma theory that it at the same time does *not* abandon problematizes the relation of "primary" perceptual experience and its "secondary" narratives. The narrative actions of psychoanalytic theory, like the actions of the pervert and the fantasies of the neurotic, enact the wish to circumvent psychologically determining referential absences and at the same time point to these absences as the determinants of psychical reality. In theory, the signifier of referential absence is the hungry baby's denial of the difference between perception and memory; in practice, its symptom is trauma's paradoxical unassimilability to and inextricability from the psychoanalytic theory of personal and collective history.

## Constructions in Analysis

### HISTORICAL TRUTH

It may seem that this reading of "Dora" is more relevant to the textual history of psychoanalytic theory than to the question how psychoanalysis, at least today's psychoanalysis, thinks historically. After all, it might be argued, the model of treatment as archeological reconstruction put forth in the opening pages of "Dora" was naive, as was Freud's practice at that time. Much has changed since then in psychoanalytic theory and practice, much more is understood about transference, countertransference, object relations, adolescent development, sexual politics. ... And of course Freud's own practice and theory changed in the years after he wrote "Dora." Still, certain nagging problems would not, and do not, go away. The epistemological difficulties opened up in "Dora" and *Three Essays* in connection with writing the "history" of a "case" or the theory of that history serve as point of departure for Freud's most mature work, itself at the center of the current debate about narrative truth and historical truth in psychoanalysis. The way this debate is often framed, it appears we must choose between two mutually exclusive versions of psychoanalysis, the scientific and the hermeneutic, roughly speaking, and such a choice might seem to offer a way out of epistemological anxiety. Those who do not choose, and who say that psychoanalysis is both, often seek a resolution through segregation. In Spence's portrait, for example, Freud seems to have two sides that coexist without obvious conflict: Freud the master stylist who uses figurative language for purposes of narrative persuasion, and Freud the positivist researcher who maintains that psychoanalysis is about reconstructing the facts, about what Spence (1982, 1987) calls the pursuit of "historical truth" according to the "archeological metaphor."[21] Spence's own narrative choice to designate two separate "voices" with which psychoanalysis "speaks"—the "rhetorical voice" and the "evidential voice" (Spence 1990)—serves the important function of giving figurative language a place in the construction of psychoanalytic theory, but tends to remove the question of reference from the question of rhetoric: "If language is all we have—if many of the referents that matter are essentially out of reach—then we have to be unusually on guard against the dangers of mere rhetoric and empty argument" (1990, 597). "Every time a piece of evidence has been captured by the rhetorical voice, we have probably lost the chance to make a new discovery" (1990, 599).

A more problematic and conflictual rhetorical dimension of psychoanalysis emerges when rhetoric is taken to be not only a method of persuasion, but also an aspect of the referential functioning of language. Reading "Dora," for example, it does not seem easy to keep the two separate.[22] When figures of speech are read among other things as ways of gathering cognitive evidence, then a tension that had seemed to lie *between* the rhetorical and the evidential "voices" of psychoanalysis is no longer so neatly encompassed. Following Derrida, one could read Spence's anthropomorphizing figure of "voice" as the symptom of a defense against this conflict, a conflict that emerges when one recognizes that in psychoanalytic theory it is not a matter of voice only, but of writing.

Starting from this expanded notion of rhetoric, I will differ from Spence: in my view, that the archeological metaphor of psychoanalysis as reconstruction of the facts was never much of a resting place for Freud. Starting again and again from the rhetorical gesture of invoking archeology, Freud seems to me never to have stopped debating with himself the question of historical truth and narrative truth, a question that goes back epistemologically to the distinction between material reality and psychical reality and, beyond that, to the distinction between perception and memory. Freud's internal debate springs up around the trauma question of the 1890s, which includes the question whether psychoanalysis recovers facts or fantasies, and is still active in texts from the late 1930s.[23] It is active not as the either/or question commentators sometimes reduce it to—trauma resulting from seduction or fantasy resulting from drives—but persistently as an undecidable pair of questions: how does real experience come to be psychologically traumatic, how does real trauma come to be psychologically experienced? As Lacan has emphasized, the principle of deferred action, *Nachträglichkeit*, governs Freud's thinking about this historical question; in the psychoanalytic sense, events are traumatic not in the present moment of occurrence, but upon recollection and reconstruction across some period of delay. The prehistorical traces of trauma are events that, like Hayden White's "chronicle," must undergo a narrative transformation in order to become part of a psychoanalytic life history.

It is under the sign of trauma that Freud opens his well-known discussion of "historical" and "material" truth in *Moses and Monotheism*, some forty years after *Studies on Hysteria*. His Lamarckian argument is that memory traces of actual traumatic events are transmitted between generations, and over hundreds of years, as an "archaic heritage." Any consideration of the psychoanalytic theory of history must take account of this quirky view of historical transmission, which Freud was as determined to maintain as he was self-conscious about this determination. Grubrich-Simitis (1988), writing about "A Phylogenetic Phantasy"—the twelfth metapsychological paper, apparently destroyed by Freud but recently found among Ferenczi's papers— argues convincingly that Freud's Lamarckianism drew its tenacity from an ongoing, lifelong attempt to reconcile his trauma theory with his drive theory. The question remains how to trace, in rhetorical terms, the path Freud has taken from the historical theory of "Dora" to Lamarck. The repression model of "Dora," represented by the unnavigable river, contained already an implicit countermodel that became more evident in *Three Essays*, as blockages in the river, although still linked to "repression," came to be associated with the enactments of perversions. A number of Freud's late texts further develop this countermodel of history, now in explicit connection with more dissociative mechanisms of defense. By way of locating a rhetorical vantage point at that far end of Freud's path, I will follow the pointer of the archeological analogy in "Dora" and turn for comparison to "Constructions in Analysis," which depends explicitly on the same analogy (*S.E.* 23:259– 60) and takes up again the question of completing the patient's incomplete account:

> What we are in search of is a picture of the patient's forgotten years that shall be alike trustworthy and in all essential respects complete. But at this point we are reminded that the work of analysis consists of two quite different portions, that it is carried out in two separate localities [*dass sie sich auf zwei gesonderten Schauplätzen vollziet*], that it involves two people, to each of whom a distinct task is assigned. It may for a moment seem strange that such a fundamental fact should not have been pointed out long ago; but it will immediately be perceived that there was nothing being kept back in this, that it is a fact which is universally known and, as it were, self-evident and is merely being brought into relief here and separately examined for a particular purpose. [*S.E.* 23:258; *G.W.* 16:44]

The complete, reconstructed account, here as in "Dora," starts out as the guiding motif of Freud's argument. But here Freud quickly interrupts himself—"But at this point we are reminded"—to introduce, in different terms, the distinction he made in "Dora" between analyst and patient. There, he described the two "aims" of the treatment, the "practical" and the "theoretical"; here, it is a matter of "two quite different portions," "two separate localities" (*Schauplätze*; more literally, "stages" or "theaters"), "two people." The disclaimer—"there was nothing kept back in this"—suggests that something *is* at stake, something, it seems, about the relationship of theory and practice.

"Constructions" begins with the question how to decide the correctness of a psychoanalytic interpretation, as Freud proposes to answer the charge "that in giving interpretations to a patient we treat him on the famous principle of 'Heads I win, tails you lose'" (257). Right away, we cannot ignore the intertextual reference to "Dora," the confluence of the two narrative streams. He will give a "detailed account of how we are accustomed to arrive at an assessment of the 'Yes' or 'No' of our patients during analytic treatment—of their expression of agreement or denial" (257). The work involves two distinct tasks. The patient's task is to remember, the analyst's task is "to make out what has been forgotten from the traces which it has left behind or, more correctly, to *construct* it" (258–59). By the end of the paper, having stated the archeological analogy—"His work of construction, or, if it is preferred, of reconstruction, resembles to a great extent an archaeologist's excavation" (259)—and given it a detailed two-paragraph development, and having said that "construction" is a more "appropriate description" for the analyst's overall activity than "interpretation" (261), Freud turns, with discernible ironic intention, to another analogy: "But none the less I have not been able to resist the seduction of an analogy [*Verlockung einer Analogie*]. The delusions of patients appear to me to be the equivalents of constructions which we build up in the course of an analytic treatment" (268; *G.W.* 16:55; *Verlockung* means "enticement"; sexual seduction is *Verführung*). And he cannot resist the further enticement of a historicizing conclusion: "If we consider mankind as a whole and substitute it for the single human individual, we discover that it too has developed delusions which are inaccessible to logical criticism and which contradict reality. ... They owe their power to the element of *historical truth* which they have brought up from the repression of the forgotten and primaeval past" (269).

Truth, in this formulation, is transmitted through human history *as delusion*. The "power" of this truth is compared explicitly to the power of the analyst's constructions, a power Freud has been manifestly concerned to defend throughout the paper, as for example when he writes that if "we have made a mistake ... we shall admit as much to the patient at some suitable opportunity without sacrificing any of our authority" (261–62). If he is unable to resist the enticement of the ironizing analogy, it is perhaps because the allure lies not just in the thematic content of the analogy (constructions:delusions), but in

the narrative act of analogizing by constructing linguistic figures. Figurative language—that siren Freud has been determined to resist, but
also to listen to, since the beginning of his writing—calls to him again,
for analytic constructions themselves are analogizing figurations, not
always securely anchored in the literal meaning of a determinate historical event:

> The path that starts out from the analyst's constructions ought to end
> in the patient's recollection; but it does not always lead so far. Quite
> often we do not succeed in bringing the patient to recollect what has
> been repressed. Instead of that, if the analysis is carried out correctly,
> we produce in him an assured conviction of the truth of the construction
> which achieves the same therapeutic result as a recaptured memory.
> [*S.E.* 23:265–66]

Does such analytic persuasion also overcome resistance through the
enticement of analogies—and is it then, *by* analogy, "seduction"? It is
important to Freud, as it should be to any practicing analyst, to go
slowly here, and not, as the translation does, to collapse the differences
between different forms of seduction; we know that analytic restraint
*does* make a difference when we find out about the harm that can be
caused when it is relinquished. Still, Freud's confessed failure here to
resist the enticement of an analogy raises questions about theory that
should concern the practicing analyst, for what is at stake is the nature
of the truth psychoanalysis unearths, and the effect on that truth of
historical "construction" as the only available method of excavation.

Questions surround the very term "historical truth." As Freud uses
it in "Constructions" and in *Moses and Monotheism*, it does not always
carry quite the straightforward meaning Spence and others give it.
Spence writes, quoting from the passage in "Constructions" about
delusions: "Out of this confusion [between narrative truth and historical truth] grew Freud's belief that every interpretation always contains a piece of historical truth and that this 'kernel of truth,' as he
calls it, is what makes interpretation effective" (1982, 27). To my
reading, the logic of Freud's sentences requires one not to equate, but
to make a distinction between, what he calls the "kernel of truth" in
a delusion and what he calls its "historical truth": "Recognition of its
[the delusion's] kernel of truth would afford common ground [between
the analyst and the delusional patient] upon which the therapeutic
work could develop. That work would consist in liberating the fragment of historical truth from its distortions and its attachments to the
actual present day and in leading it back to the point in the past to
which it belongs" (268). The "historical truth," here, is a truth that

is manifest, in the Freudian sense of the manifest dream. Distorted and displaced in a delusion, it comes to us in need of interpretation. It should be said that Freud himself is not consistent in using the term this way. Earlier in "Constructions," for example, he uses it in the more straightforward sense when he writes: "No damage is done if, for once in a way, we make a mistake and offer the patient a wrong construction as the probable historical truth" (261). But in *Moses and Monotheism*, he very clearly contrasts a distorted "historical truth" with what he calls "material truth." He is writing about the religious believer whose "pious solution" to the need for a protective presence is to believe in a single god:

> We too believe that the pious solution contains the truth—but the *historical* truth and not the *material* truth. And we assume the right to correct a certain distortion to which this truth has been subjected upon its return. That is to say, we do not believe there is a single great god to-day, but in primaeval times there was a single person who was bound to appear huge at that time and who afterwards returned in men's memory elevated to divinity. [*S.E.* 23:129]

"Material truth," here, is historical truth freed of its distortions; it is materially true, for Freud, that there was once a single, transferentially powerful figure. As Freud uses it in these passages, "historical truth" comes closer to meaning what Spence designates "narrative truth"—the truth as it is *told* from generation to generation, from patient to analyst. This usage fits with Freud's recurrent tendency in his late papers to put into question the capacity of the human mind to attain to the "truth," or to "reality": "It has not been possible," he prefaces the passage in *Moses* on historical and material truth, "to demonstrate in other connections that the human intellect has a particularly fine flair for the truth or that the human mind shows any special inclination for recognizing the truth" (*S.E.* 23:129). And in a Kantian discussion of perception in the *Outline* he states with finality: "Reality will always remain 'unknowable'" (*S.E.* 23:196).

In "Constructions," having not resisted the enticement of an analogy that ironizes the truth claims of the analyst's figurations, Freud continues, reasonably: "It will be the task of each individual investigation to reveal the intimate connections between the material of the present disavowal and that of the original repression" (268). "Each individual investigation" can be read to mean not only each psychoanalytic treatment, conducted, as Freud has said, by two persons, but also each *individual* investigating her or his own history—each analysand and each analyst. This takes us back to Freud's disclaimer that there was "nothing being kept back," when he noted that it might "seem strange that such a fundamental fact"—that analysis involves two people with different tasks—"should not have been pointed out long ago" (258). What he defensively registers there is a refusal to be daunted by the uncertainties he is about to open up by discussing not just the accuracy of the analyst's interventions, but their status as *acts* in the analysis— acts of narration. There is again, in the counterphobic tone, an echo of "Dora," and by the end of the paper the dangers have multiplied, for uncertainty has spread beyond the problem of suggestion in analysis to the problem of our grounds for knowledge.

ENACTING HISTORY: AUTOBIOGRAPHY AS THEORY

To say that Freud raises doubts about the possibility of self-knowledge is to say nothing new. It is the "path" along which these doubts arrive that matters here, the "path that starts from the analyst's constructions" and does not always "end in the patient's recollection" (265). That path was opened up by Freud's pointing to the situation of dialogue in analysis, for when he outlined the "tasks" of the two people in the analytic situation, he was also pointing, referring, to two aspects of himself: reflecting and reflected, subjective and objective, or theorizing and practicing. His splitting of the narrator into "two quite different portions . . . two separate localities"—or theaters—sets up "Constructions" as an allegorical, neo-Cartesian meditation, a text that not only describes constructions, but performs one. "Constructions" is itself a speculative construction that seeks to locate a "kernel of truth" as the starting point for psychoanalysis. The meditator, Freud, is eighty-one, and is looking back over a life's work, partly by way of review and summation, partly by way of raising doubts in order to arrive at a new certainty. To begin with, he raises the question how we can know an analytic interpretation is correct; then, he challenges the primacy of interpretation and proposes that construction is the truer form of the analyst's activity; then, he challenges construction with the thought that the analyst's construction does not always lead to the patient's recollection; then, having to this extent challenged his grounds for knowledge, he turns, like Descartes, to dreams, hallucinations, and delusions. Constructions sometimes evoke in patients "ultra-clear" recollections—and as Strachey notes, the term *überdeutlich* sends us back to two papers from the 1890s, "The Psychical Mechanism of Forgetfulness" (1898) and "Screen Memories" (1899)—not of the event that was the subject of the construction, but of "details relating to that subject" (266):

These recollections [*Erinnerungen*] might have been described as hallucinations if a belief in their actual presence had been added to their clearness. The importance of this analogy [*Analogie*] seemed greater when I noticed that true hallucinations occasionally occurred in the case of other patients who were certainly not psychotic. My line of thought proceeded as follows. Perhaps it may be a general characteristic of hallucinations to which sufficient attention has not hitherto been paid that in them something that has been experienced in infancy and then forgotten returns—something that the child has seen or heard at a time when he could still hardly speak and that now forces its way into consciousness, probably distorted and displaced owing to the operation of forces that are opposed to this return. [*S.E.* 23:266–67; *G.W.* 16:53–54]

Freud the skeptical meditator turns to hallucinations, and the delusions into which they are incorporated, in his search for certainty. In doing so he also in a way turns back to the origin of his own theorizing: the link made in his "apparatus" between perception and memory—the primitive version of memory constituted by the repetition of the hungry baby's "experience of satisfaction" in the hallucinatory wish fulfillment of a "perceptual identity." The "essence" of this "point of view," he writes here in the next paragraph, "is that there is not only *method* in madness, as the poet has already perceived, but also a fragment of *historical truth*" (267). He goes on to note, however, in what would seem an unintended *mise en abyme*[24]: "All that I can produce to-day in support of this theory are reminiscences [*Reminiszenzen*], not fresh impressions" (267; *G.W.* 16:54–55). This passing remark is evidence of the element of enactment in "Constructions," of the way it shows as well as tells the problem of the uncertainty of memory. The remark is, in the terms of J. L. Austin, a kind of performative statement.[25] Freud does not give us the content of his "reminiscences," but instead displays his mental *activity* of summoning them up: "All that I can produce to-day . . ." The word "to-day" functions as a pointer, a deictic, whose meaning is not only "in 1937" but "here, now, as I sit here writing." Freud is presenting himself in the act of reminiscing—about delusional patients he has seen in the distant past, yes, but also about the origins of his own theoretical enterprise. Strachey's footnote tracing the paragraph on "ultra-clear" recollections back to papers from the 1890s points not only to Freud's thematic return to his theoretical origins, but to his autobiographical performance.

As performance, Freud's passing remark enacts the relationship between present ("fresh impressions") and past ("reminiscences") that constitutes the topic of the paper. This enactment functions to give another twist to the quest for certainty. Freud has been preparing, if ironically, to ground analytic constructions, and through them analytic theory, in the "historical truth" that hallucinations and delusions present. His statement that he is only able to produce reminiscences in support of this theory has a paradoxical effect. Read thematically, it could be taken to disrupt the argument by grounding it in the unreliable memories of an old man. Read performatively, it could be taken instead to support the argument, for it would ground the wish that the text has thematized for a historical referent, a theoretical starting point, in an apparently certain historical moment and event, the present moment and event of the composition of "Constructions in Analysis." But this linguistic performance is empty; it establishes nothing except that Freud *is writing*, and in this sense it sends us back to the "presence" of hallucinations in the previous paragraph: "These recollections might have been described as hallucinations if a belief in their actual presence had been added to their clearness." In the certain but mnemically empty perceptual, perpetual, present that Freud autobiographically enacts in his writing, he points back performatively to the historical kernel of his theoretical enterprise, the perceptual presences of the "experience of satisfaction" in chapter 7 and the "Project."

Like all returns, the return in "Constructions" to hallucinations as the object of a theory of origins is a return with a difference. The frame is no longer the primary process/secondary process distinction, but the distinction between the two portions of the analytic task, made in explicitly narratological terms: the two persons are expected to tell different things, or in different ways. I have already introduced a term that Freud gives prominence in his late work by saying that he describes a "split" in the analytic task. In putting it this way I mean to suggest that there is a relationship between the inter- and intrapersonal narrative splits that the analyst's constructions try to bridge, and a particular defense, disavowal, the defense Freud associates with ego splitting. This takes me back to the question of a Freudian subplot in which the figure of referential mediation is not repression but denial, and to questions raised by that subplot about the limits of interpretive historical understanding in psychoanalysis. In the "Constructions," "present disavowal" that mediates between present and past is sometimes all that is available for the analyst to work with: "It will be the task of each individual investigation to reveal the intimate connections between the material of the present disavowal [*Verleugnung*] and that of the original repression [*Verdrängung*]" (268; *G.W.* 16:55). In the theory of *The Interpretation of Dreams* and "Dora," repression played the mediating role between past and present, primary and secondary processes, conscious and unconscious. "Constructions" begins by suggesting a shift in this formulation, when Freud restates the "replacement" idea from "Dora" with a difference: "It is familiar ground that the work of analysis aims at inducing the patient to give up the repressions (*using the word in the widest sense*) belonging to his early development and to replace them by reactions of a sort that would correspond to a psychically mature condition" (257; emphasis mine). By the end of the paper, he has turned his attention to disavowal—*Verleugnung*—the defense he associates with splitting of the ego—*Ichspaltung*—in several late papers: "Fetishism" (1927), *An Outline of Psycho-Analysis* (1938), and "Splitting of the Ego in the Process of Defence" (1938).

Freud's general position is that if repression defends against consciousness of internal conflict, disavowal and associated splits in the ego ward off intolerable *perceptions* of external reality. But as he tries to situate these defenses in a developmental scheme in the contemporaneous *Outline*, the notion of "original repression" seems to give way to something more like original disavowal:

> It must not be thought that fetishism presents an exceptional case as regards a splitting of the ego; it is merely a particularly favourable subject for studying the question. Let us return to our thesis that the childish ego, under the domination of the real world, gets rid of undesirable instinctual demands by what are called repressions. We will now supplement this by further asserting that, during the same period of life, the ego often enough finds itself in the position of fending off some demand from the external world which it feels distressing and that this is effected by means of a *disavowal* of the perceptions which bring to knowledge this demand from reality. Disavowals of this kind occur very often and not only with fetishists; and whenever we are in a position to study them they turn out to be half-measures, incomplete attempts at detachment from reality. The disavowal is always supplemented by an acknowledgement; two contrary and independent attitudes always arise and result in the situation of there being a splitting of the ego. [*S.E.* 23:203–4]

In "Constructions," rejection of something external comes up thematically in two ways: first in the "No" with which the patient greets the analyst's construction, then in the psychotic person's rejection of reality. In each case, the disavowal is supplemented by an acknowledgment. The patient rejects the construction relating to something perhaps first rejected in childhood, but provides various kinds of "indirect confirmation" (263, 264), which would include *überdeutlich*, hallucinationlike recollections of associated perceptual details. The psychotic rejects reality but, in the delusion, retains a kernel of the truth of the past.

Early in the paper Freud gives analytic constructions priority in practice over interpretations; in direct association, he emphasizes the primariness of disavowal as, ironically, a force of preservation and transmission in the allegory of life history. In this formulation, Freud's theory of history is inextricable from his theory of narrative, and his theory of theory. Disavowals often maintain themselves, he emphasizes, through fantasized and enacted narratives, the most common "normal" examples occurring in the mental life of children.[26] As Freud often collegially emphasizes, enactment in fantasy and play is the form taken by children's historical research, their theorizing about origins. In the 1908 paper, "On the Sexual Theories of Children," he strikingly prefigures both the "historical truth" argument of "Constructions" and the ironic comparison of the analyst and the psychotic as he discusses the child's attempts to explain where babies come from: "These false sexual theories [of children], which I shall now discuss, all have one very curious characteristic. Although they go astray in a grotesque fashion, yet each one of them contains a fragment of real truth; and in this way they are analogous to the attempts of adults, which are looked at as strokes of genius, at solving the problems of the universe which are too hard for human comprehension" (*S.E.* 9:215). The first of these theories is motivated by an anxiety Freud will come to view as inherited, through a schema he names here, for the first time, the "castration complex" (217): "It consists in *attributing to everyone, including females, the possession of a penis*, such as the boy knows from his own body" (215). It is a schema that is installed in, and transmitted by, narratives: "Legends and myths testify to the upheaval in the child's emotional life and to the horror which is linked with the castration complex—a complex which is consequently remembered by consciousness with corresponding reluctance" (217). The young researcher defensively maintains the triumph of the schema over his perceptual experience through what Freud will later name *Verleugnung*: "When a small boy sees his little sister's genitals, what he says shows that his prejudice is already strong enough to falsify his perception" (216). Earlier in the paper Freud emphasizes the defensive motivation of theory construction in general. The child "asks himself the question: '*Where do babies come from?*'—a question which, there can be no doubt, first ran: 'Where did this particular, intruding baby come from?'" (212–13). Freud asserts: "The question itself is, like all research, the product of a vital exigency, as though thinking were entrusted with the task of preventing the recurrence of such dreaded events" (213). He immediately—wishfully?—adds: "Let us assume, however, that the child's thinking soon becomes independent of this instigation, and henceforward goes on operating as a self-sustained instinct for research" (213).

Alongside its most obvious and arguable content, Freud's theory about what he would later call the phallic phase of development is also a historicizing allegory about the structural origins of theorizing. The structural problem involves an originary difference, or failure of coincidence; this emerges when one notes that Freud initially presented his general "observations" about infantile sexual theories as applying "chiefly" to males, and that he specifically theorized a disavowal of reality in the boy only.[27] Even when he attributed disavowal to the girl, in a 1925 paper, "Some Psychical Consequences of the Anatomical Distinction between the Sexes," it was not as a primary distortion of perception, but as a secondary defensive elaboration:

> There is an interesting contrast between the behaviour of the two sexes. ... When a little boy first catches sight of a girl's genital region, he begins by showing irresolution and lack of interest; he sees nothing or disavows what he has seen. ... It is not until later, when some threat of castration has obtained a hold upon him, that the observation becomes important to him: if he then recollects or repeats it, it arouses a terrible storm of emotion in him and forces him to believe in the reality of the threat which he has hitherto laughed at. This combination of circumstances leads to two reactions, which may become fixed and will in that case, whether separately or together or in conjunction with other factors, permanently determine the boy's relations to women: horror of the mutilated creature or triumphant contempt for her.
>
> A little girl behaves differently. She makes her judgement and her decision in a flash. She has seen it and knows that she is without it and wants to have it. ...
>
> The hope of some day obtaining a penis in spite of everything and so of becoming like a man may persist to an incredibly late age and may become a motive for strange and otherwise unaccountable actions. Or again, a process may set in which I should like to call a "disavowal." [S.E. 19:252–53]

The way Freud draws the difference between the sexes, the girl makes an immediate connection between accurate perception and knowledge, while the boy initially disavows both. Significantly, Freud now revises his idea about the first question the young researcher has to face, in a move that would bring the thematic origin of the child's own theory to coincide with the structural origin of the theory about the child's theorizing: "This is an opportunity for correcting a statement which I made many years ago. I believed that the sexual interest of children, unlike that of pubescents, was aroused, not by the difference between the sexes, but by the problem of where babies come from. We now see that, at all events with girls, this is certainly not the case. With boys it may no doubt happen sometimes one way and sometimes the other; or with both sexes chance experiences may determine the event" (*S.E.* 19:252 n). Freud's qualifiers signal the difficulty *he* is still having encompassing sexual difference in a general formulation, even as he places it at the origin of the child's theorizing. Theory begins in an otherness viewed as a dangerous difference, and in a denial of that difference. In such anxious asymmetry begins also a threat to the possibility for Freud of coherent, unified theory, theory that could restore to wholeness its "mutilated" objects of study. We are back to the "theoretical aim" in "Dora": "to repair [*heilen*] all the damages to the patient's memory."

Freud's theory of theoretical thinking is that it begins in the "vital exigency" of repairing, healing the threatening difference between the sexes, and in this way undertakes the impossible task of intervening in the course of the "dreaded" real world. The dream of the young researcher is a dream of power through interpretive understanding, but its enabling condition is a disavowal of perception—a suspension of reality testing. Does the older researcher, who shares the dream of interpretation, manage to shed these defensive origins? In "Constructions," the autobiographical meditation of a man in old age, Freud looks back with what appears to be a "self-sustained instinct for research" as he analyzes the archeological theories of the younger researcher of "Dora" and qualifies his youthful dream of interpreting repression. But as he theorizes about the patient's disavowal of the analyst's interpretations or historical constructions, Freud, like the child researcher, also enacts a disavowal as throughout the paper he works to sustain his claim that the analyst, even more than the archeologist, has privileged access to a unitary and complete historical past: "All of the essentials are preserved. ... It depends only upon analytic technique whether we shall succeed in bringing what is concealed completely to light" (260). At the same time he provides contrary evidence as he compellingly demonstrates the way impossibilities of translation—from action into understanding, from perception into memory—set the limits on any technique of psychoanalytic recovery, and on any historicizing psychoanalytic theory. His disavowal, like the child's, is "supplemented by an acknowledgement."

Freud points to the defensiveness of his enactment when he names "Constructions," in its opening paragraph, an "apologia": "The practicing analyst will naturally learn nothing in the course of this apologia that he does not know already" (257). An apologia is a defense, but also, like any apology, the confessional performance of an "acknowledgement."[28] In "Dora," Freud tried to defend himself—unsuccessfully, many practicing analysts would now feel—against the charges of leading the witness and subjugating practice to theory. In "Constructions" Freud again takes up the charge of suggestion, but here his self-defense cannot be separated from the text's performance of an allegorical autobiography. Allegorically, the narrator Freud enacts the history of his theorizing self, and the historicizing of his theoretical self, after he defensively proposes to single out the analyst's activity—*his* activity—for discussion. In a deceptively accessible, thematized confession, he admits, more or less, that there *is* an element of suggestion in analysis, for in his dialogue with the patient the analyst must sometimes have recourse to thought-constructions that in their evidential value are analogous to the delusions of psychotics. But in the elusive autobiographical performance, the psychoanalytic theoretician is situated in an allegorical, interpretively undecidable Cartesian dialogue between disavowal and acknowledgment as they are implicated in the two "different portions" of the task, the two "separate localities" of a split narrative self. Within both theory and practice, indeed blurring that distinction, the text's acts of narration play out a version of the defense to which Freud devoted his next paper after "Constructions": the narrative splitting of the theoretician.

As a condition of setting going the linguistic, historicizing process of psychoanalytic autobiography, such splitting always entails a loss. The analyst's constructions, like the phallic child's theories, are stories about an "external reality"—of the narrating self to itself—that cannot be attained and encompassed by repairing memory through lifting repression. Referentially, this "reality" remains split off from memory, for example in the hallucinationlike details constructions can evoke, just as, in Freud's apparatus, perceptual, material reality remained split off from its mnemic, psychical repetitions. The defensive but autobiographically enabling disavowal of this loss is both maintained and deconstructed in the narration of "Constructions." Cast as a discussion of the possibilities of psychoanalytic recovery of history that are suggested by the archeological metaphor, the text at the same time plays out allegorically the theoretician's nostalgia, equally conveyed by the archeological metaphor, for what he had lost before he started: the dream of structures outside time, of an origin—offered for narrative purposes by dreams—in which perception and thought, practice and theory, would coincide. In the face of its own claim that "all of the essentials are preserved," "Constructions" raises the question whether psychoanalysis can expect to reach interpretive understanding of the disavowals around which history is constructed, the disavowals that may be indissociable from the constitutive acts of historical narration.

THE LIMITS OF ANALYSIS

Freud's late interest in the developmental effects of disavowal, a return through theory to his early interest in defensive dissociation, accompanies in the history of his work another return to early interests, after a "lifelong *détour [Umweg]*": "My interest . . . returned to the cultural problems which had fascinated me long before, when I was a youth scarcely old enough for thinking" (*S.E.* 20:72). The content of the return to cultural problems often seemed inseparable from a manifestly allegorical form of exposition, as in *Totem and Taboo, Beyond the Pleasure Principle, Civilization and Its Discontents*, and *Moses and Monotheism*: "The story is told in an enormously condensed form, as though it had happened on a single occasion, while in fact it covered thousands of years and was repeated countless times during that long period" (*Moses and Monotheism, S.E.* 23:81). Is it simply a coincidence, to borrow Freud's way of putting it in "Dora," that as his own history evolves, a theory of disavowal and a (writing) practice of allegory seem to coincide? Or is it the sign of a sensed loss, and of an attempt to mourn that loss through the practice of theory? To put it aphoristically, Freud seems in his late work to rediscover his own discovery of the radical unconscious, and of its relation to traumatic experience. Beyond repression lie early disavowals whose schematic power to distort experience is transmitted through language, according to the theory of individual and intergenerational history, and enacted in the language of that theory. For narcissistic reasons, Freud's child researcher would disavow anatomical reality at a time when he—she?—is, as Freud often emphasizes, just learning to speak, and the disavowal would take the form of a theorizing narrative. Beginning with the theoretically destabilizing otherness of the sexes from which Freud's theory must start, the question would be whether language use does not retain the traces of this period of its history—whether a tendency toward reparative narcissistic fantasy in the service of disavowal does not stay on as the historical truth referring back to this early epoch, with inevitable distorting effects on any attempt at historical recovery through psychoanalytic autobiographical narrative.

Freud himself comes close to this question, notably, when he discusses the transmission of ontogenetically and phylogenetically early traumas through an "archaic heritage" that includes the "universality of symbolism in language" and the "very common figures of speech in which this symbolism is recorded [*Redensarten . . . in denen sich diese Symbolik fixiert findet*]": "Here, then, we seem to have an assured instance of an archaic heritage dating from the period at which language developed. But another explanation might still be attempted. It might be said that we are dealing with thought-connections between ideas— connections which had been established during the historical development of speech and which have to be repeated now every time the development of speech has to be gone through in an individual" (*Moses and Monotheism, S.E.* 23:99; *G.W.* 16:205).

In the archeology of theory, the child's denials or disavowals are inevitable consequences of linguistic attempts to institute primal differences—between internal and external reality, between perception and memory—differences that, as I read Freud, cannot be said to have antedated this linguistic institution. Such differences, on this reading, are not initially *represented* by the child's language, but *enacted* by it. With time, Freud's own attempted representational narrative of psychic origins slipped increasingly toward an allegorical schema grounded in language as action, and the consequences were not limited to theory. The often cited 1914 paper, "Remembering, Repeating, and Working-Through," for example, with its "Further Recommendations on the Technique of Psycho-Analysis," might be read differently now. The connection made in Freud's late writing between schemata of disavowal and those of allegory suggests that the "action," the "acting out" through which the patient repeats a past "he has forgotten and repressed" (*S.E.* 12:150), cannot simply be contrasted with translation into words but must be taken to include narration *as* an enactment set going by disavowal. The analyst's "perpetual struggle with his patient to keep in the psychical sphere all the impulses which the patient would like to direct into the motor sphere" (153) becomes even more Sisyphean when one realizes that language used representationally to achieve interpretive understanding has also a nonrepresentational aspect of enactment whose "practical," clinical effect can be the emptying out of the hardest-earned understanding. Like Freud's enacted disavowal in "Constructions," denial in fantasy or in act can remain invisible in a clinical psychoanalysis while the work of interpretation seems to proceed smoothly.[29] This problem is usually discussed in the clinical literature in relation to diagnosis, and it is now widely acknowledged that overemphasis on interpretation of repression from within the assumptions of conflict theory does little to help analysands with prominent "narcissistic" difficulties. In clinical accounts, "reanalysis" often figures as the moment when the problem of denial first emerges for analyst and analysand. Reanalysis of Freud seems to suggest that in theory, and perhaps also in practice, the importance of enacted schemata of denial or disavowal is not so diagnosis-specific. These schemata would shape the experience of even the analysand whose well-developed representations of inner life express the "symbolizing capacity" analysts often associate with "analyzability." A reading of "Dora" and "Constructions" with attention to the relation of representational narrative structure and enacted narrative process reveals not a conflict so much as a split within the theoretical schema that has the practical task of helping to repair life-historical experience and to make it whole. Recovered and enacted as allegory, Freud's early theory of trauma, with the implied impossibility of avoiding repetition or of fully converting acting out of the past into understanding, inscribes history in psychoanalysis, and psychoanalysis in history, as a vision of the tragic beyond all that Oedipus represents.

## Notes

I thank Joseph H. Smith, M.D., and the members of the Seminar on Psychoanalysis and History, Forum on Psychiatry and the Humanities, Washington School of Psychiatry, for the opportunity to develop ideas that form the context for this paper during our regular meetings in 1989 and 1990; Cynthia Chase, Dorrit Cohn, Stephanie Engel, Art Goldhammer, and Joseph H. Smith for their very helpful critical readings of the manuscript; and Ramon M. Greenberg, M.D., and Peter H. Knapp, M.D., in whose psychoanalytic research group at the Boston Psychoanalytic Society and Institute I presented, in 1988, an early version of the section on the "Dora" case.

1. Coleridge gives a comprehensive definition of allegory (quoted by Fletcher): "We may then safely define allegorical writing as the employment of one set of agents and images with actions and accompaniments correspondent, so as to convey, while in disguise, either moral qualities or conceptions of the mind that are not in themselves objects of the senses, or other images, agents, actions, fortunes, and circumstances so that the difference is everywhere presented to the eye or imagination, while the likeness is suggested to the mind; and this connectedly, so that the parts combine to form a consistent whole" (1964, 19). A brief definition by de Man is particularly relevant to my argument in this paper: "Allegory names the rhetorical process by which the literary text moves from a phenomenal, world-oriented to a

grammatical, language-oriented direction" (1986, 68). De Man's argument about allegory and symbol, in "The Rhetoric of Temporality," first led me to think about the relation between allegory and history in Freud: "We are led, in conclusion, to a historical scheme that differs entirely from the customary picture. The dialectical relationship between subject and object is no longer the central statement of romantic thought, but this dialectic is now located entirely in the temporal relationships that exist within a system of allegorical signs. It becomes a conflict between a conception of the self seen in its authentically temporal predicament and a defensive strategy that tries to hide from this negative self-knowledge" (1983, 208). The recent discovery of articles de Man wrote for the collaborationist newspaper *Le Soir* might cause one to read this quotation biographically, but I do not find that diminishes the power of the connection he makes between allegory, history, and negative self-knowledge—if anything, the opposite. See the collection of essays edited by Hamacher et al. (1989). Frye points to the connection between allegory and theory: "It is not often realized that all commentary is allegorical interpretation, an attaching of ideas to the structure of poetic imagery. The instant that any critic permits himself to make a genuine comment about a poem (e.g., 'In *Hamlet* Shakespeare appears to be portraying the tragedy of irresolution') he has begun to allegorize. Commentary thus looks at literature as, in its formal phase, a potential allegory of events and ideas" (1957, 89).

2. This way of putting it I borrow from Fineman, who masterfully explores the desirous dimension of psychoanalytic allegory in "The Structure of Allegorical Desire": "In thus basing itself on its own critical reflection, however, desire becomes in psychoanalysis, as in allegory, both a theme and a structuring principle, and its psychology, its theory of the human, thus becomes, in the words of another and famously ambiguous genetive, the allegory of love, whereas its metapsychology, its theory of itself, becomes the allegory of allegory" (1981, 27). Like de Man in "The Rhetoric of Temporality" (1983), Fineman emphasizes that allegory inserts structure into time.

3. "I should like to emphasize the fact that the successive registrations represent the psychic achievement of successive epochs of life. At the boundary between two such epochs a translation of the psychic material must take place" (Freud 1985, 208).

4. See in particular Frye's "Polemical Introduction" and "Historical Criticism: Theory of Modes," in *Anatomy of Criticism* (1957).

5. See Schafer (1976, 1981, 1983); White (1978, 1987). In "The Need to Connect: Representations of Freud's Psychical Apparatus" (Morris 1980), I make the argument that Freud's theory enacts in the structure of its figurative language a challenge to its own claims. A number of critics, both psychoanalysts and scholars in other fields, have taken up the question of Freud's use of figurative language. Among those who have most directly helped my thinking here are Derrida (1987), Chase (1986), Lewin (1970), Starobinski (1987), and Weber (1982, 1987).

6. Schafer's "action language" project to rid psychoanalytic theory of its outdated metaphors seems to me to stand in a relationship of some tension

with "The Psychoanalytic Vision of Reality" (1976) and *Aspects of Internalization* (1968), each of which can be read as asserting the inextricability of certain schemata from life-historical narratives, schemata based not only on literary modes but on modes of the child's psychosexual experience. But Schafer does suggest that the purpose of "action language" is more heuristic than prescriptive—more to show what is at stake in metaphors such as "inside" and "outside" than to ban their use by theoreticians or clinicians (e.g., 1983, 191).

7. See Benveniste, "The Nature of Pronouns" and "Subjectivity in Language" (1971, 217–30), and Barthes, "The Discourse of History" (1986, 127–40).

8. For overviews of narratology, see Chatman (1978), Martin (1986), Mitchell (1981).

9. See de Man (1986), Derrida (1982), Fineman (1981).

10. Genette defines "narration" as "the productive narrative act and, by extension, the whole real or fictive situation in which it takes place" (1972, 72; my translation). He equates this "narrative situation" with what he calls the "narrative instance" (76), indicating that he follows Benveniste (see note 7) in associating this "instance" with the subject—the narrator—of the *énonciation*, the act of utterance, as opposed to the subject of the *énoncé*, the (uttered) statement. The term "narration" thus suggests the relation, which my argument in this paper attempts to elaborate upon, between narratology and speech-act theory (see note 21). (For a published English translation, see Genette [1980]. See also *Narrative Discourse Revisited*, the 1988 translation of Genette's revision of his 1972 discussion. The French "*narration*" is rendered in these as "narrating.") Culler, in "Story and Discourse in the Analysis of Narrative," discusses the relation between the terms "story" and "discourse" and argues that the distinction between them "can function only if there is a determination of one by the other" (1981, 186). Freud figures importantly in his argument, as a writer "attempting to hold together in a synthesis the two principles of narrative that we have found in opposition elsewhere: the priority of events and the determination of event by structures of signification" (179).

11. See Bernheimer and Kahane (1985), Glenn (1986), Jennings (1986), van den Berg (1987).

12. I use "Freud" throughout to stand in for more precise but ponderous possibilities such as: "The linguistic figure of the narrator through which the empirical author Freud occurs in the text."

13. In his letter to Fliess of 6 August 1899, Freud takes his position on the path of the Western allegorical tradition as he describes the narrative structure of his forthcoming "dream book": "The whole thing is planned on the model of an imaginary walk [*Spaziergangsphantasie*]. At the beginning, the dark forest of authors (who do not see the trees) hopelessly lost on the wrong tracks [*irrwegereich*]. Then a concealed pass [*Hohlweg*] through which I lead the reader—my specimen dream with its peculiarities, details, indiscretions, bad jokes—and then suddenly the high ground and the view and the question: which way do you wish to go now?" (Freud 1985, 365; 1986, 400).

14. See Dorrit Cohn's discussion of the term "theoretical fiction" in chapter 2.

15. Related to my line of argument here would be the idea that even the purest "primary" process is, according to the logic of Freud's own exposition, always already characterized by a degree of "inhibition" (*Hemmung*) and detour, and therefore already "secondary." See my discussion in "The Need to Connect: Representations of Freud's Psychical Apparatus" (1980, 317–27) and Weber's in *The Legend of Freud* (1982, 34–39). Weber concludes: "The 'fictionality' of the primary process would then relate not merely to the empirical unverifiability of what it seeks to designate, but to *its own structure as a theoretical concept.* For the condition of the primary process, entailing the binding of energy to representations (cathexis), would be the inhibitory force of the secondary process Freud seeks to oppose to it" (1982, 38–39).

16. De Man develops this argument in a number of ways, for example: "The phenomenal and sensory properties of the signifier have to serve as guarantors for the certain existence of the signified and, ultimately, of the referent" (1986, 48). See also "The Resistance to Theory," in the same book. What I have called the denial of the problem of linguistic reference takes two forms in current criticism, speaking very generally. The first more explicitly argues for the intuitive connection that allows for an unproblematic lining up of linguistic signs (signifier/signified units) with their extralinguistic referents; the second decides not to treat reference as a linguistic question at all, or to say that there is no "outside" of language, nothing outside the play of signifier and signified. For a discussion of the terms signifier/signified/referent, and the Saussurian/structuralist move of bracketing the referent, see Scholes (1981). For a comprehensive, witty, and philosophically rigorous discussion of the entire problem of reference, see Avni (1990).

17. Ten years later, in the passage of "The Unconscious" (1915) I have already alluded to, Freud would explicitly install in his theory of primary and secondary processes an argument about linguistic reference, based upon the distinction between "word-presentations" and "thing-presentations": "The system *Ucs.* contains the thing-cathexes of the objects, the first and true object-cathexes; the system *Pcs.* comes about by this thing-presentation being hypercathected through being linked with the word-presentations corresponding to it. It is these hypercathexes, we may suppose, that bring about a higher psychical organization and make it possible for the primary process to be succeeded by the secondary process which is dominant in the *Pcs.* Now, too, we are in a position to state precisely what it is that repression denies to the rejected presentation in the transference-neuroses: what it denies to the presentation is translation into words which shall remain attached to the object" (*S.E.* 14:201–2). Perception is again, through the "thing-cathexes" of the objects of psychical investment, the originary referential standard, to which word presentations refer back. "Translation into words" is now theoretically even further justified as the means of undoing the referential errors of transference. The complication that words are themselves objects of perception comes up in Freud's next paragraph, but it is largely circumscribed by thematic

containment in a discussion of object loss in schizophrenia: "But word-presentations, for their part too, are derived from sense-perceptions, in the same
way as thing-presentations are; the question might therefore be raised why
presentations of objects cannot become conscious through the medium of
their *own* perceptual residues" (202). This complication poses problems
especially for the theorist, as Freud notes in an ironic aside at the end of this,
one of his most ambitious theoretical statements: "When we think in abstractions there is a danger that we may neglect the relations of words to unconscious thing-presentations, and it must be confessed that the expression and
content of our philosophizing then begins to acquire an unwelcome resemblance to the mode of operation of schizophrenics" (204). "Constructions in
Analysis" can be read—see below—as an exploration of this problem area,
where words are no longer functioning in the practice and theory of analysis
in the referentially straightforward role of translating repression, but are themselves caught up in the vicissitudes of other perceptual residues.

18. See Cohn's essay in this volume.

19. I thank Deborah Schneider for contributing to the analysis of the river
that follows here by helping me to navigate the German.

20. See Culler's discussion in *On Deconstruction* (1982, 85ff.).

21. For a literary critic's reading of Freud's archeological metaphor, see
Bowie, "Freud's Dreams of Knowledge" (1987, 14–44). Kupsit (1989) carefully traces the evolution of the figure and discusses Spence.

22. Spence gives a reading of several of the passages in "Dora" I have
discussed above (1987, 122–59).

23. For a review of the evolution of Freud's views about whether the truth
of the past, including infantile sexual trauma, is historical or psychical, or
both, see Schimek (1975).

24. "The expression '*mise en abyme*,' originally from heraldry, where it
denotes a smaller escutcheon appearing in the center of a larger one, is now
frequent in literary discussions, as popularized by Gide (*Journal, 1889–1939*
[Paris: Bibliothèque de la Pléuade, n.d.], 41), to refer to a structure in which
the whole is represented in miniature in one of its parts. An example would
be a painting of a drawing room in which a painting hung, also of a drawing
room, ideally the same drawing room, complete with painting, etc. ... The
*abyme* structure is usually said to be dizzying, unsettling." (Translator's footnote in Hartman [1978], 147–48.)

25. See Austin (1970, 1975) for the original definitions and discussions of
the terms "constative" and "performative." On the relevance of performative
language ("speech acts") to psychoanalysis, see Felman (1983) and Forrester
(1990), "What the Psychoanalyst Does with Words: Austin, Lacan and the
Speech Acts of Psychoanalysis."

26. Anna Freud (1937) gives an extensive description of the child's denial
in fantasy and in action. She argues that these are normal mechanisms only
in childhood and, if they persist, evidence of severe disturbance. In a discussion
on the topic with Joseph Sandler (1982, 1983), she qualifies this: "I suppose
we tend to call it defensive when the child prefers to turn to such denial in

fantasy or in action to an unusual degree, at the expense of coping with the real world. . . . On the other hand, people who use denial a great deal in adult life are very threatened by reality, because if they meet the reality directly, and the reality does not fall in with their method of coping, they suffer very badly" (1983, 183, 186). Her view still seems to rely on a relatively unproblematic notion of "reality." Arguments for a less pathologizing understanding of denial and disavowal mechanisms have appeared in more recent analytic literature; see Stewart (1970), Trunnell and Holt (1974), Stolorow and Lachmann (1975), Basch (1983). In 1925, Freud describes disavowal as "a process which in the mental life of children seems neither uncommon nor very dangerous but which in an adult would mean the beginning of a psychosis" (*S.E.* 19:253). His later discussions of denial and ego splitting in adulthood are less dire and could be taken to point to the idea that "reality" is itself a (negotiated) construction. For a discussion of Lacan's reading of Freud on this point, with particular reference to the question of the phallic stage and disavowal of castration anxiety, see Morris (1988).

27. "In consequence of unfavourable circumstances, both of an external and an internal nature, the following observations apply chiefly to the sexual development of one sex only—that is, of males" ("On the Sexual Theories of Children" [1908], *S.E.* 9:211). "It is self-evident to the male child that a genital like his own is to be attributed to everyone he knows, and he cannot make its absence tally with his picture of these other people" (*Three Essays on Sexuality*, 1915 edition, *S.E.* 7:195). "Unfortunately we can describe this state of things only as it affects the male child; the corresponding processes in the little girl are not known to us" ("The Infantile Genital Organization" [1923], *S.E.* 19:142).

28. Austin (1970, 175–204) and de Man (1979, 278–301) have emphasized the performative quality of apologies and excuses.

29. For a clinical discussion of the way denials of intrapsychic conflict are played out in the analysand's patterns of association, see Kris (1979): "Attempts by the analyst to approach the unconscious aim of avoidance directly in such instances lead rapidly to more denial, to devaluation of the analyst, and to withdrawal" (146). See also Kris (1983).

## References

Austin, J. L. *Philosophical Papers*. London: Oxford University Press, 1970.
———. *How to Do Things with Words*. Cambridge: Harvard University Press, 1975.
Avni, Ora. *The Resistance of Reference*. Baltimore: Johns Hopkins University Press, 1990.
Barthes, Roland. *The Rustle of Language*. Translated by Richard Howard. New York: Hill and Wang, 1986.
Basch, Michael. "The Perception of Reality and the Disavowal of Meaning." *The Annual of Psychoanalysis* 11 (1983): 125–53.

Benveniste, Emile. *Problems in General Linguistics*. Translated by Mary Meek. Coral Gables: University of Miami Press, 1971.

Bernheimer, Charles, and Kahane, Claire, eds. *In Dora's Case*. New York: Columbia University Press, 1985.

Bowie, Malcolm. *Freud, Proust, and Lacan: Theory as Fiction*. New York: Cambridge University Press, 1987.

Chase, Cynthia. *Decomposing Figures: Rhetorical Readings in the Romantic Tradition*. Baltimore: Johns Hopkins University Press, 1986.

Chatman, Seymour. *Story and Discourse*. Ithaca: Cornell University Press, 1978.

Culler, Jonathan. *The Pursuit of Signs: Semiotics, Literature, Deconstruction*. Ithaca: Cornell University Press, 1981.

———. *On Deconstruction*. Ithaca: Cornell University Press, 1982.

de Man, Paul. *Allegories of Reading*. New Haven: Yale University Press, 1979.

———. *Blindness and Insight*. 2d ed., rev. Minneapolis: University of Minnesota Press, 1983.

———. *The Resistance to Theory*. Minneapolis: University of Minnesota Press, 1986.

Derrida, Jacques. *Margins of Philosophy*. Translated by Alan Bass. Chicago: University of Chicago Press, 1982.

———. *The Post Card: From Socrates to Freud and Beyond*. Translated by Alan Bass. Chicago: University of Chicago Press, 1987.

Felman, Shoshana. *The Literary Speech-Act: Don Juan with J. L. Austin, or Seduction in Two Languages*. Translated by Catherine Porter. Ithaca: Cornell University Press, 1983.

Fineman, Joel. "The Structure of Allegorical Desire." In *Allegory and Representation*, edited by Stephen Greenblatt. Vol. 5 of *Selected Papers from the English Institute*. Baltimore: Johns Hopkins University Press, 1981.

Fletcher, Angus. *Allegory: The Theory of a Symbolic Mode*. Ithaca: Cornell University Press, 1964.

Forrester, John. *The Seductions of Psychoanalysis: Freud, Lacan, and Derrida*. New York: Cambridge University Press, 1990.

Freud, Anna. *The Ego and the Mechanisms of Defense*. New York: International Universities Press, 1966 [1937].

Freud, Sigmund. "Entwurf einer Psychologie" (1895). In *Aus den Anfängen der Psychoanalyse*. Edited by Marie Bonaparte, Anna Freud, and Ernst Kris. London: Imago, 1950.

———. *Gesammelte Werke*. Edited by Anna Freud, E. Bibring, W. Hoffer, E. Kris, and O. Isakower. 18 vols. London: Imago, 1952.

"Die Abwehr-Neuropsychosen" (1894), vol. 1.

*Studien über Hysterie* (1895), vol. 1.

"Über Deckerinnerungen" (1899), vol. 1.

*Die Traumdeutung* (1900), vols. 2, 3.

*Zur Psychopathologie des Alltagslebens* (1901), vol. 4.

"Bruchstück einer Hysterie-Analyse" (1905), vol. 5.

*Drei Abhandlungen zur Sexualtheorie* (1905), vol. 5.

*Jenseits des Lustprinzips* (1920), vol. 13.
"Einige psychische Folgen des anatomischen Geschlechtsunterschieds" (1925), vol. 14.
"Nachschrift 1935 zur *Selbstdarstellung*" (1935), vol. 16.
"Die endliche und die unendliche Analyse" (1937), vol. 16.
"Konstruktionen in der Analyse" (1937), vol. 16.
*Der Mann Moses und die monotheistische Religion* (1939), vol. 16.
————. *The Standard Edition of the Complete Psychological Works of Sigmund Freud*. Edited and translated by James Strachey. 24 vols. London: Hogarth, 1953–74.
"The Neuro-Psychoses of Defence" (1894), vol. 3.
"Project for a Scientific Psychology" (1895), vol. 1.
*Studies on Hysteria* (1895), vol. 2.
"The Psychical Mechanism of Forgetfulness" (1898), vol. 3.
"Screen Memories" (1899), vol. 3.
*The Interpretation of Dreams* (1900), vols. 4, 5.
*The Psychopathology of Everyday Life* (1901), vol. 6.
"Fragment of an Analysis of a Case of Hysteria" (1905), vol. 7.
*Jokes and their Relation to the Unconscious* (1905), vol. 8.
*Three Essays on the Theory of Sexuality* (1905), vol. 7.
"On the Sexual Theories of Children" (1908), vol. 9.
"Formulations on the Two Principles of Mental Functioning" (1911), vol. 12.
"Recommendations to Physicians Practising Psycho-Analysis" (1912), vol. 12.
*Totem and Taboo* (1912–13), vol. 13.
"Remembering, Repeating, and Working-Through" (1914), vol. 12.
"Instincts and their Vicissitudes" (1915), vol. 14.
"The Unconscious" (1915), vol. 14.
"A Metapsychological Supplement to the Theory of Dreams" (1917), vol. 14.
"From the History of an Infantile Neurosis" (1918), vol. 17.
*Beyond the Pleasure Principle* (1920), vol. 18.
"The Infantile Genital Organization" (1923), vol. 19.
"A Note upon the 'Mystic Writing Pad'" (1925), vol. 19.
"Negation" (1925), vol. 19.
"Some Psychical Consequences of the Anatomical Distinction between the Sexes" (1925), vol. 19.
"Fetishism" (1927), vol. 21.
*Civilization and Its Discontents* (1930), vol. 21.
"Postscript" (1935) to *An Autobiographical Study* (1925), vol. 20.
"Analysis Terminable and Interminable" (1937), vol. 23.
"Constructions in Analysis" (1937), vol. 23.
*An Outline of Psycho-Analysis* (1940 [1938]), vol. 23.
"Splitting of the Ego in the Process of Defence" (1940 [1938]), vol. 23.
*Moses and Monotheism* (1939), vol. 23.

————. *The Complete Letters of Sigmund Freud to Wilhelm Fliess, 1887–1904*. Translated and edited by Jeffrey Moussaieff Masson. Cambridge: Harvard University Press, 1985.

————. *Briefe an Wilhelm Fliess 1887–1904*. Edited by Jeffrey Masson. Frankfurt: Fisher Verlag, 1986.

Frye, Northrop. *Anatomy of Criticism*: Princeton: Princeton University Press, 1957.

Genette, Gérard. *Figures III*. Paris: Seuil, 1972.

————. *Narrative Discourse*. Translation of "Discours du Récit," a portion of *Figures III*. Translated by Jane E. Lewin. Ithaca: Cornell University Press, 1980.

————. *Narrative Discourse Revisited*. Translated by Jane E. Lewin. Ithaca: Cornell University Press, 1988.

Glenn, Jules. "Freud, Dora, and the Maid: A Study of Countertransference." *Journal of the American Psychoanalytic Association* 34 (1986): 591–606.

Grubrich-Simitis, Ilse. "Trauma or Drive—Drive and Trauma." *Psychoanalytic Study of the Child* 43 (1988): 3–32.

Hamacher, Werner, Hertz, Neil, and Keenan, Thomas, eds. *Responses: On Paul de Man's Wartime Journalism*. Lincoln: University of Nebraska Press, 1989.

Hartman, Geoffrey, ed. *Psychoanalysis and the Question of the Text*. Baltimore: Johns Hopkins University Press, 1978.

Jennings, Jerry. "The Revival of 'Dora': Advances in Psychoanalytic Theory and Technique." *Journal of the American Psychoanalytic Association* 34 (1986): 607–36.

Kris, Anton. "Persistence of Denial in Phantasy." *Psychoanalytic Study of the Child* 34 (1979): 145–54.

————. "Determinants of Free Association in Narcissistic Phenomena." *Psychoanalytic Study of the Child* 38 (1983): 439–58.

Kupsit, Donald. "A Mighty Metaphor: The Analogy of Archaeology and Psychoanalysis." In *Sigmund Freud and Art: His Personal Collection of Antiquities*, edited by Lynn Gamwell and Richard Wells. Binghamton: State University of New York, 1989.

Lewin, Bertram. "The Train Ride: A Study of one of Freud's Figures of Speech." *Psychoanalytic Quarterly* 39 (1970): 71–89.

Martin, Wallace. *Recent Theories of Narrative*. Ithaca: Cornell University Press, 1986.

Mitchell, W. J. T., ed. *On Narrative*. Chicago: University of Chicago Press, 1981.

Morris, Humphrey. "The Need to Connect: Representations of Freud's Psychical Apparatus." In *The Literary Freud: Mechanisms of Defense and the Poetic Will*, edited by Joseph H. Smith. Psychiatry and the Humanities, vol. 4. New Haven: Yale University Press, 1980.

————. "Reflections on Lacan: His Origins in Descartes and Freud." *Psychoanalytic Quarterly* 57 (1988): 186–208.

Sandler, Joseph, with Freud, Anna. "Discussions in the Hampstead Index on

'The Ego and the Mechanisms of Defence': VII. Denial in Fantasy." *Bulletin of the Hampstead Clinic* 5 (1982): 153–67.

———. "Discussions in the Hampstead Index on 'The Ego and the Mechanisms of Defence': VIII. Denial in Word and Act." *Bulletin of the Hampstead Clinic* 5 (1983): 175–87.

Schafer, Roy. *Aspects of Internalization*. New York: International Universities Press, 1968.

———. *A New Language for Psychoanalysis*. New Haven: Yale University Press, 1976.

———. *Narrative Actions in Psychoanalysis: Narratives of Space and Narratives of Time*. Worcester, Mass.: Clark University Press, 1981.

———. *The Analytic Attitude*. New York: Basic Books, 1983.

Schimek, J. G. "The Interpretations of the Past: Childhood Trauma, Psychical Reality, and Historical Truth." *Journal of the American Psychoanalytic Association* 23 (1975): 845–65.

Scholes, Robert. "Language, Narrative, and Anti-Narrative." In *On Narrative*, edited by W. J. T. Mitchell. Chicago: University of Chicago Press, 1981.

Spence, Donald. *Narrative Truth and Historical Truth: Meaning and Interpretation in Psychoanalysis*. New York: Norton, 1982.

———. *The Freudian Metaphor: Toward Paradigm Change in Psychoanalysis*. New York: Norton, 1987.

———. "The Rhetorical Voice of Psychoanalysis." *Journal of the American Psychoanalytic Association* 38 (1990): 579–603.

Starobinski, Jean. "Acheronta Movebo." *Critical Inquiry* 13 (1987): 394–407.

Stewart, Walter. "The Split in the Ego and the Mechanism of Denial." *Psychoanalytic Quarterly* 39 (1970): 1–16.

Stolorow, Robert, and Lachmann, Frank. "Early Object Loss and Denial." *Psychoanalytic Quarterly* 44 (1975): 596–611.

Trunnell, Eugene, and Holt, William. "The Concept of Denial or Disavowal." *Journal of the American Psychoanalytic Association* 22 (1974): 769–84.

van den Berg, Sara. "Reading and Writing Dora: Preoedipal Conflict in Freud's 'Fragment of an Analysis of a Case of Hysteria.'" *Psychoanalysis and Contemporary Thought* 10 (1987): 45–67.

Weber, Samuel. *The Legend of Freud*. Minneapolis: University of Minnesota Press, 1982.

———. *Institution and Interpretation*. Minneapolis: University of Minnesota Press, 1987.

White, Hayden. *Metahistory: The Historical Imagination in Nineteenth-Century Europe*. Baltimore: Johns Hopkins University Press, 1973.

———. *Tropics of Discourse: Essays in Cultural Criticism*. Baltimore: Johns Hopkins University Press, 1978.

———. *The Content of the Form: Narrative Discourse and Historical Representation*. Baltimore: Johns Hopkins University Press, 1987.

Translating the Transference:
Psychoanalysis and the
Construction of History

*Cynthia Chase*

H ow much of the history of psychoanalysis, and of history writing, is the history of disavowal disavowed?

Freud begins his very last article, "The Splitting of the Ego in the Process of Defence," in a curious way:

> I find myself ... in the interesting position of not knowing whether what I have to say should be regarded as something long familiar and obvious or as something entirely new and puzzling. But I am inclined to think the latter.
>
> I have at last been struck by the fact that the ego of a person whom we know as a patient in analysis must, dozens of years earlier, when it was young, have behaved in a remarkable manner in certain particular situations of pressure. We can assign in general and somewhat vague terms the conditions under which this comes about, by saying that it occurs under the influence of a psychical trauma. [*S.E.* 23:275]

Freud describes himself in a peculiar position here in relation to his own understanding. He describes himself as having "at last been struck" by something: as registering with a start, as if it were a blow or a jolt, a "fact" of the reality disclosed in an analysis, a "fact" about the past that the analysis supposedly makes manifest. This fact—the splitting of the ego, the very agency supposed to compel psychical unity— only now belatedly imposes itself as the explanation for the patient's behavior in analysis. It is as though Freud's belated acknowledgment had to struggle against a disavowal like that involved in the splitting of the ego itself, the disavowal of an impression that occurs as a trauma, a cognition intolerably at odds with "a powerful instinctual demand" or wish. Freud would have had to contend with a powerful wish for the integrity of the ego and for the integrity of the *concept* of a psychical agency defined by the "synthetic function of the ego" he describes as "of such extraordinary importance" (*S.E.* 23:276). That wish would have operated like a new edition of the male child's disavowal of castration (disavowal of his own interpretation of female genitals); like another version of his wish for an invulnerable bodily integrity unendangered by the shattering pleasure of sexual release: it would have motivated Freud's disavowal of a perception and inference that now "at last" take place with a force something like that of the past "psychical trauma" that he infers. It is as though the fact that the ego's synthetic function can be "disturbed" presents itself as a "trauma," like the possibility of a mortally wounding blow.

Freud's description of his deferred cognition of the phenomenon of splitting therefore repeats in another respect as well the phenomenon he goes on to describe, since his awareness of the phenomenon leaves him still uncertain of its status—uncertain, he says, whether it is something that has been known to him already, something "long familiar and obvious" within the parameters of psychoanalytic investigation, or on the contrary "something entirely new and puzzling." The article's opening paragraph suggests that, like "the patient in analysis," he has maintained and still maintains "two attitudes . . . side by side": that the splitting of the ego is and is not consistent with long-established psychoanalytic knowledge.

My reading of these two opening paragraphs does not aim to establish that Freud the theorist, like the patient he goes on to describe, adopts the fetishist's solution to an unacceptable reality. It aims rather at something Freud's opening gives us to read, a disturbing "fact" about psychoanalytic knowledge: that being "struck" "at last" by a piece of that knowledge does not mean that one knows its status, knows whether one had it before or not, or knows the extent to which one's own knowledge is implicated in the splitting ego's strategy of simultaneous acknowledgment and disavowal. (Freud has described that strategy in the *Outline*: "The disavowal is always supplemented by an acknowledgement; two contrary and independent attitudes always arise and result in the situation of there being a splitting of the ego" [*S.E.* 23:204]). Freud's text implies that splitting cannot be mastered by the knowledge of splitting.

What makes the splitting of the ego so disturbing or ambiguous a phenomenon that it provokes this delayed and ambivalent characterization on Freud's part—as "something long familiar and obvious" from psychoanalytic observation, as well as "puzzling and new"? Whence the uncanniness of this "fact" about the ego in analysis?

If Freud's recognition of the splitting of the ego in some respect repeats the gesture he describes, this may have to do with its disturbing implications for the possibility of treating the transference neurosis. That would have disturbing implications for history writing: trouble for the writing of history that interprets the past with a view to affecting the future. In "Analysis Terminable and Interminable" (1937), "alterations of the ego" are called fundamental obstacles to completing an analysis. In "The Splitting of the Ego," the "rift in the ego" (*S.E.* 23:276), the detachment of a portion of the ego from reality, deprives the analyst of his collaborator and interlocutor. For the historian, the phenomenon of splitting implies that the current conception of the past with which he has to work, embodied in institutions and discourses that necessarily bear upon his own practice, constitutes in unpredictable ways not only a disavowal of crucial elements of the historical past but what Lacan calls the "symbolic abolition" (1966, 388) of crucial conditions of discourse or experience, the converse of the very symbolization of reality. Such implications are explored by Freud explicitly in *Moses and Monotheism* and other texts that describe a people's relation to its past.

It may also be telling that the disturbing uncertainty about the status of one's knowledge arises as Freud invokes the notion of "psychical trauma." This old and recurrent concept would seem to have recesses and bearings capable of disrupting established psychoanalytic knowledge. It impinges upon historical knowledge as well: *Moses and Monotheism* centers its argument on the analogy between belated psychical damage by shock or trauma and the belated response to historical events reflected in an institution such as monotheism; the "latency period" that marks them both gives the discourse of the present the status of compulsions (*S.E.* 23:66–86).[1] We should note one final quietly remarkable feature of these paragraphs in Freud's last article. Defense against psychical trauma by means of the splitting of the ego is here given both a radical generality and a peculiar specificity: it is said to characterize not one sort of patient, nor (conversely) all human beings; Freud writes rather (I quote again), "I have at last been struck by the fact that the ego of a person whom we know as a patient in analysis must, ... when it was young, have behaved in a remarkable manner in certain particular situations of pressure" (*S.E.* 23:275). What analysis as such discovers, or establishes—so Freud belatedly would register—is the history of a splitting of the ego.

Establishing the history of a splitting of the ego—one of the major models of history writing that psychoanalysis would offer—raises difficulties that emerge dramatically in the history of one such construction: that of the Wolf Man case. This history involves at least three case histories of disparate status: Freud's "From the History of an Infantile Neurosis," written in 1915 just after he terminated Sergei Pankeiev's analysis, plus passages added in 1918; Ruth Mack Brunswick's "Supplement," written after her treatment of the Wolf Man in 1926–27; and Nicolas Abraham and Maria Torok's extraordinary book of 1976, *Cryptonomie: Le Verbier de l'homme aux loups* (published in English as *The Wolf Man's Magic Word*), the history of their own *rehearing* of the case through a multilingual reading of the Wolf Man's recorded words. It is the last swerve in the history of the case that I will want especially to stress, to reflect on the conception of historical experience implied in the remarkable reading practice its authors derive from an example of multilingual reading in Freud, drawn from his article on the most observable instance of ego splitting: fetishism.

Already the first case history of the Wolf Man, Freud's, brings to the fore difficulties for historiography. As is well known, "From the History of an Infantile Neurosis" comes to focus on the question of the phenomenal status of the trauma—the question of the Wolf Man's recollection or fantasy of the primal scene. Addressing that question of the ego's history turns out to be inseparable from addressing the history of such history writing: Freud places the question of the status of the primal scene in the context of his conflicts with Adler and Jung over the significance of the castration complex and "the importance of the infantile factor." Throughout its history, the Wolf Man case history carries with it the most disconcerting implications both of Freud's emphasis on an actual belatedly traumatic event (the sight of the parents' copulation) and of his construal of a traumatizing fantasy. Freud's highly deliberate nondecision between these alternatives—"I intend on this occasion to close the discussion of the reality of the primal scene with a *non liquet*" (*S.E.* 17:60)—insists on and accepts the peculiar character of the knowledge of history allowed by the concept of trauma. The consequences of the child's psychical trauma are summarized in a passage in which what will become the notion of the splitting of the ego and its bizarre implications for the nature of "knowledge" are fully apparent. Wolf Man "rejected (*verwarf*) castration," Freud writes (*S.E.* 17:84), then explains that the phrase must be understood in two ways. The child "repressed [castration]," yet later "recognized [it] as a fact," in a "second reaction [which] did not *do away with* the first," resulting in a structure similar to splitting and fetishism. Splitting, however, splits off from that structure; in a second and stricter sense, the word *verwarf* describes "a third current, the oldest and deepest, which did not as yet even raise the question of the reality of castration" (*S.E.* 17:85). To "not . . . even raise the question of the reality" of something is not to "see" it. Freud's wording evokes the omission of the very conditions of integration into psychical reality.

The nature of this repudiation or disavowal described by Freud remains ambiguous, however, because of the dubious status of what it is that is disavowed, the "reality" of "castration." The lucid commentary of Laplanche and Pontalis would suggest that this "disavowal of reality," common to "the child, the fetishist, and the psychotic," is the refusal to accept . . . what?—not a perception but a theory, castration being a theory, an "infantile sexual theory," albeit one privileged by Freud as a crucial mode of access to "reality" (Laplanche and Pontalis 1973, 168). This elucidation of "foreclosure" or disavowal is worth bearing in mind as one takes stock for instance of those indictments brought by new historicist literary historians against writers of the Romantic and Revolutionary period for their "disavowals" of history. Such "disavowal" would then mean simply the refusal to accept a concept of history tantamount to the castration theory: a refusal invariably to think in terms of a narrative of loss and endangerment, a narrative bound to a highly interpretive "perception" of absence based on its binary opposition to the presence of a significant trait.

Lacan resolves the ambiguity of Freud's account of disavowal by reconstruing it as belonging to a "primary process" made up of two complementary operations, the *Einbeziehung ins Ich*, "introduction into the subject," and the *Ausstossung aus dem Ich*, "expulsion from the subject." The first of these operations is what Lacan also calls "symbolisation"; the second "constitutes the Real inasmuch as this is the domain which subsists outside symbolisation" (1966, 388). The category of the Real radically reorients the notion of "reality" in Freud's text. Whereas Freudian "reality" is constituted by "symbolizing what ought to be symbolized (castration)," in Laplanche and Pontalis's revealing paraphrase (1973, 168), the Real is what can enter psychical experience only through hallucination. "What has been foreclosed from the Symbolic reappears in the Real" (Lacan 1966, 388). Disavowal would then be a mode of access to as well as a mode of defense against "history," now construed as that which eludes symbolization.

What eludes symbolization is once again castration, according to Freud, or more literally, the possibility of one's own dismemberment. Freud cites the Wolf Man's recollection of his hallucination at age five—"I had cut through the little finger of my (right or left?) hand, so that it was only hanging on by its skin" (*S.E.* 17:85)—and concludes strikingly: "We may . . . assume that this hallucination belongs to the

period in which he brought himself to recognize the reality of castration and it is perhaps to be regarded as actually marking this step"
(*S.E.* 17:85). This is no less than an acknowledgment of hallucination
as a mode of recognition of reality, a move Freud will make once again
in another text I shall examine, his 1937 paper, "Constructions in
Analysis." Thus the first installment in the history of Wolf Man's case
histories, Freud's 1915 text, already brings into play the difficulties
posed by the hypothesis of *Verwerfung* or disavowal for the construction of the history of a subject or the history of experience and interpretation. "From the History of an Infantile Neurosis" is perhaps chief
among the texts in which Freud had sketched the idea that would
recur to him as "new and puzzling" in 1938 in "The Splitting of the
Ego."

Abraham and Torok's construction of the Wolf Man's infantile history necessarily takes place inseparably from their reinterpretation of
his case histories, his history as a case. In Freud's 1927 essay on
"Fetishism" they descry an unidentified allusion to Ruth Mack Brunswick's treatment of the Wolf Man for (as she wrote) "a hypochon-
driacal *idée fixe*" about his nose (Brunswick 1971, 264). It is Freud's
prime example of the selection of a fetish: "For obvious reasons the
details of these cases must be withheld from publication; I cannot,
therefore, show in what way accidental circumstances have contributed to the choice of a fetish. The most extraordinary case seemed
to me to be the one in which a young man had exalted a certain sort
of "shine on the nose" into a fetishistic precondition" (*S.E.* 21:152).
Freud's text goes on to explain that the fetish was the nose; but that
this was so and how it had come to be so could only be understood
by hearing the patient's words—"*Glanz auf der Nase*"—not in German but in English, the language he had spoken with his governess as
a child, and thus as "glance at the nose," rather than "shine on the
nose," the words' translated meaning. Through this bizarre passage,
Freud's and Abraham and Torok's altogether disparate interpretations
of this case touch. Freud here shares the procedure of multilingual
decrypting that Abraham and Torok will employ, whereas they depart
entirely from his centering on the fear of castration.

Abraham and Torok note: "Freud grasped the verbal mechanism of
the fetish and its metapsychological import in this particular case: 'The
Mother has no phallus'" (1986, 32). To Abraham and Torok, the mother's lack of a phallus means precisely her lack of the father's phallus
because "he deprived her of it by diverting his desire elsewhere"
(1986, 32), in sexual play with Sergei's elder sister, a scene she would
have replayed for her younger brother. The little brother verifies her

account with adults; and it is the scandal following this event—*that* danger, not castration—that motivates Wolf Man's singular way with words. It motivates his repetition, all but undecipherably reinscribed, of the magic word *tieret* (to rub), productive of the father's, or rather of the little brother's, pleasure. The primal scene is a scene between the father and the sister that truly *takes place* in the *replay* that impels the decisive disaster: a dialogue (whose words Abraham and Torok decrypt in the dream of the wolves) in which Wolf Man's identity as witness to this scene (which he recounts first to the governess) threatens the family with scandal—and at his mother's appeal, Wolf Man suppresses and silences forever the words in which his desire is lodged. The social, legal, institutional character of this catastrophic situation contrasts with the perennial, natural, transhistorical Freudian primal scene of parental intercourse. A distinctive effect of Abraham and Torok's rehearing of Wolf Man is that his history turns, like "history," on a conflict of power within an institution (here, the family).

Yet their reconstruction of a specific, contingent episode at the origin of the illness keeps faith with the profound historiographic imperative of Freudian analysis, present independently of the polemic with Jung and Adler in the Wolf Man case when Freud defends his hypothesis of Wolf Man's childhood recollection rather than fantasy of an actual specific scene of parental coitus *a tergo*. Freud's defense of his hypothesis of the actual occurrence of a specifically circumstanced primal scene is not, I think, simply a theoretical regression, a literalistic insistence on discovering an origin in an actual external event. Its insistence needs to be heard as the obscured responsiveness to an enigma, to the enigmatic fact fundamental to psychoanalysis of the status, as *event*, of words.

The "fact" of a dream (or of the *verbal mechanism* of a fetish), the fact of the existence of a dream text: these *words* are the event from which Freud's interpretation starts, and Abraham and Torok start there too. But beginning by exercising a reading *technique*—the multilingual listening Freud practiced in hearing *Glanz* as "glance"—they arrive at a radically new interpretation of the role, in the Wolf Man's history, of words. "It is not a situation *including* words that becomes repressed; the words are not dragged into repression by a situation. Rather, *the words themselves, expressing desire, are deemed to be generators of a situation that must be avoided and voided retroactively*" (Abraham and Torok 1986, 20; their emphasis). Whence the elaborate lexical operation legible in the words the Wolf Man speaks, exercised upon the words themselves rather than on the meanings they represent. The effect is both to stifle and save, mutilate and repeat, words that *in themselves* constitute the catastrophic satisfaction of desire or the event of its prohibition and burial.

The operation consists in displacement to a lexically contiguous meaning, to its synonym, and to the synonym's translation, or inversely its homonym, in another language. An unpredictable combination of lexical, semantic, and aural displacements encrypts the original "magic word" in an inscription, which is further concealed by being cam-ouflaged by its apparent intelligibility as part of a discourse that invites the full gamut of psychoanalytic interpretation. (Here is one example among many, untypical insofar as Abraham and Torok's decrypting for once takes fewer steps than Freud's. Wolf Man reports his feeling of terror as a child on the occasion of seeing a swallow-tailed butterfly open and fold its wings. This memory is linked by Freud to an early castration threat from a nursemaid, Grusha, whose name is the same as the name for a certain sort of striped—not butterfly, but pear, also recollected by the patient [*S.E.* 17:90–91]. Abraham and Torok hear in the English name of the butterfly [about which his patient of course spoke to Freud in German] the words, "swallow the tale": "*Cry out? No! I must swallow it. ... I swallow the tale* (of the tail). What is tragic within this tale is that my desire must be eradicated within myself" [1986, 45]. Thus within a richly multidimensional text appear the relics of an entirely other drama.)

Abraham and Torok's hypothesis of a traumatic danger constituted by certain words could be seen as a new way of understanding the peculiar "more radical" "flight of the ego" taking place in that more untreatable condition than the neuroses, schizophrenia, the strange-ness of its symptoms due to "the predominance of what has to do with words over what has to do with things" (*S.E.* 14:200). As Freud writes, in "The Unconscious" (1915), "What has dictated the substi-tution is not the resemblance between the things denoted but the sameness of the words used to express them." Whereas in dreams, what is subjected to the primary process are the "thing-presentations to which the words have been taken back," in schizophrenia, it is "the words themselves in which the preconscious thought was expressed" that are so manipulated (*S.E.* 14:201, 229). Freud in these passages presumes the priority of "thing-presentations" or "preconscious thoughts" to words, conceived as their expressions or representations. Abraham and Torok instead conceive of words as *forces* "generating" a catastrophic situation, which therefore will have to be undone by work upon the words themselves. The symptom Abraham and Torok call cryptonomy takes its origin in a particular *kind* of danger rather than, as Freud suggests (*S.E.* 14:233), in the radical *degree* of the ego's withdrawal from an insupportable reality. Their hypothesis would be profoundly pertinent to the reinscription of history that we can assume informs historical or literary texts. Texts reinscribe traumatic social change inhering in the production of discourses composed in crucial part by, precisely, words—change "generated" by words, to the extent that ideology rather than economics impels the disjunctions that make up historical time, historical event. Abraham and Torok's hypothesis would imply that the displacements and "disavowals" that psychoanalytically informed deconstructive and new historicist critics have been learning to construe are in fact supplemented and undercut by encrypted repetitions and undoings of historical catastrophes lodged for the archive (which must mean, at some point, identified by individuals who write and speak) in words that have to be silenced.

Abraham and Torok's construction of encrypted words intensifies an imagination of words as the *generators of situations* that is monumentalized in Freud's concept of the transference. Freud of course came to locate the difficulty—if also the hope—of analytic treatment in the fact that the analysand uses language to repeat rather than to recollect and represent. Ruth Mack Brunswick conceived her work with Wolf Man as treating symptoms of Wolf Man's unresolved transference onto Freud. Abraham and Torok take up the complications of the treatment and the concept of transference posed by Freud's distinction between mourning and melancholia, between the introjection and the incorporation of a lost object. The piecemeal, painful work of mourning introjects the desire that linked one to the person lost, reintegrating it, dissolving it, into the self. The spell of melancholia incorporates the lost other within the self, when and because one cannot, or precisely in order not to have to, introject the desire, make it newly one's own, and also in order not to dissolve it. (Putting the distinction like this, in terms of choice or agency—a feature of Freud's, Abraham and Torok's, and their reader Derrida's texts[2]—*personifies* what also have to be understood simply as incompatible linguistic processes. Such an understanding occurs by way of Freud's opposition between consciousness and memory in *Beyond the Pleasure Principle*, for instance, which Walter Benjamin, as we shall see, takes as a clue to the character of historical experience.) Wolf Man suffers a melancholia brought on by the impossibility, the prohibition, of symbolizing his (lost) objects of love (the sister and the father) as exemplars of desire's fulfillment.

Incorporating the sister and the father, encrypting them in "an inside heterogeneous to the inside of the Self" (Derrida 1986, xvi)— within the self a sort of crypt or closed-off passageway—such a sealed-off inclusion meets the libidinal imperative that this desire neither be fulfilled (since its expression has been identified with the catastrophe of the family's destruction) nor sacrificed (which cannot be done without a substitution, that is, a symbolization). Wolf Man's melancholia is an *Ichspaltung* in which there is no transference in the usual sense, no address to the analyst that is simultaneously an address from the infantile self to the loved object. The patient's relation to the analyst does not repeat his relation to a former loved object; instead it covertly replays the imaginary relationship *between* the incorporated objects: Freud is the father, his patient is the sister.[3] The Wolf Man "'repeated' nothing of his own. he was simply not himself. He *was* his sister" (Abraham and Torok 1986, 75). The apparent transference only camouflages the prolonging of an imaginary rapport between incorporated objects that precludes the patient's utterance of the words embodying desire. Yet in the production of the cryptonyms, there takes place a form of writing that "manages somehow to pass over the heads [of the incorporated guests] and address external Objects" (21), that is to say, that includes the possibility of being read. The difficulty for the treatment is that these two modes in which the repetition of the past takes place are thoroughly heterogeneous and mutually contradictory, occurring at incompatible levels and coming from two different positions or "selves." One repetition (itself going unrecognized) blocks out the other. If the outcome of traumatic loss of libidinal objects is incorporation, the premise that analysis can proceed through treatment of the transference breaks down.

There breaks down, at least, the premise that analysis can proceed through *interpretive* treatment of the transference. If the term "transference" is still appropriate in the Wolf Man's case, it is only by radicalizing the notion of repetition, which for Freud defines transference in opposition to the remembering that ought to take place in an analysis, and only by stressing the tension between enactment or performance (in the transference) and cognition or representation (in remembering) that underlies that opposition. Interpretation will not be the "technique" required, insofar as analysis encounters not cognitive structures but words as deeds or things, and having emphasized the inevitability of the transference in this sense, Freud at last calls "construction," and not interpretation, the analyst's principal activity (*S.E.* 23:261). Abraham and Torok's construction of the Wolf Man's history *reads* his words rather than *interpreting* his statements—a radical enactment of Freud's distinctions.

As "the work of the only authentic area remaining in an alienated ego," the cryptonymic procedure would deserve, as Abraham and

Torok suggest, "the respect due any attempt at *being* in spite of every-thing" (21). One could put its significance in another way: as an unmitigated outcome of the conflict between representation and en-actment: between the semantic, cognitive, constative dimension of language and its performative status, its ability to "do" something, in the first instance simply to occur at all. The production of a sign breaks with the given array of significations, interrupts relationship and mean-ing. The words that the Wolf Man swallows and encrypts have this disruptive force. The word *tieret* embodies the threat to meaning posed by a sign that signifies by constituting an *event* in its production (the event of maximal libidinal "pleasure"), not by referring to a signification. The threat to the conditions of meaning posed by the endangerment of the position of the father, in the scandal inaugurating Wolf Man's illness, can be seen as secondary to or as a figure for this "linguistic predicament."

By the fact that it is a quotation, the Wolf Man's "magic word" *tieret* has another dimension that exemplifies the paradoxical condition of the performative power of words that Derrida calls "iterability." Only as repeated and repeatable does the "event" take place. That a sign's or an event's identity depends on being iterable, quotable, means that its meaning or identity is never whole or complete.[4] The lack of self-identity of the sign appears conspicuously in the Wolf Man's story in the lack of any moment when the word *tieret* spoken for the "first time" carried its libidinal charge or performative force. It has force as an "event" only as a quotation. Wolf Man's cryptonymic procedure seeks to meet the contradictions of these fundamental conditions of (im)possibility of language. The composition of the hidden "rhymes" of the magic words corresponds with the imperative both to produce and not to produce the mark in which is vested the very force of language to occur, the very possibility of an inscription or mark, and at the same time the interruption and potential destruction of lan-guage's capacity to mean.

Freud's papers on technique, principally his writings on transfer-ence, thematize the tension between the cognitive and performative aspects of language as the tension between the patient's "impulse to remember" and his "compulsion to repeat." "Remembering, Repeat-ing, and Working-Through" describes the usual eventual effect of the psychoanalytic rule of uncensored free association: "The patient does not *remember* anything of what he has forgotten and repressed, but *acts* it out. He reproduces it not as a memory but as an action. . . . As long as the patient is in the treatment he cannot escape from this compulsion to repeat; in the end we understand that this is his way of remembering" (*S.E.* 12:150). Repetition can be assimilated to remembering insofar as it can be construed as a mimesis of past conditions in some sense addressed to the analyst to behold and comprehend. Freud's texts oscillate between this notion of memory and a more performative one.

The same essay more explicitly describes the transference on the one hand as a continuation of the patient's illness ("we must treat his illness, not as an event of the past, but as a present-day force" [*S.E.* 12:151]) and on the other as an "artificial" illness, "conjured" into existence by the analyst's resisted insistence on recollection. The analyst's work is said to consist not in inducing the patient to resume recollection (an aim thereby implicitly acknowledged to be impossible), but rather in enforcing the view of the patient's statements as actions that are repetitions, and thereby "tracing [the patient's state of being ill] back to the past," even while it is lived through by him "as something real and contemporary" (*S.E.* 12:152). This sort of recuperation of repetition is undercut dramatically in the remarkable final sentence of "The Dynamics of the Transference": "For when all is said and done, it is impossible to destroy anyone *in absentia* or *in effigie*" (*S.E.* 12:108). Here the reality, as actions, of the patient's repetitions is central to the opportunity they offer for the treatment: not the transformation of performed actions into cognitive content as representations, but rather the enacting of new outcomes of scenarios carried over from the past. The question of the nature of the transference as repetition or representation, force or signification, remains undecidable on the basis of Freud's texts, which thereby thematize the irresolvable tension between the cognitive and the performative aspects of language.[5]

Neither of the models of the analyst's task oscillated between in "The Dynamics of the Transference"—straight cognition or straight "performance," action—would meet the necessity of dislodging Wolf Man's incorporated Objects, the others, the "guests," whose conflicts he plays out in his present relationships, especially with the analyst. Doing away with them would involve the peculiar process described by Benjamin in an introduction to his translation of Baudelaire's *Tableaux Parisiens*—"The task [or "the giving up": *die Aufgabe*] of the Translator." Paul de Man puts it like this: for Benjamin translation "kills" the original "by discovering that it was already dead" (de Man 1986, 84).[6] Freud refers to "destroying" destructive or pathological affective structures, an unsurprising aim for psychological treatment; de Man, however, refers to killing the object that translation is usually thought to value and to aim to preserve, the original text. Such a seemingly perverse or pessimistic account of translation derives from an estimate of "the original" as a structure without integrity, like the psychoanalytic conception of the "origin" of a psychical illness—not an intrinsically meaningful event, but the deferred action of an initially insignificant occurrence lent "meaning" retroactively. Translation, de Man argues following Benjamin, has to do with "what in the original belongs to language, and not to meaning as an extralinguistic correlate susceptible of paraphrase" (84). Benjamin is evoking the translator's engagement with individual words and syntactical structures, the text's devices for the production of meaning, instead of with the meaning inferred from the text (and experienced as the identity of the text) at its reception. From this perspective, the notion of "the original" delusorily conflates and identifies the production and the reception of a text. The disjunction between the syntax and the semantics of a text, the incommensurability between its devices and its meaning, makes for an ultimate "giving up" of translation, renders translation impossible.

The original is "already dead" in the sense that it consists in "language" that does not contain its meaning, and "meaning" that does not inhere in its language. This is the case too for those performances of a relationship between his incorporated objects (the father and the sister) that are the Wolf Man's substitute for a transference. Those performances, the Wolf Man's exchanges with his analyst, are merely the means or pretext for the mechanics of the production of the magic word; its significance does not inhere in them. Such a situation invalidates standard assumptions about treating the transference neurosis—above all, the expectation of gaining access to the original illness through interpreting the interpersonal bearing of the analysand's present discourse.

"Killing the original by finding it already dead": what de Man's strange formula *does* readily describe, unlike the canonical (and pious) view of translation (including the translation of the transference back into the terms of the past), is the work of mourning. This is the task of the analyst confronted with a melancholia such as Wolf Man's incorporation of his father and sister. Freud writes of the bitter work of melancholia, "Just as mourning impels the ego to give up the object by declaring the object to be dead and offering the ego the inducement of continuing to live, so does each single struggle of ambivalence loosen the fixation of the ego to the object by disparaging it, denigrating it and even as it were killing it" (*S.E.* 14:257). But what if ambivalence—say, the tension between rapt pleasure in and aggressivity toward the sexual scene—strengthens rather than loosens the fixation, sustains, as in the Wolf Man's case, the structure of the crypt? In place of melancholia's work would have to come a "killing" by finding already "dead": devalorizing the significance of the "original" scene, demystifying the father's pleasure, crime, and endangerment, through a disclosure of the limited, illusory validity of "the juridical code that permitted the [English] nurse's blackmail in the first place" (Abraham and Torok 1986, 76), which rendered the father-daughter scene a crime.[7] The patient's freeing from fixation on the incorporated objects and the "original" structure of their relationships could happen through such a process as Abraham and Torok's peculiar labor of "translation," which is also the renunciation of translation: their attention to the material elements of the *language* of the illness, not to its reception or ostensible meaning (i.e., what is understood by Freud and by the Wolf Man, who accepts his interpretations) nor finally even to the *latent* "meaning" of Wolf Man's exchanges with his analysts, the replayed scenario of seduction and prohibition. For the nucleus of the illness is not the illicit asymmetrical sexual relationship, but rather the attachment of explosive force to certain words. An analysis concentrating on the peculiar labor of "translating" their reinscriptions finds the original characters (in both senses) "already dead" by disclosing what in them belongs to language, after all, "and *not* to meaning."

Considering texts from the perspective of "the task of the translator" involves attention to their materiality in a way that is profoundly congruent with psychoanalytic theory, and particularly with reflections around the motif of "trauma." *Nachträglichkeit* ("deferred action"), the syntax of psychical trauma, of experience subjected to repression, is one version of the disjunction between "language" and "meaning," between the production and the reception of an experience or text. Another way of thinking about trauma, which arises very early in Freud's thought and recurs very late, is the model of a psychical apparatus combining distinct, separate systems for perception and consciousness and for memory.[8] Freud's speculation on the origins of life, in an organism for which *warding off* is far more important than receiving stimuli, leads to the counterintuitive notion of consciousness as a "defensive shield" or "screen." The implications of this line of thought for the historiographical status of literary and other texts, its consequences for a conception of how history impinges upon writing, were explored by Walter Benjamin in "On Some Motifs in Baudelaire" (1980, 1.2: 605–54; 1969, 155–200). Benjamin focuses on some remarkable assertions in *Beyond the Pleasure Principle*:

> On the basis of impressions derived from our psychoanalytic experience, we assume that all excitatory processes that occur in the *other* systems [other than the perception-consciousness system] leave permanent traces behind in them which form the foundation of memory. Such memory-traces, then, have nothing to do with the fact of becoming conscious; indeed they are often most powerful and most enduring when the process which left them behind was one which never entered consciousness. [*S.E.* 18:24–25]

The limits that would be set upon "the system's aptitude for receiving fresh excitations" by its retaining "permanent traces" suggest that any "excitatory process becomes conscious in the system *Cs.* but leaves no permanent trace behind there; ... the excitation is transmitted to the [other] systems, ... and ... it is in *them* that its traces are left" (*S.E.* 18:25). These inferences thus "lead one to suspect," as Freud writes (in the hypothesis that Benjamin singles out as decisive), "that becoming conscious and leaving behind a memory-trace are processes incompatible with each other within one and the same system" (*S.E.* 18:25).

Where an impression was conscious it leaves no record, and where it leaves a record, it was never conscious: strange inspiration for a theory of history, but it accords with Benjamin's conception of history in terms of shock or trauma. Unlike Bergson, who "rejects any historical determination of memory," Benjamin is concerned to describe the nature of writing that has "as its basis an experience for which the shock experience has become the norm" (Benjamin 1969, 157, 162). "On Some Motifs in Baudelaire" sketches how Baudelaire exemplifies and thematizes writing as a form of consciousness, as the parrying of shocks. In its own resolute negativity, Benjamin's essay resembles Freud's "Papers on Technique" (*S.E.* 12). "On Some Motifs in Baudelaire" should be read with Freud's "Constructions in Analysis" as an account of how historiography may proceed in conditions in which consciousness and recollection fail; in which (as Baudelaire affirmed) consciousness loses its duel against the world;[9] in which usually no memory can be recovered, like early childhood experiences and reality the self finds insupportable.

The key image in Benjamin's description of these conditions is Baudelaire's figure of "M.G.," a portrayal of his friend Constantin Guys, which for Benjamin's reading also describes Baudelaire himself, engaged in the "fantastic combat" of "parrying" impressions:

> How he stands there, bent over his table, scrutinizing the sheet of paper just as intently as he does the objects around him by day; how he *stabs*

*away* with his pencil, his pen, his brush; ... how he pursues his work swiftly and intensely, as though he were afraid that his images might escape him; thus he is combative, even when alone, and parries his own blows. [Benjamin 1969, 163–64; Baudelaire 1968, 553]

Guys was a draughtsman who produced pictures and sketches of such ephemeral subjects as Parisian fashions, performances of opera and ballet, travels in Spain and Turkey, and episodes in the Crimean War. Painting or writing is here consciousness as shock defense, *preventing* impressions from entering the (involuntary) memory by *noting* them as they occur. These images do not attain or aspire to the fullness of recollection or the past recaptured. They are datings; they are notes. The more efficiently consciousness is on the alert as a screen against stimuli, Benjamin writes, "the less do these impressions enter experience (*Erfahrung*), tending to remain in the sphere of a certain hour of one's life (*Erlebnis*). Perhaps the special achievement of shock defense may be seen in its function of assigning to an incident a precise point in time in consciousness *at the cost of the integrity of its contents*. This would be a peak achievement of the intellect; it would turn the incident into a moment that has been lived (*Erlebnis*)" (Benjamin 1969, 163; my emphasis).

Crucial in this description is the impoverishment, abstractness, reductiveness, of what counts as (psychical and aesthetic) achievement. It should not be obscured for us by the misleadingly positive sound of the word *Erlebnis* nor the plenitude evoked through its deceptively lyrical translation. Emphasizing and identifying these qualities with "a peak achievement" is the force (and the virtue) of Benjamin's reading. In Baudelaire's own text, "*Le peintre de la vie moderne*," the stress on these features undercuts the essay's idealizing portrayal of "a swiftness that would transcend the latent opposition between action and form" (de Man 1983, 158). The tension is reflected in a passage that describes Guys's achievement of a "synthesis" of the impression through a technique that supplements with filled-in details a sketch that indicates the whole image right from the start ("at each point of its elaboration, each drawing seems sufficiently completed; you may call this a sketch, if you like, but it is a perfect sketch" [Baudelaire 1968, 555; quoted in de Man 1983, 158]). In the description of this method, an ideal of organic form contends with an emphasis on technique and on the "disincarnation and reduction of meaning" (de Man 1983, 158). Baudelaire's portrayal of M.G., "the painter of modern life," is plainly an idealization—of a deliberate and rhetorically self-conscious kind.

One finds the same ideal—and an idealizing apparent perhaps in the very idea of consistent or normative *success* in "synthesizing" impressions—in a shrewd and suggestive recent account by Robert J. Lifton of "traumatic syndrome," the "compulsion to repeat" in survivors of accidents or of combat that Freud addressed in *Beyond the Pleasure Principle*. Lifton describes it as the state of being haunted by images "that can neither be *enacted* nor cast aside" (Lifton 1979, 1972; my emphasis). It is caused by a perception of death or drastic damage, an impression that interrupts the "flow" from the image or impression of drastic damage or death to the "action" in relation to it—precluded by the suddenness or danger of the situation; "action," Lifton writes, in the sense of "the psychic equivalent" of forms of action, such as pity or anger. Lifton locates the origin of the accident neurosis in "the gap between image and enactment" (1972), and much of *The Broken Connection* is given to arguing for the significance and value of feelings of guilt about such a disjunction, not because the survivor is really guilty, but because his sense of guilt reflects his commitment to humanistic values and a norm centrally including the assumption of *continuity* between "image and enactment," "feeling" and "knowledge" (175), perception and cognition, "language" and "meaning." What is made clear by Baudelaire's essay is that this norm reflects an *aesthetic* ideal, or rather a mistakenly idealist conception of the aesthetic. The aesthetic illusion that Baudelaire's text evokes and undoes is that of an operation of consciousness that would be at once an action and a work: human being, as *the* work of "art." This operation of consciousness is rather of the order of M.G.'s sketches or notations, dating impressions that they reduce rather than restore: premised—like Freud's model of the "psychical apparatus"—on the *non*integrity of perception, on the disjunction and heterogeneity between the impression and its knowledge.[10]

Benjamin reads Baudelaire's description of M.G.'s sketching as an account of the successful functioning of the "shock defense": as the operation of *consciousness* rather than memory, though Guys draws, of course, from memory. (Baudelaire's essay describes him as *looking* during the day and drawing at night.) Yet we need to read this as a description—not just a metaphor—of the functioning of consciousness "itself." Benjamin's interpretation as "consciousness" of the frenetic sketching of M.G. has the same significance as Freud's conception of the psyche as a writing machine in "Note upon the 'Mystic Writing Pad'" (*S.E.* 19)—namely that consciousness, in Freud's conception, is always already supplemental, technical, a material process. Stressing "the disincarnation and reduction of meaning" that consciousness entails, its assigning an incident a precise point in time "at the cost of the integrity of its contents," brings out the proximity between "presence" or "presence of mind" and its "incomplete substitute[s]" (*S.E.* 23:266): notes, writing, the sketches or notations of others.

It brings out the proximity between the successful operation of the shock defense and the measures that must meet its failure: the *constructions* that Freud concedes a crucial role in a psychoanalytic reconstrual of the past. The historiographer, for Benjamin, is a figure like M.G., or like the analyst confronted with the bizarre, abstract "images" in which the patient repeats his past (hallucinations, rebuses, scenes that stage magic words); "History in the strict sense," he writes, "is an image from involuntary memory, an image which suddenly occurs to the subject in the moment of danger. The historian's credentials rest on a sharpened awareness of the crisis that the subject of history has entered at any given moment. . . . Historiography . . . has to test its presence of mind in grasping fleeting images." (Benjamin 1980, 1.3: 1242–43; cited in Cadava 1991). Techniques for producing schematic sketches of what "suddenly occurs" (the image, as much as the traumatic incident, "occurs to" the subject of history): such are the resources of the historian; and the artist, "the painter of modern life," the subject of history fully "present" to historical experience, has no resources of another order (more immediate, natural, or complete).

Such would be the reasons for what Freud puts aside as another issue "for a later inquiry" in "Constructions in Analysis":

> Quite often we do not succeed in bringing the patient to recollect what has been repressed. Instead of that, if the analysis is carried out correctly, we produce in him an assured conviction of the truth of the construction which achieves the same therapeutic result as a recaptured memory. The problem of what the circumstances are in which this occurs *and of how it is possible that what appears to be an incomplete substitute should nevertheless produce a complete result*—all of this is matter for a later enquiry. [*S.E.* 23:265–66; my emphasis]

The construction is a schema or a figure; my point is that it is in this way *like* the image achieved by consciousness and like the recollection that association in the absence of resistances may produce.

"Constructions in Analysis" introduces an "analogy" between two sorts of texts, constructions and delusions, both of which include hallucinatory memories and an attempt to contextualize them. "The delusions of patients appear to me to be the equivalents of the constructions which we build up in the course of an analytic treatment—attempts at explanations and cure," writes Freud, and further, "Just as our construction is only effective because it recovers a fragment of lost experience, so the delusion owes its convincing power to the element of historic truth which it inserts in the place of rejected reality" (*S.E.* 23:268). The persuasive power of the construction is a function of the power of disavowed impressions to return and of the totalizing tendency that extends their felt authenticity to contiguous elements of the analyst's discourse. Freud's theory of the disjunction between consciousness and memory here shows its power as a dialectical model. "Constructions in Analysis" extends the argument of the earlier papers on technique that it is the transference—the compulsive repetitions that are the patient's "way of remembering"—that makes analysis possible. Hallucinations and delusions are here considered to involve the return of the repressed, to which the hallucinatory return of the "disavowed" is assimilated. The past *failure* of the shock defense is here envisaged as a crucial condition for cognition.

Freud's comment, "I have not been able to resist the seduction of an analogy" (268) calls attention to the not necessarily trustworthy allure of the comparison between constructions and delusions, which enlists a dialectical model of tremendous recuperative power, through a chiasmus ascribing to delusions the cognitive content of constructions and to constructions the persuasive power of delusions. But if Freud's paper implies that delusions (i.e., psychoses) are subject to analytic treatment, it also suggests that the material of analysis's quest for "historical truth" is delusions: constructs around the opaque, nondiscursive contents (like Wolf Man's word-things) of disavowals. Freud is explicit if brief about the constraints under which analysis of disavowal will labor: these "attempts at explanations and cure . . . ," he writes—delusions *and* constructions—"under the conditions of a psychosis, can do no more than replace the fragment of reality that is being disavowed in the present by another fragment that had already been disavowed in the remote past. It will be the task of each individual investigation to reveal the intimate connections between the material of the present disavowal and that of the original repression" (*S.E.* 23:268). The intricacy of such connections, their reliance on a mode of repetition different from either transference or manifest hallucinations or hallucinatory memories, we have seen exemplified in the Wolf Man's reheard case. The promise of the dialectical model (disavowals are involuntary memories; they contain the past) is betrayed by the dependence of analytic interpretation upon *technique*, which is also to say upon chance, in the absence of continuity between consciousness and memory, the absence of predictable correspondence between the "repetition" and what it repeats. Readings like Abraham and Torok's suggest how radically analytic technique is exposed to the chance of error. Proust's conclusion haunts Freud's lodging of "historical truth" in involuntary memory: that though the past is "unmistakably present in some material object (or in the sensation which such an object arouses in us), . . . we have no idea which one it is. As for that object, it depends entirely on chance whether we come upon it before we die or whether we never encounter it" (1954, 44; quoted in Benjamin 1969, 158). This is just as much the case when the material instance bearing the "element of historical truth" is the elusive, protean material object, a word.

There is a *caveat* for historians in the material I have been discussing. For if "mankind as a whole" may be functioning "under the conditions of a psychosis"—as Freud's closing generalization from individuals' delusions to mankind's would suggest (*S.E.* 23:269)—then the most the historian could do would be to replace "the fragment of reality that is being disavowed in the present by [one] that had already been disavowed in the remote past": at best, in the sense that the historian would provide knowledge of past historical events (reading through the disavowals *in* the past *of* the past), but without thereby preventing their displacement onto the present; at worst—reproducing the delusions the historian would claim to read—in the sense that the historian would interestedly, yet unknowingly, replace historical events of the present with belatedly experienced events of the past. Freud's reflections point to a permanent lag in the "experience" of history, to the "inherent latency" of historical occurrences (Caruth 1991, 187).

Is there a sense in which we could assert, like Benjamin, the "historical determination of memory," the historical determination of such a relation to history? Freud's hypothesis about memory and consciousness proves fruitful in explaining "situations far removed from those which Freud had in mind when he wrote" (160), says Benjamin, because impressions that are excessive, too sudden, or "insupportable" in their contradiction of the self's integrity become part of daily adult life. But rather than the mark of a historical—the "modern"—period, this could be said to be the character of history as such: of change incommensurate with and never fully explainable by preceding conditions.

Derrida ascribes a kind of historical determination to Freud's model of the psyche and a fundamental historicity to the psyche as such. In the first place, Freud's analogy between the psyche and a writing apparatus would not be possible without the historical existence of such an apparatus: without "the historico-technical production" of "a supplementary machine, *added* to the psychical organization in order to supplement its finitude" (Derrida 1978, 228). Freud's conception of memory is in this sense historically determined: by the historical, not "natural," occurrence of a supplementary machine. But in the second place, that process of supplementation is *not* itself historical in the sense of being limited to a specific era. "The very idea of finitude is derived from the movement of this supplementarity." There is no such thing as the psychical without it. This is what we saw in the proximity of consciousness to the activity of historiography, and in Benjamin's deft assimilation of Baudelaire's account of Guys's sketching from memory to Freud's conception of the workings of consciousness. Derrida writes:

> Far from the machine being a pure absence of spontaneity, its *resemblance* to the psychical apparatus, its existence and its necessity bear witness to the finitude of the mnemic spontaneity which is thus supplemented. ... This resemblance [of memory to the machine]—i.e., necessarily a certain Being-in-the-world of the psyche—did not happen to memory from without, any more than death surprises life. It founds memory. [228]

The psychical is defined by an "original" possibility and necessity of supplementation, an openness of the psychical to the nonpsychical, which constitutes the *historicity* that is the condition of possibility of historical events. That materiality of the psyche is what Abraham and Torok accept and acknowledge in giving up the transference and displacing the possibility of meaning to untranslatable but writable words. Historiography would have to start, as they do, from Freud's avowal of the inevitability and uncertainty of "constructions."

## Notes

1. On the implications of *Moses and Monotheism*, especially the analogy between historical event and trauma, for the concept of history and the referential status of texts, see Caruth (1991). Caruth's account of the "inherent latency" of historical occurrence goes to the heart of Freud's analogy. "What in fact constitutes the central enigma revealed by Freud's example," she writes, "is not so much the period of forgetting that occurs after the accident, but rather the fact that the victim of the crash was never fully conscious during the accident itself: the victim gets away, Freud says, 'apparently unharmed.' The experience of trauma, the fact of latency, would thus seem to consist, not in the forgetting of a reality that can hence never be fully known, but in an inherent latency within the experience itself" (187).

2. Derrida has written about Nicolas Abraham and Maria Torok's work in

"Me—Psychoanalysis" (1979), and in a foreword to *The Wolf Man's Magic Word*, "*Fors*: The Anglish Words of Nicolas Abraham and Maria Torok" (1986, xi–xlviii).

3. "The Ego proper," Abraham and Torok write, "whose function it is to be Hand for the Libido, Hand for Sex, will have become Sex for *another* Hand, Hand for *another* Sex. Its own activity will consist in satisfying or counteracting the desires lent to its Guests, or to their respective Ego Ideals, and of thus maintaining them within itself" (21).

4. Derrida elaborates this point and its implications in regard to the "performative utterances" first identified and theorized by J. L. Austin (1975); for a clear discussion of this issue, see Jonathan Culler (1984, 110–25). Derrida stresses the following: such an utterance—for instance, the formula pronounced in order to open a meeting, name a ship, or perform a marriage—could not succeed if it did not repeat a coded or iterable utterance, "if it were not identifiable in some way as a 'citation.'" And "given that structure of iteration, the intention animating the utterance will never be through and through present to itself and to its content. ... This essential absence of intending the actuality of utterance, this *structural unconscious*, if you like," prevents the context of the utterance from being exhaustively determinable, and so prevents certainty of its meaning (1988, 18; my emphasis).

5. I am grateful to Humphrey Morris for making this point in these terms.

6. So de Man characterizes history, critical philosophy, and literary theory, as well as translation, all of which are secondary and derivative, yet, he observes, "do not resemble that from which they derive." "They all are intralinguistic: they relate to what in the original belongs to language, and not to meaning as an extralinguistic correlate susceptible of paraphrase and imitation. ... They reveal that their failure, which seems to be due to the fact that they are secondary in relation to the original, reveals an essential failure, an essential disarticulation which was already there in the original. They kill the original, by discovering that the original was already dead" (1986, 84).

7. Abraham and Torok envisage doing this by setting in opposition to the English governess's condemnation of the scene between father and sister an "analytic understanding of the father" that would involve extending the analysis to the paternal grandparents and great-grandparents, "so that the Wolf Man could be situated within the libidinal lineage from which he was descended. Under such circumstances it is conceivable that the extreme emotional charge of the traumatic scandal would gradually have been diluted. ...." The work would have had to be done "without expecting any form of transference." It would consist in essence in "challeng[ing] the *juridical code* that permitted the nurse's blackmail in the first place" (76; my emphasis).

8. Versions of the *Pcpt.-Cs.* model appear in the "Project for a Scientific Psychology" of 1895, part I, section 3, in chapter 7 of *The Interpretation of Dreams* (1900), in chapter 4 of *Beyond the Pleasure Principle* (1920), and in the "Note upon the 'Mystic Writing Pad'" (1925).

9. If reflexion is lacking, "there would be nothing but the sudden start, usually the sensation of fright which, according to Freud, confirms the failure

of the shock defense," writes Benjamin. "Baudelaire has portrayed this condition in a harsh image. He speaks of a duel in which the artist, just before being beaten, screams in fright. This duel is the creative process itself. Thus Baudelaire placed the shock experience at the very center of his artistic work" (Benjamin 1969, 163; 1980, 1.2: 615). The prose poem to which Benjamin refers is "Le *Confiteor* de l'artiste" (Baudelaire 1968, 149).

10. Baudelaire's description of *l'art mnémonique* (555), his term for the art practiced by "the painter of modern life," reveals a line of thought congruent with the implications of Hegel's distinction between the symbol and the sign: the aesthetic—rigorously conceived as the mode in which the idea makes its appearance in the world—would be of the order of the sign and not the symbol. A conception of the aesthetic as crucially connected with the use of signs, mnemonic devices, and memorization, as opposed to symbols or symbolic forms purportedly uniting form and content, is a powerful undercurrent in Hegel's *Aesthetics* and in the dominant tradition of valorizing symbolic form. Freud's account of the disjunction between consciousness and memory contributes to this countercurrent of thought about the aesthetic. See de Man (1982) and, on Hegel and Baudelaire, Chase (1986).

*References*

Abraham, Nicolas, and Torok, Maria. *The Wolf Man's Magic Word: A Cryptonomy* (1976). Translated by Nicholas Rand. Minneapolis: University of Minnesota Press, 1986.
Austin, John L. *How to Do Things with Words.* Cambridge: Harvard University Press, 1975.
Baudelaire, Charles. *Oeuvres complètes.* Paris: Seuil, 1968.
Benjamin, Walter. "The Task of the Translator" (69–82). "On Some Motifs in Baudelaire" (155–200). In *Illuminations.* New York: Schocken, 1969.
———. "Ueber einige Motive bei Baudelaire," vol. 1:2, 605–54. "Ueber den Begriff der Geschichte," vol. 1:2, 691–704, and 1:3, 1222–53. "Die Aufgabe des Uebersetzers," vol. 4:1, 9–21. *Gesammelte Schriften.* Frankfurt: Suhrkamp, 1980.
Brunswick, Ruth Mack. "A Supplement to Freud's 'History of an Infantile Neurosis.'" In *The Wolf Man by the Wolf Man*, edited by Muriel Gardiner. New York: Basic Books, 1971.
Cadava, Eduardo. "Words of Light: Theses on the Photography of History." *Diacritics* (1992) (in press).
Caruth, Cathy. "Unclaimed Experience: Trauma and the Possibility of History." *Yale French Studies* 79 (1991): 181–92.
Chase, Cynthia. *Decomposing Figures: Rhetorical Readings in the Romantic Tradition.* Baltimore: Johns Hopkins University Press, 1986.
Culler, Jonathan. *On Deconstruction.* Ithaca: Cornell University Press, 1984.
de Man, Paul. "Sign and Symbol in Hegel's Aesthetics." *Critical Inquiry* 8 (Summer 1982): 761–75.

――――. "Literary History and Literary Modernity." In *Blindness and Insight*. 2d ed., with five additional essays, edited by Wlad Godzich. Minneapolis: University of Minnesota Press, 1983.

――――. "'Conclusions': Walter Benjamin's 'The Task of the Translator.'" In *The Resistance to Theory*. Minneapolis: University of Minnesota Press, 1986.

Derrida, Jacques. "Freud and the Scene of Writing." In *Writing and Difference*, translated by Alan Bass. Chicago: University of Chicago Press, 1978.

――――. "*Fors*: The Anglish Words of Nicolas Abraham and Maria Torok." Foreword to Abraham and Torok (1986).

――――. "Me—Psychoanalysis." *Diacritics* 9, no. 1 (1979): 4–12.

――――. "Signature, Event, Context." In *Limited Inc.* Evanston, Ill.: Northwestern University Press, 1988.

Freud, Sigmund. *The Standard Edition of the Complete Psychological Works of Sigmund Freud*. Edited and translated by James Strachey. 24 vols. London: Hogarth Press, 1953–74.

"Project for a Scientific Psychology" (1950 [1895]), vol. 1.

*The Interpretation of Dreams* (1900), vol. 5.

"Papers on Technique" (1911–15), vol. 12.

"The Dynamics of Transference" (1912), vol. 12.

"Remembering, Repeating, and Working-Through" (1914), vol. 12.

"The Unconscious" (1915), vol. 14.

"Mourning and Melancholia" (1917), vol. 14.

"From the History of an Infantile Neurosis" (1918), vol. 17.

*Beyond the Pleasure Principle* (1920), vol. 18.

"A Note upon the 'Mystic Writing Pad'" (1925), vol. 19.

"Fetishism" (1927), vol. 21.

"Analysis Terminable and Interminable" (1937), vol. 23.

"Constructions in Analysis" (1937), vol. 23.

*Moses and Monotheism* (1939), vol. 23.

*An Outline of Psycho-Analysis* (1940), vol. 23.

"The Splitting of the Ego in the Process of Defence" (1940 [1938]), vol. 23.

Lacan, Jacques. "Reponse au commentaire de Jean Hyppolite sur la 'Verneinung' de Freud." In *Ecrits*. Paris: Seuil, 1966.

Laplanche, Jean, and Pontalis, J.-B. *The Language of Psychoanalysis*. Translated by Donald Nicholson-Smith. New York: Norton, 1973.

Lifton, Robert Jay. *The Broken Connection: On Death and the Continuity of Life*. New York: Basic Books, 1979.

Proust, Marcel. *A la recherche du temps perdu*. Paris: Gallimard, 1954.

# 5 Mourning, Art, and Human Historicity

## *Joseph H. Smith*

> *By picturing our wishes as fulfilled, dreams are after all leading us into the future. But this future, which the dreamer pictures as the present, has been moulded by his indestructible wish into a perfect likeness of the past.* —Freud (*S.E.* 5:621)

I begin with the inferred, original imaging of the newborn, and I hardly move beyond that beginning. By imaging I refer to the way an infant, when hungry, remembers some percept connected with the mother and a prior feeding. The percept remembered in the image might have been a sensation in the lips, the mother's voice, touch, odor, or something similar. In accord with this assumption the original image is molded as a wish for the repetition of the "perfect likeness" of the prior feeding.

My purpose, beginning within imaging itself, is to trace out a possible difference of fate of special sensitivity to loss and transience in the artist on the one hand, and in the depressive on the other. That context provides the basis for considering how the work of mourning, the work of art, and working through as it occurs in analysis and in everyday life pertain to the assumption of human historicity and subjecthood.

Historicity means more than just having a history by virtue of language and memory. It denotes, rather, the dynamic effects in the present and in present futural projects of our *being* our past. What happened back then is not so important as what one can do with that now and in the future. The psychoanalytic importance of elucidating what happened back then, as Schafer has suggested (1983, 208), is that such understanding clarifies what one *is* doing and planning in present and anticipated interactions and projects. Of course, the opposite is also true: understanding the present sheds light on obscure aspects of the past. Present change allows for reinterpretation of the past, and reinterpretation of the past can allow for present change.

The subject comes into being with a concern for that being. That concern is one's historicity. It is a concern that can be overtly avowed or overtly disavowed, but by virtue of being with others, language, ongoing lack, memory, and anticipation, concern for one's being is never absent. Subjecthood is oxymoronic through and through in that it denotes a unity marked by lack. But lack is not just a mark or feature of subjecthood. The subject comes into being by reason of lack; lack, concern regarding lack, and concern for the subject that has arisen in lack sustain subjecthood.

To be without language, without words, would be not to be human; to be only with words would be an impossible extreme of obsessional defense. Before words, the world comes to light in affectively charged images. This predifferentiated world, a world in which the difference between self and other is not yet established in the mind of the infant, is a world in which an image of the other, an image of the "not yet" other, nevertheless appears. One comes to be in imaging, in imaging the other, in an image of the other.

The image is at once a memory, a wish, and an anticipation—a memory of a prior experience of satisfaction now newly wanted and anticipated. But the memory, perception, and anticipation of an event (the past, present, and future) are not yet differentiated. Thus, not only is the image a call for the return of the mother, but also it is a mode of recreating the mother and thus an overcoming of the danger of her absence. To recreate the mother—who is at that stage the infant's all in all, its world—is, for the moment, to *be* omnipotent.

The image as wish represents the need[1] of the infant and, at the same time, is an image *of* the mother. The not-yet self and the not-yet world are condensed and sustained in the image. The image is of the mother as *object*; the image in some primitive way *means* the mother. If, as Lacan insisted, there is no object that is not metonymical and no meaning that is not metaphorical, potentialities for both metonymy and metaphor are already features of the first image.

The image anticipates language. It anticipates both words and a beyond of the conventional use of words. Only in the poetic word and in imagery and art beyond words is the fullness of the predifferentiated image recovered and surpassed.

Difference, to be sure, is, first of all, introduced by lack—by the need that awakens the infant to imaging. In the preverbal, founding sentence, "I need you," the subject-to-be, the "I" of the not-yet sentence, arrives already covered over and decentered—there, in the lack, which can only be represented in consciousness as an affect-laden image of the object that promises resolution of that lack. The "you," the image, the image of the mother, is a call, like a one-word sentence, standing for "I need you." But only the mother can "read" this sentence; the infant, for the moment, experiences her image as, "I have you. I am you." The you/image stands for everything—you and me together. Complete.

In this fashion, difference signaled by lack is disavowed in the (presumed) hallucination of the mother's presence that Freud (*S.E.* 5:566–67) called the identity of perception. However, in imaging played out against lack and the memory and anticipation of actual satisfaction, multiple differences are established and effectively avowed. In this interplay of the real and the imaginary, the difference between the mother and an image of the mother comes to be known. Knowing this difference also marks a difference between "me" and "my mother," between "me" and "my image of her," between "my" need and "my" image of the object of that need. The establishment of these differentiations Freud called the identity of thought (*S.E.* 5:602).

Before such differentiations, since each image in a primitive sequence is of the mother and thus *means* the mother, it could be said that each image is equivalent to the other. But from the standpoint of internalizing a relationship with the object, each image, though unbeknownst to the infant, represents a discrete facet of the object, a discrete facet of the infant's wish, and a discrete facet of the relationship with the object.

Need evokes original wishing. The way in which a present but futurally oriented wish is shaped by memory of the past is both the means of internalization through repetition and a fundament of human historicity as concern for one's present and future being. History, Ricoeur wrote somewhere, is the hope of history. In early life, internalizations, each conditioned by the formative record of prior internalizations, build toward a complex separateness, historicity, and subjecthood—a separateness, historicity, and subjecthood that are announced with the advent of speech.

This portrayal of primitive development, it seems to me, is the necessary context for emphasizing that knowing the difference between the mother and the image of the mother not only is the precondition for being able to refind the actual mother—Freud's main interest (Smith 1991, 73)—but also is the precondition for being able to take an interest in the multiple potential meanings of the image as such. The meaning of the image is no longer limited to being *only* the representative of the drive. Even though every image remains tied to an image-making subject marked by lack and is ultimately reducible to its drive-determined dimension, that dimension of significance fades in either a successful analysis or a work of art.

The multiple images, multiple vantage points on the object, constitute a metonymical treasury from which metaphor can arise. The capacity to take an interest in the image (aside from and beyond the fact that it is both a representative of the drive and an image *of* the object) allows for a departure from the closed completeness by which the future is "moulded," as Freud put it, "into a perfect likeness of the past" (*S.E.* 5:621). "To bring the subject to recognize and to name his desire," Lacan wrote, "... is the nature of the efficacious action of analysis. But it is not a question of recognizing something that would have already been there—a given—ready to be captured. In naming it, the subject creates, gives rise to something new, makes something new present in the world" (*Séminaire* 2.267, as cited in Felman 1987, 131).

If "desire," for any purposes here, can stand for original wishing, demand, or desire, primitive imagery is the indicator of both desire and danger, either of which would be total. Desire is wholly for the mother's absolute presence, danger the dread of her absence, which is experienced as absolute loss. Prefigured in such primitive absoluteness is that to be with the mother is to be and that dread of her absence is dread of nonbeing.

Imaging, I have said, is a mode of recreating the mother in her absence. It is love, work, and play. Urgently wishing for the mother is the first mode of love. The image is a work. The materials of memory, present need, and anticipation are subjected to displacement and condensation in such fashion that an image of the mother, in whatever form is right for that infant at that time, can be beheld. Imaging is also a work in that it provides one's own set of meanings against which the actual mother (in what Freud [*S.E.* 1:331, 336] called her unassimilable thingliness) can be measured and eventually differentiated. Finally, although the play of imaging would presumably occur at moments of less than peremptory need, the imaging of infancy is play just as surely as is the older child's *Fort/Da* verbal playing with presence and absence, which Freud described in *Beyond the Pleasure Principle.*

Danger and loss differ from each other in that danger is anticipated in the future and evokes anxiety, whereas loss that evokes mourning has already occurred. Pathological attunement to danger, a being obsessed with danger that is alloyed with an even stronger motive not to face or an inability to know the specific danger, is phobia or paranoia. Pathological attunement to loss, on the other hand, the effort to face loss that refuses to or cannot acknowledge specific losses, is depression. Notwithstanding these differences, danger and loss come together in that danger is seen to be an anticipated loss. The series of danger situations that Freud listed—loss of the mother, castration, loss of the love of the superego (*S.E.* 20:136–40; see also 128, 165, and 169), or being abandoned by the protecting superego or the powers of destiny (*S.E.* 20:130)—is a series of impending or possible losses anticipated as dangers.

Freud believed that death as such could not be an unconscious danger because "the unconscious seems to contain nothing that could give any content to our concept of the annihilation of life" (*S.E.* 20:129). At a glance, it is an argument that hardly fits with the emphasis he gave to castration anxiety. However, that also may be seen as not so much a fear of literal castration as a dread of that which castration symbolizes. Perhaps anticipated literal death symbolizes the actually experienced repeated loss of the only transiently established self and world in primitive experience. By extension each person's fear of literally dying, with its unknown time and mode, would be conditioned by various modes of dying throughout life. Death and threatening death as absence, lack, alienation, separation, and loss enter in with the first imaging. Death symbolizes all of these, and all of these symbolize death. This is the meaning of castration. Castration—symbolic castration— refers to a dying out to the symbiotic mother and the coming to terms with love and hate toward both the mother and father in the achievement of oedipal separateness.

Here is the dream of a forty-one-year-old male musician subject to insomnia at the time of the dream and previously prone to depression.

> I was in a cell with a childhood friend, but we were our present ages. There was affection between us but also danger that rendered it unsafe to sleep. There was a gun in the cell and the feeling that if I did not shoot him he would shoot me. Then my mother appeared at the cell door. I felt protective toward her and was concerned that if a shot were fired she might be harmed.

The patient's attitude toward the analysis was that it would not cure him but was holding him together and so would have to be indefinitely prolonged. This is to say that there could be no killing of me by him or him by me, no dying out of the relationship with me nor, ultimately, with the mother or father. It was a position that I had directly challenged for the first time about a month before the dream by interpreting the content of one session as pertaining to termination.

By comparison and contrast with the dream (and also with the severe depression that brought him to treatment), the relationship between us at the time was characterized by mutual affection and playfully expressed rivalry—a rivalry, that is, that was going on as if there were no lethal weapon or dire threat at hand. Rivalry with colleagues, on the other hand, or at least more direct assertiveness and looking out for his own interests, had recently become more open.

As opposed to depression, insomnia with moderate anxiety was a less obdurately defended position. In this instance it allowed for the formation of a dream in which was embedded an accessible interpretation of what was keeping him awake.

Lines such as "to sleep, perchance to dream" or ordinary euphemisms such as putting our ill and aged pets to sleep, might suggest that insomnia as fear of sleeping is always connected at some level with fear of dying. However, to raise that connection to the level of workable insight probably requires elucidation of the whole history of a person's way of dealing with loss. This man had experienced notable losses in his preoedipal and preadolescent eras that I shall not here detail.

From early childhood, the patient harbored rather vivid negative feelings toward his mother and staunchly maintained the preoedipally established affection for and identification with his father. I associate this with what Freud called identification with the father of individual prehistory (S.E. 19:31), a preconflictual, affectionate bond with the father that shapes and paves the way for oedipal transactions and is at the core of both the girl's and the boy's ego ideal.

The father of individual prehistory enters as a third term between the symbiotic mother and infant. But the intervention is not just a no-saying to the child's wish to perpetuate merger with the mother. The father is also both a model for the child's own developing separateness and an object for primary, nonconflictual affection.

Just as the oedipal crisis is recapitulated in adolescence, the boy's preoedipal affection for the father and the girl's preoedipal affection for the mother[2] are recapitulated in preadolescent attachments. A displaced object of the patient's love for his father was the friend of his preadolescence who appeared in the dream. The friend thus represents both father and analyst—the father of individual prehistory and the transference position of the analyst at the time of the dream. But in this dream the friend has come to occupy the position of Laertes, who in the duel stands for both the king and the king's brother, all in the presence of the queen. The queen, emptying the cup, is carousing, as she said in the scene, to Hamlet's fortune—to

Hamlet's fortune/destiny, to Hamlet's and her own destiny, to the destiny of all.

The primary bond with the father had already been a major means of relinquishing the symbiotic mother. The bond also is the basis for some faith that both child and father can survive the prospective relinquishment, experienced as the killing of each other, or dying out of each to the other in the oedipal denouement. The patient's dream stages these issues. The primary affectionate bond is to end. The weapon is at hand. After half a lifetime of being recurrently compelled by love and guilt to be dead/depressed, or having to deny rather than mourn the maternal paradise lost, the son recognizes the new option of kill or be killed by the father in the presence of the mother, who is also to be finally renounced as symbiotic or incestuous object. This option is not so much the one in *Oedipus Rex* of killing the father in order to have the mother, or being killed as punishment for incestuous desire. The much stronger story line, evoking *Oedipus at Colonus*, is that all three are faced with death; each is called upon to assume, here and now, that destiny. The loss of a particular level of love and relatedness *is* a death and, in some way, a killing in which each participant takes part (Loewald 1980, 389–95). The death of the nonconflictual bond with the father is also a further step in dying out to the earlier bond with the mother, from whom the tie to the father was in some measure transferred.[3]

Loss is the impetus for love, work, and play, but the capacity for love, work, or play is hampered to the extent that losses remain unacknowledged and unmourned. Mourning works toward ratification of death as destiny. One's history, one's historicity, can be recognized ultimately only from the stance of having assumed this destiny. Mourning is a work of love, reparation, and ratification in which every aspect of the relationship with the lost object is repeatedly reenacted internally. In that process, certain aspects of the relationship are relinquished and certain others internalized and made one's own. Such internal change is in the context of the child's play or in a variety of work or playful projects undertaken by the child or the adult.

Mourning, in this view, is not merely feeling sad. Mourning the ordinary losses of everyday life is, typically, not even accompanied by sadness. Such losses are nevertheless worked over in fantasy, dreaming, humor, play, and work, all of which can occur in a variety of moods. To assert that play is meaningful is to assert that it is a kind of work.

Were we to know all the conscious and unconscious meanings of the thought, dreams, play, and work pertaining to either major mourning or the ongoing mourning of everyday life, we would be less likely, I believe, to see so radical a distinction between dealing with loss by some creative endeavor, or letting time take care of it. Creative working over of the relationship with the lost object is what goes on in time in each instance of major or minor mourning. The artist, however, gathers these meanings into a work that all can behold as a signifier of transience, which time, nevertheless, will not likely erase. Art honors the necessity and validity of the mourning of all.

Thus far I have specified a little of what I mean by love and a lot of what I mean by mourning in order to clarify the claim that a work of art is a work of love and mourning. I shall now approach that claim from another vantage point—a consideration of Freud's remarks on art and sublimation.

In "applying" psychoanalysis, it was the work of art before which Freud claimed he would lay down his sword. Ricoeur, strong man of peace that he is, would like to take Freud at his word in this regard and presents a convincing argument for so doing (Ricoeur 1976). But there may have been more torment than humility in Freud's "surrender." As Ricoeur himself notes, others, perhaps responding to the militancy of Freud's metaphor, suspect the surrender itself of being only a ruse to seduce his readers into following his way of applying psychoanalysis to art (1976, 4). In an effort to redouble such suspicion, I myself have raised the question of whether Ricoeur's taking sides with Freud—taking Freud at his word—is also a ruse to cut Freud off at the passage to psychoanalytic explanation of art, thus limiting him, on the near side of the pass, to the "modesty" of surrendering in advance, whether or not that was Freud's real intent. It was, considering that both Freud and Ricoeur are heroes of mine, a mean idea, but not necessarily for that reason wrong, nor cause for marring my pleasure in having the idea.

The enigma of art, for Freud, was tied to the enigma of sublimation. Sublimation is a wonder to behold—a product of "specially perfect" moments when id, ego, and superego all work together. It is a solution involving neither repression nor symptom formation. How might the capacity for such functioning come to pass?

Everyone shares, in some degree or other, the artist's sensitivity to loss and transience, to which imaging was the original response. As a refinding of the mother, the first image, for an instant anyway, cannot fail to get her right. It doesn't matter *how* she is pictured, but only that she *is* pictured. In this predifferentiated state, everything cannot do otherwise than work together. Might there not remain traces of such fabulous success, even though the memory of the image itself fades? The formation of that image, being in the presence of that image, being, in fact, merged/identified with that image is what Freud, as I have noted, named the identity of perception.

The fate, though, of this identity of perception depends on whether the emphasis falls on one's imaging or one's need. From the point of view of the need for satisfaction, the identity of perception utterly fails one. The image as such must be abandoned in favor of the delayed coming of the actual mother. But from the point of view of the remembered, though momentary, perfect recreation of the mother, a new need for repetition of such creation is established.

Being able to follow out an interest in the image as such, the image for its own sake so to speak, would occur in moments where need is not at a peremptory level. In such moments the emphasis would not be on the fact that taking the image to *be* the mother is a *false* connection but on the fact that it *is* a connection. That the image is *of* the mother initially sustains interest in the image as such.

The artist and the depressive may both be even genetically endowed with a special sensitivity to loss and transience. Whether the fate of a person so marked would be depression or art could depend on further genetic marking, or on differences in the degree and nature of delays and losses suffered in early life together with the degree and nature of successful recreations. Either endowment or experience or, more likely, both could determine whether the effects of early imaging would leave the emphasis more on the efficacy or the failure of imaging. At this time when we have learned how to "ask" intricate questions of very young infants regarding various modes of recognizing the mother (Stern 1985, 47–53, 90–94), we might even find ways of asking about the differential effects of early imaging.

The artist's heightened capacity for sublimation might derive from, among other factors, heightened sensitivity to loss, paired with a special capacity to take an interest in the image as such and in the satisfaction wrought by its creation. Such a person would be spared, in some measure, the dismay that the image did not satisfy the original need from which it arose. The emphasis would instead be on the new center of interest established by the discovery that an image of the object can be made.

If sublimation has its *anlage* here, it could still be said to be a solution to conflict, but it is a solution achieved through bypassing, in some measure, the ordinary drive/defense conflict. By so doing it can be a solution that involves neither repression of the drive nor the compromise between drive and defense that appears as inhibition or symptom. Still, it is not a complete bypassing. The drive originally gives rise to and is represented by the image. The nonprimitive working out of such raw imagery into a work of art is still a way of dealing with the basic drive, even though the dominant satisfaction achieved is in relation to the artistic interest established at another level in the wake of the success of original imaging.

In the depressive, undue delay or excessive loss undermines faith that basic needs will be met and prohibits attention to the image as successful recreation of the mother. The increased urgency based on such experience would lead to dismayed dismissal of the "mere" image as incapable of satisfying the basic need. That the image is right nevertheless yields to an emphasis in the depressive on the missing actual mother, which, in turn, means that everything is wrong. The (not yet) object is absent and the (not yet) self is wrong/bad. This is the story of primitive—one could even say original—guilt (Smith 1986).

This differentiation of the artist and the depressive calls for adjustment. Some artists are subject to depression and the interim creativity of depressive persons has long been noted. Freud, in fact, asserted that his best work was in the context of being mildly depressed. Let us pursue the idea of the divided meaning of derivative motivation in terms of motives arising from the drives, but also always from other centers of interest established through primitive and later imaging.

At a point of intense need, recreation of the mother is an emergency procedure in the face of impending death/castration/nonbeing. Repeated experiences of recreating and refinding the mother gradually establish the decentered, desiring "I" implied by such loss and recreation of the object. But even before the "I" is established, the very precise knowledge the infant has of its mother is not merely the passive product of visual, olfactory, acoustic, and other sensory endowments. From the start these capacities would be activated and their objects remembered by virtue of the urgency of primitive need and primitive imaging. No infant, even with the best of mothering, is spared the urgency of such experience. No infant that survives, on the other hand, even with the worst of mothering, misses the repeated experience of recreating the mother and getting her right, getting her.

I cannot but believe that each instance of developmental advance, all working through, every work of art, every solution to conflicts or problems bears the marks of this loss/recreation, death/rebirth sequence. All are facilitated by a readiness, usually unconscious, to undertake—one might even say happily undertake—the mourning of everyday life as an ongoing task.

A final vantage point for viewing imaging, art, and human historicity is that of metonymy and metaphor. For some purposes, I believe, too sharp a distinction can be drawn between the uses and meaning of metonymy and metaphor. Metaphor, in which one thing can substitute for another, is usually thought to occur only after the differentiation of image and object; of memory, percept, and anticipation; of the "I" and the other. Metaphor, in other words, is thought to await the advent of speech—language as such. Imaging, on the other hand, is ordinarily seen as the product of desire as metonymy, a movement from one image to another on a basis of similarity or contiguity—for instance, a sequence of imaged attributes of the mother—in which each image almost *is* the other and with which the desiring subject is more merged than separate.

In such a metonymic series of images—in relatively uncharged imaging along, we could say, with desire at a nonperemptory level— the movement is from one image to another contiguous or similar image. However, an element of substitution is still here; each image may be said to substitute for those prior in the series, and each is also an image of, a substitute for, the object of desire. As need, and thereby interest, in the object mounts to a peremptory level, metaphor may be prefigured in its seeming opposite—taking the image to *be* the object. The latter could be the forerunner of recognition that the image is an image *of* the needed object. This is to say that substitution is not limited to metaphor or that metaphor itself, or a forerunner of metaphor, is a feature of original imaging. Perhaps metaphor and metonymy, at that level, are not to be differentiated simply on the basis of features such as similarity or substitution but also in the context of the urgency or the lack thereof in imaging. Peremptory imaging can be or usher in metaphor. Nonperemptory imaging is likely to be metonymy.

Nonperemptory images are unknowing signifiers of both self and other. From such a metonymic sequence of images, metaphors involving primitive recognition of self and other arise. In more advanced functioning, if anticipated danger blocks a metaphor, what remains is the metonymic debris from which the metaphor should have arisen and in which it remains embedded. The task of the therapist is, in that case, to find the clues of a solution, or to assist the patient in finding such clues, within the metonymic debris of failed metaphor.[4]

Crucial differentiations, the establishment of the self and the other, are wrought in primitive imaging that is motivated by absence of the needed object. Speech announces these differentiations; it is by virtue of language that differentiations so established are both recognized and augmented. Differentiation allows for more complex, higher-order interests and gives rise to more complex, higher-order problems that call for more complex, higher-order solutions.

In conclusion, a work of art would not enter the cultural order if it did not recapitulate the loss and recreation sequences beyond infancy that are universal in human development. Nevertheless, no matter the other levels of meaning wrought, the work of art, I suggest, ultimately recapitulates original loss and celebrates the original imagistic recreation of the mother. But so also does each instance of working through and mourning through which the assumption of one's historicity and subjecthood is achieved. A work of art takes its place as an object in a cultural order by reason of being a more perfect example of the kind of solution universally wrought as necessary mourning in the everyday lives of ordinary mortals.

## Notes

An English/Spanish version of this chapter is scheduled for simultaneous publication in *EOS Rivista Argentina de Arte y Psicoanálisis.*

1. To phrase it in less condensed form, the wish represents instinctual drive, the latter being the first-level psychological representative of bodily need.

2. The "father" of individual prehistory is a function of both parents, but Freud noted, "In order to simplify my presentation I shall discuss only identification with the father" (*S.E.* 19:31n; for mother's role see Smith 1991, ch. 6).

3. Any loss worthy of grief—and what loss is not?—is experienced in one dimension as total loss. Perhaps such death-in-life losses (through which symbolic castration, the assumption of one's history, and the endorsement of one's destiny are achieved) would be more adequately portrayed if the specimen story of psychoanalysis moved, as Lacan suggested, beyond *Oedipus Rex* to *Oedipus at Colonus.* The kind of killing and dying portended by the patient's dream *is* a movement toward the question posed by *Oedipus at Colonus,* "Is it now that I am nothing that I am made to be a man?" (from Lacan's reading of *Oedipus at Colonus, Séminaire* 2.250, 1978, as cited in Felman 1987, 132).

4. This paragraph derives from my reading of the 13 November 1957 session of Lacan's unpublished *Séminaire* 5, *The Formations of the Unconscious,* to which I had access through a transcription by Cormac Gallagher.

## References

Felman, Shoshana. *Jacques Lacan and the Adventure of Insight: Psychoanalysis and Contemporary Culture.* Cambridge: Harvard University Press, 1987.

Freud, Sigmund. *The Standard Edition of the Complete Psychological Works of Sigmund Freud.* Edited and translated by James Strachey. 24 vols. London: Hogarth Press, 1953–74.

"Project for a Scientific Psychology" (1895), vol. 1.

*The Interpretation of Dreams* (1900), vols. 4,5.

*Beyond the Pleasure Principle* (1920), vol. 18.

*The Ego and the Id* (1923), vol. 19.

*Inhibitions, Symptoms, and Anxiety* (1926), vol. 20.

Loewald, Hans. "The Waning of the Oedipus Complex." In *Papers on Psychoanalysis.* New Haven: Yale University Press, 1980.

Ricoeur, Paul. "Psychoanalysis and the Work of Art." In *Psychiatry and the Humanities,* vol. 1, edited by Joseph H. Smith. New Haven: Yale University Press, 1976.

Schafer, Roy. *The Analytic Attitude.* New York: Basic Books, 1983.

Smith, Joseph. "Primitive Guilt." In *Pragmatism's Freud: The Moral Disposition of Psychoanalysis,* edited by Joseph H. Smith and William Kerrigan. Psychiatry and the Humanities, vol. 9. Baltimore: Johns Hopkins University Press, 1986.

———. *Arguing with Lacan: Ego Psychology and Language.* New Haven: Yale University Press, 1991.

Stern, Daniel. *The Interpersonal World of the Infant: A View from Psychoanalysis and Developmental Psychology.* New York: Basic Books, 1985.

# 6　Echoes of the Wolf Men: Reverberations of Psychic Reality

## Robert Winer

> Wolf Man: *Well, how did Freud explain it? You know better than I.*
> Obholzer: *Better than you? No, no.*
> Wolf Man: *It's paradoxical but that's the way it is.*
> —Obholzer (1982, 52)

I practice an unsharable profession. Psychoanalysts teach their students rules with which they can make orderly their encounters with their patients. But, teach psychoanalysis? Our instruction is equivalent to explaining love by detailing the mechanisms of the sex act. What lies at the heart of the analytic encounter is unteachable, beyond communication. We can only learn from experience. Psychoanalytic training, however, is based on the illusion that we can know each other's experience.

The shift to thinking of psychoanalysis as a hermeneutic enterprise, an elaboration of meanings rather than of positivist universals, brings us closer to an appreciation of the subjective, thus unsharable, nature of our work. As we come to understand that our work is the elaboration of a dialogue, we must reconsider how we think, as psychoanalysts, about historicity, intercourse, and truth.

### Now and Then

Psychoanalysis as a narrativizing project is both drenched in history and at the same time quintessentially ahistorical. This tension between past and present has been with us from the start, often intermixed with the tension between fantasy and fact. In his case histories, Freud indeed led us on archaeological digs, demonstrating how current odd

140

behaviors could be understood as transformations of past traumas, desires, and misunderstandings. These early accounts read like detective stories, as Peter Brooks (1984) and Donald Spence (1987), among others, have pointed out, boldly announcing the certainty that dogged investigation will lead to certifiable truth. The analytic present, however, seemed less important for the telling until the patient either failed to get well in spite of the explanation or, more to the point, rebelled against her position as evidentiary specimen and fled the treatment. After a number of these confrontations, Freud discovered the transference.

In the paper that was the centerpiece of his early writings on psychoanalytic technique, "Remembering, Repeating, and Working-Through" (1914), Freud instructed us that "the patient does not *remember* anything of what he has forgotten and repressed, but *acts* it out. He reproduces it not as a memory but as an action: he *repeats* it, without, of course, knowing that he is repeating it" (150). In particular, the reenactment would be directed at the analyst, giving birth to the transference; the past would be *recreated* as the analytic present. The detective genre could no longer be the format for case histories: analytic tellings would now have to implicate the transference dialogue. Freud's choice, however, was to stop his extended case writing, and his circumspection became a model for the profession.

The tension between past and present continues to shift: we have come to see the task of analysis not as clarifying the transference to uncover the past, but as clarifying the past to uncover the transference. It is in this sense that I described psychoanalysis as quintessentially ahistorical—in our work with our patients, only the present ultimately counts. Our notion of time is changing. Hans Loewald points out that time, psychoanalytically, is a field, not a progression: "We encounter time in psychic life primarily as a linking activity in which what we call past, present, and future are woven into a nexus. . . . Past, present, and future present themselves in psychic life not primarily as one preceding or following the other, but as modes of time which determine and shape each other, which differentiate out of and articulate a pure now" (1980, 143–44). He speaks of "the modification of the past by the present" (144), recognizing that the psychoanalytic past is always a creation: "any historical truth—whatever Freud might have thought of the status of objective reality and of the truth of objectivity—is a reconstruction or construction which restructures in novel ways what already at the time when it actually happened had been a mental construction" (146). The moral act of appropriating the past transforms that past into present (Loewald 1978).

In psychoanalysis I can only explore psychic reality; in that sense, the past only exists as it is now constructed. Transference is the precipitate of that past, the joining together of the critical elements in one's life, crystallized from the ocean of experience. And transference is the *coming to life* of that past in the way in which present experience is interpreted. Memories are not transcriptions of past experience, archives open to any interested reader, independent data that can be recalled in an analysis to confirm an interpretation—albeit we often treat them as such. Although in our work we are constantly in search of the past, we must remember that the memories we encounter are in fact always *interpretations* of events (and I include here childhood fantasies themselves as events that are immediately interpreted)[1] organized by the patient for particular purposes, and these interpretations are continually being reshaped both by new experiences and by new agendas. My father died when I was eleven. How I remember his dying changes as my need to use his dying for various explanatory purposes changes; as I no longer need to use that event to justify certain ways of leading my life, for example, the memory itself changes, and I remember his dying in a different way.

Thus memory is tendentious, and motives are always creations of the present. To carry this argument all the way, I now need to assert that remembering itself is often (and especially early in treatment) a symptomatic act, a turning away from present intensities—in Schafer's terms, a form of disclaimed action (1976). The "I" whom I remember is a former me, a curious character whom I observe with bemused detachment; in time I will approach the painful recognition that we are the same person, that that person is also the present me, and the past will then no longer be a refuge, it will lose its interest for me.[2] (Of course for some patients the past has been so traumatic that it cannot even be remembered in this distanced way.) Schafer observes that "reconstruction of the infantile past is a temporally displaced and artificially linearized account of the analysis in the here and now" (1983, 203); while he is referring to the analyst's act of reconstruction, I am suggesting that this statement is equally true of the patient's remembering. James Hillman (1975) proposes, along these lines, that historicizing can be an intermediate step toward understanding: historicizing is "a means of *separating an act from actuality*," moving acts "from confession into fiction, where they can be looked at in another light" (164).

Working as an analyst I can only know my patient in his present psychic reality, and that is where he will come to know me. As I listen to his recounting of his life I will have this question in my mind: how do I understand his choosing to tell this to me now? As I develop ideas about his past experience, and even as I arrive at reconstructions about his early past, I need to keep in mind that I am making sense of his *current* interpretations of these ancient events, whether those interpretations are presented to me directly as ideas or are enacted with me in the transference. (Transference enactments are themselves always interpretations, constructions the patient is privately making of what I must really be about.) R. A. Sharpe (1987) makes the useful analogy that as analysts we are not kin to historians, but to historiographers—we are studying our patients' formulations of their lives, interpreting their interpretations.

*The Word and the Words*

There are no facts in psychoanalysis that have independent standing outside the refraction of interpretation. We find this truth hard to keep in our grasp. In his otherwise excellent defense of a hermeneutic understanding of psychoanalysis, R. A. Sharpe, while discussing the formation of the narrative, lapses into, "Either way he is now in possession of an accurate mental history" (1987, 340). "Accuracy" implies that there are objective criteria outside the analysis against which insights are measured—this implodes his argument. Freud had a great deal of difficulty with this issue. He was constantly at work in his case studies to arrive at reconstructions of actual events, his demurrer in the Wolf Man case (1918 [1914]) about the actuality of the primal scene notwithstanding. (That he even came to the point of arguing about the reality of his invention toward the end of that exposition is in its own way remarkable.) Paul Jacobsen and Robert Steele observe that "for Freud such events are both bedrock and first causes; in fact they are the culmination of psychoanalytic speculation" (1979, 361). They suggest that one motivation for this driven emphasis was Freud's attempt to refute those who opposed his psychology with evidence that seemed more material; could he really take on Jung and Adler by simply offering them his constructions of *psychic* reality?[3]

Hillman, however, takes the argument a step further, and in the process sheds light on one of our deepest anxieties in the transactional trade. Starting from A. J. Ayer's observation that in philosophy empiricism is a response to "the egocentric predicament," he continues:

> Empiricism is not only a defense against Platonism (innate ideas, universals, deductive idealism), it is, psychologically, that fantasy which makes us safe from solipsism, its isolation, its paranoid potentialities.

Therefore, since psychological material is essentially subjective and the therapeutic situation a reinforcement by mirroring or doubling (the closed vessel) of this isolated subjectivity, *the appeal to empiricism of therapy is a direct consequent of the solipsism of therapy*. The empirical disguise in case histories is an inevitiable defense against the solipsistic power of the fictions with which therapy is engaged. [1975, 134–35]

As Roy Schafer reminds us in his chapter in this volume, and in his earlier work, psychoanalytic meaning is *created* in the patient-analyst dialogue. "Purported life-historical facts that are intially presented by analysands become *psychoanalytic* facts" (1983, 188) as they ricochet between the partners in the conversation. There is no Word, we have only the words. And Schafer continues:

In this light, the history that the analyst comes to believe in with most justification is the history of the analysis itself. That history includes the varied tellings and contemporary reconstructions of the past. These tellings and reconstructions are both verbal and nonverbal, and both explicit and implicit, and they occur both within the bounds of the sessions and, through acting out, beyond these bounds. [206]

This analytic dialogue is organized, given direction, by the fact that the participants have agreed upon a task: the clarification of the patient's experience. With this purpose established, it becomes possible to declare that, in the main, and in good faith, the patient's interpretations of the analyst can be taken to constitute transference distortion, and the analyst's constructions of the patient constitute impartial psychoanalytic interpretation (without that definition of task, this assertion would be absurd—which nevertheless should not obscure our recognition that both parties' interpretive activities always serve both defensive and organizing ends). This sense of direction offers us hope that we won't be drawn down into a confounding intersubjective swamp. And yet I know from experience that I will be taken over by my patient's subjective reality at times, that I will lose my bearings, that this is in the nature of the work, and that my job is to work my way free again to the clearing. (Despite the current often voiced anxiety that our interest in the concept of projective identification will lead us to blame our confusions and misadventures on our *patients*, it has been my experience that young therapists are intent on attributing the intensities of their experience in therapy hours to the rumblings of their *own* dispositions. It seems much more threatening, in fact, to consider that their patients might have been intent on evoking this rage, that guilt, this envy outside their awareness—the danger is of feeling inhabited by another being. Empirical grounding becomes a defense against lightning catastrophe.) Harold Searles (1959) and Robert Langs (1976) have demonstrated to us that both partners in the therapy relationship are driven to make each other mad and to make each other well; Langs sees this as avoidable (the therapist's error) while Searles views it as intrinsic to the encounter (the therapist's ordeal).

The idea that I am working my way toward here is that psychoanalysis is an inescapably private encounter. The truths arrrived at are private truths, known only to the participants. Patient and analyst have come to know something together about why the patient experiences in the way that he or she does, and that knowledge has no demarcatable reference outside their shared subjectivity. Neither person could offer proof of what had been learned to an outsider (although they have offered proofs to each other). In this sense, to return to an idea with which I opened this essay, the experience is most like making love, like being in love, from the loving of the mother and her infant to that of the couple fifty years married. You cannot know my love.

*Authors and Stories*

I do not know how my colleagues work. I am not there and I listen to their descriptions of their work with skepticism. All accountings are tendentious, none more so than the case report. The case report, since Freud, has been the favored way to share our work with each other, but case reports, since Freud, have been written with an agenda in mind, a point to make. The data are organized to make that point. Not, of course, that we could do otherwise. In telling the story of our work with a patient, we must always both organize the work and be selective, presenting one aspect and not another, and generally presenting the work as we finally understand it, not as we understood it at the time. But we are always organizing our experience with our patients, from the first moment that we see them, and that organizing is always as much about us (us as analysts, us as persons) as about them. Case reports are never, in fact, about patients; they are always about treatments, our view of an interaction in which we've participated, whether we've chosen to recognize or to conceal that.

Actually, analysts rarely present their clinical work in detail; case reports are usually focused on a particular aspect of the treatment about which the analyst wishes to write. It is equally rare that a course of treatment is presented in our professional meetings and classes. The preservation of privacy is at stake, we are told—the analyst's as well as the patient's, truth be told. That caution is not unwarranted, because the analyst foolhardy enough to risk such exposure reliably gets shredded. The shredding occurs not only because the material is always open to many interpretations, not only because people have axes to grind and not only because we are relentlessly competitive. I believe that we go after each other because what we are being offered is a view into an intimate experience, a primal scene; at once anxious about being drawn in and enraged by our exclusion, we force ourselves in and destroy the scene in appropriating the case (alternatively, we revise the scene, making ourselves the protagonists). The exception to this rule, not unexpectedly, is case discussions in small study groups that have been meeting over a course of years. In that setting the members' regard for each other, their investment in their group, counterbalances the narcissistic tensions generated by feeling too drawn in or too left out.

I find a case report useful if it persuasively demonstrates to me an idea that I can apply to my work with patients or if it assists me in my own model construction. I may find the report unconvincing if its internal logic seems faulty, or if I can offer a more satisfying explanation of the clinical events. (I won't *know* that my interpretation is more accurate—I can't know that—but plausibility will carry the day.) I will also fail to find it useful if I can't align it in some measure with my own conceptual models. In one sense that is my problem, not the author's, and yet dismissal is so often the fate of theorists who construct their own metapsychologies—only those with a cadre of loyal friends survive (perhaps this is the reason Heinz Kohut succeeded where Harry Stack Sullivan had failed). I cannot imagine taking the treatment material as data from which I could build a testable alternate theory because the material is densely encased in its author's interpretation—at most, I might have contrary interesting hunches (see below).

Persuasiveness is determined by the author's ingenuity and rhetoric. Stanley Fish (1980) tells us that works acquire their authority when they are well received by interpretive communities; success is determined by the appeal to the audience. The power of Freud's rhetoric, Schafer explains in this volume, is attested to by the amazing way he can "be felt to be holding up his end of a lively and invariably refocusing conversation" with subsequent generations of readers. Donald Spence (1987), on the other hand, is deeply concerned about the way we work our rhetoric. He urges us to provide more of the relevant data, explain our rules of inference, avoid the narrative smoothing that conceals cracks in our argument, so that alternative hypotheses can be constructed. He accuses us of trying to sneak into the scientific community by concealing the hermeneutic basis of our work and presenting our findings as if they were based on deductive logic. His effort to dispatch our wanton seducers to a nunnery is misguided. As savvy readers, we generally know when we're being handed a line. The problem, as both Spence and Schafer point out, is that too often the hustlers seem compelled to dress in mourning clothes, hoping that we'll be impressed by their sobriety when what we really want is to be engaged.

Then again, being engaging can backfire. Janet Malcolm points out that Freud got himself into such trouble over the Dora case because of the vividness of his telling. The facts, she reminds us, are Freud's facts—he chose, for example, to believe Dora's account of the seduction over Herr K.'s. I'll let Malcolm tell the story herself:

> As Freud structured his account of it, the truth and goodness of the girl and the falsity and badness of the father and Herr K. are as unarguable as are the traits of princesses and ogres in fairy stories. The feminists . . . —who charge Freud with insufficient understanding of and sympathy for the beleaguered girl's plight at the hands of the creepy men around her—should understand the extent to which their own understanding of and sympathy for the girl are artifacts of Freud's rhetoric. [1987, 98]

Contretemps of this sort, backgrounded by the inherent subjectivity, dramatic structure, and intimate privacy of the therapeutic encounter, have prompted many critics to think of the better case reports as well-constructed fictions.

This idea receives a useful application in the hands of Jonathan Culler (1981) and Peter Brooks (1984). Culler examines story and discourse and shows the interrelationship between reading case history as discourse (narrative) determined by story (events) and as story shaped by discourse (the meaning of events created by their telling). This parallels the dialectic between present and past in the clinical situation, as described above, and lets us see from another vantage point how we are simultaneously driven by the structure of events and by our effort to narrativize the events in our work. Brooks, who is also taken with the possibilities in the analogy to fiction, points out that the logic of the clinical narrative is most crucially driven by desire, thus highlighting the instinctual underpinnings of our work.

The problematic aspect of considering case histories to be fiction, as Dorrit Cohn elaborates in her chapter in this volume, is that it blurs the issue of referentiality. Although we cannot know what actually

happened to Dora by the lake, we read the case knowing that something, in fact, did or did not happen, however Dora and Freud chose
to remember and understand it. We will form our own ideas about
that, and about all the romantic entanglements in the case, and will
find Freud's account more or less plausible in relation to structures
of meaning based on our sense of how people work. While structures
of meaning will also inform our reading of a novel, the question of
believability has far different implications. It matters to us whether a
case history is believable—we want to be able to use what we learn
from it. In fiction, believability is a parameter of style. That we are
always working with *psychic* reality only means that we have a less
tangible referential field, but my fantasy of revenge is as real as the
car that cut across my lane.

We might define reality, for these purposes, as that which can be
located in history. Why do we have such difficulty allowing for the
referentiality of psychic reality? Are we afraid that its elusiveness means
we're more likely to be conned? Do we fear that there's no mast we
can be tied to to protect us from the Sirens' call? If we feel uneasy
about Freud's persuasive powers, Stanley Fish (1986) warns us that
we should be. Patrick Mahony (1984), in an exhaustive and remarkable
study of the Wolf Man case, demonstrates that Freud, through devices
of rhetorical wizardry, sold us (and for over a half century kept us in
the thrall of) a thoroughly implausible reconstruction of a primal scene
putatively witnessed in astonishing detail by a malaria-struck one-and-
a-half-year-old. Mahony argues that Freud's writing mimes in various
stylistic dimensions both the Wolf Man's symptomatology and Freud's
theories. (As one example, the issue of the deferred effect of a trauma
is represented by Freud's moving backward and forward in time in
his report.)

Fish, however, turns it the other way around and argues that the
case reflects the telling. Freud, he says, is quite caught up with per-
suading us, while denying that he is doing so, and constructs the case
or at least his telling of it, to enact that conflict. To wit: "The real
seduction in this chapter . . . is the seduction not of the patient by his
sister, but of both the patient and reader by Freud, who will now be
able to produce interpretive conclusions in the confidence that they
will be accepted as the conclusions of an inevitable and independent
logic." For Fish, all is persuasion, but Malcolm challenges this, pointing
out that Fish was not persuaded. I, on the contrary, imagine that on
first reading he was thoroughly seduced, and that a subsequent unease
brought him back for a deconstructive reprise, an undoing of the spell.

Mahony links Freud's overidealization by the analytic community to his rhetorical facility.

Fish takes as an epigraph for his essay the Wolf Man's thoughts during his first hour on the couch: this man is a Jewish swindler; he'd like to use me from behind and shit on my head. (Fish's point is that the Wolf Man got it right!) According to Jones, however, Fish got it backward; citing Freud's letter to Ferenczi, Jones reports: "He initiated the first hour of treatment with the offer to have rectal intercourse with Freud and then to defecate on his head" (1955, 2: 274). In his effort to persuade us (and to create a great epigraph), Fish made the victim into the perpetrator.

*The Wolf Men: A Cautionary Tale*

One response to the relative absence of case reports has been an interest in taking on the cases reported by others, most notably by Freud (as demonstrated above). To be sure, part of the motivation for this work comes from the need each analyst has to take his own measure of Freud, to destroy and resurrect him, Freud being every analyst's father and straw man cluttering the road to professional growth. What better way to take on Freud than at the heart of his practice? And, in another sense, those cases are simply there—Dora, Schreber, Little Hans, the Rat Man, the Wolf Man—like Everest, K-2, Fuji, and Annapurna, peaks demanding to be scaled. My ambition here is more modest: to take on the mountaineers.

The Wolf Man chronicles read like a gothic novel. We follow the transformation of this man from a troubled young Russian in Vienna to an artifact of the psychoanalytic profession—from person to persona. The eighty-eight-year-old pensioner we encounter in German journalist Karin Obholzer's interviews and in Muriel Gardiner's final reporting (1971, 1983) is a man wrestling to reclaim himself from his proprietors. From reading Gardiner's accounts of what begin to sound like pilgrimages to Mecca ("I received many letters, from analysts and others, wishing to meet him, asking his name and address, asking me questions about him or requesting some information from the Wolf Man directly. I was often in a quandary as to what to do" [1983, 867]), one senses that the Wolf Man had become a talisman for psychoanalysts, a magical link to Freud. Kurt Eissler spent many hours tape-recording interviews with him. While according to Gardiner, Eissler's purpose was primarily diagnosis and research ("One cannot consider this an analysis" [1983, 888]), the Wolf Man complained, not without admiration, that Eissler could not stop analyzing him, apparently in the sense of interpreting childhood sexuality and unconscious process. Eissler's doggedness with this elderly, fading man, who considered himself by this time well beyond help, suggests to me some uneasiness about simply taking from him for archival purposes without offering something in return, whether helpful or not. Perhaps Eissler sensed that he was part of an outrageous business that was turning analysis on its head and was trying to rescue his calling. We work in this remarkably fragile profession.

The Wolf Man begins his memoirs with a description of strange happenings on his father's estate:

> The estate was well known throughout the surrounding country-side, because part of our land was used as a marketplace where fairs were held every now and then. As a small child I once watched one of these Russian country fairs. I was walking in our garden and heard noise and lively shouting behind the garden fence. Looking through a crack in the fence, I saw campfires burning—it was wintertime—with gypsies and other strange people clustered around them. The gypsies were gesti-culating wildly, and everyone was loudly shouting at the same time. There were many horses and the people were evidently arguing about their price. The scene created an impression of indescribable confusion, and I thought to myself that the goings-on in hell must be pretty much like this. [Gardiner 1971, 4–5]

This haunting description is in sharp contrast to the banal renderings of childhood events that follow.

This chapter, we learn, was written at the end, and only in response to concerted pressure. In fact, he finally put pen to paper only when he was told that the book would go to the publisher a month hence, with or without the childhood accounting (another deadline, as Gar-diner observes). One can imagine a variety of reasons for his reluct-ance, certainly including the difficulty in writing about the era that was the heart of Freud's report. In later years at least, the Wolf Man was troubled by the sense Freud had made of those early times; he and Freud had always seemed to have divergent views of the analysis. But beyond that, I imagine that the Wolf Man was disturbed by the imminent publication of his affairs. The story of the country fair is foreboding: it speaks of intruders, riffraff on the estate, strange com-merce, "indescribable confusion," the gates of hell opened on earth. He wants us to know what this is costing him, this presentation of a life lived as another's creation.

Harold Blum thought that "the analysis was more enriching for

Freud than it was for his famous patient ... possibly ... an indication that the analysis was primarily elucidated and organized in the mind of the analyst" (1974, 721–22). Blum thus reflects a typical experience of the reader—that of being dazzled by an astonishing tour de force that sailed right over the Wolf Man's head. Janet Malcolm (1987) comments that only Freud is alive in the narration, the Wolf Man being an anesthetized body (dream, free association, enactment) undergoing surgery. Others argue that Freud, to follow the dream's metaphor, was barking up the wrong tree; they claim that he ignored the relationship with the mother, or that he missed the Wolf Man's paranoid (Meissner 1977), narcissistic (Gedo and Goldberg 1973), psychotic (Frosch 1967), or borderline (Blum 1974) psychopathology. Balancing these depreciations of Freud's work, yet others remind us that the Wolf Man came to Vienna "in a pitiful psychological state" (Gay 1988, 285), "unable even to dress himself or face any aspect of life" (Jones 1955, 2: 274), in Freud's own words "in a state of complete helplessness" (1937, 217). The Wolf Man, this argument goes, with the help of Freud and later of Freud's analysand and student Ruth Mack Brunswick, was eventually able to carry on a self-sufficient life in spite of substantial external hardship, including loss of his family's fortune: he married, worked competently at a career, enjoyed painting, and developed intellectually.

Efforts to vindicate Freud by emphasizing the Wolf Man's recovery are doubly misguided. In his interviews with Obholzer, the Wolf Man claims that statements of his incapacity were great exaggerations, passed on uncritically within Freud's circle. While this assertion also cannot be taken as the last word, in reading his autobiography one senses a vitality in the child and adolescent suggesting that his breakdown in late adolescence or young adulthood was probably traumatic in origin—a response perhaps to his gonorrhea, or more likely to his sister's and later his father's death. The Wolf Man himself suggests that in seeking out Kraepelin he was trying to find a replacement for his father. By this reasoning, it was likely that the Wolf Man would have in time recovered in any event, that Freud had not miraculously rescued a drowning man. (This would not, of course, deny the Wolf Man's substantial character pathology, however one chooses to characterize it.)

On the other hand, Freud's treatment, as presented in his report, does not require absolution. Freud made it clear that he was not by any means presenting the entirety of the treatment, that he was selecting certain aspects of the work to elaborate for purposes of developing his clinical and developmental theories. His arguments about infantile sexuality, the impact of the primal scene, deferred action, unconscious homosexuality, the role of reconstruction and of forced termination, and his conjectures about fantasy and reality stand or fall as they are supported or refuted by experience with new cases. These ideas can hardly be proven or rejected by this case because ideas are never in fact proven by an author's cases.

In reviewing the various sources, furthermore, the reader might reasonably conclude that Freud did help the Wolf Man, although not in the ways he believed he had. After reading the Wolf Man's auto-biography and the interviews, it stretches both faith and the imagi-nation to believe that he assimilated Freud's formulations about his infantile sexual conflicts. On the contrary, one can imagine the Wolf Man being obsessed throughout the treatment with his relationship with Theresa, the main issue for him being whether Freud would permit the relationship, just as during his later years he tortured every-one who spoke with him (Obholzer not the least) with the question of how he should deal with the woman who he then claimed was persecuting him, the woman Obholzer calls Luise. He says he went to Freud in the hope that he would be given this esteemed man's per-mission to see Theresa (a relationship that everyone else in his life seemed to oppose), and it's not clear that he ever got much past this.

The reader senses, however, that the Wolf Man found himself in a meaningful relationship with a person of intelligence and integrity who was determined to come to terms with him, at least on his own terms. This affirmation, internalized as a relationship with a supportive other, seemed to sustain the Wolf Man over the years. Such support is often understood as the nonspecific therapeutic aspect of analytic treatment and is simply attributed to the analyst's commitment, reliability, and presence. In reading these accounts, however, one hears something more at work, a relentless effort to reach understanding that brooked no evasion: the Wolf Man seemed grateful to Freud (and later to Brunswick, Gardiner, and Eissler) for that.

The problem the analysis created for the Wolf Man was that he swallowed it whole and came to see himself through Freud's eyes, not his own. It seems impossible to tell whether that happened in the course of the treatment or after the publication of the case report, but in any event we hear the Wolf Man offering formulations of his character and his illness that ape Freud. He has not internalized an understanding, he has taken in a persona: Freud's most famous case, the Wolf Man, the man who had the wolf dream, the man who wit-nessed his parents copulating as an infant, and so on. It becomes *uncanny* how much he sounds like Freud when he discusses psychology: "Theoretically, it is interesting how insidious the 'id' can be. How it can dissemble, apparently following the commands of the 'ego' and the 'superego,' but in secret preparing its 'revenge' and then suddenly triumphing over these higher courts" (Gardiner 1971, 337). The literate world has become fascinated with him, but not him as he is, rather as the man Freud made him out to be. This is the cloak that he obsessively tries to make fit and to tear to shreds. His life becomes, in large measure, the unwinding of his analysis.

The Wolf Man is not the only one, however, who has come to confuse person and persona. Subsequent analysts take up Freud's interrogation, not recognizing that they are not analyzing Sergei Pankejeff but Freud's Wolf Man, a creation of Freud's analysis. What is available for scrutiny, of course, is a rendering of a psychoanalysis, and this can relevantly be approached with the tools of literary analysis, leading to a critique of Freud's capacity for representation and communication. Some writers have tried to strengthen their arguments by including material from the Wolf Man's memoirs, as though this were a primal source and not itself a tendentious representation, the Wolf Man as seen through the eyes of the Wolf Man as transcribed by Sergei Pankejeff, if you will. (The memoirs could easily be read, for example, as a reproach to Freud that Theresa was what mattered in his life after all. Apart from the opening paragraphs, this is the only section this reader finds poignant.) Neither are the reminiscences of the Obholzer interviews, for that matter, simply liquid truths; behind their ingenuous surface lie levels of refraction—Obholzer's agendas and editing, the Wolf Man's agenda in having the interviews, his transference to her and hers to him, to name a few.

It has been argued, by Mahony among others, that the Wolf Man used the various psychoanalysts who had contact with him as self-objects. While this seems plausible, it also seems plausible that in so doing he was mirroring their use of him as a transitional object, a link to Freud. Those of us who have analyzed the Wolf Man have kept it unclear (because we have been unclear) whether we were talking with Sergei Pankejeff or the Wolf Man, a person or a creation. As Winnicott told us (1971), transitional objects are experienced as both persons and creations (remember that he instructed the mother that she was not to ask her toddler whether he had created the object or received it, for it was always to be both and neither). Laboring between our ambitions regarding Freud and our refusal to accept the inaccessibility of another practitioner's patient (our refusal to accept the Wolf Man as a narrative creation), we have given birth to a monstrosity: the wolf in Sergei's suit.

We have one Sergei Pankejeff, many Wolf Men. But this assertion raises a question: who are the wolves—our renderings of him or ourselves? This brings us to the heart of subjectivity and transference—transference being the great conception psychoanalysis brings to our understanding of subjectivity. Ironically, one senses that Freud was too determined to be the master, too intent on making psychoanalysis an objective science, to allow himself to appreciate the depth and power of his conception, and thus it remained for him a conceit. One senses that he could feel chagrined when misled by a patient, but not shattered, in the way in which we now understand that we must bear shattering so that we can recrystallize an understanding. How else, for example, could he bear to tell and retell the story of his encounter with Dora? Or, for that matter, with the Wolf Man? (To be more generous, as Schafer certainly is, we might say that Freud did not yet have the tools to fully understand himself.)

There is a remarkable locution that has crept in around the Wolf Man case. It begins with Freud's footnote at the end of the report, added a decade later, in which he comments on the Wolf Man's brief return to treatment with him toward the end of the First World War: "After a few months' work, a piece of the transference which had not hitherto been overcome was successfully dealt with" (*S.E.* 17: 122). Referring back to the case in "Analysis Terminable and Interminable," Freud comments on the brief attacks of illness that brought the Wolf Man to treatment with Ruth Mack Brunswick: "Some of these attacks were still concerned with residual portions of the transference" (*S.E.* 23: 218). Brunswick echoes this in saying that "the source of the new illness was an unresolved remnant of the transference" (Gardiner 1971, 264). The phrase "unresolved remnant" becomes standard fare in discussions of the case, as though we were considering a scrap of cloth Freud had accidentally mislaid. The Wolf Man himself is hardly so sanguine here; he comments ironically, changing metaphors, "Mack [Brunswick] thought there was a little grain, as it were, that had remained undissolved, and that grain was paranoia" (Obholzer 1982, 57). "Transference," he assures us, "is a dangerous thing" (31). For the Wolf Man, late in life and speaking retrospectively, his transference to Freud has been the bane of his existence. By "transference" he meant helpless dependency on another, a state of mind in which he felt he had led far too much of his life. He saw his dependent relations with subsequent figures as extensions and displacements of his transference to Freud. And he used this argument to blame others and exculpate himself: had it not been for his transference to Freud, he argues, he might have returned to Russia and rescued his fortune.

(Transference, of course, is never a little bit of anything; it is always all of everything.)

For Freud, the treatment was an exercise in reconstruction, the reinterpretation of childhood memories and especially of a childhood dream. The Wolf Man's transference is treated as an obstacle to this unfolding, a resistance to be gotten rid of through education and limit setting. The crucial information that emerged in the last stages of treatment became available because, "under the inexorable pressure of this fixed limit his resistance and his fixation to the illness gave way" (*S. E.* 17: 11). We might now say that Freud did not work through the Wolf Man's transference, but manipulated it to create a state of compliance; in fact, he comments that "the patient gave an impression of lucidity which is usually attainable only in hypnosis" (11). Despite Freud's engaging presentation, the absence of an analytic process, as we now understand it, makes this case report ultimately unsatisfying to the contemporary reader.

Consider, however, the possibilities—the wolf dream, for example. Freud does not tell us the context in which the patient remembered the dream, presumably considering the context irrelevant. The telling of a dream, however, like any act in analysis, occurs in a transference setting; encoded within the telling is a communication about the analysis. In reading the Wolf Man's memoirs, I was caught by this passage: "[Freud] was a genius. Just imagine the work he did, remembering all those details, forgetting nothing, drawing those inferences. He may have had six, seven patients a day" (Gardiner 1971, 32). I immediately thought of the dream's wolves in the tree—the Wolf Man had said there were six or seven—and of Freud's speculations about the meaning of those numbers and of the uncertainty. I wondered if the wolves represented for the Wolf Man Freud's daily patients, six or seven, depending on whether he included himself. We are aware of his intense rivalry with his sister for his father's affection, and it is easy to imagine that he felt a similarly intense competition with his analytic siblings; he asked Freud about the people he saw coming and going, and Freud identified them to him by occupation and circumstance, although not by name. At the point at which Freud finally succeeded in analyzing this dream, might the Wolf Man have been retelling it because he was facing rejection by Freud, imagining the siblings poised outside the consulting room door, motionless, ready to spring, a projection of his own wish to break in on Freud's life and make his claim, a protest against the exclusions, both the forced termination date and the Sunday absences, the one day of the seven Freud didn't receive him, the omission blurred by the phrase "six or seven"?

This is all, to be sure, wildly speculative,[4] but it is evocative, bringing the treatment to life. Perhaps "six or seven" was a locution the Wolf Man habitually used, picked up in childhood, entirely incidental to the possibilities I am suggesting. But perhaps not. (In the spirit of full disclosure, I should report that the theme of rivalry with a sister for a lost father is hardly irrelevant to my own life. Does this create my interpretation as a projection of my own competitive strivings, or does it sensitize me to recognizing something present in the treatment? That is an unanswerable question; the appeal of the interpretation, as always, depends on the resonance it evokes in readers.)

The lesson of transference is that we cannot stand outside a subjective position. My choosing to use the case of the Wolf Man as a vehicle for exploring these issues is dense with personal meanings, only one of which I have briefly acknowledged. I do not begin to imagine that I could sort out my countertransferences understood as my own distortions of the material from my countertransferences understood as empathic responses to the material. In the literature on treatment, the capacity to make this distinction is held to be absolutely critical, and yet it always eludes us. Every moment in an analysis is created by two minds, two psychologies, two lives intersecting. The notion that we could perceive our patients without our own transferences is unanalytic. Bion's conception that we should approach our patients without memory and desire I take to be his acknowledgment of the absolute impossibility of that task. We hesitate to share our cases because we know they reveal as much about ourselves as about our patients. (One rhetorical tactic has been to expose more fully the treatment of patients we worked with as candidates; they, we imagine, were treated by someone else.)

Each reader creates his own Wolf Man, as each analyst, each interviewer, and each author has. The irony, in terms of received theory, is that we find ourselves more engaged in certain treatments, in certain readings, in which we have more personally at stake, less clear about our bearings; those are probably the treatments in which we have the potential to be of greatest use, the readings to which we can best respond with our own interpretations. In any event, and in all events, we work by adding our meaning to the layers of meaning that existed before us; if what we have to offer is useful it will be added to the fabric of meanings. In contrast to Freud's vision of analysis as archaeology or sculpture, a process of unearthing and subtraction, I understand analysis as a process of addition, in the way that an artist might return to a painting and see a new possibility, add new paint to the canvas, reach a new synthesis.

## Notes

1. Psychoanalysts, of course, beginning with Freud, have been quite interested in the question of whether memories refer to events or fantasies. Reality traumas and disturbing fantasies indeed have different effects on development; actual events are more difficult for the child to encompass within his sphere of omnipotence (the fantasy, on the other hand, was of his own construction) and are thus more likely to result in unresolvable guilt. Scott Wetzler (1985) points out the ways in which it makes a difference clinically which one is reconstructing. To say that we are in any event working with the patient's interpretation does not erase the need to find out how and why the patient arrived at that understanding, how and why he reworked the trauma or fantasy. It may also be useful to the patient to discover facts that were concealed from him, for secrets often leave ghost trails that are scented but not understood, or omissions that must be filled with confabulation.

2. We must in fact recognize that all thoughts about ourselves are self-objectifying and thus self-estranging.

3. Both Strachey and Freud tell us that an impetus for writing up the Wolf Man case was that it gave Freud the chance to refute the challenges to psychoanalysis coming at that time from Jung and Adler. Jung's claim was that the child's sexual memories are adult fantasies displaced backward, while Adler felt that Freud was missing the aggression inherent in apparent sexual activity. The straw men we set up for ourselves, however, represent one side of a dialectic in which we are momentarily frozen; we set them up so that by struggling with them we can work our way free. By the end of the case report, Freud was having to sort out his own thinking by considering whether the latent content of his patient's dream was a fantasy projected backward by a four-year-old child onto an infant; the issues of displacement in time and the relationship between psychic and material reality were very much on his mind. And it was not long after the publication of the case that Freud began to consider with greater freedom the vicissitudes of aggression.

4. Otto Rank's speculation about the six or seven wolves proved to be even wilder. He opined that the image represented the six photographs of Freud's committee members hung on the consultation room's wall; were this so, the Wolf Man would have had to have dreamed his dream during his analysis. But a delighted Jones (1957, 3: 76) refutes this claim by pointing out that during the Wolf Man's analysis there were only three committee members—Ferenczi, Rank, and himself. Unlike me, Rank had made the mistake of offering a refutable hypothesis! And I find support, of sorts, for my conjecture in Nicolas Abraham and Maria Torok's (1986) linking of the Russian words for "six persons" and "sister."

*References*

Abraham, Nicolas, and Torok, Maria. *The Wolf Man's Magic Word: A Cryptonymy* (1976). Translated by Nicholas Rand. Minneapolis: University of Minnesota Press, 1986.

Blum, Harold P. "The Borderline Childhood of the Wolf Man." *Journal of the American Psychoanalytic Association* 22 (1974): 721–42.

Brooks, Peter. *Reading for the Plot: Design and Intention in Narrative*. New York: Alfred A. Knopf, 1984.

Brunswick, Ruth Mack. "A Supplement to Freud's 'History of an Infantile Neurosis' " (1928). In Gardiner (1971).

Culler, Jonathan. *The Pursuit of Signs: Semiotics, Literature, Deconstruction*. Ithaca: Cornell University Press, 1981.

Fish, Stanley. *Is There a Text in This Class? The Authority of Interpretive Communities*. Cambridge: Harvard University Press, 1980.

———. "Withholding the Missing Portion: Power, Meaning, and Persuasion in Freud's 'The Wolf-Man'." *Times Literary Supplement*, 29 August 1986.

Freud, Sigmund. *The Standard Edition of the Complete Psychological Works of Sigmund Freud*. Edited and translated by James Strachey. 24 vols. London: Hogarth Press, 1953–74.

"Remembering, Repeating and Working-Through" (1914), vol. 12.

"From the History of an Infantile Neurosis" (1918 [1914]), vol. 17.

"Analysis Terminable and Interminable" (1937), vol. 23.

Frosch, J. "Severe Regressive States during Analysis." *Journal of the American Psychoanalytic Association* 15 (1967): 491–507.

Gardiner, Muriel, ed. *The Wolf-Man by the Wolf-Man*. New York: Basic Books, 1971.

———. "The Wolf Man's Last Years." *Journal of the American Psychoanalytic Association* 31 (1983): 867–97.

Gay, Peter. *Freud—A Life for Our Time*, New York: Norton, 1988.

Gedo, John E., and Goldberg, Arnold. *Models of the Mind: A Psychoanalytic Theory*. Chicago: University of Chicago Press, 1973.

Hillman, James. "The Fiction of Case History: A Round." In *Religion as Story*, edited by J. Wiggins. New York: Harper and Row, 1975.

Jacobsen, Paul B., and Steele, Robert S. "From Past to Present: Freudian Archaeology." *International Review of Psycho-Analysis* 6 (1979): 349–62.

Jones, Ernest. *The Life and Work of Sigmund Freud*, 3 vols. New York: Basic Books, 1953-57.

Langs, Robert. *The Bipersonal Field*. New York: Jason Aronson, 1976.

Loewald, Hans W. *Psychoanalysis and the History of the Individual*. New Haven: Yale University Press, 1978.

———, "The Experience of Time" (1972). In *Papers on Psychoanalysis*. New Haven: Yale University Press, 1980.

Mahony, Patrick, J. *Cries of the Wolf Man*. New York: International Universities Press, 1984.

Malcom, Janet. "Reflections: J'appelle un chat un chat." *New Yorker*, 20 April 1987, 84–102.

Meissner, W. W. "The Wolf Man and the Paranoid Process." *The Annual of Psychoanalysis* 5 (1977): 23–74.

Obholzer, Karin. *The Wolf-Man: Conversations with Freud's Patient—Sixty Years Later*. New York: Continuum Publishing Company, 1982.

Schafer, Roy. *A New Language for Psychoanalysis*. New Haven: Yale University Press, 1976.

———. *The Analytic Attitude*. New York: Basic Books, 1983.

Searles, Harold. "The Effort to Drive the Other Person Crazy—An Element in the Aetiology and Psychotherapy of Schizophrenia." *British Journal of Medical Psychology* 32 (1959): 1–18.

Sharpe, R. A. "Psychoanalysis and Narrative: A Structuralist Approach." *International Review of Psycho-Analysis* 14 (1987): 335–42.

Spence, Donald P. *The Freudian Metaphor: Toward Paradigm Change in Psychoanalysis*. New York: W. W. Norton, 1987.

Wetzler, Scott. "The Historical Truth of Psychoanalytic Reconstructions." *International Review of Psycho-Analysis* 12 (1985): 187–97.

Winnicott, Donald W. *Playing and Reality*. London: Tavistock, 1971.

Wolf Man. "The Memoirs of the Wolf-Man." In *Wolf-Man by the Wolf-Man*, edited by Muriel Gardiner. New York: Basic Books, 1971.

7    Freud on His Own Mistake(s):
     The Role of Seduction in the
     Etiology of Neurosis

*Rachel B. Blass and
Bennett Simon*

A *mistaken idea had to be overcome which might have been
almost fatal to the young science.*—Freud (*S.E.* 14:17)

If this chapter had been written in the eighteenth century it would
have had a title like "The True History of Freud's Seduction Hypothesis:
Being an Essay on the Real and the Fantastic in the Misguided Accounts
of the History of a Theory of the Real and the Fantastic." Our thesis
is that writing the history of Freud's dealing with the problem of the
actual and the imaginary in the realm of seduction and incest has been
plagued by short-circuiting the complexities, and that the result is an
imaginary history of the actual steps in the development of Freud's
thinking about seduction and incest. Our underlying assumption is
that the problem of the relationship between the actual and the imaginary has both animated and haunted psychoanalysis from its very
beginning and that psychoanalysis has recurrently succumbed to the
temptation to oversimplify this crucial problem.

In this chapter we focus first on what Freud documents in the
course of the years 1893–1906 about how he was actively wrestling
with the relationship between neurosis and seduction, actual or fantasied. Here we have the relatively unedited data of Freud's own thinking. Second, we review Freud's *later accounts* of his thinking during
those early years, which characterized that thinking as mistaken and
dangerous to the development of the science of psychoanalysis. We
introduce these topics with a brief presentation of two antithetical
historical versions of Freud's work on seduction during 1893–1906.
Finally, we conclude with a discussion of the implications for contem-
160

porary psychoanalysis of the way psychoanalytic history has been written, rewritten, and miswritten. Recent critiques of the seduction theories, the greater availability of historical data, and new perspectives on research possibilities all make this an auspicious time for psychoanalysis to further its necessary process of self-analysis.

*Two Antithetical Histories of Freud's Seduction Theories: The "Received View" and the "Revisionist View"*

What we call the received view of Freud's seduction theories is a composite of the formulations of Ernest Jones, Anna Freud, and Ernst Kris. It draws heavily on Freud's formal recantations of his early ideas of seduction and neurosis (as presented in 1914, 1925, and 1932). It emerges through Anna Freud's and Ernst Kris's editing of the Freud-Fliess correspondence (Freud 1954) and also through Ernest Jones's discussion of that correspondence (Jones 1953). The received view has dominated psychoanalytic writing and training and has become a building block in classic explorations of the history of psychoanalysis.

This view runs as follows: Psychoanalysis began with Freud's adoption of Breuer's trauma theory of hysteria and his modification of Breuer's method for treating this disorder. Working within this framework, Freud came to an astonishing revelation that was to mark a turning point in the development of psychoanalysis. What Freud found was that in tracing the patient's associations to the first appearance of the pathological manifestation, what invariably emerged were recollections of sexual assault in which the father was most usually described as the perpetrator of the involuntary seduction. Freud took these recollections at face value and drew the conclusion that it was not, as Breuer believed, just any trauma that could precipitate the outbreak of a neurosis. It was, rather, a trauma of a specific kind, a sexual trauma resulting from incestuous relationships, that lay at the basis of the disorder. It was at this point that Breuer, finding sexual formulations of this kind threatening and distasteful, parted paths with Freud. Left to develop his ideas on his own, Freud emerged with a comprehensive theory of neurosis—the seduction theory. The theory centered on what he referred to as "paternal etiology" and relied on the verbal reports of patients for its confirmation.

The received view of the seduction theory goes on to explain that this theory was only briefly maintained. Its duration according to different authors is somewhere between two and four years, 21 September 1897 being the consensual date of its abandonment. It disappeared as soon as Freud recognized the improbability that incest was as widespread as hysteria. More important from the standpoint of psychoanalytic theory, it disappeared with the recognition of the centrality and power of fantasy. Through self-analysis and the concomitant discovery of the Oedipus complex, Freud discovered the etiological role of fantasy. Consequently, he recognized the error of assuming that patients' reports were veracious; they were products of wishes and defenses, not recollections of actual events. Fantasy seduction rather than actual seduction thus became crucial in the etiology of neurosis. The analysis and the interpretation of fantasy became the essence of psychoanalysis, and hence the seduction theory was dismissed. As Freud in a popular passage in 1932 explains: "In the period in which the main interest was directed to discovering infantile sexual traumas, almost all my women patients told me that they had been seduced by their father. I was driven to recognize in the end that these reports were untrue and so came to understand that hysterical symptoms are derived from phantasies and not from real occurrences" (*S.E.* 23:120).

According to the received view described here, the seduction theory should be recalled as a stepping stone and an error. It contained the first insights into the sexual etiology of the neuroses but erroneously considered the sexual causes to be real events. Freud, this view continues, was great enough to admit his error, to discard his briefly, albeit tenaciously, held position on the role of actual incestuous seduction, and thus to open the way for his new and innovative ideas, which constitute the basics of psychoanalysis as we know it today.

What we call the revisionist view of seduction is primarily the creation of two controversial psychoanalysts, Jeffrey Masson (1984, 1990; Freud 1985) and Alice Miller (1984). It has also been developed, adopted, and augmented by other therapists and investigators, especially those outside of orthodox psychoanalytic circles, such as Herman (1981) and Russell (1986). This view crystallized in the early 1980s and has rapidly become as canonical in its own way as the received theory.

The revisionist view holds that Freud was correct in his early account of the importance of paternal seduction and abuse for the etiology of mental illness. This view has it that there was no justification for Freud's reevaluation and redefinition of patients' reports as products of fantasy; the evidence weighs heavily in favor of the veracity of the reports. Accordingly, it was in the dismissal of this evidence that Freud erred or, perhaps it would be more appropriate to say, failed. Proponents of this view go on to assert that it was not theoretical considerations that led Freud to change his views, but rather a conglomerate of motives outside the boundaries of science. Such motives include Freud's wish to acquit his father and an entire generation of fathers of the crimes the patients described; his wish to absolve his friend and colleague Fliess from the accusation of malpractice he faced for nasal surgery performed on one of Freud's patients (Emma Eckstein) to cure her of her neurosis—surgery that due to negligence almost resulted in death; and Freud's wish to undo his rejection by the Viennese medical community on account of his seduction theory.

This view maintains that Freud's distortion and dismissal of the true claims of patients have been perpetuated by generations of analysts. There are rare exceptions such as Ferenczi (1933 [1955]; 1933 [1988]), who was shunned by his contemporaries, and Robert Fliess (1953, 1956, 1961, 1973; Masson 1984), whose work was not fully understood. The growing recognition in recent years that indeed seduction and incest are as frequent as Freud had originally found should bring the truth of the seduction theory back to center stage in psychoanalytic theory and practice.

In brief, our researches indicate that neither the received view nor the revisionist one encompasses the actual history of Freud's early ideas on seduction. Similarly, each view distorts the complex history of what other analysts have held about the role of fantasy seduction and actual seduction. Note that the received view describes Freud's renunciation of the seduction theory exclusively in terms of organic developments in his scientific thinking (aided by his self-analysis), and the revisionist view describes the change entirely in terms of self-serving conscious and unconscious motives. These antithetical views of psychoanalytic history are themselves of interest as specimens of mythmaking and distortion in psychoanalytic thinking, instantiations of a propensity to premature closure on complicated issues (Blass, in press; Simon, in press). For the remainder of this chapter we examine Freud's writings.

*Freud's Theory(ies) of Seduction*

Between the years 1893 and 1898 Freud maintained several etiological theories of the neuroses, all of which different authors at different times have referred to as *the seduction theory*. The neglect of the distinctions between the different theories is one of the more immediate sources of error concerning Freud's views on seduction, his abandonment of the seduction theory, and the factors that influenced this move. It should be noted at this point that Freud himself never employed the term "seduction theory." The earliest reference we have found is by Kris (Freud 1954). In using the term we refer to the theories Freud maintained from 1893 to 1898, all of which in varying degrees and in regard to varying meanings of the term ascribe significance to seduction in producing the psychoneuroses. Another point that is important to bear in mind here is that to distinguish the different theories requires an awareness of the different ways in which terms such as *seduction, abuse, trauma,* and *assault* are used and the context in which they appear. Freud, for example, maintained a very early theory of the traumatic effect of abusive seduction. What he had in mind by "abusive seduction," however, as is apparent from his clinical illustration, is the overworking of the adult male's sexual apparatus by an overeager adult female sexual partner, his mistress (letter to Fliess, 27 November 1893, Freud 1985, 61). In our account, we have tried to exclude such use of the terms and to adhere to a more conventional understanding of *abuse* and *seduction.* Given Freud's varied use of the terms, this task was not always easy. In general, it should be noted that looseness of terminology has over many decades characterized psychoanalytic discussions of trauma, abuse, and seduction.

THE THEORY OF TRAUMA AND DEFENSE: 1893 [1888]–7 FEBRUARY 1894

We have termed Freud's first theory of seduction the theory of trauma and defense. It appears in Freud's joint work with Breuer, *The Studies on Hysteria* (*S.E.* 2), in the preliminary communication to that work (1893), in his 1894 paper, "The Neuro-Psychoses of Defence" (*S.E.* 3), and in some of Freud's letters to Fliess during this period. While first appearing in 1893, the theory seems to have already guided Freud in his earliest therapeutic endeavors in 1888. The letter to Fliess of 7 February 1894 (Freud 1985, 65-66) can be taken as the end of this period. The theory of trauma and defense is not a theory of seduction per se. Seduction, however, plays a prominent role within it. According to this theory, intense excitation of the psychical apparatus that cannot be worn away through associative pathways (i.e., thought) becomes manifest in hysterical symptoms. These symptoms constitute symbolic reproductions of the excitatory event and allow for the discharge necessary for the maintenance of "constancy." Freud and Breuer elaborated the nature of the intense excitatory event, the trauma. Fright, anger, and anxiety, but most important, traumatic sexual experiences, including seduction and the "retention" of ideas relating to sexual longings and needs, were noted in this regard. Their main focus of attention, however, was directed toward the elucidation of the feature that prevented the normal discharge of excitation through the associative pathways. It is here that Freud's fundamental concept of defense is introduced. This blocking of the pathways, or the "splitting of the mind" as it is often referred to, is seen to be the result of defense. At this point, "defense" denotes a deliberate, self-imposed amnesia aimed at avoiding a range of unpleasurable feelings. Accordingly, when an associatively linked event reawakens the repressed memory of an unpleasurable or traumatic one, neurosis becomes manifest. The question of why certain unpleasurable excitatory events evoke defense and others do not was not to be satisfactorily resolved during this period.

THE TRANSITIONAL THEORY: 7 FEBRUARY 1894–15 OCTOBER 1895

The second theory of seduction is known to us primarily from a series of letters from Freud to Fliess written between 7 February 1894 and 15 October 1895. In a secondary way, it is alluded to in the final chapter of the *Studies on Hysteria*, which was written in 1894 and 1895. This theory of seduction may be referred to as one of transition. It develops ideas that facilitate the shift from the theory of trauma and defense to what will soon be seen to be Freud's formal seduction theory.

Two ideas gradually become central in this context. The first is the ubiquity of the sexual foundation of the psychoneuroses. Freud contends here that in *all* cases the neuroses are derived from some form or another of sexual occurrence. With this assertion Freud feels that he is breaking away from Breuer, who refused to acknowledge the primacy of sexual factors. The second idea that over a period of months begins to take shape is the notion of early trauma. That is, beyond the immediate excitatory event associated with the onset of the neurosis, and beyond the more intensely traumatic events it may conceal, lies an early, prepubertal trauma. This early trauma and its sexual nature account for the differential employment of defense. In adulthood defense may emerge *only* when the event to be forgotten and isolated is in association with the memory of an early sexual trauma. Freud does not specify ages, nor does he note the specific nature of the sexual trauma. Within this model it is clear, however, that the trauma involves a sexual interaction that, at the time of its occurrence (in the prepubertal period), was experienced as unpleasurable, being accompanied, Freud ultimately concludes, by feelings of "revulsion and fright."

THE FORMAL SEDUCTION THEORY: 15 OCTOBER 1895–6 DECEMBER 1896

The next theory of seduction to emerge, the formal seduction theory, provides an answer to the question of why specifically sexual traumata constitute the foundation of later defense. This theory is first revealed and then discussed in the Freud-Fliess correspondence but is most fully elaborated in the "Project" (*S.E.* 1) and in three different essays published in 1896: "Heredity and the Aetiology of the Neuroses," "Further Remarks on the Neuro-Psychoses of Defence," and "The Aetiology of Hysteria" (*S.E.* 3).[1] Theoreticians, in their attempt to clarify Freud's early formulations (e.g., Laplanche and Pontalis 1968; Sadow et al. 1968; Schimek 1975, 1987; Schusdek 1968; Stewart 1967; Sulloway 1979), have often referred to this formal theory as *the* seduction theory, neglecting the less systematically presented ideas that preceded and followed it. The formal seduction theory centers on the idea of *nachträglichkeit*, the "deferred action" of a memory of an infantile seduction. Continuing from where the previous theory of seduction left off, this means that (*a*) the early sexual event was always a seduction, and more importantly (*b*) the early seduction was not experienced as traumatic at the time at which it occurred, but is so experienced in its postpubertal revival.

The course of events leading up to the neuroses may be described as follows (focusing here on hysteria): A prepubertal sexual seduction occurs. At this point Freud limits prepubertal to an upper range of eight years old but usually stresses that seduction should occur by age three or four, at the latest. The early seduction, which must include the excitation of the infant's genitals, is not, in and of itself, traumatic and has no immediate effect on the child's well-being. At some later, postpubertal period another seduction occurs. This later seduction, which may range in severity from an almost inadvertent brush of the knee to consummated incest, is not per se traumatic either. It indirectly exerts a powerful effect, however, in that it revives the memory of the early seduction. This memory, which at the time of its registration was not experienced, is first experienced in its postpubertal revival. The intensity of the later primary experience of the early seduction (in the "Project," "posthumous primary affective experience," 359) is traumatic and consequently must be defended against. The early memory must not be allowed into consciousness, repression is invoked, and neurosis appears.

This theory, it should be recalled, is predicated on a view of the infantile, prepubertal period as presexual. There is no experience of the early seduction because sexuality cannot at that time be experienced. Thus it is only when the memory is revived in the postpubertal period that its original charge is activated and sexual feelings of traumatic intensity are experienced. The fact that under these conditions the memory of the sexual seduction is more unpleasurable than the seduction itself explains why defense is so intimately tied to memories of sexual encounters.

THE THEORY OF PATERNAL ETIOLOGY: 6 DECEMBER 1896–LATE 1897

On 6 December 1896, the formal seduction theory implicitly under-
goes a major revision, one that changes its basic nature. On that date,
in a letter to Fliess, Freud discloses that "the essential point of hysteria
is that it results from *perversion* on the part of the seducer [and] that
heredity is seduction by the father" (1985, 212). Freud was shortly
to refer to this essential point, namely, that neurosis is the result of
not just any early seduction but an incestuous one, perpetrated by a
perverse father, as the "paternal aetiology" of neurosis (28 April 1897).
It is noteworthy that Freud never explains what he seems to posit as
the theoretical necessity that the father specifically is the perpetrator
in cases where neurosis develops. Importantly, this etiological theory
gains strength and remains dominant in the Freud-Fliess letters right
up to the abandonment of the seduction theory, but *it is never publicly
presented*. Strangely, it is this formulation of the seduction theory that
is most directly addressed in Freud's later, public comments on early
psychoanalytic theory.

While on 21 September 1897 Freud writes of his loss of belief in
his "neurotica," his final theory of seduction—that paternal seduction
leads to neurosis—continues to be intermittently presented for a
while longer, at least until 12 December 1897 (Freud 1985, 285–87),
and remnants of the theory can still be seen in the Dora case (Blass,
in press).[2]

It may be seen that this brief presentation of the actual and detailed
history of Freud's seduction theories in and of itself suffices to dismiss
many of the claims both of the "received" and the "revisionist" histories of Freud's theorizing. For example, once we acknowledge the
late date (6 December 1896) of the appearance of the theory of
paternal etiology, the claim that Freud's guilt surrounding the death
of his father determined the retreat from it can no longer be held.
Freud's father died three months *before* Freud introduced his theory
of the father's involvement. Further (though we have not presented
all the data here), there is now little basis for the "revisionist" argument
that Freud's wish to be in the good graces of the Viennese medical
establishment motivated his turn away from the seduction theory(ies).
While Freud was bothered by the indifferent reception of his 1896
presentation, "The Aetiology of Hysteria," there are abundant indications that he was also afraid of ridicule and rejection of his ideas
on infantile sexuality.

In a more general way, it may be seen that the centrality ascribed
to "paternal etiology" by both the received and the revisionist ap-

proaches does not correspond to the actual development of Freud's early theories. The primitiveness of Freud's seduction theory emphasized by the received approach similarly distorts Freud's work. While the actual event of seduction is prominent in all Freud's early formulations, his theory was never a simple one of cause and effect. Complex internal mechanisms, such as conflict and repression, were also essential, and the specific nature of these mechanisms underwent many changes as Freud developed his ideas.

Thus, underlying the complexity of Freud's formulations can be seen his grappling with certain basic theoretical questions. Prominent among these questions are the following:

1. What is the ultimate and universal origin of the motive force behind the neurotic symptom? In a broad sense, Freud, through his various formulations of the seduction theory, starts from the position that the motive force is the intense excitation of the external world set up within the person in such an immediate form that it cannot be "worn away." He moves to the position that it is sexual excitation, caused by the environment's premature stimulation of the organism (dissociated from the person's experiential world), that serves as the pathogenic force.

Such a theory is entirely compatible with a theory of fantasy and internal drives. Internally motivated sexual and self-preservational drives and their ideational representation, the wish, are postulated as well. If not gratified, these internal motives lead to unpleasure. They are not, however, the source of pathology. Pathology, according to the seduction theory(ies), is the product of the intervention of the external world. It is the external world that creates the person's basic conflicts by inserting and arousing motives that run counter to the organism's natural and age-appropriate strivings (see Friedman 1977).

2. What is the ultimate and universal origin of the specific form and ideational content of the neuroses? In brief, Freud also sought through the seduction theories to reveal the ultimate factor that determines the *uniformity* of the way in which motives manifest themselves in pathology. While intense stimulation is, in and of itself, the source of pathology, additional factors of a qualitative kind come into play that determine the nature of the mental contents, the nature of the disorder. Most notable among these factors are the specifics of the setting in which the stimulation took place, the specifics of the "original scene." These are inherent components of the memory of the pathogenic event, and they serve as templates for the later expression of the pathogenic force. Thus in regard both to the motive force in psychopathology and to the qualitative determinants of the form

and content of the pathology, Freud sought to locate the external, experiential factors that shaped the person's inner world.

Freud's interest in the nature of the revived "scene" grows in the course of the development of his theory and becomes increasingly focused on revealing a single universal factor. His final hypothesis that the father is in *all cases* the perpetrator of the seduction is now intelligible in the context of a search for a universal cause of both the motive *and* the factor that gives specific shape to the neurosis.

3. What is the source of repression? Through the formulations of the seduction theories, Freud struggles with the question of how and why certain kinds of intense stimulation are prevented from discharge and hence how they and the memories to which they are attached become pathogenic structures. Although Freud's formal conceptualizations in this regard become more theoretically sophisticated, he continues to maintain the simple and theoretically inadequate notion that the social and moral unacceptability of these ideas and memories leads to their repression. While the conceptually sophisticated notions were intimately tied to the quantitative factor—the motive force— the more intuitive and theoretically deficient one was tied to the qualitative factor—the specific content of the pathogenic "scene."

*Evidence for the Seduction Theory—Confirmation and Bias*

Confirmation of the various formulations of the seduction theory was, according to Freud, obtained primarily from patients' reports and re- productions during treatment, as well as from the fact of the clinical success of the treatment. Contrary to popular belief, Freud was not naive regarding the validity of these three kinds of evidence— memory, reproduction in a session of a purported childhood scene, and clinical improvement. Already in *Studies on Hysteria* Freud strug- gled with issues of the trustworthiness of patients' reports, the effect of suggestion, the verification of the permanence of cure, and the possibility of alternate explanations being as valid as or better than his own etiological explanations. In "The Aetiology of Hysteria" (1896) he puts aside his doubts and presents a convincing argument in favor of the validity of the evidence he has at hand; he also argues for the a priori likelihood of his theories.

As we follow the development of Freud's ideas, it becomes apparent that his concern with forming a good theory was not consistently translated in practice to mean scrupulous use and presentation of his data. It was not the evidence alone or even primarily that guided the evolution of his seduction theory. This does not mean that Freud was indifferent to facts. Rather, relying on his "feel" for the plausibility of a theory, as well as on what is referred to among creative scientists as a theory's "aesthetics," Freud, in order to develop and discover, had to suppress and ignore certain facts within the maze of data— had to draw the best possible curve through the scatter of points, as it were. Discrepancies between the available clinical data in 1896 and Freud's theoretical formulations at that time attest to this state of affairs (Schimek 1897). Further testimony for this discrepancy can be seen in Freud's private complaints concerning the absence of sufficient confirmatory evidence (e.g., letter of 30 May 1896, Freud 1985, 187) for the very formulations that he publicly professed to be clinically proven![3] There is additional evidence that Freud took liberties in his process of discovery in his own reports on the data he was collecting. For example, emergence of the (hypothesized) initial seduction in the course of treatment is taken as major confirmation of this hypothesis. In his case reports and discussions, however, the nature of this emergent material is often unclear. Is it a reproduction (i.e., an affective mimetic enactment of a scene of seduction) in the session of the "original" scene, which had been unconscious? A recollection of a scene? A recall of a memory that had been at some time consciously available to the patient? This lack of precision is critical because at different points Freud argues that the existence of one or another of these possibilities to the exclusion of the others gives his clinical data evidential value. That is, that the patient has a reproduction and not a recollection is offered as powerful evidence.

It seems to us that Freud's predilection for certain kinds of scientific solutions to his fundamental theoretical questions interdigitated with certain biases that may have had a more personal and autobiographical origin. This combination helped lead Freud to fundamental discoveries and also led him to maintain his theories in spite of refuting evidence. His single-minded search for sexual determinants plays an important role here. The personal bias becomes more apparent in his presentation of his "paternal etiology" formulation of the seduction theory. Elements of seduction or coercion in his style appear more prominently, for example, as he reports to Fliess the "forceful" and "penetrating" interpretations that he presents to disbelieving female patients. A case in point is the story of paternal seduction described in a letter with the punning caption, "Habemus Papam" (We have a Pope! We have caught the papa!) (3 January 1897, Freud 1985, 220-21). Freud "thrust" his interpretation of paternal etiology at his patient on the basis of such evidence as her presenting symptom—a tic involving the mouth and tendency to accumulate saliva in her mouth, a process that reminds Freud of fellatio. His own notions of confirmation are subsequently disregarded. The patient's acceptance of his interpretation is considered to be confirmation of its truth. The patient's later rejection of the interpretation, after her confrontation with her father met a solemn oath of innocence, is here also considered to be a confirmation of the truth of Freud's reconstruction. Freud construes her rejection as an identification with the father's [purported] untruthfulness as reflected in *her* oath swearing. The patient's rejection of Freud's idea is then countered by Freud's threat to send her away (221). Freud's coercive and seductive tendency in this period of his work is in line with his later revelation through self-analysis that his earlier, supposedly *inevitable* conclusion that his own father was the "prime originator" of his neurosis was "no doubt ... an inference by analogy from myself unto him" (1985, 268). The discovery of his own seductive wishes [here, as a child toward his mother] led him to project the accusation of seduction onto his father. But as if partially undoing his discovery of the direction of wishes, from the child to the adult, his self-analysis also revealed to him seductive wishes toward his daughter, that is, from parent to child (letter of 31 May 1897, 1985, 249).

In a broader sense, we see Freud's preference for formulations that posit a clash between the external world and the person's internal strivings, and that place the responsibility for the perverse and immoral sexual motives on the external environment. This preference at this point in his career probably represents a confluence of his scientific style of theorizing with conflicted personal issues emerging in his self-analysis (Laplanche and Pontalis 1968).

In his letter to Fliess of 21 September 1897 (Freud 1985, 264–67), Freud lists four reasons for losing faith in his seduction theory: his failure to bring a single case to conclusion, the unlikelihood of such a high incidence of seductive fathers, the theoretical impossibility of distinguishing between actuality and affectively cathected fantasy, and finally, the recognition that the unconscious can never be fully tamed by consciousness and hence that treatment, if seduction were the cause, could never be complete. Inasmuch as (*a*) Freud was aware of these arguments throughout, (*b*) some of them stand in sharp contrast to his explicit statements at earlier points, and (*c*) he retained his seduction theory for several months after this date, it is likely that additional factors influenced his writing, specifically at this time, a letter that was later construed as a formal letter of "abandonment." These factors may be better understood in light of Freud's later discussions of his early theories.

*Freud on His Mistakes*

The received and the revisionist histories of Freud's theorizing on seduction, antithetical versions of Freud's mistake(s), have in a major way neglected the details of Freud's own later accounts of his mistakes, accounts that are at some variance each from the other. By being attuned to these different versions offered by Freud, we can see some of the complexity of Freud's career-long struggle with his ideas on seduction, actual and imaginary.

The first mistake that Freud notes in his retrospective discussions of his early theories is his belief in the *etiological significance* of actual seduction. This mistake is prominent in Freud's first renouncement of his "neurotica" (letter to Fliess, 21 September 1897, 1985, 264–67), in his first *public* admission in 1906 (nine years later!) (*S. E.* 7) that his "seduction theory" was mistaken, and in a more implicit way in several writings before 1914 that touch upon the early theories (especially between 1905 and 1907). Freud's claim here is that in ascribing etiological significance to actual seduction and incest he had misestimated the general incidence of this phenomenon. Recognizing the disparity between the true incidence and that required by his seduction theory, it must be concluded that his theory is mistaken. However, Freud's statements about the direction of his mistaken estimate of the frequency of seduction are contradictory. In one place he asserts that the prevalence of seduction is too high, in another too low, for seduction to qualify as the etiological factor. In the famous September 1897 letter, for example, Freud writes of his realization of the "unexpected frequency of hysteria" and his concomitant realization that "surely such widespread perversions against children are not very probable." Similarly, in 1906 (*S.E.* 7:274) Freud discusses his error in terms of the "overestimat[ion of] . . . the frequency" of sexual seduction, which resulted from the chance fact that his sample contained a disproportionately large number of cases in which seduction played a part. In contrast in 1905, in *Three Essays on Sexuality* (*S.E.* 7:190), Freud asserts that in his early works on seduction he did not exaggerate "the frequency or importance" of actual seduction, but that he "did not then know that persons who remain normal may have had the same experiences in childhood" as neurotics. This position regarding the mistake is reiterated in 1907 (letter to Abraham, 5 July 1907, Abraham and Freud 1965).

The second mistake that Freud refers to in his discussions of his early views on seduction is his belief in the truth of his patients' reports concerning their alleged seduction. This mistake is first discussed in

1914 and is maintained throughout Freud's subsequent discussion of the topic. In *On the History of the Psycho-Analytic Movement* Freud describes his almost fatal mistake as follows: "Influenced by Charcot's view of the traumatic origin of hysteria, one was readily inclined to accept as true and aetiologically significant the statements made by patients in which they ascribed their symptoms to passive sexual experiences in the first years of childhood—to put it bluntly, to seduction" (*S.E.* 14:17).

In 1925 when he discusses his error in having "believed these [seduction] stories," the stories he refers to are more specific. "The part of seducer was almost always assigned to their father" (*S.E.* 20:34). This shift to the father continues and by 1932 Freud contends that "in the period in which the main interest was directed to discovering infantile sexual trauma, almost all my women patients told me that they had been seduced by their father" (*S.E.* 22:120).[4]

In contrast to the statistical argument that he puts forth in his discussion of his first mistake, here Freud claimed that what convinced him of his error was the discovery that the patients' reports were simply untrue—that they were found to be contradictory "in definitely ascertainable circumstances" (1914, *S.E.* 14:17).

Both the change in the nature of the mistake that Freud admits regarding his seduction theory and the relationship between his admissions and the actual course of events provide important information on Freud's theorizing on seduction and his own difficulties with that theorizing.

Regarding the relationship between the errors Freud admits to and the actual course of events, the following points should be noted:

1. In the course of the development of his ideas on seduction Freud was not oblivious to the various statistical arguments that could be leveled at his theories. On the contrary, he carefully developed counter-arguments and forcefully presented them in his defense. Freud's address to the Verein für Psychiatrie und Neurologie in 1896 (published as "The Aetiology of Hysteria") is relevant here, for he demonstrates the invalidity of "two mutually contradictory objections" (*S.E.* 3:207), namely, that the incidence of seduction is too high, and that the incidence is too low for seduction to count as an etiological factor.

2. Freud was well aware of the data on incidence. His various almost contemporaneous claims regarding his miscalculations of the incidence of seduction are inherently contradictory (i.e., too low; too high; low, but his sample was biased and had too high an incidence). Further, these claims also stand in contradiction both to Freud's admitted familiarity with the early data (before Havelock Ellis) on the

high incidence of seduction (1896, *S.E.* 3:209–10) and to his later claims that the reports of seduction presented to him by almost all his female patients were fantasized.

3. Freud's claim that he was misled by his patients' reports is questionable inasmuch as it is not at all clear that the evidence that emerged in the clinical setting was in the form of confession or admission of incest or sexual seduction. As suggested in our earlier discussion of Freud's evidence for his seduction theories, the conclusion that seduction occurred was often based on interpretation and reconstruction rather than on a simple announcement. Schimek (1987) argues this point convincingly, adding that Freud did not discredit reports about incest and seduction from the late childhood and adolescent years of his patients. In fact, sexual seduction that becomes known to the analyst through a simple announcement of its occurrence is, from the purely theoretical perspective of most of Freud's formulations of his seduction theory, of minor or no etiological relevance. As Freud explains, it is only unconscious memories of early infancy that have a pathogenic effect. As previously noted, Freud is inconsistent on the issue of the form in which the seduction is represented in the course of analytic treatment. However, from the purely theoretical perspective, the emergence of these infantile memories would have to be in the form of reproduction and thus open to and requiring interpretation.

4. Freud's assertion (from 1925 onward) that the reports, which he had mistakenly believed, incriminated fathers contradicts most of the data on the reports of seduction as presented while he maintained his seduction theories and as he described these reports in his renunciations before 1925. Particularly clear instances of contradiction become apparent from the examination of Freud's cumulative publications of his data in "Heredity and the Aetiology of the Neuroses" and "The Aetiology of Hysteria" (1896, *S.E.* 3). In the first, Freud refers to thirteen cases, in the other to eighteen cases. While the exact number of fathers is not noted, the possible range constitutes a small percentage of the broader group of perpetrators, which includes strangers, nursemaids, siblings, and others.[5]

These discrepancies between the actual course of Freud's theorizing and the course described in his retrospective views of that theorizing, as well as the changes these descriptions undergo with time, point to covert theoretical difficulties. Specifically, these difficulties pertain to obstacles in the development of Freud's specific theories, but in a broader sense they pertain to Freud's struggle with the process of theorizing within psychoanalysis. There is the struggle with the desire to discover the truths of the mind and their origin, and the fear that these discoveries are solely imaginary creations of our own observing minds, bearing little or no relationship to the real. While these different kinds of difficulties are intertwined, in the following passages we try to highlight some of the specific difficulties that at least in part determined Freud's contradictory presentations of his own theories.

We hypothesize that it was not the appearance of new evidence or form of argumentation per se that influenced Freud's original abandonment of his seduction theories. As we have seen, the evidence and arguments that Freud brings forth in his first public and private recantations of his theories of seduction were already known to him during the time when he was championing those very theories. We suggest rather that it was Freud's concerns with his own irrationality that played a crucial role in his 1897 turnabout. The Fliess correspondence documents Freud's concerns with his own "wildness," his own craziness. The Yiddish word for crazy, *meshugge*, occurs a number of times, especially in the letters in the period after his September 1897 renunciation of the seduction hypothesis (the letters of December 1897). Anna Freud and Ernst Kris struck out one important instance of this word (letter of 2 December 1987, Freud 1954) as part of their overall pattern of toning down Freud's own reports of his swings of thought and mood. But Freud himself censored such reports, primarily by never later referring to, let alone citing or publishing, his correspondence with Fliess. Basically he smoothed over the rough terrain—namely, his fears that the very theories he was devising about patients' confused use of fantasy and reality were also mixtures of fantasy and reality. We believe that it was Freud's self-analysis and the conscious and unconscious recognition gained therein of his personal influence on the data and the "wild" uses he made of it as he plunged forward with his new discoveries that led him to lose faith in the validity of his previous ideas.

One form of personal influence of particular interest is related to oedipal fantasy. It has been suggested by some analysts, and implied at points by Freud that it was the recognition that oedipal fantasy was the etiologically significant factor that led to the abandonment of the seduction theory. We have found that there was a more gradual development over a period of many years of the primacy of the oedipal fantasy as a causative factor in neurosis (Laplanche and Pontalis 1968; Simon and Blass 1992). Furthermore, the seduction theory is not instantly replaced with a theory centered on oedipal etiology. While the discovery of oedipal fantasy is thus not directly the basis for the abandonment of the seduction theory, we have found that Freud's growing recognition of its centrality exerted an important indirect effect. Our review of the relevant material leads to the speculation that it was the confrontation with his oedipal fantasies, which included seductive fantasies involving "the daughter," that led Freud to some form of awareness of the effect of these fantasies on his theory, his methods, and his relationships with his young female patients. He saw that the patient's reports of their fathers' acts were in accord with his own oedipal fantasies and thus were likely to be fantasy. But he also seems to have become more in touch with his fear that his seductive fantasies were having a real seductive effect on his patients and the kind of material they produced. Freud's "overaffectionate" dream about his daughter Mathilde (letter of 31 May 1897, 1985, 249) and his associated dream of being caught naked are part of the evidence for this speculation, as is his letter of 17 January 1897 about hysteria, the inquisitorial methods of questioning witches, and the indirect comparison of his treatment methods to the Inquistion's method of obtaining proof (1985, 224–25).[6]

With the entire foundation of his theory now cast in doubt, Freud tried to put aside for a while the whole complicated question of patients' reports and from whence they are derived. His focus shifted instead to the elaboration of a factor that could replace external sexual stimulation as the pathogenic motive force. When his ideas on the psychosexual stages and on their fixation were sufficiently elaborated, he believed he had found such a factor. Only then could he openly break with his earlier theories.[7] This explains the late date—1906—of the public announcement of his "mistake." Within this context we can understand Freud's acknowledgment between 1905 and 1907 of the very high incidence of seduction. With the move away from external factors and the shift to constitution (defined as the sequence of psychosexual stages), accidental influences were no longer considered very relevant. It would appear, furthermore, that the two early points at which Freud denies the high incidence mark his beginning to wonder why, if seduction is etiologically so irrelevant, the analyses repeatedly lead back to this event. Freud, however, seemed quite content to avoid dealing with that question for quite a few years. Both the question itself and Freud's willingness to put it aside appear to be related to his reluctance to take a closer look at what he had done in his early analyses.

Freud returns to this question when his theory of fantasy begins to be sufficiently strong to stand at the foundation of his explanation of patients' reports. This took quite some time, 1912–18 being the major years of its consolidation. Essential to the consolidation is the development of the idea that certain fantasies derive from our biological-historical heritage, the "phylogenetic phantasy" (Grubrich-Simitis 1988). Only with the emergence of this idea does Freud's nagging question of the internal origin of fantasy find a solution. With a "real" basis for fantasy secured, Freud can provide a more complete theoretical understanding of his patients' reports of seduction. It is thus in 1914 that Freud begins to talk of his mistake in believing those reports instead of recognizing them as oedipal fantasies.

It is important to take note here of what this focus on oedipal fantasy involves. It is often implied by psychoanalytic writers that what Freud recognized was that the reports were *derived* from oedipal fantasies—that is, that what was previously believed to be actual seduction in early childhood is now considered a fantasy created in early childhood. Close examination of Freud's writings, however, reveals that this view is not fully suggested and discussed until after 1918. Until that time Freud maintained that the fantasies that emerged in the course of analysis were later creations retroactively assigned to early childhood. This retroactive assignment is considered a defensive maneuver aimed at the concealment of infantile masturbation. Note, for example, Freud's remarks in 1914:

> If hysterical subjects trace back their symptoms to traumas that are fictitious, then the new fact which emerges is precisely that they create such scenes in *phantasy* ... This reflection was soon followed by the discovery that these phantasies were intended to cover up the autoerotic activity of the first years of childhood, to embellish it and raise it to a higher plane. And now, from behind the phantasies, the whole range of a child's sexual life came to light. [*S.E.* 14:17–18]

Freud here is still involved in the defensive creation of fantasies.

It would appear that one reason why even after having produced the conception of the phylogenetic fantasy Freud still focused on the defensive uses of oedipal fantasy has to do with the issue of age of the child. The universal fantasies that Freud introduces focus on the child's wishes between the ages of two and five. It is difficult to reconcile this with Freud's conception of infantile sexuality, which posits that from day one the person is vulnerable to pathogenic events. Freud struggles to establish a tie between fantasy and infantile experience. But can the preoedipal infant have oedipal fantasies? If he cannot, is there a period in which fantasy does not play a role? It seems that Freud could not ascribe fantasy a more causative role in the formation of neurosis until these questions were resolved. It would seem furthermore that Freud's ultimate solution to these questions emerges through the development of a theory of preoedipal fantasy.

We may now better understand Freud's later description of his patients' implications of their fathers. The claim that the father was always involved became theoretically consistent only after Freud had established for himself the universality and centrality of the oedipal fantasy. Further, he needed to integrate his conception of the oedipal fantasy with his idea that the motive forces of pathology lie in infantile sexuality beginning from earliest infancy. Thus, the present necessity for the role of the father in the oedipal fantasy led Freud to rewrite the earlier history of his theory. This rewriting made it seem that he had long and consistently held that the father was always, in one way or another, the agent of seduction.

Interestingly, once the universality of the fantasy and its early origin were firmly established it became increasingly difficult for Freud to maintain a clearcut distinction between neurosis and normality, both being directly motivated by the same internal fantastic forces. In this version of the central role of fantasy, paradoxically, the identity of the seducer is relatively accidental (though not unimportant). Thus Freud, in line with his notion of the early origin of neurosis, allowed the mother to play a major role as the first seducer. As Freud explains in 1931:

> Girls regularly accuse their mother of seducing them. This is because they necessarily received their first, or at any rate their strongest, genital sensations when they were being cleaned and having their toilet attended to by their mother. . . . The fact that the mother thus unavoidably initiates the child into the phallic phase is, I think, the reason why, in phantasies of later years, the father so regularly appears as the sexual seducer. When the girl turns away from her mother, she also makes over to her father her introduction into sexual life. [*S.E.* 21:238]

Importantly, the relationship between the actual conduct of the parent and the inborn fantasy remains problematic. That problematic relationship was imported into the notion of the preoedipal period even as the notion of the preoedipal period was devised in part to solve the problem of the relationship between the real and the fantastic in the oedipal period.

*Broader Implications*

As may be seen from this overview, Freud's writing and rewriting of his ideas on seduction had many explicit and implicit determinants.

We would like to briefly make note of two of them. The first is Freud's focal concern with the unitary and ultimate origin of neurosis. Freud struggles to understand the relationship between innate and environmental factors. His theoretical conceptualizing, however, contains, and is strongly influenced by, an undaunting search for the original source of motive, fantasy, and neurosis. The second determinant is Freud's preoccupation with the neuroses. While he was intrigued by all forms of thought and behavior, it was the neuroses that remained the source and the arena for his theorizing on pathology and the mind. Two important negative consequences derive from this preoccupation with neurosis. Firstly, his poignant awareness in his early writings of the distress and pain caused by adult seduction of the child is gradually eclipsed. Whatever his feelings may have been about the child's distress, that awareness could not easily find a place within his theorizing.[8] The second consequence is that it was difficult for Freud to appreciate and develop the idea that there were important pathological consequences of seduction and incest that contributed to disorders other than the classical neuroses. In this regard attention to one part of the field, the etiological role of fantasy for the neuroses, led to a relative neglect of the pathogenic trauma.

We began this chapter with a statement about the true history of an account of the real and the fantastic. Such phrases go to the heart of the matter in the writing of the history of Freud's seduction theories. Overall, we believe that psychoanalysis is constituted by a dialectic between fantasy and reality. This dialectic operates within the patient's efforts at constituting her or his own history, within the analyst's efforts to constitute the patient's history, and within the field's perception and construction of its own history. We must be prepared to accept the inevitable swings, too far in one direction or the other, in all three areas. Further, it is clear even in this brief survey that the definitions of the nature, influence, and origins of both reality and fantasy change over the course of the history of the field. The best of Freud's legacy is to take the relationship between reality and fantasy as a challenge to exploration and understanding. The worst is to opt for one or another form of final closure. The "received" view and the "revisionist" view of Freud's theorizing both exemplify reductionist allegiance to either reality or fantasy. Freud himself illustrates the best and the worst of Freud; this can be seen in our account of his writing and rewriting about the role of seduction.

As Freud struggled to elucidate the relative roles of fantasy and reality, he kept encountering his own worst fear, that his theories about reality and fantasy were all fantasy—"a fine frenzy," quotes Freud from Shakespeare's *Midsummer Night's Dream* (act 5, scene 1), also evoking "We are such stuff as dreams are made on" (1985, 251-52). At times he moved gracefully, at other times he lurched wildly, in his attempt to find the reality behind the fantasy and the fantasy elaboration of the reality. The reality of fantasy and the fantasy of reality were two solutions Freud formulated, as instantiated in infantile sexuality and phylogenetic inheritance. Within these and many other of Freud's attempts at solution we find both an insistence on some reality and, at the same time, an insistence on the "real" power of fantasy.

Man is a fantasy-making animal, and this is the unavoidable reality of the psychoanalytic method of inquiry. Hermeneutic approaches, taken to their extreme, have understood this reality as legitimizing a view that psychoanalysis only creates fantasies about fantasies. Causal explanatory approaches, taken to their extreme, have, in contrast, refused to accept this reality of fantasy. What we are proposing is that there is a real history, whether of the field or of the person. The delineation of that history is not immune from all of the forces that psychoanalysis has posited as shaping and distorting the person's account of his own life.

In our account of Freud on his mistakes we have exemplified how complicated is the task of laying out a full account of even the bare facts of what he wrote and when he wrote it. While we may have mistakes in our assemblage of the facts, let alone in our interpretations, there is an ascertainable factuality to the history. Remaining with the confusion of the known and the uncertainty about all that is unknown is indeed daunting, whether for an individual or for the field of psychoanalysis. Freud failed at points to strike some ideal balance, but his example is a cautionary tale. We know more now about the nature of his errors, but the "cautionary" part should remind us that we may be in the midst of creating other errors of which we are not yet aware.

We have also suggested that Freud's use of evidence, or rather the interplay of theorizing and evidence, was imperfect. Here, too, there is no one final answer, one final formula for arriving at the "perfect" admixture of theory and evidence. Like the problem of the relationship between reality and fantasy, this is an ongoing issue in psychoanalysis. This is the *reality* of our field—that we have a complex, shifting, dialectical relationship between evolving theories and evolving evidence.

## Notes

This work is supported by the Smolen Fellowship granted to Rachel Blass.

1. The last paper cited is based on a lecture Freud gave to the Verein für Psychiatrie und Neurologie. Freud reports that it was given "an icy reception," and Krafft-Ebing said it sounded like a scientific fairy tale (*S.E.* 3:189–90).

2. Masson (1984) points out that Anna Freud and Ernst Kris omitted this 12 December 1897 letter in their edition of the Freud-Fliess letters. Masson (1990) claims that Anna Freud wanted this letter omitted, lest "it confuse people." If Masson's report is accurate, it documents an important step in the construction and propagation of the "received view," an act of holding back contradictory evidence.

3. His anxiety about whether or not he is suggesting or coercing data is further seen in his discussion of the Inquisition's prosecution of witches and the implicit analogy to the analytic situation (Freud 1985, 224–25).

4. See his 1940 *An Outline of Psycho-Analysis* (*S.E.* 23:187–89) for his last "compromise" on the questions of etiology and incidence. Also, his statements there need to be considered in relation to all his efforts at integrative theories of the relationship between actual and fantasied experience. This topic requires detailed treatment in its own right.

5. Part of Freud's evidence for his seduction theories was his interviewing or treating several perpetrators of incest or seduction. He never renounces, reviews, or even mentions this evidence in his publications after 1897.

6. This is our reading of the dream of "Hella" (Mathilde) and the rest of the letter in which the dreams are reported. It is different from the interpretation given by Freud and by his biographers, e.g., Jones (1953, 322) and Gay (1988, 94).

7. Until 1906 Freud tended to emphasize the continuity of his early and later ideas. See, for example, the first volume of his collected works, published in 1906, shortly before his first public recantation of his seduction theories. In the preface he stresses that although he has at points gone beyond some of his early opinions, he has nevertheless "been able to retain the greater part of them unaltered and in fact [has] no need to withdraw anything as wholly erroneous or completely worthless" (*S.E.* 3:5–6).

8. At certain points Freud's early writings on the distress suffered through actual seduction (e.g., *S.E.* 3:215) resemble both in form and content Ferenczi's writings on the issue (1933 [1955]; 1933 [1988]). Ferenczi's writings, of course, were in part influenced by the early Freud but were denounced by the later Freud (Masson 1984; Simon, in press).

## References

Abraham, Hilda C., and Freud, Ernest L. *A Psychoanalytic Dialogue: The Letters of Sigmund Freud and Karl Abraham.* New York: Basic Books, 1965.

Blass, Rachel B. "Did Dora Have an Oedipus Complex? A Re-examination of the Theoretical Context of Freud's 'Fragment of an Analysis.'" *Psychoanalytic Study of the Child* (in press).

Ferenczi, Sandor. "On the Confusion of Tongues between Adults and the Child" (1933). In *Final Contributions to the Problems and Methods of Psychoanalysis*. New York: Basic Books, 1955.

―――. *The Clinical Diary of Sandor Ferenczi* (1933). Edited by Judith Dupont. Cambridge: Harvard University Press, 1988.

Fliess, Robert. "The Hypnotic Evasion." *Psychoanalytic Quarterly* 22 (1953): 497–511.

―――. *Erogeneity and Libido*. New York: International Universities Press, 1956.

―――. *Ego and Body Ego*. New York: International Universities Press, 1961.

―――. *Symbol, Dream, and Psychosis*. New York: International Universities Press, 1973.

Freud, Sigmund. *The Standard Edition of the Complete Psychological Works of Sigmund Freud*. Edited and translated by James Strachey. 24 vols. London: Hogarth Press, 1953–74.

"The Neuro-Psychoses of Defence" (1894), vol. 3.

"Project for a Scientific Psychology" (1895), vol 1.

*Studies on Hysteria* (1893-95), vol. 2.

"Heredity and the Aetiology of the Neuroses" (1896), vol. 3.

"Further Remarks on the Neuro-Psychoses of Defence" (1896), vol. 3.

"The Aetiology of Hysteria" (1896), vol. 3.

"Fragment of an Analysis of a Case of Hysteria" (1905), vol. 7.

*Three Essays on the Theory of Sexuality* (1905), vol. 7.

"My Views on the Part Played by Sexuality in the Aetiology of the Neuroses" (1906), vol. 7.

*On the History of the Psycho-Analytic Movement* (1914), vol. 14.

*An Autobiographical Study* (1925), vol. 20.

"Female Sexuality" (1931), vol. 21.

*New Introductory Lectures on Psycho-Analysis* (1932), vol. 22.

*An Outline of Psycho-Analysis* (1940), vol. 23.

―――. *The Origins of Psychoanalysis. Letters to Wilhelm Fliess, Drafts and Notes: 1887–1902*. Edited by Marie Bonaparte, Anna Freud, and Ernst Kris. Translated by Eric Mosbacher and James Strachey. New York: Basic Books, 1954.

―――. *The Complete Letters of Sigmund Freud to Wilhelm Fliess, 1887–1904*. Translated and edited by Jeffrey M. Masson. Cambridge: Harvard University Press, 1985.

Friedman, Lawrence. "Conflict and Synthesis in Freud's Theory of the Mind." *International Review of Psycho-Analysis* 4 (1977): 155–70.

Gay, Peter. *Freud: A Life for Our Time*. New York: Norton, 1988.

Grubrich-Simitis, Ilse. "Trauma or Drive—Drive and Trauma: A Reading of Sigmund Freud's Phylogenetic Fantasy of 1915." *Psychoanalytic Study of the Child* 43 (1988): 3–32.

Herman, Judith L. *Father-Daughter Incest*. Cambridge: Harvard University Press, 1981.

Jones, Ernest. *The Life and Work of Sigmund Freud*. Vol. 1, *The Formative Years and the Great Discoveries, 1856–1900*. New York: Basic Books, 1953.

Laplanche, J., and Pontalis, J.B. "Fantasy and Sexuality." *International Journal of Psycho-Analysis* 49 (1968): 1–18.

Masson, Jeffrey M. *The Assault on Truth*. New York: Farrar, Straus, Giroux, 1984.

———. *Final Analysis: The Making and Unmaking of an Analyst*. Boston: Addison-Wesley, 1990.

Miller, Alice. *Thou Shalt Not Be Aware: Society's Betrayal of the Child*. New York: Farrar, Straus, Giroux, 1984.

Russell, Diana E. H. *The Secret Trauma: Incest in the Lives of Girls and Women*. New York: Basic Books, 1986.

Sadow, Leo, Gedo, John E., Miller, James, and Pollock, George. "The Process of Hypothesis Change in Three Early Psychoanalytic Concepts." *Journal of the American Psychoanalytic Association* 16 (1968): 245–73.

Schimek, Jean G. "The Interpretations of the Past: Childhood Trauma, Psychical Reality, and Historical Truth." *Journal of the American Psychoanalytic Association* 23 (1975):845-65.

———. "Fact and Fantasy in the Seduction Theory: A Historical Review." *Journal of the American Psychoanalytic Association* 35 (1987): 937–65.

Schusdek, A. "Freud's 'Seduction Theory': A Reconstruction." *Journal of the History of the Behavioral Sciences* 2 (1968): 159–66.

Simon, Bennett. "'Incest: See Under Oedipus Complex': The History of an Error in Psychoanalysis." *Journal of the American Psychoanalytic Association* 39 (1991): 641–68.

Simon, Bennett, and Blass, Rachel B. "The Development and Vicissitudes of Freud's Ideas on the Oedipus Complex." In *The Cambridge Companion to Freud*, edited by J. Neu. New York: Cambridge University Press, 1992.

Stewart, Walter A. *Psychoanalysis: The First Ten Years*. London: George Unwin, 1967.

Sulloway, Frank G. *Freud: Biologist of the Mind*. New York: Basic Books, 1979.

# 8    The Quicksands of the Self:
Nella Larsen and Heinz Kohut

## Barbara Johnson

Nella Larsen's first novel, *Quicksand*, was published in 1928, at the height of that period of black migration from the rural South to the urban North that led to the explosion in cultural and artistic creativity known as the Harlem Renaissance. The novel was immediately greeted with enthusiasm: it won second prize in literature from the Harmon Foundation, and W. E. B. Du Bois called it "the best piece of fiction that Negro America has produced since the heyday of Chesnutt."[1] Readers then and now have indeed read the novel as a dramatization of racial double consciousness,[2] in the form of the all-too-familiar topos of the tragic mulatto. Nathan Huggins, in *The Harlem Renaissance*, writes:

> Nella Larsen came as close as any to treating human motivation with complexity and sophistication. But she could not wrestle free of the mulatto condition that the main characters in her two novels had been given. Once she made them mulatto and female the conventions of American thought—conditioned by the tragic mulatto and the light-dark heroine formulas—seemed to take the matter out of the author's hands. [Huggins 1971, 236]

In other words, Larsen's attempt to present the inner life of her main character was subverted by the force of a literary cliché designed to rob the character of any inner life by subjecting her to a tragic "condition."

The mulatto image, a staple of nineteenth-century literature both by white "plantation school" writers and by black and white abolitionist writers, is less a reflection of a social or sociological reality

184

than it is a literary and mythic device for both articulating and concealing the racial history of this country. Critics such as Barbara Christian, Hazel Carby, and Hortense Spillers have analyzed the ways in which the mulatto represents both a taboo and a synthesis, both the product of a sexual union that miscegenation laws tried to rule out of existence and an allegory for the racially divided society as a whole, both un-American and an image of America as such. In an essay entitled "Notes on an Alternative Model—Neither/Nor," Hortense Spillers writes:

> Created to provide a middle ground of latitude between "black" and "white," the customary and permissible binary agencies of the national adventure, mulatto being, as a neither/nor proposition, inscribed no historic locus, or materiality, that was other than evasive and shadowy on the national landscape. To that extent, the mulatto/a embodied an alibi, an excuse for "other/otherness" that the dominant culture could not (cannot now either) appropriate, or wish away. An accretion of signs that embody the "unspeakable" of the Everything that the dominant culture would forget, the mulatto/a, as term, designates a disguise, covers up, in the century of Emancipation and beyond, the social and political reality of the dreaded African presence. Behind the African-become-American stands the shadow, the unsubstantial "double" that the culture dreamed *in the place of* that humanity transformed into its profoundest challenge and by the impositions of policy, its deepest "un-American" activity. [Spillers 1989, 165–66]

Nella Larsen herself suggests that her novel should be read through the grid of the mulatto figure by choosing as her epigraph a stanza from a Langston Hughes poem entitled "Cross":

> My old man died in a fine big house.
> My ma died in a shack.
> I wonder where I'm gonna die,
> Being neither white nor black?

Where one might expect a both/and, we find, as Spillers and Hughes suggest, a neither/nor. Nella Larsen's project in *Quicksand* is to tell the story of the neither/nor self from within.

The question of that neither/nor of racial designation is tied, both in the epigraph and in the novel, to the question of *place*: shack or big house, North or South, Europe or America. In the Hughes poem, the father is white, the mother black. This corresponds to the historical realities of the sexual abuse of slave women by white slaveholders. Nella Larsen's protagonist's parentage, however, is reversed: her mother is a Danish immigrant and her father is a black American. This, I think, further complicates the question of race and place, both socially and geographically. The first sentence of the novel, "Helga Crane sat alone in her room," echoes not only the "ins" of the epigraph but even its very rhythm. The last clause of the opening paragraph of the novel continues that rhythm: "Helga Crane never opened her door." It is as though the novel originates within the "stanza" (which etymologically means "room") of its epigraph. The question of place thus intersects with a question of space, of personal space, of the inside/outside boundaries of the self. Helga Crane's closed door circumscribes a space filled with small luxuries: a Chinese carpet, a brass bowl, nasturtiums, oriental silk. Her room symbolizes the issue of the self as a container (of value, positive or negative). And the title, *Quicksand*, extends the metaphor of space in a nightmarish direction: the self is utterly engulfed by the outside because there is nothing outside the engulfing outside to save it.

What, then, is the nature of the quicksand into which Helga Crane sinks in Nella Larsen's novel? Critics have offered various answers. Hiroko Sato writes: "The title, *Quicksand*, signifies the heroine Helga Crane's sexual desire, which was hidden beneath her beautiful and intelligent surface and came up at an unexpected moment and trapped her" (1972, 84). For Deborah McDowell, Hortense Thornton, and Cheryl Wall, on the other hand, it is not Helga's sexuality that has trapped her but rather her attempts to disavow it—her own and society's contradictory responses to it. To be respectable as a "lady" is to have no sexuality; to have sexuality is to be a jungle creature, an exotic primitive, or an oppressed wife and mother. These readings, which focus on the centrality of black female sexuality, are responses to earlier readings (mostly by male critics), which focused on the problems of the biracial self. As Deborah McDowell puts it explicitly, "In focusing on the problems of the 'tragic mulatto,' readers miss the more urgent problem of the female sexual identity which Larsen tried to explore" (Larsen 1986, xvii). And Cheryl Wall writes:

> Helga's interracial parentage—her father is black and her mother white—troubles her too, but it is not the primary cause of her unease. Her real struggle is against imposed definitions of blackness and womanhood. Her "difference" is ultimately her refusal to accept society's terms even in the face of her inability to define alternatives. . . . *Passing*, like *Quicksand*, demonstrates Larsen's ability to explore the psychology of her characters. She exposes the sham that is middle-class security, especially for women whose total dependence is morally debilitating. The absence of meaningful work and community condemn them to the "walled prison" of their own thoughts. . . . As these characters deviate from the

norm, they are defined—indeed too often define themselves—as Other. They thereby cede control of their lives. But, in truth, the worlds these characters inhabit offer them no possibility of autonomy or fulfillment. [Wall 1986, 109]

As these critics make clear, *Quicksand* is a complex analysis of the intersections of gender, sexuality, race, and class. It seems, therefore, somehow regressive and discordant to ask what use a psychoanalytic perspective might be in understanding the novel. How can any insight be gained into all these structures by focusing on intrapsychic processes? Yet the inside/outside opposition on which such scruples are based is one that the novel constantly forces us to reexamine. It will also, I hope, force us to reexamine that opposition in the assumptions and interpretive frames of psychoanalysis.

As we have seen, critics often praise Larsen for her psychological sophistication, but then go on to interpret the novel in social, economic, and political terms. Such readings illuminate many aspects of the novel but leave certain questions untouched. How, for example, can one account for the self-defeating or self-exhausting nature of Helga Crane's choices? At several points, Helga achieves economic autonomy—when teaching in a southern black college or when working for an insurance company in New York—but she seems each time all too ready to flee to dependency. Economic autonomy does not provide something that economic dependency seems to promise. Then, too, Helga repeatedly reaches states of relative contentment—in Harlem, in Denmark, in Alabama—only to fall into depression again for no obvious reason. Chapter breaks often occur where psychological causation is missing. It is the *lack* of precipitating cause that calls for explanation. And it is the difficulty of defining the causes of Helga's suffering that leads to irritation in many readers. Mary Helen Washington summarizes a common reaction to the novel, before going on to critique the terms of such a reaction:

> Nella Larsen ... published two novels, *Quicksand* and *Passing*, which dealt with this same problem: the marginal black woman of the middle class who is both unwilling to conform to a circumscribed existence in the black world and unable to move freely in the white world. We may perhaps think this a strange dilemma for a black woman to experience, or certainly an atypical one, for most black women then, as now, were struggling against much more naked and brutal realities and would be contemptuous of so esoteric a problem as feeling uncomfortable among black people and unable to sort out their racial identity. We might justifiably wonder, is there anything relevant, in the lives of women who arrogantly expected to live in Harlem, in the middle-

class enclave of Sugar Hill, to summer at resorts like Idlewild in Michigan, to join exclusive black clubs and sororities? Weren't the interests that preoccupied Larsen in her work just the spoiled tantrums of "little yellow dream children" grown up? [Washington 1987, 159–60]

The Harlem Renaissance was indeed the literary coming-of-age of the black middle class, but as Hazel Carby and others have pointed out, it was as much a critique of middle-class values as an espousal of them. But the description of Helga Crane's problems as "esoteric," "arrogant," and "spoiled" suggests to me a parallel with the vague, ill-defined complaints of the middle-class patients treated by Heinz Kohut under the category of "narcissistic personality disorders." I will therefore turn to the work of Kohut as a framework for understanding what Larsen understood about the psychological effects of social conflicts, and then I will take Nella Larsen as a framework for questioning the limits of Kohut's description of the phenomenon he calls narcissism. But first, a summary of the novel and of Kohut's theory of narcissism.

The novel opens with Helga Crane's resolution to leave Naxos, the stifling black school where she teaches, because rather than stimulating growth and creativity in its students, it teaches conformity, low horizons of expectation, and imitation of middle-class white values. She goes to the office of the principal, Robert Anderson, to hand in her resignation and is momentarily tempted by his discourse on service into reconsidering, until he inadvertently insults her and she flees to Chicago, where her white uncle, her mother's brother, Peter Nilssen, lives. Hoping to enlist Nilssen's support while she looks for a new job, she encounters his new white wife, who wants nothing to do with her husband's sister's mulatto daughter. Thrown on her own resources, Helga is rejected for a library job because she lacks "references" and for domestic work because she is too refined. Eventually she gets a job as a speech editor for a prominent "race woman," Mrs. Hayes-Rore, through whom she finds work in an insurance company in New York.

In New York, Helga lives with Mrs. Hayes-Rore's elegant niece, Anne Grey, through whom she gets to know Harlem's glittering society life and, for a time, feels quite contented. But her contentment doesn't last, and when a check arrives from the remorseful Uncle Peter, Helga sails to Denmark, where she lives with her mother's relatives, the Dahls. There, she is treated as an exotic treasure, dressed and wined and dined in splendor, and courted by the famous painter Axel Olsen, who paints her portrait, propositions her sexually, and, in the face of her nonresponse, asks her to marry him. Insulted by the way in which the proposal expresses his generosity and her objectification, she refuses. Homesick for Harlem, she returns to New York for the marriage of Anne Grey and Robert Anderson. Later, at a party, Anderson kisses her, and she is overwhelmed with desire. At a later meeting she intends to give herself to him, but he wants only to apologize and reestablish distance. In despair, she walks into a church, has an intense conversion experience, sleeps with the black minister, Rev. Pleasant Green, marries him, and goes south with him to his rural congregation, where she is soon buried in the physical exhaustion of bearing and caring for four children. As the novel ends, she sees nothing in her environment to value and is pregnant with her fifth child.

Heinz Kohut is known for having developed a psychoanalytic theory of what he called "self-psychology." Lacanians have seen this theory as an example of entrapment in the fictions of the autonomous self generated by the mirror stage. While such a critique may be justified, I prefer to see Kohut's work as a parallel and much richer exploration of structures of mirroring, of which the mirror stage is one example.

What does Kohut mean by a self? The self, he writes, should not be confused with the ego. The self is not a subject. The self is an image, a representation. Indeed, simultaneous contradictory self-representations may exist in a person. "The self, then, quite analogous to the representations of objects, is a *content* of the mental apparatus but is not . . . one of the *agencies* of the mind" (Kohut 1971, xv). How is the self formed? Kohut answers: through empathic mirroring. The self is the internalization of the gaze of the other, generally the mother in Kohut's account. Instead of Lacan's statuelike visual self-representation in the mirror, for which the mother serves only as a baby stand, Kohut's self-representation derives from the approval-conveying "gleam in the mother's eye." In the early stages of the formation of the self, therefore, other people are not perceived as separate, true objects, but as parts of the self, as "selfobjects." Other people, including sexual partners and, especially for Kohut, psychoanalysts, can continue to function as selfobjects throughout a person's life.

The psychological structures appropriate to the earliest phase in the development of the self, according to Kohut, are the grandiose, exhibitionistic self ("I am perfect") and the idealized, omnipotent selfobject based on the parent ("you are perfect, but I am part of you"). "The need of the budding self for the joyful response of the mirroring selfobject, the need of the budding self for the omnipotent selfobject's pleased acceptance of its merger needs, are primary considerations." If the child is not appropriately mirrored, is not given the message, "What you are is valuable," at this stage, then the grandiose self and the desire to merge with the idealized selfobject do not fade away but become split off and retain their archaic demands. Rather than being progressively reality-tested and integrated, they keep the unfilled hunger for validation intact, like an open wound. This, I think, is what Helga refers to as "a lack somewhere." Like Helga, the patients Kohut analyzes often have considerable talent and strong aesthetic investments. And, like Helga, they have a tendency to "react to sources of narcissistic disturbance by mixtures of wholesale withdrawal and unforgiving rage" (65). Periods of heightened vitality and contentment are followed by a renewed sense of depletion, often brought about either by the anxiety that arises from an uncomfortable degree of excitement or by a rebuff or merely a lack of attention from the environment. Kohut's theory is, among other things, a revaluation of the moral valence of the term "narcissism," which is based not on self-satisfaction but on hollowness. Helga's apparent selfishness is based not on an excess of self but on a lack of self.

What does the novel tell us about the origins of Helga's narcissistic deficit? What kind of early mirroring did she receive? Her father, a black man she refers to as a gambler and a "gay suave scoundrel," deserted her mother, a Danish immigrant, before Helga could form any definite relation to him. The mother, "sad, cold, and remote," remarried, this time choosing a white man who treated Helga with malicious and jealous hatred. Helga thus has no early relations with black people, except the image of her father as both desirable and unreliable, and she has increasingly negative relations with the white people who are her only family. But instead of becoming enraged at their lack of empathy for her, she actually learns to empathize with their view of her as a problem *for them*. "She saw herself for an obscene sore in all their lives, at all costs to be hidden. She understood, even while she resented. It would have been easier if she had not" (Larsen 1986, 29). In other words, she learns to identify with the rejecting other, to desire her own disappearance. Intimacy equals rejection; the price of intimacy is to satisfy the other's desire that she disappear. To be is not to be. It is no wonder that Helga's mode is flight and that her first spoken words in the novel are, "No, forever." The culminating scene of orgasmic conversion in the church is a stark acting out of the logic of self-erasure in a merger with the omnipotent other. As the church service begins, a hymn is being sung:

> Oh, the bitter shame and sorrow
> That a time could ever be,
> When I let the Savior's pity

Plead in vain, and proudly answered:
All of self and none of Thee,
All of self and none of Thee. . . .

As the hymn continues, the refrain changes:

Some of self and some of Thee,
Some of self and some of Thee. . . .

Then:

Less of self and more of Thee,
Less of self and more of Thee. . . .

Then, at the moment Helga surrenders to the conversion, the moment
the text says, "She was lost—or saved," the hymn's final refrain is
acted out, but not stated:

None of self and all of Thee,
None of self and all of Thee.

The religious conversion, the merger with the omnipotent selfobject,
momentarily overcomes the self's isolation but at the cost of the self's
disappearance. The narcissistic plot here merges with the oedipal plot:
Helga's life, like her mother's, is drastically transformed by a moment
of blind surrender.

This ecstatic disappearance is only the culmination of a series of
encounters in the novel that present the narcissistic logic in other,
less drastic, terms. Each time, Helga's vulnerable and defensively haughty
self approaches a potential mirror and is, or perceives itself to be,
mismirrored. I will analyze two of these moments, the opening encounter with Robert Anderson and the encounter with the Danish
painter, Axel Olsen.

Robert Anderson is the principal of the black school in which Helga
is teaching at the start of the novel. She has become enraged at the
school for its low, self-denying expectations of its educational mission;
it accepts the image of blacks as hewers of wood and drawers of water,
which has just been repeated to the assembled school by a white
preacher. Helga has decided to leave the school immediately and must
tell Anderson her reasons. As she waits for him to receive her, she
thinks about the school's disapproval of her love for bright colors and
beautiful clothes. Upon entering his office, she sees "the figure of a
man, at first blurred slightly in outline in that dimmer light." She feels
confusion, "something very like hysteria," then a mysterious ease. She
begins to explain her resignation to Dr. Anderson in an exchange that
very much resembles an initial psychoanalytic session: he remains

detached, prompting her to elaborate on her remarks, probing for her thoughts. She explains that she hates hypocrisy and the suppression of individuality and beauty. He then begins a discourse of "wisdom," telling her that lies, hypocrisy, and injustice are part of life that dedicated people put up with when their goals are high. The text describes Helga's reactions:

> Helga Crane was silent, feeling a mystifying yearning which sang and throbbed in her. She felt again that urge for service, not now for her people, but for this man who was talking so earnestly of his work, his plans, his hopes. An insistent need to be a part of them sprang up in her. With compunction tweaking at her heart for ever having entertained the notion of deserting him, she resolved not only to remain until June, but to return next year. [20]

In this scene, then, Helga enters with a sense of her embattled grandiose self (her esthetic difference, her individuality and creativity) but is drawn toward the appeal of the omnipotent selfobject, the merger with the idealized other. That merger can only exist, however, on the basis of perfect empathy. Anderson inadvertently breaks that empathy in the very words he uses to solidify it:

> "What we need is more people like you, people with a sense of values, and proportion, an appreciation of the rarer things of life. You have something to give which we badly need here in Naxos. You mustn't desert us, Miss Crane."
> She nodded, silent. He had won her. She knew that she would stay. "It's an elusive something," he went on. "Perhaps I can best explain it by the use of that trite phrase, 'You're a lady.' You have dignity and breeding."
> At these words turmoil rose again in Helga Crane. The intricate pattern of the rug which she had been studying escaped her. The shamed feeling which had been her penance evaporated. Only a lacerated pride remained. She took firm hold of the chair arms to still the trembling of her fingers.
> "If you're speaking of family, Dr. Anderson, why, I haven't any. I was born in a Chicago slum."
> The man chose his words, carefully he thought. "That doesn't at all matter, Miss Crane. Financial, economic circumstances can't destroy tendencies inherited from good stock. You yourself prove that!"
> Concerned with her own angry thoughts, which scurried here and there like trapped rats, Helga missed the import of his words. Her own words, her answer, fell like drops of hail.
> "The joke is on you, Dr. Anderson. My father was a gambler who deserted my mother, a white immigrant. It is even uncertain that they

were married. As I said at first, I don't belong here. I shall be leaving at once. This afternoon. Good-morning." [20–21]

In the act of delivering a compliment, Anderson puts his finger on a wound. By juxtaposing the word "lady" (which at Naxos signifies the denial of sexuality) and the word "breeding" (which for Helga is the name both for forbidden sexuality and for lack of family), he shows not only that he is not omnipotent (since he does not really know anything about her) but that what he wants to value in her is something she thinks she does not and cannot possess. The mirror breaks, the pattern in the rug loses its design, Helga fragments into chaotically scattering pieces, and she departs in a narcissistic rage.

In Denmark, Helga is drawn to the symmetrically opposite kind of narcissistic satisfaction. There, it is her grandiose exhibitionism that is initially mirrored, rather than her desire to merge with the idealized other. Whereas Helga's difference and fine clothes have been met with hostility and disapproval in the United States, the Danes are fascinated. They urge her to become more exhibitionistic, more exotic, more sensuous. Yet they are at the same time cold and detached. Instead of being repressed, Helga's exhibitionism is expropriated, objectified, commodified, alienated. This process comes to a head in her relation to Axel Olsen, the portrait painter. When she looks at the portrait he has painted of her, she is represented as thinking "it wasn't herself at all, but some disgusting sensual creature with her features. Bosh! pure artistic bosh and conceit! Nothing else." This has often been read as her refusal to acknowledge her own sexuality. But I think that, far from constituting a mirror designed to confirm her sexuality, this mirror gives her only someone else's narcissistic appropriation of it. She refuses the painter's offer of marriage out of a refusal to be owned by a white man. It is in Denmark that she first feels homesick for Negroes and first identifies with, and forgives, her father. She returns to Harlem.

Several times in the novel, the potential mirror is not a person but a race, a "world." When Helga first arrives in Harlem, she feels keenly a "joy at seeming at last to belong somewhere." When she first arrives in Denmark, too, she tells herself that "this, then was where she belonged." Yet each time the surrounding mirror is incapable of sustaining the role of selfobject which she asks of it. The promise of belonging flips over into a pressure to conform. Each mirror limits even as it embraces. But instead of seeing that therefore she herself is composite, a mixture, a process rather than a product, that wholeness itself is a fiction—the problem and not the solution—she goes on believing that both she and the environment can be perfected, made whole, non-self-different. For Helga, there is no middle, no compromise, no gray area—satisfaction must be total, pure, and therefore unreal, short-lived. She seeks to fill her narcissistic deficit with the environment, not for its own properties but in the attempt to substitute for a missing part of the self. The line between remedy and poison is thin: the magical selfobject must inevitably oppress and disappoint.

What is different about Nella Larsen's treatment of these dynamics is that she shows race itself to be a kind of selfobject from which a self can derive both positive and negative mirroring. Kohut occasionally suggests as much, as when, in a footnote, he writes:

> It may be helpful to say that the grandiose self ... has such analogues in adult experience as, e.g., national and racial pride and prejudice (everything good is "inside," everything bad and evil is assigned to the "outsider"), while the relationship to the idealized parent imago may have its parallel in the relationship (including mystical mergers) of the true believer to his God. [1971, 27]

As an analysis of the narcissistic roots of racism and race pride, this is quite convincing. But it fails to account for the fact that what is a narcissistic structure for the individual is also a social, economic, and political structure in the world. Racial pride and prejudice are not merely interpersonal phenomena but institutionalized structures in history and culture. In dealing with individual patients, Kohut generally neglects or subsumes the *social* mirroring environment in favor of the dynamics of the nuclear family. The following is a fairly striking example:

> Over and over again, throughout his childhood, the patient ... had felt abruptly and traumatically disappointed in the power and efficacy of his father just when he had (re-)established him as a figure of protective strength and efficiency. ... After an adventurous flight via South Africa and South America, the family had come to the United States when the patient was nine years old, and the father, who had been a prosperous businessman in Europe, was unable to repeat his earlier success in this country. ... Most prominent among the patient's relevant recollections of earlier occurrences of the idealization-disappointment sequence concerning his father were those of the family's first years in Eastern Europe. ... Suddenly the threat that the German armies would overrun the country interrupted their close relationship. At first the father was away a great deal, trying to make arrangements for the transfer of his business to another country. Then, when the patient was six, German armies invaded the country and the family, which was Jewish, fled. [58–60]

The minor role played in the last sentence by the fact that the family was Jewish is an indication of Kohut's overestimation of the nuclear family as the context for psychic development.

What Nella Larsen does is to articulate the relation between the mirroring environment of the nuclear family and the social messages from the environment, which *also* affect the construction of the self. It is as though, for Kohut, the child has no independent experience of history, no relation to the world that is not filtered through the parental imagoes. Yet the social world can indeed set up an artificially inflated or deflated narcissistic climate for the child. Racial privilege would offer an unearned archaic narcissistic bonus that, when threatened, would lead to the characteristic narcissistic rages of racism just as surely as the undeserved narcissistic injury resulting from the insertion of a black child into a hostile white environment would lead to the kinds of precarious self-consolidation Larsen documents in the absence of a strong black mirroring environment.

No matter how empathic a mother or father might be, a parent cannot always offset the formative mirroring of the environment. Indeed, in Kohut, the burden of good mirroring falls, again and again, on the mother. His case histories sound like accusations against the mother, whose own context or needs are not analyzed. What Nella Larsen does is to locate the failures of empathy not in the mother but in the impossible ways in which the mother finds herself inscribed in the social order. Neither for Helga's mother nor for Helga herself as mother at the end of the novel is the social order nourishing, or even viable. And the split between fathers—the absent black father and the rejecting white father—cannot be understood apart from the stereotypical overdeterminations of such a split in American society as a whole.

The therapeutic desire to effect change in the self alone amputates the energies of change from their connections with the larger social and economic world. As Hazel Carby has written of *Quicksand*,

> Alienation is often represented as a state of consciousness, a frame of mind. Implied in this definition is the assumption that alienation can be eliminated or replaced by another state of consciousness, a purely individual transformation unrelated to necessary social or historical change. Helga does question the possibility that her recurrent dissatisfaction with her life could be due to her state of mind and that if she could change her attitudes she could be happy. But against this Larsen has placed an alternative reading of Helga's progress, that her alienation was not just in her head but was produced by existing forms of social

relations and therefore subject to elimination only by a change in those social relations. [Carby 1987, 169]

As this quotation makes clear, Larsen herself does not ask the reader to *choose* between a psychic and a social model, but rather to see the articulations between them. To see Helga purely from the inside or purely from the outside is to miss the genius of the text. It is the inside/outside opposition itself that needs to be questioned.

In addition to questioning the inside/outside opposition as an adequate model for the relation between the self and society, Larsen's novel also provides material for a critique of the conception of the self as a locus of value. Throughout this chapter, I have echoed and extended Kohut's economic vocabulary of narcissistic investments, deficits, and assets, emphasizing the ways in which Helga Crane alternates between surplus value and lack, grandiosity and worthlessness, between an image of herself as a luxury item and an image of herself as garbage. What luxury and garbage have in common is that each is a form of excess with respect to an economy of use or need. Thus, for instance, after humiliating rejections by Uncle Peter's new wife and by the library personnel, Helga spends what little money she has on a book and a tapestry purse, "which she wanted but did not need," and resolves to go without dinner, attempting to fulfill a narcissistic hunger in preference to a physical one. As long as need is ignored, however, the narcissistic imbalance cannot be rectified. This emphasis on the isolated self as a locus of value (positive or negative) risks duplicating, in the psychological realm, the structures Marx identified as "the fetishism of the commodity"—the belief that the commodity, abstracted from both labor and use, "contains" value in and of itself. Both Larsen and Kohut indeed analyze a self that is very much structured like a commodity. This returns us to the perceived middle-classness of both Larsen and Kohut: it may well be that both the concept of the self and the analytical framework through which we have been discussing it can themselves be analyzed as artifacts of class.

I would like to pursue this question indirectly by turning to a domain that lies in an intermediary position between the psychic and the social and economic. This is the domain of cultural forms. Kohut often mentions the role of aesthetic investments in consolidating a cohesive self, even in the face of early traumatic environments (an incubator baby, children from concentration camps). Larsen has often been criticized for her lack of investment in African-American cultural forms, which appear in ambivalent or degraded guises in her novels (the black church, the rural folk, the black educational establishment, the cabaret, the singers Helga sees in Denmark). But these forms also exert a powerful attraction in the novels, which is what gives the forms so much power to disappoint. Hearing the strains of "Swing Low, Sweet Chariot" in Dvorak's *New World* Symphony, Helga is over-whelmed with the desire to be carried home.

The final chapter in Larsen's life as a writer is instructive in this context as a bringing together of questions of culture, narcissism, and economics. After her two very successful novels, Larsen wrote a short story entitled "Sanctuary," in which a black woman harbors a fugitive from justice only to find out that the man she is protecting has killed her own son, Obadiah. The last paragraph of the story reads

> It seemed a long time before Obadiah's mother spoke. When she did there were no tears, no reproaches; but there was a raging fury in her voice as she lashed out, "Git outen mah feather baid, Jim Hammer, an' outen mah house, an' don' nevah stop thankin' yo' Jesus he done gib you dat black face." [Larsen 1930, 18]

The character and the plot were an unusual affirmation of black folk speech and racial solidarity for Larsen. But upon its publication she found herself accused of plagiarism: another writer, Sheila Kaye-Smith, had published a strikingly similar story entitled "Mrs. Adis" about white laborers in Sussex eight years earlier. Larsen responded by saying that she had heard the story from an old black patient in the hospital where she worked as a nurse, and her publisher produced several of her drafts. She was more or less exonerated. Mary Dearborn, in *Pocahontas's Daughters*, raises questions about the nature of ethnic authorship on the basis of this event:

> Whether Larsen plagiarized from "Mrs. Adis," was influenced by or unconsciously borrowed from it is not the point. . . . Rather, it is sig-nificant that Larsen's choice of material left her open for such a charge in just this way. Again, ethnic authorship seems to hinge on the own-ership of stories. Does the woman who sets down a folk tale then own the tale? Are folk tales fit matter for fiction? Because Larsen set down a story told her by another woman, is she then the author of that fiction? If Larsen had set it all down as it happened—recounting her meeting with the black patient, then the story—would "Sanctuary" be fiction? [Dearborn 1986, 57]

What becomes clear in this discussion is that the question of the boundaries of the self can arise in ways that transcend the purely psychic domain while still opening up the possibility of a devastating narcissistic wound. If authorship is ownership, how can folk material be one's own? When oral sources are written down, to whom do they belong? (This question could indeed be asked of the debt psychoanalytic theory owes to the oral histories of analysands.)[3] What is the property status of a common heritage? In this case, it is not even clear that the story "belongs" to the black tradition, since the other version concerns white workers. If Larsen was writing out of a sense of still precarious loyalty to a tradition and a people about whom her other works express more ambivalence, then there is an ironic parallel between the story and its publication. Like the protagonist of the story, Larsen, out of an act of racial solidarity, has harbored a fugitive who turns out to take away her own literary offspring. This is not the fault of the sanctuary, or of the fugitive, but of the laws of ownership and cultural heritage that define the self as property and literature in terms of the authorial proper name. We will never know what Nella Larson might have written next, or what other stories her patients told her. After the exposure and shame of her aborted "Sanctuary," she traveled on a Guggenheim fellowship to Europe and then returned to nursing for the next thirty years. She never published again.

Nella Larsen has often been conflated with her heroines, whose narcissistic predicaments she is seen to share. In ending my discussion with her silence, I am making the same equation. But while her disappearance from the publishing world may well be a narcissistic withdrawal, I think it is important not to equate her novels with her psyche. As fully realized representations of intricate social and psychic structures, they are more like analyses than like symptoms. The Helga Crane of the novel is never in a position to write the novel *Quicksand*. As is the case for many similar writers — Baudelaire and Dostoevsky come immediately to mind — it is, after all, Nella Larsen who provides all the insight that enables readers to feel that they understand more about Nella Larsen than Nella Larsen does. Which does not mean that the insight is the cure. The literature of narcissism does not satisfy the desire for a workable program for social change, but it does offer the warning that any political program that ignores the ways in which the self can refuse to satisfy need or can seek self-cancellation in place of self-validation will not understand where certain resistances are coming from.

## Notes

1. Quoted by Deborah McDowell in her introduction to Nella Larsen, *"Quicksand" and "Passing"* (1986, ix). All references to *Quicksand* are to this edition.

2. Cf. Du Bois's famous formulation from *The Souls of Black Folk*: "It is a peculiar sensation, this double-consciousness, this sense of always looking at one's self through the eyes of others, of measuring one's soul by the tape of a world that looks on in amused contempt and pity. One ever feels his twoness,—an American, a Negro; two souls, two thoughts, two unreconciled strivings; two warring ideals in one dark body, whose dogged strength alone keeps it from being torn asunder" (1965, 215).

3. I would like to thank Beth Helsinger for suggesting this.

## References

Carby, Hazel. *Reconstructing Womanhood*. New York: Oxford University Press, 1987.

Dearborn, Mary V. *Pocahontas's Daughters*. New York: Oxford University Press, 1986.

Du Bois, W. E. B. *Three Negro Classics*. New York: Avon, 1965.

Huggins, Nathan. *The Harlem Renaissance*. New York: Oxford University Press, 1971.

Kohut, Heinz. *The Analysis of the Self*. New York: International Universities Press, 1971.

Larsen, Nella. "Sanctuary." *The Forum*, January 1930.

———. *"Quicksand" and "Passing."* New Brunswick: Rutgers University Press, 1986.

Sato, Hiroko. "Under the Harlem Shadow: A Study of Jessie Fauset and Nella Larsen." In *The Harlem Renaissance Remembered*, edited by Arna Bontemps. New York: Dodd, Mead, 1972.

Spillers, Hortense. "Notes on an Alternative Model—Neither/Nor." In *The Difference Within*, edited by Elizabeth Meese and Alice Parker. Philadelphia: John Benjamins, 1989.

Wall, Cheryl. "Passing for What? Aspects of Identity in Nella Larsen's Novels." *Black American Literature Forum* 20 (1986): nos. 1–2.

Washington, Mary Helen. *Invented Lives*. Garden City, N.Y.: Anchor, 1987.

# 9    Transformations:
      Psychoanalytical and Political

## Richard H. King

Central to the narrative of modernity is the theme of the de-mystification of the world and the growing secularization of culture. Despite this historical development, the search for ways to transform the self has scarcely abated. Indeed, the decline of institutional religion may have exacerbated a desire for self-transcendence and led to its pursuit in areas hardly considered earlier. The two most important spheres of self-transformation under the conditions of modernity are the "personal" and the "political." Specifically, psychoanalysis, a theory and (normally) an individual experience, and revolution, a collective, public event and experience, have emerged in this century as the two dominant sources of vocabularies of transformation.

Though it is not exactly a secret that the therapeutic experience, however defined, often serves as a replacement for the religious experience, the therapeutic and even redemptive power of politics is less obvious, at least in what Richard Rorty has referred to as rich North Atlantic bourgeois polities. So-called "normal" politics—parliamentary jostlings, party rivalries, and modern mass elections—is rarely considered an effective or appropriate site for individual or group conversion. Nor does a liberal political culture offer its members what John Rawls (1985) has called a "comprehensive conception of the good" to be inculcated by its political institutions.

With revolutionary politics it is another matter. Though the distinctions are arbitrary, most would understand revolutions to be about fundamental changes in political, economic, and social structures, often accomplished through armed struggle by "the people" against the established regime(s). But in *The Old Regime and the French Revo-*

200

*lution* (1848 [1955]), Alexis de Tocqueville identified a unique characteristic of the revolution that had turned his country and the Western world upside down a half-century before. Because it aspired to be "world-wide" and was concerned with "man-in-himself" rather than just "Frenchmen," Tocqueville suggested that "the ideal the French Revolution set before it was not merely a change in the French social system but nothing short of a regeneration of the whole human race" (10–13). In the ensuing two centuries, an increasingly explicit goal of modern revolutionary struggles has been the creation of a new sort of human being, one shorn of old ways of thinking, feeling, and acting. What is of significance in such a "cultural revolution" is the emphasis upon the transformation of human nature in all its manifestations. Many ostensibly secular revolutionary efforts are species of what has been called "redemptive politics" (Heller and Feher 1987).

With this in mind I want to consider the questions that have been around since the early days of psychoanalysis—what is the relationship between self-transformation in politics and self-transformation in the psychoanalytic sphere? Is there any way to understand one in terms of the other, particularly the latter in terms of the former? More pointedly, can psychoanalysis explain what is needed in order to effect those transformations to which revolutions aspire?

To do this I would like briefly to review the political dimensions of psychoanalysis in its classic phase, roughly up to World War II, and then focus on what psychoanalytic "action" language offers by way of bringing psychoanalysis and politics (and ultimately history) into closer contact. Then I would like to analyze a quite modern attempt by Frantz Fanon to link violent political action with therapeutic, even redemptive, effect. And finally I want to suggest an alternative historical model for thinking of the relationship between private and public, psychological and political change.

*I*

Freud's attitude toward politics and the political realm was a highly ambivalent, at times dismissive, one. According to Carl Schorske, politics was "the side of human affairs from which he had expected most in youth and had suffered most in manhood" (1980, 182). As Freud grew older he became less concerned with, and indeed hostile to, political change, not to mention revolution, an attitude that both grew out of his personal experience and was a general trait of the fin-de-siècle Viennese bourgeoisie.

This personal predilection did not remain merely personal and without implications for Freud's theory, which was always superintended by what Hayden White (1973, 31–35) called the "ironic" or the "metonymic" trope, or by both; In Paul Ricoeur's well-known phrase psychoanalysis exemplifies a "hermeneutics of suspicion." It is not surprising that a theory that focuses on the unconscious, hidden, and complexly encoded motives of human thought and action would deny fundamental (as opposed to secondary) importance to the public realm of action. Moreover, Freud's controversial abandonment of the seduction theory, whatever its particular justification, indicated that his theory was organized around the assumption that a wish or fantasy had the same psychic effect as a deed, that desire and action had equal psychic status.

Though Freud's later work on more general cultural and political topics is often provocative and suggestive, its perduring effect has been to undermine the independent and separate status of "the political." As Philip Rieff (1961, 252) has put it, "The independent intelligent citizen, cherished by Rousseau, is given no more credence psychoanalytically than the increasingly rational proletarian of Marxist utopianism." The "Führer is by definition a Verführer" (259). All politics reduces to a variation on the oedipal story, for, suggests Schorske, in Freud's work "patricide replaces politics" (1980, 197). What is important to emphasize here is that even when Freud granted the unavoidable importance of politics, he—like Marx for different reasons—could never quite grant it an independent causal status. Rather, it always reflected or derived from something more basic.

This, needless to say, is not the whole story about the psychoanalytic movement or the "culture of psychoanalysis" roughly up to World War II. Many of the second-generation analysts (those born around 1900), Russell Jacoby notes, considered themselves socialists or even Marxists, the two best known being Wilhelm Reich and Otto Fenichel. After World War I psychoanalysis was seen as an ally of the feminists and was thought to offer valuable aid to artists in their cultural rebellion against the philistine, bourgeois world. But these radical strands in psychoanalytic circles worked against the grain of Freud's personal and theoretical proclivities. It was easier for analysts to be politically engaged in Berlin than in Vienna, where the founder's influence was so pervasive. Once the central European diaspora began after 1933, this spirit of political and cultural rebelliousness was even further diluted. Exile in (usually) America and the professionalization (meaning medicalization) of psychoanalysis contributed to what Jacoby with some exaggeration has referred to as psychoanalysis's "repression of its own past" and its subsequent depoliticization (Jacoby 1983, 6). As a result, when there was a resurgence of interest in the radical potential of psychoanalytic theory in the 1950s and 1960s, the essential work would be done outside the professional psychoanalytic community by thinkers such as Herbert Marcuse and Norman O. Brown.

Freud had himself determined quite early what the nature of the movement's "repressed" would be. In his confrontation with the first two psychoanalytic heretics, Jung and Adler, Freud took a position firmly in the "center" against Jung's right-wing, religiously tinged dissent and against Adler's more left-oriented, politically and socially engaged work. Freud objected to Adler's one-dimensional emphasis upon the primacy of the aggressive or ego instincts in their efforts to (re)assert the individual's desire for equal status and insisted that not just ego components but libidinal feelings and unconscious motives were at work as well (*S.E.* 14:52). Put another way, Freud denied the primacy or even coequal status of the ego's conscious plans and projects, the very stuff of normal and revolutionary politics. But however much orthodox psychoanalysis has tried to excise the positions represented by Jung and Adler from its own historical narrative and the narratives of their patients, neither religious nor political concerns have disappeared. As suggested at the beginning, each has kept turning up disguised as the other within the orthodox psychoanalytic camp.[1]

One might reasonably wonder what more there is to say about the connection between psychoanalysis and politics, given Freud's personal and theoretical rejection of the latter as unworthy of his theoretical attention. Recently, both Philip Rieff (1966) and Richard Rorty have claimed that there is no useful connection to be made between the two fields of action or thought. Psychoanalysis is primarily concerned with self-understanding and a certain kind of recreation of the self, while politics concerns itself with the proper arrangement of the public world and forms of action within it. Generally, according to Rorty, there is "no way to bring self-creation together with justice at the level of theory," whether it is a question of Freud or anyone else (Rorty 1989, xiv).

Rorty's assertion is controversial and powerful. Though the evidence is a bit confusing, he does seem to approve of the attempt to bring personal and communal narratives (as opposed to theories) together (1986, 20).[2] Since we experience ourselves as the same character in both stories, it would be strange if the impulse to bring our personal and communal narratives together were not a valid one. The desire to make our stories mesh is not necessarily a capitulation to metaphysics or some sort of intellectual "escape from freedom." But even if one speaks of bringing narratives rather than theories together, foundational claims for a psychoanalytically informed narrative are still being made if the latter provides the story of all other stories, the master narrative of individual and collective lives. Rather psychoanalysis should be seen as offering us one kind of vocabulary— and one way of organizing memory—for constructing personal and collective narratives.

There have been several valuable attempts in the intellectual history of psychoanalysis to subsume collective and individual narratives under the same vocabulary. On the utopian left, Wilhelm Reich and the figures associated with the Frankfurt school stressed the connection of sexual repression and passivity toward those who hold political power. More descriptively, and from a less obviously radical viewpoint, Erik Erikson has studied religious and political leaders such as Luther and Gandhi to try to understand how their inner lives and personal development were linked with the historical, social, and political realities facing them, and thus how these men initiated major changes in human institutions and culture. Followers of Erikson such as Robert Jay Lifton have also emphasized the need for a sense of permanence and immortality in the face of historical-cultural instability and biological mortality. Underlying all these efforts is the belief that changes in the world beyond the individual and the family significantly shape the individual self and that neither sphere can be understood in isolation from the other. But by no means are all these efforts intended to serve some totalizing "comprehensive conception of the good" or what John M. Cuddihy once called "wholeness hunger" (Cuddihy 1974).

Some recent developments in psychoanalytic theory ring further changes on this theme of the relationship between the individual and the communal. Roy Schafer has suggested that the best way to understand the self is to place it in an on-going narrative and that "action" is the central idea linking personal and collective narratives. Schafer's claims for the efficacy of action language go back to *A New Language for Psychoanalysis* (1976), where he jettisoned the Freudian metapsychology based on "mixed physiochemical and evolutionary biological language" as implying that individuals neither were nor could be made responsible for their lives (3). The point of psychoanalytic therapy—a change in self-understanding—was at odds, claimed Schafer, with psychoanalytic theory's epistemology and metaphysics.

To replace the older metapsychology, Schafer suggested that an action language be adopted. Psychoanalytic action language assumes that "each psychological process, event, experience, or behavior [is] some kind of activity." Furthermore, action displays "goal-directed or symbolic properties." Finally, an action is characterized by "intentionality" because it is undertaken by an agent. "Action," Schafer insisted, "is human behavior that has a point" (1976, 9–10, 100, 139). Beyond that, as a being-in-time, the individual needs to narrativize the acting self: "In the course of analysis, the analysand comes to construct narratives of personal agency." (1980, 42).

At first glance Schafer's recasting of psychoanalytic theory and practice in terms of narrative and action promises to bring psychoanalytic and political theory closer together. Approaching the topic from the side of political theory, it might be observed that while much modern liberal and radical political thought employs the language of "interest," "power," "force," and "necessity," the appropriate keywords in the language of politics should, according to Hannah Arendt, be "action" and persuasive "speech," not "interests" or "power" (Arendt 1959). Moreover, according to Arendt, poets and historians play a crucial political role by remembering and memorializing past actions, while the political thinker maintains the political realm by remembering and reinvoking the stories of those past actions (Benhabib 1990, 170). Human action and speech make sense only if remembered as taking place in a particular setting and remembered as part of a narrative. If both politics (and the historical narratives about it) and psychoanalysis make central the narration of an agent's action, then the way seems open to bring them together in the terms suggested by both Schafer and Arendt.

There are problems, however. First, Schafer's definition of action encompasses too much and too little. On his account, action is predominantly private. That is, action in Schafer's work refers to any interior state or process that has meaning and purpose and for which responsibility can be taken. Aside from motor reactions and bodily processes, it is difficult on his account to understand what is *not* an action. Thus we are back to Freud's tendency to lend equal weight to a fantasized wish and acting on that wish. By way of contrast, Alasdair MacIntyre's definition of an action as an "occurrence ... flowing intelligibly from a human agent's intentions, motives, passions and purposes" and "for which someone is accountable" dovetails well with Schafer's, *except* that MacIntyre (like Arendt) assumes that an "occurrence" differs from "intentions, motives, passions and purposes" (1981, 195). In Schafer's hands the psychoanalytically informed narrative of the self still refuses to consider the distinction between internal/external, private fantasy/shared reality to be of any great moment. And that, in the context of psychoanalytic theorizing, has tended to mean that action in the normal sense and a public, shared reality tend to receive short shrift.

All this suggests the apolitical nature, or at least bias, of Schafer's action/narrative language. Though Schafer and Arendt both embrace the vocabulary of action, Arendt emphasizes instead that the political realm is "the organization of the people as it arises out of acting and speaking together," of "sharing of words and deeds," even if such sharing need not be confined to a specific "physical location" (1959, 177). The analyst and analysand share words and act together in a sense, but not in the same way as people who act together in public. The point of psychoanalytic treatment is not the health of the *res publica* but the well-being of the individual patient. Moreover, according to Arendt, what distinguishes action from "behavior" is that action refers not just to any internal state or bodily movement but to those that "take the initiative" (1959, 257). The motivation for action is less crucial for her than that the action promises to begin something anew by breaking an established pattern or process. For that reason, Arendt rejected all metahistorical determinisms, whether the liberal grand narrative of progress or the Marxian narrative pointing toward the end of history or purely naturalistic accounts of human existence. Each kind of determinism denies the possibility of acting "otherwise" or changing the course of history. In short, they deny freedom, and for Arendt it is through action that freedom manifests itself in the world among human beings.

But this last notion of Arendt's—action as manifestation of freedom—bears some resemblance to one Freudian understanding of cure. In Freud's classical formulation, the patient suffers from "repetitions," the tendency to repeat past thoughts, feelings, and actions; recollection and working through are the means by which these fixed patterns of feeling and behaving are to be destroyed. On this account, cure would be represented by the possibility of acting (and feeling and thinking) contrary to what the determinants of past experience, in the form of unconscious wishes and fantasies, would have predicted. One could see psychoanalysis as a preliminary to, or a propaedeutic for, action in the world rather than, as Rieff would have it, a way of disillusioning the individual about the importance of such action. "The work of the analyst," writes Joseph Smith, "is directed toward enhancing the analysand's capacity to decide on the basis of a maximum understanding of himself or herself and the situation" (1986, 53). Finally, though Schafer and Arendt differ on what action means or implies, they share a certain vision of what "healthy" or "free" action entails.

Still, they do differ significantly; and even this brief examination of the meaning of action suggests the difficulty of imagining how the psychoanalytic and political meanings of action could be reconciled.

Yet Frantz Fanon made such an attempt. Fanon's thinking on the therapeutic effects of violence illustrates the dangers of the theoretical effort to bring together individual and political transformation through political action. Such an attempt is symptomatic of a "wholeness hunger" and represents the idea of some comprehensive, collective cure for individual psychological and spiritual distress.

*II*

The Martinique-born psychiatrist Frantz Fanon can be placed within several contexts. His work, particularly *Black Skin, White Masks* (1952 [1967]) and especially *The Wretched of the Earth* (1961 [1966]), is of utmost importance in understanding the psychological and cultural legacy of racial and colonial domination. Both books were of considerable importance in shaping the radical consciousness of Third World liberation movements during the 1960s, including the black power/black consciousness movement in the United States as articulated by leaders of the Black Panther party and of the Student Nonviolent Coordinating Committee.[3]

Fanon's work was shaped most saliently by the intellectual legacy of the francophone Negritude movement, the idiom of postwar Left-Existentialism in France (where Fanon received his medical and psychiatric education), and by contemporary psychiatric and psychoanalytic thought. Of the radical thinkers of the 1960s, Fanon is one of the most intriguing, having been engaged in the independence struggle in Algeria against the French as well as having written powerfully and eloquently about it. Black radicals in America articulated the effects and reconstructed the history of racial domination but lacked the training to "theorize" it. Fanon was able to demonstrate that a theoretical account of racial and colonial domination could retain the immediacy of the experience of the dominated population.

Left-Existentialism, which derived from Jean-Paul Sartre's work, particularly *Anti-Semite and Jew*, reflected the pervasive influence of Alexandre Kojeve's lectures on Hegel in the late 1930s in Paris and supplied Fanon with an anthropology and theory of action. For Fanon, as for Kojeve's Hegel, the basic human drive was the desire for recognition. Risk and struggle (and the violence implied) were not the manifestations of biological drives à la Darwin; the difference between animals and humans lay precisely in the fact that humans risk their lives for prestige and honor. Resorting to violence is not merely a response to frustration; rather, choosing violence is a sign of and a means toward freedom. Finally, Fanon assumed that individuals (and by extension, groups) construct themselves or, more pertinently, are constructed by others rather than created according to a preordained plan or essence.

The other intellectual tradition from which Fanon drew extensively was modern depth psychology. As a psychiatrist (though not a trained psychoanalyst), Fanon wanted to conceptualize the relationship between the self-consciousness or self-image of colonized people and the structures of colonial domination that had generated that self-image. In *Black Skin* he laid bare the social etiology of what manifested itself as individual psychic disturbance. Though he cited Freud and Jung, Fanon questioned Freud's intrapsychic emphasis and Jung's essentialist theory of the collective unconscious. In fact, while he also questioned Adler's emphasis on the individual, Fanon's concern was with the sense of inferiority and negative self-image of the individual qua member of an oppressed group. The tradition of Left-Existentialism referred to above, including the early work of Jacques Lacan, who attended Kojeve's lectures and whom Fanon made use of in *Black Skin*, comported quite well with the "repressed" Adlerian tendencies within orthodox psychoanalysis. Fanon found in Lacan's work a kind of psychoanalytic version of role psychology, one that emphasized the origins of the self/identity in the misrecognitions of what Lacan named the mirror stage: "a drama whose internal thrust is precipitated from insufficiency to anticipation ... and, lastly, to the assumption of the armour of an alienating identity" (Lacan 1977, 4). On Lacan's account one's identity is marked by a false sense of coherence and underlain by jealousy and aggressivity toward the other. Identity is not the solution but the problem; it is not to be strengthened but undermined.

It is not difficult to understand the appeal of this for Fanon. But he also attempted to synthesize and move beyond Hegel, Adler, and Lacan. He noted that Lacan's mirror stage allowed him to see that for white colonizers the black man is the "real Other" — "and conversely." But what turns that dialectic of misrecognition into a frozen opposition is that whites perceive the black Other as purely "body image" rather than as a form of self-consciousness. According to Fanon, black people were not even misrecognized by whites; they were seen rather as natural resources or impulse centers, hardly entering into the dialectic at all: "what he [the white man] wants from the slave is not recognition but work" (1952 [1967], 161–63). But domination was not simply physical and economic; it was psychological and linguistic as well. Ultimately, how whites represented blacks determined how blacks represented themselves to themselves. On such an understanding, the distinction between personal identity and a socially imposed role all but disappeared.

By the early 1950s Fanon had forged a theoretical account of the nature of racial and cultural domination. His "project" became one of arriving at a "cure" for social, cultural, and political domination. At the end of *Black Skin* Fanon outlined his political-cultural diagnosis in the following terms: "Historically the Negro steeped in the inessentiality of servitude was set free by his master. He did not fight for his freedom.... He went from one way of life to another but not from one life to another" (1952 [1967], 219). Put in terms of the languages of freedom, Fanon was saying that the oppressed can be given their negative freedom (freedom from) but not a new sense of being a free self (freedom for). That must be chosen and created rather than received.

Moreover, for Fanon the relationship between cure and action, between a new sense of self and political involvement, was one of priority and causality. As a psychiatrist he wrote: "My objective, once his [the patient's] motivations have been brought into consciousness, will be to put him in a position to *choose* action (or passivity) with respect to the real source of the conflict—that is, toward the social structure" (1952 [1967], 100). In more abstract terms this would mean: "To educate man to be actional, preserving in all his relations his respect for the basic values that constitute a human world, is the prime task of him who, having taken thought, prepares to act" (1952 [1967], 222). To be fully human it was necessary to live in a world in which one was recognized as a subject and in which that recognition had been won rather than granted. In order to arrive at this position, the patient would have to become aware of the intrinsic relationship between the oppressive structures of domination and his or her negative self-image. Only then could the patient choose to act to change those structures.

Between the publication of *Black Skin* and the posthumous appearance of *The Wretched of the Earth* Fanon went to Algeria as a doctor/psychiatrist and became active in the struggle for independence against the French. Taking his distance from conventional Marxism, he wrote on the composition of a new revolutionary social class and also developed the outlines of a theory of culture. Having moved beyond his early allegiance to the Negritude movement, he rejected the ideas of "black" or purely "African" culture as dead ends, since indigenous African cultures had become "closed, fixed in the colonial status," and had undergone "cultural mummification" (1967, 34). Nor was any form of theocratic-religious state, even then a tendency in Islamic cultures, desirable. Rather Fanon's notion of culture, like his notion of politics, was an existentialist one. Culture arose out of concerted action in the present rather than being passively inherited from the past. Authentic culture was to be created in and by the revolutionary struggle. This new revolutionary culture would incorporate but transcend the corrupted European culture of humanism, which perpetuated racism at the same time that it advocated universal values, and point the way toward a new humanism and "new man." Fanon's therapeutic politics had become transferred into a redemptive vision.

Up to this point Fanon's vision of the individual and cultural change was fresh and insightful but not radically new. His social analysis in *Wretched* was much the same as earlier. "The settler," he asserted, "brought the native into existence." The result was a kind of "Manichean" standoff between the two worlds of the colonizer and colonized. If, he asserted, "decolonization is quite simply the replacing of a certain 'species' of men by another 'species' of men," then colonial domination can only be "called into question by absolute violence" (1961 [1966], 30, 33, 29).

But Fanon did not then spell out the usual justifications for violence in a revolutionary struggle. Where he had once considered therapy to be a preparation for action, in the chapter entitled "Concerning Violence" Fanon reversed the causal relationship: violent action became the instrument of change in the colonized self. Violence is "a royal pardon. The colonized man finds his freedom in and through violence. This rule of conduct enlightens the agent because it indicates to him the means and the end." Furthermore, violence creates solidarity among its perpetrators; it "invests their characters [those of the colonized] with positive and creative qualities ... bands them together as a whole ... mobilises the people" (1961 [1966], 67). Finally, "at the level of individuals, violence is a cleansing force. It frees the native from his inferiority complex and from his despair and inaction; it makes him fearless and restores his self-respect" (1961 [1966], 73). In sum, Fanon was now claiming that violence had a therapeutic and even redemptive effect on those who wielded it. Nor was therapeutic effect to be felt by the individual alone. Violence was part of a larger struggle within which one acted in and from solidarity with others. Fanon's theory was a psychological claim about action on the way to becoming a redemptive vision, a form of what Marie Perinbam has called "holy violence" (1982, 107).

Apotheosizing violence is not totally unknown in the annals of revolutionary struggle, even in America. Many American abolitionists, for instance, accepted what Lawrence Friedman refers to as John Brown's "righteous violence" against slavery, and black abolitionists such as Frederick Douglass were eager that black men demonstrate their manhood by fighting for their freedom in the Civil War—the occasion and theme of the film *Glory*. Christianity and Judaism (as well as Islam) have traditionally distinguished between "just" and "unjust" wars and thus sanctified violence, while the civic humanist political tradition has historically emphasized the willingness of the citizen to give his life for the common good. Fanon's politics of therapeutic violence is different, however, in this way: while the willingness to suffer or incur violence for a cause is usually seen as the sign of an existing faith or commitment to certain values or of a state of mind such as courage and honor, for Fanon the use of violence was a means of creating that faith or commitment or new state of mind. It was not, in other words, a way of demonstrating the existence of a quality or virtue but the very means of engendering it.

*III*

Fanon can be assessed in several contexts. The obvious one is in terms of political ethics and morality, but I will eschew that one here as such. More to my point, Fanon, like Marx and Freud, is one of those thinkers whose understanding of what shapes us as agents can scarcely be distinguished from a normative vision of what type of intervention into, or action from within, history would be appropriate to change us. Their theories encompass a visionary component that strongly suggests some action or intervention in ways, say, that an academic history of capitalism or a psychobiography of a political leader or an account of the French or Algerian revolution does not.

Specifically, Fanon's work exemplifies a certain type of historical consciousness and hence of narrative. In "The Politics of Historical Interpretation: Discipline and De-Sublimation," Hayden White (1987) focuses on what it means for a body of knowledge and set of methods to become a discipline. White's concern is with (professional) historical rhetoric: what its characteristics are and what it excludes. According to White, professional historiography has adopted a kind of "middle" voice or nonrhetorical rhetoric; it aims at scientific objectivity and transparency to reality and particularly excludes what White calls the "sublime" in the form of the transcendent or the grotesque. Thus the proper tone of the historical narrative is sober and fairly detached; it stresses the complexities of historical judgment and the necessity of documenting those judgments, and it rules out ecstasy or terror. Finally, it seeks to turn "memory" into "history," no longer to be driven by a desire to "avenge the people" but to strive to be balanced and fair (White 1987).

From this perspective, psychoanalysis, the tradition that still takes Freud to be its founder and lawgiver, emerges as a form of theory/narrative that also seeks to exclude or tame the sublime. Although as a Jew, Freud might have been tempted to see himself as "charged with avenging the people," and although anti-Semites, including Jung, have come close to suggesting as much in condemning psychoanalysis as a "Jewish science" intended to lead us astray, Freud finally intended psychoanalysis to serve a reintegrative, not a disruptive, function. Like Lenin's "infantile leftism," the term "wild psychoanalysis" was meant, among other things, to damn those who lacked the discipline to proceed patiently through the long and arduous process of analysis. In the end Freud sought to drain the swamps, not to disappear into them—to tame the savage beast, not release it on the world.

What White's analysis suggests about Freud enables us to better place Fanon's redemptive narrative of decolonization. Though certainly never a member of the orthodox psychoanalytic community, Fanon is perhaps the clearest contemporary example of a psychoanalytically oriented thinker who plumped for the sublime in the form of violence; rejected the "analytic" for the "therapeutic" and the disciplinary for the transgressive imperative; and devoted his life and work to "avenging the people" for the humiliation and shame that Western domination had imposed on and created in them. This led Fanon to reject the efficacy (and glory) of the politics of persuasive speech and action, which Arendt, among others, saw as the fundamental alternative to the compulsions of violence. Where Arendt saw violent action as fundamentally antipolitical, Fanon saw it as the essence of revolutionary politics.[4]

Fanon's work is also a part of an ongoing debate about the nature of the self-other relationship, particularly the role of the "other" in self-formation. The central questions in this debate can therefore be addressed to Fanon's work. To what extent do we internalize and introject the roles we play, and to what degree is there a self somewhere behind or beyond the various roles we assume?

One of the central themes in historical and sociological studies of domination has been the degree to which the slave—and by extension members of oppressed groups generally—internalizes the negative self-image imposed by the master or oppressor; to what degree, for instance, does the slave learn to play the slave role but retain enough of an "inner" or "core" self to change his or her behavior when outside of the master's or oppressor's control. Those who focus on the damaging effects of domination tend to stress regression and internalization as central in the formation of what historian Stanley Elkins calls the "Sambo" personality type. In contrast, sociologist Orlando Patterson claims that "there is absolutely no evidence from the long and dismal annals of slavery to suggest that any group of slaves ever internalized the conception of degradation held by their masters" and thus emphasizes the ability of oppressed people to maintain a space of difference and freedom from the roles they must play as slaves (1982, 97).

How Fanon fits into this debate is not hard to see. Where the emphasis in *Black Skin* tended to fall precisely upon mask and role, *Wretched* was organized around a strong theory of internalization, the recourse to the therapeutics of violence being eloquent testimony to the strength of the internalized shame and self-hate of the colonized. As Erik Erikson has written, what all "theories and ideologies of action" share is "the intuition that violence against the adversary and violence against the self are inseparable; what divides them is the program of dealing with either" (Erikson 1969, 437). This is also where Sartre's influence was crucial in Fanon's writing. For the essential thesis of Sartre's work was that the Jew "is one whom other men consider a Jew," a contention that egregiously ignored the entire history and tradition of Judaism as something more than a function of anti-Semitism (1965, 69). In sum, Fanon's depiction of the dominated (un)consciousness bore more than a passing resemblance to Elkins's "Sambo," a figure stripped of cultural traditions or humanizing resources.

Despite Fanon's psychiatric experience, and perhaps because of his exclusive attention to social and cultural determinants of individual personality, he offered very little by way of a theory or model of psychic structures or functioning. He had no theoretical way to describe or explain how social and cultural forces were internalized and became part of the personality structure. His central claim—"violence is a cleansing force.... It makes [the individual] fearless and restores his self-respect"—indicates that Fanon was working with incompatible models of the psyche: that is, he was mixing conceptual metaphors. The "cleansing" metaphor sees the essential effect of action as quantitative, similar to the view of repression as a "damming up." Action removes that which hinders or restrains, or is a "cleansing force" to expunge something. But the other model he deploys is that of the psyche as the receiver and generator of meanings of images rather than of powers and forces. On this view, the problem is not that the energies or actions of the colonized are repressed but that his or her self-image is a negative one. The goal becomes one of replacing one meaning with another, of destroying an old identity or self-representation and creating a new one through remembered action.

This is no mere literary quibble. The quantitative model, having to do with unblocking and cleansing, suggests that cure for domination can be achieved through a cathartic action alone, while the concept/trope of self-respect suggests that, along with action, achievement of a new self-understanding is essential. In this context it is important to remember that psychoanalysis is not concerned with releasing frustrations per se but with re-experiencing, understanding, and then working through the reasons for and causes of resistances and repressions. A modified form of psychoanalytic action theory helps here, since Schafer emphasizes the importance of getting the patient to reclaim rather than disclaim actions. The form this reclaiming assumes is a narrative of and by the patient.

If this model of self-transformation is given a political dimension, the implication is that the self-image of the members of a collectivity is not changed simply by action, whether violent or not. The self-image or *imago* of the colonized is grounded in unconscious processes, structures, and images internalized from the colonizer's world. But to maintain that action would destroy such a self-image is to beg the question of the nature of these unconscious images and desires. And to assume that action destroys repression assumes that it is possible to attain the original object of desire. This is not to say that literally confronting the oppressor and even engaging in violence makes no psychological difference. It's that it doesn't seem to make all the difference. The limited evidence from *Wretched* itself suggests that the use of violence by individual Algerians against the French often had profoundly disturbing rather than therapeutic effects upon those who perpetrated it. And it is the collective, not violent, nature of political action that frequently is experienced as so exhilarating and therapeutic. Nor did victory over the French create a strong base for the emergence of a new culture and new men and women in Algeria. Put another way, the psychoanalytic notion that "acting out," a way of repeating old patterns rather than superseding them, is not a solution but a symptom of the problem has a profound truth to it. In what might be called "political" acting out, the passive colonized person becomes the active colonized person. Though action rather than passivity is the mode, the old self-images of dependency remain unanalyzed. But in genuinely free political action, the passive colonized becomes the active free man or woman.

## IV. Coda

Fanon's work would seem to be a classic example of the dangers of eliding the distinction between personal and political transformation, of using the political sphere as a way of resolving personal problems— in short, of seeing political action as a way of assuaging "wholeness hunger." To that extent I would agree with Rorty's position, except to say that it is probably not that a satisfactory theoretical way of linking the private and the public self cannot be attained, if that is desired. It is rather that the two spheres should not be conjoined in the ways suggested by the model of therapeutic or religious transformation. The problem with total conversion is that very few people or groups can be recreated anew in short periods of time, however deeply the conditions of their lives may have been changed. Nor, one suspects, does a "Saul-to-Paul" conversion last in its original form. Moreover, the work and subtlety required of secular therapeutics is hard to imagine on a mass scale. As a result of such difficulties, the temptation is always toward seeing action as a shortcut.

Granting all that, people engaged in political action often do talk of their experience of politics in terms of a change in their sense of self. Such descriptions of self-transformation must be respected. In the American civil rights movement, for instance, there was much talk of achieving a new sense of "somebodyness" or "self-respect" or a new feeling of freedom. "What did we win?" asked a black newspaper editor. "We won self-respect. It changed all my attitudes" (quoted in Watters 1971, 158). Or in the words of activist John Lewis, "Being involved tended to free you. . . . You saw yourself as the free man, as the free agent, able to act" (quoted in Beardslee 1983, 8). One reason for Fanon's appeal to black radicals in America was that he promised a new way to achieve this self-respect after the mid-1960s, when the momentum of the civil rights movement had been lost.

If Fanon's concept of the self and its transformation is neither effective nor desirable, what concept of self-transformation would neither envisage a total transformation through violent means nor settle for Rorty's rigid distinction between the personal and political spheres?

The obvious alternative to both of these extremes might run something like this. The process of self-transformation by and through political action should not be couched in the language of either religious conversion or psychological cure. Rather, emphasis should fall upon self-transformation as a form of education, a much slower process that builds in a component of self-examination and criticism, not only of the self but of the process. Gandhi and Martin Luther King, to take two examples, emphasized the need to prepare for action through self-examination and self-education, as did the early Fanon in his emphasis upon the need for the individual to be in a position to choose to engage in action. Action should be that which education prepares one to undertake, not the reverse.

With extensive preparation or education, there is less need to emphasize the personal transformational capacities of action itself, whether violent or not. This is not to say that political involvement, even including risk of life and confrontation with the oppressor or enemy, will have no effect on one's sense of self. The testimony is too overwhelming on this point to think otherwise. The point is that changes in the self deriving from action should be a by-product rather than the main point of political action.

Finally, the most desirable outcome is not to be a "new man" or "new woman" but a people united by a history of action together who have come to tell a new story about what they have become through that collective action. Such a narrative implies an agent possessing the temporal dimension of "pastness" rather than a character who has just emerged *ex nihilo*. The past must not, as Schafer emphasizes, be disowned but incorporated into an expanded and enriched narrative. It is no accident that both Gandhi and King built on the existing cultures of their people rather than urging them to discard their old way of life. Elements of continuity, as well as of transformation, are essential.

Do these changes in self experienced by participants in political movements last? Is there any way to answer the question in a psychoanalytically convincing way? The answer to the second question is probably no, since a mass psychoanalysis of a postrevolutionary population is not possible (or desirable). Erikson's work has been valuable in suggesting, at least in the case of individual leaders, that changes in self-identity were possible even after early childhood and that participation in a mass struggle means different things to different people, according to the point in their lives at which they find themselves. But beyond that, we have to depend on the testimony elicited by interviewers and oral historians from participants in the civil rights movement. After conducting extensive interviews with a number of people involved in the civil rights movement and reinterviewing them several years later, William Beardslee writes:

> The fundamental concerns they voiced before—the overwhelming importance of closeness to others, . . . the handling of anger, the new sense of self, the taking of action rather than being passive, the development

of faith in the work over time, the reconciliation of Movement experience with the rest of their own life experiences, and the acceptance of self with limitations—all remain true. What is different, and in some ways even more unusual than in the original observations, is the length of the commitment of these men and women, now extending over twenty years in most cases. [1983, 163]

Clearly, for those Beardslee interviewed, the transformation of the self was no superficial or momentary thing.

Perhaps, then, Freud's famous definition of what holds a community together—"work ... and the power of love" (*S.E* 21:101)—should be augmented with a third human capacity: "action." What might be suggested is a comparison between the emergence of a new sense of self in conjunction with political action and the phenomenon we name "falling in love." Though romantic love has been labeled a cultural myth and thereby passed off as illusion, it is nevertheless an idea/ideal deeply embedded in Western cultural experience. Similarly, the experience of political action and the new sense of self-respect attendant to it can be dismissed as transitory or even as a dangerous phenomenon, the result of a kind of mass intoxication that threatens political stability and civility. In fact, Freud's view of political engagement was not far from what I have just described, and Rorty's liberal distaste for eliding the distinction between the personal and political derives in part from a similar suspicion.

But such an attitude is not the only one possible. From another perspective, if the experience of romantic love is one of our culture's most "exalted" private experiences, political action as freedom is perhaps its most "exalted" public moment. In both cases, the original experience of exaltation and transcendence is necessarily modulated over time and assumes different forms. To note that two people who have lived together for twenty years no longer feel the same surge of emotional and erotic current or the same commitment of passion between them is not to say that their original experience was somehow spurious or nonexistent. Similarly, neither the exaltation of what Arendt has named "political happiness" nor the liberation from fear and shame and rage that comes with acting together in public lasts in its original form. But this is not to say that such experiences were illusions or swindles. For they provide those who experience them, those who witness the action, and those who record and memorialize the action a reminder of the best we can do and be as public beings.

*Notes*

1. See Philip Rieff, *The Triumph of the Therapeutic* (1966), and Paul Roazen, *Freud and His Followers* (1975), for more detailed discussions of the ongoing relationship of Jung and Adler to orthodox psychoanalytic theory and institutions.

2. But see Rorty in *Contingency, Irony, and Solidarity*, where he writes: "Ironist theory ran its course in the attempt to achieve this same synthesis through narrative rather than system" (1989, 120).

3. The material on Fanon is taken from my longer study (in process) of the political thought of the civil rights movement.

4. White edges toward self-contradiction when he suggests that narratives of vengeance are best labeled as "fascist" or have been "conventionally" associated with such positions. Though a cult of violence cum cultural transformation has been an important ingredient historically in fascism, it is part of White's larger point that labels such as "fascism" are ways of "disciplining" rather than understanding such phenomena.

*References*

Arendt, Hannah. *The Human Condition*. Garden City, N.Y.: Doubleday Anchor, 1959.
———. *Men in Dark Times*. New York: Harvest Books, 1968.
Beardslee, William. *The Way Out Must Lead In*. 2d ed. Westport, Conn.: Lawrence Hill, 1983.
Benhabib, Seyla. "Hannah Arendt and the Redemptive Power of Narrative." *Social Research* 57 (Spring 1990): 167–96.
Cuddihy, John Murray. *The Ordeal of Civility*. New York: Basic Books, 1974.
de Tocqueville, Alexis. *The Old Regime and the French Revolution* (1848). Translated by Stuart Gilbert. Garden City, N.Y.: Doubleday Anchor, 1955.
Elkins, Stanley. *Slavery*. Chicago: University of Chicago Press, 1959.
Erikson, Erik. *Gandhi's Truth*. New York: W. W. Norton, 1969.
Fanon, Frantz. *Black Skin, White Masks* (1952). New York: Grove Press, 1967.
———. *The Wretched of the Earth* (1961). New York: Grove Press, 1966.
———. *Toward the African Revolution*. New York: Grove Press, 1967.
Freud, Sigmund. *The Standard Edition of the Complete Psychological Works of Sigmund Freud*. Edited and translated by James Strachey. 24 vols. London: Hogarth Press, 1953–74.
"On the History of the Psycho-Analytic Movement" (1914), vol. 14.
*Civilization and Its Discontents* (1930), vol. 21.
Friedman, Lawrence J. *The Gregarious Saints*. New York: Cambridge University Press, 1982.
Heller, Agnes, and Feher, Ferenc. *Eastern Left, Western Left: Totalitarianism, Freedom, and Democracy*. Atlantic Highlands, N.J.: Humanities Press, 1987.

Jacoby, Russell. *The Repression of Psychoanalysis: Otto Fenichel and the Political Freudians.* New York: Basic Books, 1983.

Kojeve, Alexandre. *Introduction to the Reading of Hegel.* Edited by Allan Bloom. New York: Basic Books, 1969.

Lacan, Jacques. *Ecrits: A Selection.* Translated by Alan Sheridan. New York: Norton, 1977.

Lifton, Robert Jay. *The Life of the Self.* New York: Touchstone Books, 1976.

MacIntrye, Alasdair. *After Virtue.* Notre Dame, Ind.: University of Notre Dame Press, 1981.

Patterson, Orlando. *Slavery and Social Death.* Cambridge: Harvard University Press, 1982.

Perinbam, Marie. *Holy Violence: The Revolutionary Thought of Frantz Fanon.* Washington, D.C.: Three Continents Press, 1982.

Rawls, John. "Justice as Fairness: Political not Metaphysical." *Philosophy and Public Affairs* 14 (Summer 1985): 233–51.

———. "The Priority of the Right and Ideas of the Good." *Philosophy and Public Affairs* 17 (Fall 1988): 251–76.

Rieff, Philip. *Freud: The Mind of the Moralist.* Garden City, N.Y.: Doubleday Anchor, 1961.

———. *Triumph of the Therapeutic.* New York: Harper and Row, 1966.

Roazen, Paul. *Freud and His Followers.* New York: Alfred Knopf, 1975.

Rorty, Richard. "Freud and Moral Reflection." In *Pragmatism's Freud: The Moral Disposition of Psychoanalysis,* edited by Joseph H. Smith and William Kerrigan. Psychiatry and the Humanities, vol. 9. Baltimore: Johns Hopkins University Press, 1986.

———. *Contingency, Irony, and Solidarity.* New York: Cambridge University Press, 1989.

Sartre, Jean-Paul. *Anti-Semite and Jew.* New York: Schocken Books, 1965.

Schafer, Roy. *A New Language for Psychoanalysis.* New Haven: Yale University Press, 1976.

———. "Narration in the Psychoanalytic Dialogue." *Critical Inquiry* 7 (Autumn 1980): 29–53.

Schorske, Carl. *Fin-de-Siècle Vienna.* New York: Alfred Knopf, 1980.

Smith, Joseph H. "Primitive Guilt." In *Pragmatism's Freud: The Moral Disposition of Psychoanalysis,* edited by Joseph H. Smith and William Kerrigan. Psychiatry and the Humanities, vol. 9. Baltimore: Johns Hopkins University Press, 1986.

Watters, Pat. *Down to Now.* New York: Pantheon Books, 1971.

White, Hayden. *Metahistory: The Historical Imagination in Nineteenth-Century Europe.* Baltimore: Johns Hopkins University Press, 1973.

———. "The Politics of Historical Interpretation: Discipline and De-Sublimation." In *The Content of the Form: Narrative Discourse and Historical Representation.* Baltimore: Johns Hopkins University Press, 1987.

# 10    Psychoanalytic Culture: Jacques Lacan and the Social Appropriation of Psychoanalysis

## Sherry Turkle

F reud believed psychoanalysis so deeply subversive of people's most cherished beliefs that only resistance to psychoanalytic ideas would reveal where they were being taken seriously. In 1914 he wrote that the final "decisive struggle" for psychoanalysis would be played out in "the ancient centres of culture, where the greatest resistance has been displayed" (*S.E.* 14:32). By that point it was already clear that it was in France, country of Mesmer, Bernheim, Charcot, Bergson, and Janet, France with its long literary tradition of exquisite sensitivity to the psychological, that resistance to psychoanalysis was greatest. "In Paris itself," reflected Freud, "a conviction still seems to reign ... that everything good in psycho-analysis is a repetition of Janet's views with insignificant modifications, and that everything else in it is bad" (*S.E.* 14:32-33). Despite early interest by the surrealists, there was no French psychoanalytic society until 1926, and for nearly a quarter of a century it remained small, its members badly stigmatized by medical peers. Before World War II, the French had rejected psychoanalysis as a German inspiration; after the war the discipline fared only a little bit better under its new image as an American import.

In the 1960s, all of this seemed to change. An acceptance, indeed a growing thirst for things psychoanalytic, became a hallmark of French intellectual life. Ready to satisfy this thirst was a peculiarly French brand of psychoanalytic thinking embodied in the work of Jacques Lacan. His Cartesian, poeticized, linguistic, and politicized psychoanalysis constituted a French reinvention of Freud.

In the early 1970s, I went to France to study this indigenous psychoanalytic movement and how it had "reinvented" Freud for the

French taste, adapting psychoanalytic ideas in a way that fit the needs of the French structuralist intelligentsia of the 1960s. But it soon became clear that my framing of the problem was insufficient to capture the scale and complexity of the situation I found on arrival. I was there at a time when it was possible to study a larger process: the popular appropriation of Freudian ideas about mind, the creation of a widespread "psychoanalytic culture."

My notion of a psychoanalytic culture and its contrast with a psychoanalytic movement is central to this essay. A psychoanalytic movement is made up of analysts, their patients, their analytic societies, and the intellectuals they directly interact with and write for. A psychoanalytic culture includes intellectual circles, but goes beyond them to include far less exalted folk. In the French case, this would mean the kindergarten teacher who takes a training course that includes a watered-down Lacanianism, the *lycéen* who learns about Lacan when she prepares the new "Freud question" for the baccalaureate, the writer and reader of advice in the newly psychologized agony columns in the French popular press. Psychoanalytic culture refers to a diffusion of psychoanalysis that influences how people think about their past, their present, and their possibilities for change, whether or not they have ever visited a psychoanalyst or have any specific interest in psychoanalytic theory.

The quality of a theory that facilitates the generation of a culture from a movement needs a name: I refer to it as that theory's appropriability. Using the name focuses a general question: what makes some theories of mind more appropriable than others? I shall argue that psychoanalytic ideas, like computational ideas (that other currently fashionable approach to the representation of mind), have a quality that makes them inherently appropriable. They incite people to play with them in an active way.

Given this intrinsic quality, what makes certain psychoanalytic ideas more appropriable than others? The answer to this second question lies in the interaction between ideas and the social and cultural contexts in which they are deployed. The psychoanalytic ideas that are appropriated are not the ideas as written but the ideas as "read," the ideas as reconstructed by what, in the context of literary criticism, Stanley Fish (1980) has called an "interpretive community." In the case of psychoanalysis as in the case of literature, displacing political and social effects from the text to its reading has the advantage of moving the debate from the question of what a theory is to "what the theory does—in a particular place, for a particular public, ... at a particular time" (Suleiman 1990, 193).

In previous writings on the sociology of French psychoanalysis (Turkle 1978) I have focused on Lacan and Lacanians because it was their theoretical and political positions that had served so effectively as a bridge between Freudian theory and larger French social and political currents in the 1960s. Toward the end of that decade, what might have been confined to the hothouse world of the intellectuals was carried beyond it by the passions of May 1968. The May events were a festival of speech and desire, and psychoanalysts were perceived as the professionals of both. In the context of May, Lacanianism had a special cachet. It was linked to Althusser's Marxism and Dali's surrealism, both excellent credentials for a movement that found itself caught between Marx and street theater. "Lacanianism served as an ideological alternative to Catholicism and gauchism," remarked *L'Express* (19-25 May 1989, 81). "It was a blessed time when Jesuits seized by doubt and stalled Althusserians could join the new Lacanian institution." Elisabeth Roudinesco went further, believing that without the "Lacanian adventure," a certain number of young French intellectuals of the 1968 generation would have "drifted toward terrorism" (1991, 398).

On a more down-to-earth level, by 1968, Lacan had spent more than twenty years criticizing American psychoanalysis as imperialistic and adaptationist. Antiestablishment and anti-American in his politics within the psychoanalytic movement, Lacan became a symbol of the larger social protest. There was even the story, so much a part of the folklore that it made its way across the Atlantic to be reported in the *New Yorker* (4 July, 1977, 72), of Lacan putting student leader Daniel Cohn-Bendit in the back of his own Jaguar and successfully smuggling him across the border into Germany. Like all myth, the story speaks its own truth. May '68 and its aftermath helped to sweep Lacanianism, already lionized by intellectuals, onto a more public stage.

In the years after '68, French psychoanalysis became more permeable to politics and politics more permeable to it. A failure of radical politics led to the politicization, at least in its discourse, of a significant segment of French psychoanalytic thought, a politicization that facilitated its infiltration into French culture as a whole. Education, social work, psychiatric training, film criticism, talk shows, women's magazines, and the Sunday supplements all "went psychoanalytic" (Turkle 1978). John Forrester correctly notes that for Lacan, "the brilliant innovative phase was more truly the 1950s than any later date," and characterizes a focus on its "fashionable prominence in post-1968" as the "shorter view" (1990, 2). From my perspective, it is not the shorter view but a different view. The disagreement here turns on whether one focuses on the history of the psychoanalytic movement or on the study of what I am calling the psychoanalytic culture. From the point of view of a high-minded history of the psychoanalytic movement, the rapprochement of the Lacan takeoff and the arrival of psychologically minded advice to the lovelorn laced with "Lacan speak" implies an ignorant or vulgar juxtaposition. But a psychoanalytic culture is made up of precisely such little vulgarities, little pieces of this and that taken up and woven into larger wholes. And from the perspective of psychoanalytic culture, the story of how 1968 became a turning point for Lacanianism depends less on the emotions of displaced intellectuals and disaffected militants than on those of a larger group of people whose lives were touched by the spirit and the aspirations of May.

In this essay I use the French experience to elaborate a set of ideas about the appropriation of psychoanalysis as a science of mind. However, even with this focus on the sociology of psychoanalytic *culture*, the story of the psychoanalytic *movement* continues to play a crucial role for many reasons. First, the movement provides the seeds for the development of the culture; we cannot make sense of the culture without some knowledge of the movement. Second, movement and culture are involved in a two-way relationship: the culture influences the movement as well as reflecting it. Third, for the sociologist of culture, the history of psychoanalysis provides a precious resource for understanding the development of other intellectual movements. Such complex issues as the role of *Maître* in the transmission of ideas take a particularly acute and informative shape in the case of psychoanalysis; the enterprise itself provides a theory of its contradictions.

Thus, in part I of this chapter I use an account of crises in the Lacanian movement during the last years of Lacan's life and since his death to raise larger questions about how intellectual schools mourn their leaders, transmit their teaching across generations, and relate to other social institutions.[1] First, there was a crisis of institutional forms. Does a psychoanalytic school belong to *Maître*, or is it a public institution like any other? Second, there was a crisis of textual authority. To what degree can theorists dictate what version of their spoken teachings will be disseminated? To what extent should they be allowed to do so? Third, there was a crisis of familial authority. The final years of Lacan's life—years in which his son-in-law, Jacques-Alain Miller, was put in the place of dauphin much as Freud made his daughter Anna his Antigone—brought to the surface the complex and self-contradictory nature of psychoanalytic transmission as a family affair, whether by blood or by marriage or by transferential bond. The last chapter of the Lacanian saga never strayed far from family romance.

Plaguing the Vienna circle as much as the Paris circle of fifty years later, the issue of familial authority shows psychoanalysis struggling against itself.

Fourth, there was a crisis of professional authority. Psychoanalysis, like many other intellectual movements, has an "applied" as well as a theoretical side. Since Freud's day, the two have been in tension. The tension comes both from within the movement and from the larger culture because democratic societies have a declared responsibility not only to encourage the free circulation of ideas but also to control and license a wide array of therapeutic practices. Lacan spent a professional lifetime arguing that the kind of discipline appropriate to a medical conception of psychoanalytic work would kill psychoanalytic science. The question came up with increasing force in the years after his death.

In part II of this essay, I turn from the specifics of the French case to a general and cross-national discussion of the relationship between psychoanalytic movements and cultures. Given the intrinsic appropriability of psychoanalytic ideas, what social conditions encourage a psychoanalytic movement to grow into a psychoanalytic culture? What stands behind the development of a psychoanalytic thirst? What has to happen in order for psychoanalytic ideas to influence "thinking about thinking," not just by professional psychologists but by the amateur psychologists that we all are? There is a tradition of writing on such questions that emphasizes large social forces and, in particular, conditions of social fragmentation, as preconditions for psychoanalytic appropriation (Rieff 1966). Here I try to place this tradition in the context of a more intimate sociology, the way ideas come to connect with individuals, an "inner history" of sciences of mind. By comparing the social appropriation of psychoanalysis with that of computational ideas, I hope to underscore the importance of an active "constructionist" model for trying to grasp how intellectual "movements" give rise to "cultures" in the understanding of mind.

Finally, I come full circle when I discuss an issue dramatically raised by Lacan's psychoanalytic career and by events of the "après-Lacan." I call it the myth of the well-analyzed analyst. The psychoanalytic movement and the psychoanalytic culture both support a fantasized relationship among personal cure, professional authority, and theoretical legitimacy. In all intellectual fields other than the natural sciences, which have been traditionally assumed to present "objectively" verifiable results, authorial judgments are to some degree validated by reference to personal history and personal qualities. For example, there is the widely debated issue of whether the politics of literary theorists and philosophers should challenge the validity of their ideas. In the sociology of sciences of mind, the question of the moral status of the mind that reflects on itself is posed even more sharply. The myth of the well-analyzed analyst dramatizes the complex interplay between psychoanalytic movement and culture and illustrates the eloquence with which psychoanalysis speaks to general issues in the sociology of knowledge.

## Part I: Looking Back on Lacan

### THE LACANIAN DISSOLUTION

Within the psychoanalytic movement itself, Lacan was a controversial figure. Disagreement over his unorthodox practices (in particular his short sessions, sometimes of five minutes' duration) and his equally unorthodox ideas about psychoanalytic training precipitated three postwar schisms in the French psychoanalytic movement. And in the heat of yet another controversy, Lacan dissolved his Freudian School shortly before his death in 1981, which in turn produced a chain reaction of schism so that at one point there were more than thirty identifiable psychoanalytic groups in Paris.

Lacan had founded the Freudian School in 1964. Unlike traditional psychoanalytic societies, it welcomed nonanalysts as full members. There Jacques-Alain Miller and a small group of his fellow Althusser students formed a study group on "the theory of discourse." In January 1966, this group, known as the Cercle d'Epistémologie de l'Ecole Normale Supérieure, began to publish its own journal, *Cahiers pour l'analyse*. It promoted Lacanianism as a model for a new kind of Freudian science, purified of all reference to the psychological subject. From 1966 to 1969, *Cahiers pour l'analyse* built up an extra-analytic, theoretical Lacanianism, oriented toward logic, formalism, and science. It became a vanguard for the Lacanian colonization of the worlds beyond psychoanalysis. In its issues, Lacan appeared next to such writers as Georges Canguilhem, Louis Althusser, Jacques Derrida, and Georges Dumézil.

In 1969, after its tenth issue, Miller interrupted publication of *Cahiers pour l'analyse* to turn his full attention to politics. He was now a committed Maoist, a member of La Gauche prolétarienne. At this turn of events there were already those at the Freudian School who were relieved that the very ambitious and very brilliant Miller would be occupied elsewhere than on their home turf. But they were naive to rejoice so soon. In 1966, he had married Lacan's daughter Judith. In 1969 he began his step-by-step takeover of the Department of

Psychoanalysis at Vincennes, a campaign waged to full victory by 1976, when Vincennes was his, a fiefdom within the University of Paris. And in 1972, while still a member of La Gauche prolétarienne, Miller was passed what in retrospect was clearly Lacan's most potent symbol of succession. Lacan decided that Miller should edit and control the texts of his seminars. Miller would inherit the rights to the Word.

In this transaction, Lacan bequeathed Miller a life's work. Miller would not simply "edit" but would "establish" the text of Lacan's seminars. Miller added language where there were gaps, he removed contradictions and ambivalences. In the course of this work, Lacan's dependence on Miller grew; some would say their relationship became the dominant force during the last fifteen years of Lacan's life. On the one hand, Miller was a scribe, writing out what the *Maître* had said, or perhaps, meant to say. On the other, Miller revised and changed Lacan's work as he "established" it. To some degree, Miller renounced his own voice to pledge himself to his version of Lacan's (Miller 1985, 23). On his side, Lacan accepted Miller's formulations and, to all appearances, came to see them as his own. The resulting symbiosis was to have fateful consequences for the history of Lacanianism. If by the 1980s, Miller seemed to feel justified in speaking for Lacan, by that point he was acting not only out of habit but out of a profound sense of Lacan's wanting and needing him in this role.

In 1974, Miller's relationship with the Lacanian enterprise entered a new phase. He went into analysis with Charles Melman, a prominent Freudian School analyst. Now, on his way to becoming an analyst, he could present himself as the legitimate heir not only of Lacan's science but of his analytic kingdom as a whole.

By 1979, Miller's time had arrived. The Freudian School was increasingly factionalized; Lacan had become withdrawn and silent. The school was a powder keg waiting to explode. It had grown to 609 members, and from Miller's point of view, "Lacan no longer held an ideological majority."[2] An incident in which Lacan acted imperiously (but no more so than he had done many times before) finally set it alight. Perhaps he did not realize that by distancing himself from his "subjects" and imposing Miller on them, he had broken his side of the political contract that kept the school together. There could be an absolute monarch, but it had to be Lacan, not his designate. Perhaps Lacan wanted the keg to explode.

In February, Denis Vasse, a vice president of the Freudian School, had participated in a meeting of Confrontation, a group that assembled psychoanalysts from all schools. As the formal and mathematical Millerian line became more dominant at the Freudian School, many of its analysts had turned toward Confrontation, which served them as a kind of counterweight. Lacan had never taken a public position against Confrontation, although he clearly was upset by its role as a meeting place for his disaffected students. Now, however, Lacan dismissed Vasse from the vice presidency. The response within the Freudian School was immediate outrage. In the wake of the protest, a special general assembly was called for 30 September 1979; it was marked by an almost comic series of parliamentary irregularities, which rode roughshod over all objections to Lacan's imposition of his will.

The decision to disband the Freudian School was made at a meeting at Miller's house on 30 December 1979. Lacan was ill; those close to him knew that he had been diagnosed with cancer of the colon and had refused surgical intervention. According to Solange Faladé, a school vice president, there was a pressure to act quickly "in order to create something with him while there was still time ... Lacan could no longer write. It was decided that Miller would compose the letter and Lacan would correct it. He eliminated passages that were not to his liking. I did not return to Guitrancourt [Lacan's country home], but during the first weekend of the new year, Miller telephoned me to say the letter was typed up and ready to be sent out" (Roudinesco 1991, 652). Miller has a somewhat different version of these events. He claims that on 6 January, at the Lacan country home, Lacan gave him a text of the letter of dissolution (Roudinesco 1991, 651–52).

In his essay on Poe's *Purloined Letter*, Lacan uses a letter to describe the power of the signifier. All of the actions of all of the characters in the story are determined by the presence of the letter, a signifier whose contents are unknown, a unit of signification that takes on meaning by its opposition to other units. The deployment of Lacan's letter of dissolution had odd echoes of the Poe story. No one questioned Lacan's commitment to its contents. But the circumstances around the origins of the letter—that is, whether it was Lacan himself who took pen to paper—took on far greater importance than what the letter said.

In the crisis of dissolution, the osmotic, some said fusional, relationship between Miller and Lacan, which Lacanians implicitly tolerated when they accepted Miller's words as Lacan's seminar, became intolerable. People became preoccupied with the degree to which Lacan was *alone* responsible for the dissolution of the school.

On Tuesday, 8 January, at the usual time for his seminar, Lacan read the letter of dissolution, dated Guitrancourt, 5 January. He called on those who wished to avoid "the deviations and compromises nourished by the Freudian School" to make their wishes known to him within ten days. By the following Friday, Lacan had the stenographic transcripts of his seminars withdrawn from the Freudian School library.

When he founded the Freudian School, Lacan had said: "I hereby found—as alone as I have always been in my relation to the psychoanalytic cause—the Ecole Française de Psychanalyse" (Lacan 1990, 97). (The name of the school would change three months later to the Ecole Freudienne de Paris.) In his mind, since he had founded it alone, he could now dissolve it alone. Others felt differently. The Freudian School was a public institution. It was not Lacan's to dissolve. It belonged to them as well. The battle lines were clearly drawn between those who saw psychoanalytic organizations as about personal power, theoretical brilliance, and transferential bonds and those who thought they were organizations that also must obey the law. "We are not questioning his [Lacan's] right to found elsewhere or to disavow whomever he wants," said Michèle Montrelay, one of the younger analysts who opposed the dissolution. "That's his right and we respect it. But why can't Jacques Lacan bear that what he removes himself from should continue to live?" (Roudinesco 1991, 662).

The parallel with Vienna is, of course, inexact, but imagine that in the early 1930s Freud had informed his disciples that with the support of his daughter Anna he was shutting down the Vienna Psychoanalytic Society to begin a new group and that Jones, Sachs, Rank, Erikson, Deutsch, and Abraham insisted that since they had participated in the development of the organization, Freud could really not act without their approval. Freud treated psychoanalytic organizations as though he owned them. Lacan was stunned that there should be any question of the Freudian School's not belonging to him.

Week after week, month after month, the French press ran the story of the Freudian School dissolution as front page news. The dramatis personae were in costume for a spectacle that crossed *King Lear* with *Dynasty*. There was the dying *Maître* who pronounced the words, *Delenda est*, and announced the destruction of his kingdom; the scheming son-in-law, positioned to inherit the property, the woman, and the power; the obedient daughter, dominated by father and husband; and the jealous students, divided in their frustration at not having familial access to their beloved *Maître*, reduced to fighting over the spoils of the kingdom. Finally, there were the *Maître's* aging comrades, the "barons," who had never had their deserved place in the sun. Remarkably, for a troupe of psychoanalysts, the actors in the drama played willingly on the most public of stages. During the May events, psychoanalysts had anguished over speaking and writing in public forums. Now, they behaved as though it were perfectly natural for them to heap invective and venom on each other in the pages of *Le Monde* and *Libération*, and on the airwaves of Europe no. 1.

Meanwhile, Lacan's call to his true followers produced a remarkable result. In the week that followed his public presentation of the letter of dissolution, Lacan received over a thousand letters from people wanting to continue with him, or in his terms, *père-severe*, persevere with a severe, punishing, and severing father. Only about three hundred of these letters were from members of the Freudian School. The rest were from teachers, psychiatry interns and residents, social workers, psychologists, and physiotherapists who had in one way or another affiliated themselves with the Lacanian adventure. The popular success of the Lacanian movement had rested upon this waiting, fascinated public who had occupied the couches of the ever-swelling ranks of Freudian School analysts. They were the underclass of the French psychoanalytic movement, and they had responded to Lacan's call for love and allegiance. To almost everyone's great surprise, on 21 February 1980, they all received an invitation to a new dance: "To the thousand whose letters attest their desire to go with him, Jacques Lacan replies that as of today, 21 February 1980, he founds the Freudian Cause."

On 22 October 1980, modifications to the original statutes of the Freudian Cause were filed with the Paris Prefecture of Police over Lacan's signature. These amendments dealt a final blow to any semblance of democracy at the new organization. The cause was transformed into a political party and Miller into its Mao. By now, hundreds of pages have been written that agonize over the question of whether Lacan wrote or approved these new statutes. There had of course been controversy over the authorship of the first letter of dissolution, but in that case, even if Lacan didn't write the letter, he clearly intended and supported its contents. But now Lacan seemed too weak and confused for his actions to indicate clear intentions. Yet his signature, his "letters," were still being used to give direction to the "thousand" of the cause. If before, Miller might have taken the intentions of a weakened Lacan, turned them into prose, and submitted these words for Lacan's signature, knowing that his father-in-law stood behind them, now the procedure would have to be different. Among the architects of the dissolution there were now those who accused Miller of using a senile Lacan as a rubber stamp for political intrigues that he could not possibly understand. Having supported Miller in Lacan's name, it was now difficult for them to denounce Miller in Lacan's name. Yet it would seem that for many analysts this solution was preferable to

facing the painful truth that Lacan had done everything he could to
ensure that his legacy (his money, his property, his daughter, his texts,
and his school) would go to Miller. It was easier for them to think of
a feeble, trapped, even imprisoned *Maître*, powerless against the energetic, obsessed, tyrannical Miller. Miller presented an enemy that
you could love to hate. Perhaps being enraged with Miller was a way
of refusing to mourn Lacan, of refusing to accept that Lacan wished
to give his legacy not to a great clinician or to a lifelong follower, but
to a philosopher and a member of the family.

In December 1980, tensions at the new Freudian Cause broke to
the surface in a crisis nominally about real estate. Miller had asked his
analyst, Charles Melman, to help him secure permission for the cause
to rent the Freudian School's former headquarters. This accomplished,
Miller submitted a lease to Melman, which the latter found unacceptable because among other things, it stipulated that it could be
rescinded by the tenant alone. Furthermore, Miller announced plans
for a renovation of the headquarters so that they could be used as a
library and editorial office. The renovations would effectively close
the space to analytic teaching. In this symbolic harbinger of the "après-
Lacan," the philosopher was taking yet another revenge on the clinicians. Melman, who had loyally supported Miller throughout the
crisis of the dissolution, was enraged and was about to break all the
rules. He could have simply rejected the lease Miller submitted. Instead
he used the occasion to denounce his patient.

On 7 December, Melman sent three hundred former members of
the now defunct Freudian School a letter attacking Miller, although it
did not mention him by name. The letter aired grievances about Miller's ambition and dishonesty and about the questionable legality of
the 22 October amendments to the statutes of the cause. Most important, Melman said what no member of the inner circle had yet
dared to say: he questioned the authenticity of the many letters supposedly sent by Lacan over the past year. Melman spoke of "apocryphal
texts," with the inference that Miller had been running the show all
along, manipulating Lacan's supposed "wishes" and his signature. "The
Freudian Cause, although in its cradle, has a malformation which runs
the risk of killing it or turning it into a monstrosity. Why? Because
everything is decided and inscribed in Lacan's name although it is
clear that he himself has nothing to do with these actions except for
adding his signature, now become automatic. That is the painful fact"
(Dorgeuille 1981, 28).

In a failed and futile effort to show respect for the principles of
clinical confidentiality, Melman insisted that his letter did not draw

on information confided to him in the privacy of the analytic encounter. Psychoanalytic politics always mixes institutional and analytic affairs—the internal conflicts of a psychoanalytic society are fought out among people who are or were each other's patients, analysts, supervisors, lovers, ex-lovers, spouses, and ex-spouses. But even in the Lacanian mileu, which by the 1980s had more or less seen everything, Melman's letter went beyond acceptable bounds.

Although most analysts could not condone Melman's letter, many believed its allegations to be true. January 1981 brought a flood of resignations from the Freudian Cause, so many, in fact, that it was decided to abandon the organization and start a new one, calling it the *School* of the Freudian Cause. Created on 19 January 1981, the school's statutes were attributed (as usual) to Lacan. Tragedy had already repeated itself as farce. This third act was pure politics. Miller was not going to take the chance of having powerful psychoanalyst barons again. At the School of the Cause, no titles were to be permanent. (The much coveted status of school analyst would be held for only three years.) Nor would Miller tolerate grass-roots democracy or coalition politics. In this organization, all votes would be by a public show of hands. Dissenters would be seen before they could be heard. Six days later, a group of twenty-two former school analysts who had been loyal to Miller through the dissolution resigned. Within six months, most would be heads of their own schools in the post-Lacanian diaspora.

The day after the group resignation, another letter signed by Lacan appeared in the mail: an appeal for love and for the School of the Freudian Cause. "It is the School of my students, those who still love me. I open its doors to them. I say to the thousand: 'This is worth the risk. It is the only solution possible—and decent' " (Ecole de la Cause Freudienne 1985, 42). This letter merely inflamed the debate about whether Miller was writing Lacan's texts.

THE LACANIAN DYNASTY

Lacan died as the decade of the 1970s ended: the one that followed had a very different political tenor. In the 1960s and 1970s, the Left had been in the opposition; in the 1980s, the Left was in power but no longer recognizably on the Left. In the structuralist 1960s, French intellectual culture was predominantly Marxist; in the postmodernist 1980s, this was no longer the case. In the 1960s, when intellectuals spoke of conservative forces, they were likely to be referring to the Communist party; in the 1980s, the Communist party all but disappeared as a force to contend with; conservatives were now on a reborn, nationalist Right. In the 1960s, social theory nurtured the idea of the decentered subject; in the 1980s, there was a rebirth of liberalism and humanism; theories that spoke of an intentional actor were newly relegitimated in political thought (Ferry and Renaut 1990).

The "Lacanian moment" on the French Left had made a commitment to a program that integrated politics and epistemology, social action and personal reflection. The tone of that moment survives in French feminist writing, some of which still takes Lacanianism as a discourse of liberation, and in the School of the Freudian Cause—headed by Miller—which has consecrated itself to keeping the flame alive.[3] If the organization seems authoritarian in its management style and doctrinaire in its theoretical commitments, this is at least in part because it functions as would a group of embattled militants, protected and defended by a publishing house (Navarin), a literary and cultural magazine (*L'Ane*), a university stronghold, now at Saint-Denis, and an international organization.

In the years before his death, Lacan (through Miller) had put in place an instrument of potential revenge against those who had banished and humiliated him. The Foundation of the Freudian Field, originally created in 1979 to organize international conferences, gradually took on a political vocation: to organize the non-French Lacanian world under the umbrella of the Paris organization. In most cases, what the more than sixty affiliated groups want and get is simply Miller's blessing, a sign that they are part of the true Lacanian family. The organization is headed by Lacan's daughter, Judith Miller, which enhances the sense that it is "of the family." Unlike the International Psychoanalytic Association, the foundation does not dictate an acceptable training program or other rules. In practice, however, affiliates are under pressure to maintain a certain ideological purity. Perceived disloyalty to Miller is not well tolerated.

Indeed, what is most characteristic of the School of the Freudian Cause is its tone of political militancy. For example, on its seventh birthday, the school published a four-point overview of its history (Ecole 1988, 2). It detailed deviationism to fight and a slogan to fight it under and also evoked the memory of its charismatic founder, who had passed the torch to a new generation of leaders. In this official history, social crisis has created an accelerating demand for psychoanalysis; Lacan had termed it "epidemic." This demand was being met by a false and bureaucratic psychoanalysis, the kind of psychoanalysis that Lacan spent his life opposing. It is the school's mission to confront and challenge this false psychoanalysis by preaching the word of Lacan. Here we have an explicit rewriting of the history of psychoanalysis from the inside. In this revisionist history, key actors make decisions rather than do the best they can under the pressure of events. For example, Lacan's departure from the International Psychoanalytic Association is represented as his response to its deviations. In fact, he was excluded from the association against his will because of *his* deviations. The rhetoric here is dialectical and Maoist: extend true psychoanalysis and challenge the symptom-psychoanalysis; spread the word of Lacan in the university and participate in the deconstruction of the university.

Throughout the 1980s, the School of the Freudian Cause had been involved in a series of controversies, most of them centered on its relation to Lacan and its right to claim legitimacy through him. In one sense, there was ample room to invoke the sturdy French aphorism, "The more things change, the more they are the same." Controversy had been a cornerstone of Lacanian psychoanalytic politics for over a quarter of a century. However, unlike the politics of previous generations, these controversies brought the school into direct contact with the legal system. A first lawsuit concerned Lacan's intellectual legacy. Lacan had granted Miller exclusive rights to his literary estate, including the responsibility to "establish" the texts of all his seminars for publication at Le Seuil. In 1985, however, a group of analysts joined together in an Association for Research and the Establishment of the Seminars, known by the acronym APRES. APRES published in the journal *Stécriture* a version of Lacan's seminar of 1960-61 based on stenographic transcripts. Miller tried to stop APRES, but the organization insisted that Miller's "establishment" of the seminars was an admitted act of literary *interpretation*. In its view, the seminars were a spoken act, and not allowing the original words to circulate was inadmissible censorship. Thus did the "question of the passage of Jacques Lacan's spoken work through writing" come before the French courts. In December 1985, Miller won his case. The court upheld Miller's right to declare illegal the circulation of any traces of Lacan's words except those he chose to let out.

Two years later, Miller was back in court. This time he was being sued by Gérard Pommier, an analyst at the School of the Freudian Cause who had been a staunch supporter during the period of the dissolution. The media tended to portray this case as part of a struggle for the "après-Lacan." Pommier saw it otherwise: as a struggle to clarify the relationship between psychoanalysis and the law.

In September 1985, Pommier wrote several confidential letters to Spanish colleagues in which he criticized Miller and the School of the Cause and discussed plans for a new psychoanalytic review. One of the Spaniards with whom Pommier corresponded was in analytic treatment with Jacques-Alain Miller and gave Miller one of Pommier's letters. Pommier accused Miller of using information from this letter against him and claimed a violation of the principle of professional confidentiality, traditionally thought of as protection for patients, not for colleagues.

The court dismissed Pommier's lawsuit for lack of evidence, but Pommier continued his pursuit of Miller. He saw the professional confidentiality case as only one manifestation of larger problems endemic to psychoanalysis and flagrant at the School of the Freudian Cause: analytic practice tempts analysts to think of themselves as above the law, and analytic legitimacy tends to become a family affair. In April 1989 Pommier wrote directly to his colleagues about his concerns.[4]

> Since the death of Freud, we have seen the repetition of a ludicrous mode of transfer of legitimacy. The I.P.A. claimed a legitimacy by its association with Anna Freud, although neither her practice nor her theories justified it. As long as family ties serve as the means of recognition, to speak of ethics in psychoanalysis is senseless.
>
> Today, Judith Miller, who has never even undergone analysis, heads a foundation whose objectives are the same as those of the I.P.A.: to control theory and to install bureaucracy. It is true that in France the methods and objectives of J.-A. Miller have been rejected by the vast majority of psychoanalysts, obliging him to look abroad for the recognition he didn't receive in Paris. Furthermore, he allows himself to practice psychoanalysis even though he never received the training normally required by all schools of psychoanalysis. (It is known that his analyst refused to continue his training. At the time, J.-A. Miller was writing the last "Lacan" texts which were then signed by J. Lacan.)
>
> It is once again a serious problem of ethics which is posed and because of repeated manipulations of patients for political ends, I have decided to bring the question before the courts.

Pommier was clearly looking for a way to challenge Miller; not surprisingly, the two were soon on opposite sides of another legal proceeding. In the fall of 1989, Pommier published *La Névrose infantile de la psychanalyse*, which elaborated his ideas about the familial transmission of psychoanalysis, noting the case of Anna Freud and that of the Lacan family. In doing so he revisited the question of whether Miller had authored Lacan's last seminars and the many letters that appeared over Lacan's signature during the period of the dissolution and the foundation of the successor organizations to the Freudian School. In his mind there was no doubt: "Jacques-Alain Miller wrote

Lacan's last seminars" (45). Pommier's controversial book was published right before the fall scientific meetings of the School of the
Cause on 14 and 15 October. Books published by school authors are
often sold at these meetings, and Pommier wanted his book to be
among them. It was not to happen that way. Pommier was denied
permission to sell his books, but since he claimed that the school
bylaws did not require that he have permission, he displayed them
despite the official interdiction. When they were repeatedly removed
from the sale table, Pommier blew up and in his anger knocked over
the exhibit table on which books were displayed. That evening, Pommier distributed a press release claiming censorship.

The School of the Freudian Cause expelled Pommier, accusing him
of lying to the press and committing an act of public vandalism that
had humiliated the school in front of twelve hundred conference
participants. Pommier sued the School of the Cause in court and won
on the grounds that he had been discouraged from bringing a lawyer
to a key meeting of the school's internal investigation of his behavior.
Pommier again made it clear that in his view, the current fracas was
a smokescreen for a larger scandal concerning the legitimacy of the
school and the authorship of Lacan's final seminars. Pommier insisted
that it was now time to end the fiction that Lacan had founded the
School of the Cause. "Jacques-Alain Miller should stop trying to profit
from these ambiguities. He should clarify this past or start his own
[psychoanalytic] group. Doing so, he would have the right—and for
the first time—to my respect and he would moderate the scorn that
most French psychoanalysts, both Lacanians and non-Lacanians, feel
for him" (Pommier 1989b, 6).

At the start of this second lawsuit Miller officially declared the
school to be in crisis, and as Lacan had done, he asked for love. Miller
wrote an open letter to the membership and announced a cultural
revolution. Against Pommier's charges, Miller insisted that Lacan's last
wishes did legitimate the school's authority, but that it must now be
born again, its challenged foundations made once again transparent.
Born in crisis, the school would know how to nourish and replenish
itself through crisis. "The crisis of 1990," said Miller; "I want it cold,
clean, and without acrimony" (Miller 1990, 1).

Four months later, the school announced that the crisis was over;
the support for Miller had been overwhelming and it was time to get
back to work (Clastres et al. 1990). When the school's governing body
was informed that Pommier had won his lawsuit because of their faulty
procedures, they began new ones to exclude him, this time conforming
to the requirements set by the courts. Once again Pommier was charged

with "vandalism and public scandal," but four new charges were added, concerning Pommier's general attitude toward the school, for example, "participating in or helping groups that were deliberately founded against the School of the Cause and its friends" (Silvestre 1990, 3–4). In some respects, things seemed to have come back full circle to the logic of the Freudian School dissolution when Lacan removed Denis Vasse from his post as vice president for participating in Confrontation. But the 1990 School of the Freudian Cause was a very different kind of organization from the 1979 Freudian School. Its dissidents were already gone. Its members were prepared to take the role of militants, increasingly stigmatized by the rest of the French analytic and even Lacanian landscape. Indeed, in the 1990s, French psychoanalysis faces the prospect of a new myth in the making. It goes roughly like this: good Lacanians, defined as Lacanians who abandoned Miller, can get along with almost everybody, and the only significant cleavage is between the School of the Freudian Cause and the others.

Miller interprets analysts' animosity toward him as a projection of their guilt for having abandoned Lacan: "I am their 'living tort' [*leur tort vivant*], their insupportable object." And he believes that at bottom they cannot tolerate that Lacan chose him over them.

> It was I, still a student at the time, whom he invited for weekends at his country house! It was I, to whom he gave the mission of transcribing [the seminars]. . . . He put his hand on my shoulder; we made a pact. He gave me this task, he didn't give it to the others. And he chose me from the crowd to make me promise that I would take on all of the seminars. . . . It is this that they cannot tolerate: they dream to get from me that which they lost of the Freudian field because of their conflict with Lacan. I symbolize the living signifier of their castration! [*Libération*, 16 July 1985, 29]

Whether or not one agrees with Miller's interpretation, on one point he is right. French Lacanians (and non-Lacanians) without Lacan are preoccupied with Miller as a member of Lacan's family, the inheritor of his literary estate, the favored disciple, and finally, as the one who dared to put himself in Lacan's place in the establishment of the seminars. During Lacan's life, analysts found the notion of Miller as Lacan's extension and alter ego hard to take. With Lacan gone, it seemed to become intolerable.

Preoccupations with Miller are apparent in recent discussions of proposals about the licensing of psychoanalysts. Since the early 1980s, French analysts have feared that the government might decide to require state certification to practice, a "statut de la psychanalyse."

More recently, these fears have been heightened by the economic integration of the European community; neighboring EEC countries enforce strict controls over the analytic profession. In France, where all analytic schools have been influenced by Lacan, such a plan is profoundly countercultural. Lacan believed that psychoanalysis is more like a calling than a traditional profession, more like the priesthood than the law. The only person, insisted Lacan, who can know if an analysand is ready to assume the position of an analyst is that analysand. No official certification can validate an analyst's right to practice. "Only the analyst can authorize himself as an analyst." Self-authorization was a cornerstone of what I have termed Lacan's "Psychoanalytic Protestantism" (Turkle 1978, 16). But when self-authorization became a popular slogan, it had unintended effects. In the 1970s in France, the label "analyst" became prestigious, chic, and financially rewarding. The doctrine of self-authorization gave a wide range of French therapeutic practitioners (marriage counselors, group therapists, social workers) who had had some experience with a personal analysis the justification they were looking for to declare themselves analysts. By the end of the decade, there was no longer any straightforward way to know who was doing what. The chaotic situation was exacerbated by the dissolution of the Freudian School; after the dissolution many analysts never again formally joined any psychoanalytic organization. Indeed, by 1989, half the analysts practicing in France were working outside of any institutional framework.

Most French analysts do not want government intervention, but many found it hard to resist an opportunity to use discussion of it as a forum in which to denounce Lacanians, or if they were Lacanians, to denounce Millerians. The sentiment grew among them that they needed to put their own house in order before the government did it for them. In December 1989, Serge Leclaire, one of Lacan's closest collaborators during the early days of the Freudian School, led an effort that proposed that analysts create a formal mechanism for self-regulation, an Order of Psychoanalysts.[5] The organization would determine which practitioners had a right to call themselves analysts, in the hope that all designated analysts would then be treated equally by the tax and social security systems, putting an end to the present financial discrimination against analysts who are not also licensed physicians.

Leclaire's proposals, which would require selecting "true" from "false" analysts, revived controversies of the early 1960s, when the International Psychoanalytic Association expelled Lacan and his colleague Françoise Dolto for not meeting its "standards" but was willing to welcome their students on condition that they renounce their mentors. The paradox was apparent: if the trainers were flawed, what made the trainees acceptable? To the generation of French analysts who had grown up in an atmosphere charged with this history, it was clear that psychoanalytic standards often boil down to psychoanalytic politics, and this seemed no less true in 1989, when analysts were motivated by a desire to exclude Miller, than it had been in the 1960s, when they wanted to exclude Lacan.

### Part II: The Cultural Appropriation of Psychoanalysis

PSYCHOANALYTIC MOVEMENTS VERSUS PSYCHOANALYTIC CULTURES

The French psychoanalytic takeoff and the explosive growth of a psychoanalytic culture were phenomena of the 1960s, but three decades later they are still going strong. There are an estimated fifteen thousand analysts in France, which translates into an annual business figure of about 1.5 billion francs a year.[6] Unlike the situation in America, where the number of patients in classical analysis has decreased and analysts usually fill their practices with patients in analytically inspired psychotherapy, most reports have it that French analysts are able to find analytic patients. There is also widespread testimony about a democratization of the analytic cure, even in the provinces. Paul Mathis describes his full-time analytic practice in Toulon, a city that had two analysts in 1960 and more than a hundred analysts in 1989, claiming that it includes "doctors, lawyers, judges, high school and grade school teachers, naval officers, and a few workers from the naval shipyards. The only people I have never seen in my office are policemen." In a 1986 survey, 18 percent of all French adults knew someone in psychoanalysis (*L'Express* 19–25 May 1989, 75).

This growth and democratization of clientele has gone hand in hand with increasing coverage of matters psychoanalytic in the French popular media. Eric Cantona, a young French soccer star, described to *L'Express* how he had to cut his analysis short to make a career move from Auxerre to Marseilles:

> When I stopped, we had barely begun to explore the real questions, emotional problems, sexual problems, problems with my family. So I had to begin again—once again I felt a lack, no one to speak to, to really speak to. ... When I am in analysis, it is like an oil change, I am in my best form, I play my best. Yes, I must start again. It's no longer a curiosity but a necessity. As a matter of fact everyone should have the courage to have done one. Everyone should at the very least, read Freud and Groddeck. [72]

It is a public testimonial that is hard to imagine from an American baseball or British cricket star.

Beginning with Marie Cardinale's 1976 *The Words to Say It*, the French "psychoanalytic novel" or "report from the couch" became a new French literary genre. Two of its most recent manifestations, *Seductions on the Couch* (Anonymous 1989) and *My Analyst and Me* (Augerolles 1989), portray patients who after being sexually exploited by their analysts find salvation *through a second psychoanalysis*, this time with a more serious practitioner. Patients find psychoanalysts through the yellow pages of the phone directory, through computerized information systems available on home networks, and through personal advertisements that sometimes include the analyst's photograph. The best known of French analysts, including Lacan, Serge Leclaire, Françoise Dolto, and Gérard Miller, turned to radio and television to bring their messages to the public.

The French psychoanalytic takeoff speaks to larger issues about the growth of psychoanalytic cultures. A psychoanalytic culture is not something that a psychoanalytic movement can create in the outside world; the outside world has to be ready. This is an area of inquiry where it is wise to be reticent about "providing comprehensive accounts or global theories." The relationship of elite to popular cultures cannot be reduced to any simple "two-culture" argument; "the network formed by family, educational system, state, organized religion, and commodified economy," all of these loci of psychoanalytic culture, "has complex connections with levels of culture and psychic processes" (LaCapra 1987, 242). Comparisons among different national cultures and between psychoanalysis and other philosophies of everyday life help to place global theories in the context of a more concrete sociology of psychoanalytic thirst.

Philip Rieff has written that psychoanalysis flourishes during what he calls a moment of "deconversion," a time of rapid mobility and social dislocation, a time when the old rules and traditional, collective ways of interpreting experience no longer seem to apply (1966). In a traditional society, it is the community and its values that cure; when tradition breaks down, the community no longer serves this function and the individual must create a personal world of symbols and meaning. G. Stanley Hall, Freud's American host, informed Freud in 1909 that he had come to America at an auspicious "psychological moment." I would say rather that he came at an auspicious sociological moment: traditional forces of community and cohesion were dissolving. In France, the moment of deconversion arrived far later, having had to wait for the end of the extraordinary synthesis of state, society, and individual that marked France's republican period.

In contrast to America, France had a smaller and poorer middle class as well as a rigidly centralized educational establishment that was unreceptive to new, not to mention foreign, ideas. In America, psychoanalytic absorption in the history of the individual helped to compensate for the absence of a collective past in the American nation of immigrants. The American habit of public self-congratulation was superimposed on a collective insecurity about parvenu status, which encouraged a compulsive self-examination. In France, on the contrary, ancestors were known by their names and their habits; the past was secure and the future began in it. For the French, psychoanalysis threatened a sense of reassuring continuity by stressing that the past can live within us as an insidious rather than benign presence.

American social fragmentation threw the individual back on the private sphere, where he or she was positioned to become an anxious consumer of reassurances about authentic subjectivity, hidden and deep inner life, and the primacy of intimate experience. In a reflection on the social dislocation of American society and the American splitting of private and public life, sociologist Peter Berger remarked that in America, "If Freud hadn't existed, he would have had to be invented" (1965, 38). One might say that when they faced an analogous situation, the French *did* invent their own Freud, as their society evolved in directions that brought it closer to the loss of community that characterized early twentieth-century America. In a recent study of cultural responses to psychoanalysis, Barry Richards stressed the historical relationship between the appropriation of psychoanalysis and the experience of modern urban life. Expanding on Rieff's thesis, Richards isolates the cultural specificity of psychoanalysis in its ability to help people integrate fragmented urban experience, but "unlike the holistic syntheses promised by contemporaneous cults, it was intended—at least by Freud—to remain truthful to the conflictual core of experience. Its goal was to manage tensions, not to transcend them" (1989, 24).

Following the model suggested by Berger, Rieff, and Richards, one can speculate about the causes of the continuing cultural reticence toward psychoanalysis in Great Britain. There, unlike the situation in France and the United States, a strong psychoanalytic movement exists in relative cultural isolation (Forrester 1990; Kurzweil 1989; Roazen 1990). Psychoanalysis has had little impact on British academic life, and for the most part cultural criticism, political discussion, and social analysis proceed without psychoanalytic referent. British psychoanalytic theory of the object relations school increasingly dominates American clinical discussion, but this international success is coupled with cultural isolation at home.[7]

To put it too simply, the British psychoanalytic movement is not situated in a British psychoanalytic culture. There are powerful psychoanalytic theories but little psychoanalytic thirst. British society seems to have retained certain traditional values that have shielded it from the full implications of deconversion—for example, in the community of British intellectuals, few of whom have turned toward psychoanalysis as have their French and American counterparts. In the early days, the Freudian movement was taken up by a certain literary culture through Bloomsbury, but things did not go much further. For some British intellectuals, the traditional virtues of rationality and logic, an intact sense of caste privilege, and the intellectual aesthetic of analytic philosophy, have served as a shield against what they perceived as the unseemly Freudian onslaught. For others, the role of traditional intellectual values has been played by a style of Marxism hostile to psychoanalysis, which it condemns as reductionist and bourgeois.

The current experience of the Soviet Union gives a new opportunity to reflect on the experience of psychoanalytic thirst. There, in recent years I have been able to observe the development of a situation where psychoanalysis is very much in demand in a context of virtually no cultural supply. Freud had been unofficially banned since the 1930s, but with *glasnost* and the relaxation of censorship, there has been a race to republish his texts; in 1989-90 more than a million copies of the first official publication of Freud's essays were printed and sold before they made their way into bookstores.

In the Soviet Union today, people are visibly eager to understand their experience in psychoanalytic terms. Freud is one symbol among many others for democratization, free expression, and the growth of a new individualism in personal and economic life. The Soviet situation is intriguing because it is the mirror image of that in Britain. Again, to put it too simply: Britain has a psychoanalytic movement and no psychoanalytic culture; the Soviet Union has no psychoanalytic movement but the first precondition for a psychoanalytic culture, a widespread psychoanalytic thirst.

Not surprisingly, life in Moscow in 1991 is characterized precisely by a crisis of community and traditional values characteristic of a period of deconversion. With the communist party and its view of history delegitimated, the Soviet individual is thrown into the uncharted waters of having to define individual purpose. In Berger's terms, something has to be invented or reinvented. On the side of reinvention, Eastern Orthodox religion is the main contender. But its appeal is conservative: the reintegration of the individual into a collectivity, a collectivity that looks to the past. On the side of invention, there are classical models of free enterprise, Social Darwinism, and a range of psychologies of the individual, among them psychoanalysis. In the Soviet Union today, psychoanalysis is perceived as an ideology for the invention of a new kind of person who can make it alone and who has meaning alone, without party or state.

On my first visit to the Soviet Union, in 1987, I met Soviets who held tattered Freudian texts, translated and printed in the 1920s and banned in the 1930s, as though they were precious religious icons. The analogy to the icons is more than metaphorical. For the most part, Freud's works were kept in locked rooms in libraries. And when there was private possession, their reverent study tended to be kept a guarded secret. In 1988, I met philosophy students who had been analyzed by their elders, and their elders by their elders, a small and somewhat clandestine community that took its direction from Freud's earlier writings, largely because these were the most readily available. By 1989, the situation was far more open. Among students, intellectuals, teachers, and therapists of all varieties, there was interest in and demand for analysis—indeed, repeated demands that I undertake training analyses during a three-week visit to Moscow. (My objections to this procedure were repeatedly challenged with the comment: "Isn't that how Freud analyzed his first students on their visits to Vienna?")

By spring 1989, the question of publishing Freud had become one symbol of stronger demands for freedom of speech and press. The first publication of Freud in the Soviet Union since Stalin's ban was not by the state publishing office but by a member of the new class of free enterprise entrepreneurs, Marat Akchuran. Akchuran headed a small private business that, in the somewhat confusing lexicon of Soviet free enterprise, is called a "cooperative." In May 1989, he printed 100,000 copies of *Three Essays on Sexuality*, using a text taken from a small provincial library. But the law that established cooperatives did not permit these "private" organizations to publish books, a right reserved for state publishing houses. Freud's *Three Essays* became a test case to challenge that law.

The edition of the *Three Essays* was seized. The reasons given by the state bureaucracy: Freud was still banned, these ideas were bad for youth, the texts were pornographic, and finally, only the state could publish books. In Moscow 1989, publishing Freud became a symbol of the right to repressed knowledge and of the rights of free enterprise to trade in the marketplace of ideas. By the following September, a state publishing house, Prosvichenia, had released a collection of Freud essays that ran through two editions and sold one and a quarter million copies within six months.

Looking at psychoanalysis in different national settings suggests that while one level of understanding psychoanalytic appropriability stresses the large social processes that constitute what Rieff called deconversion, a second needs to be on the level of a more intimate sociology: the way that ideas come to connect with individuals, the "inner history" of sciences of mind. Deconversion creates the context for individualistic ideologies to flourish. But which ones will flourish? Which ones will be able to make a connection? Here, two factors come into play. A first relates to a theory's *intrinsic* appropriability because of its internal structure, a second to the "fit" between a specific theory and moment in the life of a specific society or group within it.

Psychoanalytic ideas are intrinsically "appropriable," chiefly because people can take them up and play with them in an active way. In the popular appropriation of psychoanalysis, what people play with are Freudian "objects" such as dreams, slips, and jokes. The "Freudian slip" as an "object to think with" provided one important way for psychoanalytic ideas to weave themselves into the fabric of everyday life. Freudian ideas about slips became well known and gained wide acceptance for reasons that had little to do with positive assessments of their scientific validity and a great deal to do with the fact that they are almost-tangible ideas. You can analyze your slips and those of your friends. Slips are manipulable and thus appealing. As we look for slips and play with them, both seriously and not so seriously, psychoanalytic ideas, at the very least the idea that there is an unconscious, begin to seem more natural.

The play of manipulable objects also stands behind the appropriability of other theories of mind that have easily passed from the world of high science to the larger culture. In the domain of education, "constructionist" theory puts the emphasis on the active engagement and personal construction of knowledge by learners; when looking at the development of psychoanalytic culture, constructionism puts the emphasis on the same active qualities in the potential consumers of ideas about mind. To clarify this point, I consider a classical "slip" (one from Freud's own collection) from the perspective of two highly appropriable theories of mind: the psychoanalytic and the computational.

At the beginning of a meeting, recounts Freud, its chairman rises to greet the participants and says, "I now declare this meeting closed."

For Freud it is obvious that the slip is a source of information about the real wishes of the chairman: "The President secretly *wished* he was already in a position to close the sitting, from which little good was to be expected" (*S.E.* 6:59). From a computational perspective, however, things need not be so emotionally complex. People, like computer programs, can become momentarily derailed. And when this happens and a slip occurs, it doesn't necessarily reflect secret wishes or hidden ambivalence. It may simply reveal the mechanisms of computation. The computational perspective on the chairman's slip begins with a view of the brain as a computer that contains information in something like a dictionary.[8] In an ordinary dictionary, the words *closed* and *open* are far apart. But when information is stored in a computer, opposites are commonly represented by the same symbol, with another symbol to represent negation. In other words, hot = ( − )cold, dry = ( − )wet, and of course, open = ( − )closed. In the computer's storage medium, open and closed would be right next to each other, precisely because they are so far apart in meaning. Thus, in the case of a computationally modeled slip, all that has happened when *closed* is substituted for *open* is that a minus sign, a bit of information, has been dropped. As one of my students at MIT once put it, reflecting on Freud's example of the unhappy chairman: "All that has happened is that a bit has been dropped. There has been a power surge. No problem."

When what was once seen as a Freudian slip comes to be theorized as an information-processing error, there has been a shift in focus from meaning to mechanism. From the point of view of content, the two models, psychoanalytic and computational, are dramatically different. However, from the perspective of our inquiry into what makes theories of mind appropriable, what is most striking is not their differences but their similarity. Each offers accessible and manipulable objects to think with. Each allows its objects to be easily anthropomorphized.

The appropriation of computational ideas about slips, and through these, the idea of mind as computer, takes place through a process of personal identification with objects or agents within the machine. You pour catsup into your coffee instead of cream. The computational model, as I have argued elsewhere (1984, 300), allows you to imagine a computer in your place and think of its workings as a process involving numerous subprograms. One program is called up to locate the cream, another to locate the coffee, another to get a fix on the location of the hand, another to get it going in the right direction, and others to check that it is on the right path, to verify that the position of hand, creamer, cup have not changed, and so on. In this buzz of activity it is hardly surprising that one of these programs might go wrong. At a given moment, the program that verifies that the position of $X$ has not changed might "mistakenly" take $X$ to be catsup instead of cream, because another program on which it depends is still registering catsup as "the object of greatest salience," a morsel of information left over from a previous phase of the meal during which catsup was appropriately being poured on a cheeseburger. Once you have identified with the computer you cannot fail to identify with the error, since each of us knows that we make many more errors when "we" are consciously involved in a scenario as complex as this one. People are able to identify with the programs and so become sympathetic to their confusion.

Computational models of slips are appropriable because their description of how a computer works sounds so much like a confused person that people identify with the computer to the point of believing that it makes slips for the same reasons they do. Computational theories of mind are appropriable because the anthropomorphization is direct: one is asked to imagine programs and subroutines as inner agents in a computer's "society of mind."[9] Similarly, psychoanalytic theory offers a compelling cast of inner agents and games to play with them. To take the simplest case (which is the only case that matters when examining the reasons for a theory's appropriability), when you think about psychoanalysis, you can imagine the rational ego, dirty id, and censoring superego as inner personae. In the case of psychoanalysis and computational models of mind, people imagine themselves in the role of the psychic entities, and acting out these roles feels enough like an acting out of the theories to give the sense of understanding them. *Whether or not one really understands computational and psychoanalytic theories in their technical detail, each offers active experiences that break down resistance to seeing mind in its terms.* So one way to describe the appropriability of specific theories of mind is to talk about the possibilities they offer for concrete manipulation.

For this point of view, Lacan's genius was that although he was an extremely abstract theorist, he also gave psychoanalysis a new set of concrete objects to think with. His integration of linguistics and its notation into psychoanalytic discourse provided a highly manipulable object language. Whether or not one thinks this new language moved psychoanalytic thinking in a desirable direction, its cultural power was unquestionable. It gave psychoanalysis new relevance for those who took text as their object; it opened up what Lacan termed the "Freudian field" to the larger study of discourse. And taken as a formal game, Lacan's play of equations, of little letters and big letters, of bars and ratios of signifiers to signified, was easy to pick up and experiment with, even if crudely. Indeed, towards the end of his life, Lacan embodied the process of theorizing in the manipulation of complex knots whose configurations symbolized the structure of the mind as he understood it. At a seminar at MIT in 1976, he spoke of how manipulating and perforating the spheres of string knots is "the thing to which the spirit is most rebel." The knots "so contradict our global sense of our bodies as enveloped and enveloping that to try oneself in the praxis of knots is to shatter inhibition" (Turkle 1978, 237).

For Lacan, doing the theory, working on the knots, practicing the manipulations, was an integral element in the emergence of insight about the self, in the same sense that psychoanalytic insight grows out of the lived relationship with an analyst. In the case of the knots, Lacan believed that the *objects themselves* carried the theory.[10] Claude Lévi-Strauss wrote of the power of *bricolage*, a theoretical tinkering at the heart of a science of the concrete (1968). Lacan himself was a bricoleur; beyond this, he facilitated the work of bricolage on a cultural level.

Lacan's discussion of the fears and inhibitions provoked by the practice of the knots raises another issue relating to the appropriation of theory through active manipulation and construction. Some constructions are more evocative than others because they are more threatening. Freud's theory of slips is a theory of why people make them: we try to repress unacceptable wishes, but they break through all the same. It is also a theory of why people like to think about slips: they offer a way to get closer to these taboo wishes. And most central to my subject here, it is a theory of why people are attracted to Freudian ideas in general: they offer us a way to come close to aspects of ourselves, such as sexuality and aggression, which we censor but at the same time want to be in contact with, the uncivilized that makes us human. In my own research, I have observed that this is equally true of computational ideas (1984). If behind popular acceptance of Freudian theory was a nervous, often guilty preoccupation with the self as sexual, behind the widespread interest in computational interpretations of the self is an equally nervous preoccupation with the self as machine. Playing with psychoanalytic and computational theories allows us to play with aspects of our nature that we experience as taboo.

Discussing the appropriability of a psychological theory in terms of its ability to offer concrete "objects to think with" puts the emphasis on a theory's intrinsic or formal qualities. But raising the question of what is taboo at a given moment in the life of a society points to the necessity of another level of analysis. Appropriable theories must be available for a process of sculpting by the culture into which they are deployed. Anthropologists have long stressed that to be effective, models of healing must be congruent with the values, structure, and symbols of the surrounding culture (e.g., Lévi-Strauss 1963; Turner 1967); psychoanalysis is no exception. "Every country creates the psychoanalysis it needs, although it does so unconsciously," said sociologist Edith Kurzweil, whose work on comparative psychoanalysis provides rich material for thinking about the cultural plasticity of psychoanalytic ideas (1989, 1). To take the present example, the "French Freud," whose idiom invaded French life and language in the 1960s, was a very different animal than "American Freud" ever was or is today.

In America, a special mix of optimism, individualism, and voluntarism contributed to the acceptance of a psychoanalytic therapy founded on the belief that people can change themselves by their own efforts if they want to. American individualism tends to represent the individual as a virtuoso or entrepreneur of his or her own self. Although it underscores autonomy, it does not assume that we each possess an inviolable inner core that constitutes our "human nature." Thus, it is very different from traditional French ideas about individualism that focus on the individual's boundaries and isolation from others. French notions about the immutable self were hard to reconcile with an active notion of psychoanalytic interventionism. But they are reflected in Jacques Lacan's style of psychoanalytic theory, which places the emphasis on psychoanalysis as an interpretive science in which images of analytic listening and analytic understanding are more salient than promises of analytic cure.

From the beginning Lacan scorned any vision of psychoanalysis as a medical and therapeutic technique that could be placed in the service of social adaptation. In large measure he got his point across by contrasting a radical French School with adaptationist American ego psychology. By the late 1960s, the idea of psychoanalysis as antiauthoritarian, even "subversive," had become one of Lacan's lasting contributions to French psychoanalytic culture. The cultural presence of this idea has a potential "*effet de retour*" on the movement. For example, when in 1989 Serge Leclaire and his colleagues proposed a professional association that would certify psychoanalytic practitioners, the "Order of Psychoanalysis," the popular (one might even say establishment) "leftist" press, from Le Monde to Libération, consistently raised the question of whether such an "order" was compatible with psychoanalysis's radical vocation.

In contrast, Americans accepted psychoanalysis, but they shaped it to their image of what would be helpful. American psychoanalytic ego psychology, directed toward an active adaptation of the patient to reality, toward what came to be called "coping," brought Freudianism in line with American beliefs about the virtue and necessity of an optimistic approach. This version of psychoanalysis, considerably more optimistic than Freud's own, could then be presented as a recipe for individual change.[11] Ego psychology was the version of the conscious most acceptable to the unconscious.

Aspects of psychoanalytic theory that could not be brought into line were rejected or reshaped. So, for example, American optimism would naturally rebel against that part of the Freudian message that suggested an early and irrevocable determination of character. Erik Erikson's work is a good example of how psychoanalytic theory was able to take on a more acceptable American form. Erikson's emphasis on adolescent and adult development and on a life cycle in which early themes get to be replayed at later stages suggests that we all get second chances, as do Heinz Kohut's ideas about reparenting, another image that aptly fits American dreams. In America, where there is no strong intellectual tradition of the Left, optimistic revisions of Freud focused on an adaptation to a reality whose justice was rarely challenged. In France, on the other hand, where there is a strong political and intellectual Left, psychoanalysts became deeply involved in radical social criticism, and French social criticism became deeply involved with psychoanalytic thinking. In France, Lacanian psychoanalytic premises became the common reference shared by Communist party and nonparty Marxism, utopian and anarchistic *gauchisme*, and feminism.

The political valence of the general French psychoanalytic culture is a striking example of how a specific historical movement creates the psychoanalysis it can use, shaping theory into forms best suited to its special needs. When in the early 1970s, disappointed American student radicals turned toward psychology and the self, they felt that they were turning *away* from politics (Turkle 1978). In France after 1968, this was not the case. French students and intellectuals maintained a sense of political continuity as their activities and language took on a psychoanalytic tone. Given the almost total disjuncture of psychoanalytic and radical political discourse in France before 1968, it seemed clear that something new was going on.

What was going on was the emergence of a Lacanian reading of Freud that served as a bridge between politics and psychology. Psychoanalysis had long been associated with bourgeois thought, but Lacan rehabilitated it for radicals. Lacan came to personify a conception of psychoanalysis not as a quasi-medical technique focused on cure but as a scientific discipline and individual research program that needs no further therapeutic justification. This therapeutic indifference goes hand in hand with a radical critique of the psychoanalytic institution. For Lacan, becoming and being a psychoanalyst involve processes of scientific discovery and self-development that have nothing to do with having a particular academic degree, with belonging to the bureaucracy of a psychoanalytic institute, or with following a set of rules on how to conduct psychoanalytic sessions. For example, the orthodox length of a psychoanalytic session has long been set at about fifty minutes. Lacan would shorten or lengthen the session according to what was happening with a particular patient on a particular day, thus using time as well as speech to punctuate analytic discourse. The fact that Lacan's perspective has been, at least in theory, resolutely anti-institutional, pitted for decades against the psychoanalytic "church," seen as American and adaptationist, made it easier for Lacan's ideas to filter through the world of French radical politics. But the reconciliation between psychoanalysis and radical politics was due to more than Lacan's well-known stands against bureaucracy. In Lacan's psychoanalytic theory Marxists were able to find ways to neutralize some of the complaints they had traditionally lodged against Freud and his followers.

For example, the Marxist complaint that psychoanalysis "adapts" people to bourgeois society seemed to have been disarmed by Lacan's insistence that only a perversion of psychoanalysis conceives of itself in terms of adapting people to the social status quo. He presented psychoanalysis as a form of truth seeking. If cure came at all it came *par surcroît*, as a bonus, or a form of secondary gain. From this vision, the Left was able to extract a notion of psychoanalysis as a facilitator of political consciousness raising. A second Marxist reproach to psychoanalysis has been that in the face of human misery, psychoanalysis eschews societal analysis to focus on the individual ego. For Lacan, however, the coherent autonomous ego is an illusion, and one of the goals of psychoanalytic science is to explain its social construction, a view that places Freud's contribution, like that of Marx, at the center of interest for those who want to understand the individual in society (Althusser 1964–65). A third Marxist objection has been the alleged biological determinism of psychoanalysis. Does anatomy make destiny, or does destiny derive from the individual's place in a social system of production? Lacan's reading of Freud is militantly antibiological, shifting all descriptions from a biological-anatomical level to a symbolic one. According to Lacan, Freud never meant to say anything about anatomy, and where he seems to be talking about anatomy, he is really talking about how culture imposes linguistic meaning on anatomical parts. To put it too simply, for Lacan, when Freud seems to be talking about organs, he is really talking about information. In sum, Lacan mediated a French connection between Marxism, feminism, political antipsychiatry, and psychoanalysis.

Richards has observed that psychoanalysis has historically been "available to diverse and often quite divergent political appropriations" (1989, 128). The unconscious has been "inserted and with equal conviction into both historical materialism and classical liberalism" (128). He concludes that the contributions psychoanalysis makes to particular political outlooks "are not a matter of logical affinities between abstract forms of discourse ... but of whether there are the people around, able and willing to do the intellectual work required to establish cooperative relationships between psychoanalytic thinking and any particular kind(s) of political perspective" (128–29). Indeed, what makes the story of Lacanianism so important for the sociology of sciences of mind is the size, the passion, and the diversity of the "interpretive community" it was able to mobilize in post-1968 France.

In the years following the events of 1968 there has been an ongoing debate on whether Lacan was "really" a radical. This debate has tended to focus on the exegesis of Lacan's texts, looking for their political implications.[12] However, once we take a perspective that shifts the emphasis away from "text" to its active reconstruction by a reader or community of readers, the limitations of this kind of analysis become clear. Any question about a theory's "real" politics looks for a message within the theory to reveal itself with final clarity. But for a theory to be taken up and reconstructed by a large and diverse group of readers, the criterion is not that the theory have a clear message but that it be evocative. And evocative theory can be ambiguous rather than clear (Turkle 1984, 1–25), just as evocative objects, objects that provoke thought, are most often liminal, posed betwixt and between our standard categories (Turner 1966). Ambiguity makes ideas evocative and appropriable because different people can make them their own in their own way. From this point of view, the appropriability of Lacanian ideas may follow less from their specificity than from their lack of specificity. They left space for personal construction and personal appropriation.

Thus, the growth of psychoanalytic cultures is facilitated by a movement of social deconversion and by the presence of theory in a form that is both concrete and culturally malleable. There is a crucial third factor as well: *theories most easily pass into popular culture when they offer a way for people to "think through" a collective issue of political and social identity.* The notion of using theory to "think through" a historical event is well illustrated by a nonpsychoanalytic example. French existentialist writers began writing before the war, but it was only in the postwar years that, in a sense, history caught up with them. Their philosophy of extreme situations and of action for extraordinary individuals was resonant with the French experience of the Occupation and Resistance. Part of existentialism's popular appeal was that it provided a way to think through the issues of choice and individual responsibility that had been raised by the war years: to collaborate or not to collaborate, to betray or not to betray those who did.

The infatuation with Freud and Lacan that followed the events of May 1968 drew on a relationship between psychoanalysis and the May events that was in many ways similar to the one between existentialism and the Occupation and Resistance. Both theories offered historically appropriable "objects to think with," theoretical materials for a cultural process analogous to the concrete manipulations that Lévi-Strauss called "bricolage" or tinkering. Both theories mobilized interpretive communities who were both motivated and able to build the bridges between abstract ideas and everyday life. Both theories were available at a historically appropriate moment for audiences who would build with them. When people "build with ideas," timing is all-important. Lacan's ideas were present for many years, contributing to an intellectually vibrant psychoanalytic movement. In the late 1960s, there was a new combination: good materials available at the same time as motivated builders.

May–June 1968 was an explosion of speech and desire. It called for the invention of new political forms that looked not to the politics of traditional political parties but to a politics of the person. For a short while the events looked like a revolution in the making, but then suddenly they were over. After the events, people were left hungry for a way to continue to think about sexuality and self-expression as part of a revolutionary movement; people were left hungry for a way to think about the personal as the political and social. "Thinking through the events" required a theory that integrated the political and the personal, addressed the tension between society and individual. Lacan provided materials for building that theory in his ideas about the transition from an imaginary to a symbolic realm, the transition from presocial to social with the acquisition of language.

Lacan's theory of the construction of the symbolic order, when language and law enter men and women, allows for no real boundary between self and society: human beings become social with the appropriation of language, and it is language that constitutes human beings as subjects. In this way of looking at things, society doesn't "influence" an autonomous individual but comes to dwell within him or her at the moment of the appropriation of language. In the description of this moment, Lacan, like Rousseau, described a powerful myth of passage that was able to serve as a framework for thinking about the relationship between the individual and society in a way that Wilhelm Reich's discussion of a "natural man" deformed by a crass society could not. In Lacan's version of the banishment from Eden *there is no natural man* and therefore no way of thinking about society as coming *after* to thwart his nature. The infant is alienated in the imaginary realm, a realm of mirrors and misidentifications, an imaginary order that always remains with us, as does the structure of the social order when we pass into the symbolic.

People who thought of themselves as being on the Left were able to read Lacan as suggesting that the notion of a private self is itself a construct of capitalism and that the distinction between private and public, the very touchstone of bourgeois thought, exists only as bourgeois ideology. This interpretation was surely far from Lacan's intent when he wrote, and such appropriations might well have seemed off the point both to him and to dedicated members of his psychoanalytic movement. But such appropriations are the stuff of psychoanalytic culture.

Lacanianism offered images that were "good to think with" for addressing the issues that surrounded the May events. The Lacanian mythology, his vivid and richly imaged portrait of the social and linguistic construction of the subject in the symbolic dimension, became a common idiom in French discourse in the years that followed 1968. For several years, much of French social thought situated itself in what one could term "Lacanian space." That is to say, French social and political theory tended to accept the fundamentals of Lacan's theoretical scaffolding, in particular the notions that people are constituted by language, that our discourse embodies the society beyond, and that there is no autonomous ego. People who disagreed profoundly with each other—and people who disagreed profoundly with Lacan—nevertheless situated themselves in this space.

In writing about the May events and the psychoanalytic takeoff, Richards describes a historical puzzle. Was the philosophy that grew out of May 1968 congruent with psychoanalytic thought, or did people turn to psychoanalysis because of their disappointment and disillusion (1989, 122)? However, when we put the emphasis on active appro-

priation of theory, it is clear that this puzzle assumes a false dichotomy. After 1968 a community did the work to make an ambiguous
and multivalent Lacanian theory congruent with their politics and
philosophy. Psychoanalysis did provide an escape from the disappoint-
ments of May, but not in any simple sense. Part of its appeal was
precisely that it kept the events in focus.

"Thinking through the May events" required a theory that could
integrate politics and the person. In the "après-mai," this theory was
psychoanalysis. When I speak of "thinking through the Resistance" by
"thinking existentialism" or "thinking through the May events" by
"thinking psychoanalysis," I am not describing a use of theory to
*explain* social conditions, but rather a way of using theory to work
through powerful cultural images, to help to arrange these images into
new and clearer patterns. In the case of the May events and psychoanalysis, people used contact with the theory to keep in touch with
the stuff of which the events were made. For a person to use theory
in this way does not require a full understanding of its subtleties.
Understanding the power of theory in such cases constitutes a "sociology of superficial knowledge" that does not trivialize the meanings
of that theory in the life of an individual or culture. In this spirit, the
widespread phenomenon of "coffee-table Lacan" does not imply de-
nigration of those who used him in that way. The books on the coffee
table are a serious object of study for social epistemology.

In the Soviet Union today, the people who talk so much about
psychoanalysis often don't even have a psychoanalytic book to put on
their coffee table, if indeed they have a coffee table. The psychoanalytic
discourse there is impressionistic and fragmented, based largely on
images of psychoanalysis frozen in the 1930s. And yet, the images
drawn from this "time-capsule Freud" serve urgent current purposes.
Soviets *want* to talk about repression, the unconscious, the things they
feel but were not allowed to say, the things they have trained themselves not even to feel. In this context, psychoanalysis carries a heavy
symbolic burden. Traditional Soviet psychiatric doctrine argued that
all mental distress was born in the material illness of the body or in
the lack of integration of the individual into the socialist collectivity.
In a striking analogy with the meanings carried by psychoanalysis in
the years after May 1968, it has become symbolic of the individual,
the idiosyncratic, the power of new and previously unliberated forces
for change. Psychoanalysis has become symbolic of the symbolic itself.

When psychoanalysis carries such symbolic baggage, the burdens
may be heavy. To the extent that psychoanalysis is a subversive science,
undermining all accepted truths, what does it mean when it becomes

acceptable, "the thing to do"? Freud thought he was bringing America "the plague." Instead, cultural diffusion occurred at the price of normalization, of medical and social acceptability. In America today, the specificity of the Freudian field sometimes seems lost in the morass of self-help and therapeutic homilies. In France, where psychoanalysis has been deployed as social ideology, there is the associated risk that the psychoanalytic movement will be consumed in psychoanalytic culture. Psychoanalysis, like anarchism, is a system committed to breaking down systems. Does the continuing power of the psychoanalytic movement, like that of anarchism, depend on permanent revolution rather than social acceptability?

Today's French psychoanalytic culture stands in a complex relationship to this issue. It could even be described as schizophrenic. On the one hand, I have noted that the years since Lacan's death in 1981 have been marked by an ever-increasing normalization of the enterprise. On the other hand, Lacan's dissolution of the Freudian School, the debates that followed upon it, and the ensuing struggle for power after his death dramatized central paradoxes in the psychoanalytic movement that have been reported as front page news for nearly ten years: If psychoanalysis is a theory that challenges the power of all bonds, then is the psychoanalytic society a contradiction in terms? Is there a contradiction between a stance of radical self-doubt and the presence of a *Maître*? Does the master-disciple relationship that is built into psychoanalysis subvert what is most subversive about it? In France, the passage of time has made it clear that the politics of self-authorization in the Lacanian movement was in conflict with the presence of a *Maître* whose authority authorized the self-authorization. Lacan, dead or alive, has remained the living legitimating presence.

THE MYTH OF THE WELL-ANALYZED ANALYST

The dissolution, the Melman scandal, the Pommier lawsuits, all of these are chapters in recent French psychoanalytic history in which patients denounce their analysts, analysts denounce their patients, and colleagues of long standing turn against each other. What are we to infer from their bitter quarrels?

Does the fact that these men and women are psychoanalysts call psychoanalysis itself into question? Isn't it the job of psychoanalysts to help people understand and thus master such emotions? Are these out-of-control institutional warriors able to do that kind of work? What do their political struggles say about their qualities as analysts? And what do their public scandals say about their analytic theories?

In physics, theories are not shaken by the neuroses of their creators. But in our scientific culture, opinions about psychoanalytic theory are colored by an image of the well-analyzed analyst, a person whose judgment is legitimated by a degree of calm and distance about his or her own life. Just as each new analysand develops a fantasy about the successful analysis of his or her analyst, the analytic movement perpetuates myths about the successful analyses of its founder and major theorists. In the psychoanalytic movement and the psychoanalytic culture a myth of the well-analyzed analyst is used to legitimate analytic theory.

Analysts are anxious about the release of Freud's private papers because they fear scandal—an affair or indiscretion. But more important, they fear the banal. Will Freud be further revealed as a man who struggled like the rest of us with his demons and his pettiness, man whose self-analysis got him so far and no further, and most damagingly, a man whose unresolved conflicts are transparently spelled out in his theories?

In every part of the world where psychoanalysis has flourished, *the myth of the well-analyzed analyst brings together the psychoanalytic movement and the psychoanalytic culture.* The myth is in the culture because it speaks to common sense. After all, asks the reasonable man and woman, how could Lacan have been a good clinician if he was so obviously hysterical? And the myth has the complicity of the professionals who want to use it to legitimate both their theories and their right to practice. The importance of the myth helps to explain why the identity of Anna Freud's analyst was kept in the shadows for so long (Roazen 1990, xiv). Would a well-analyzed Freud have undertaken the analysis of his daughter? And could a daughter analyzed by her father be well analyzed? Was she in a good position to train a new analytic generation? What is the status of theoretical ideas born of such illegitimate unions?

Freud was protected by well-guarded secrets when he was alive and by a loving biographer and closed archives when he died. In contrast, Lacan's life was an open book. His private affairs were public knowledge, his indiscretions, jealousies, rages, and pettiness were covered as front-page news. The man whom many hailed as the greatest psychoanalytic theorist since Freud was from the beginning hard to place in the category of the "well analyzed." His own analyst testified against him. In a 1953 letter to Marie Bonaparte, Rudolf Loewenstein wrote that Lacan never completed his analysis. Although he promised Loewenstein he would continue, Lacan dropped out of analysis as soon as he had been elected to membership in the Paris Psychoanalytic

Society. "One does not cheat on such an important point with im-
punity," wrote Loewenstein (Oliner 1988, 44). And Lacan's analysands
testified against him. For example, Didier Anzieu, who left Lacan during
the schism of 1963, recounted his experience of what it was like to
be on Lacan's divan.

> During the sessions, Lacan was intermittently attentive. Sometimes, in-
> stead of sitting in his analyst's chair, he paced back and forth in the
> room in order to stretch his legs, to take a book; he sat at his work
> table and read, leafing pages covered with Chinese letters, which,
> apparently, he was learning. ... Sometimes, his maid knocked on the
> door, to bring tea, sandwiches, the mail, or to alert him that he was
> wanted on the telephone. Lacan gave instructions for the answers or
> even went to answer himself. "Don't let this prevent you from contin-
> uing your session during my absence" he told me once as he disappeared
> from the office. [Anzieu 1986, 34]

In France, such examples of Lacan's self-indulgence and aggression
have been talking points for challengers to his theory for nearly half
a century. The state of thinking about the relationship of theorist and
theory is, however, more complex in both the French movement and
culture. Within the French movement, the need to come to terms
with Lacan has provoked a way of thinking about the tensions between
theorist and theory that goes beyond denigrating the scientific contribution by reference to personal failings. Beginning in the 1970s, a
series of works on the cycle of dependence on a beloved *Maître*,
conflict with a dominating *Maître*, and preoccupation with a lost *Maître*
helped to forge a new, more balanced, and sympathetic discourse for
talking about the paradoxes of psychoanalysis. They produced insights
as applicable to the psychoanalytic politics of the "après-Lacan" as
they were to the stormy years before Lacan's death (Granofff 1975;
Roustang 1976) and as applicable to other national settings as they
were to France (Anzieu 1975).

Certainly, in the popular press, the thousands of pages written about
Lacan's bad behavior and the ongoing squabbles among his closest
descendants have often implied that psychoanalysis is delegitimated
by psychoanalysts who are portrayed as unpleasant, unethical, and
unanalyzed. But there is a new trend here as well: indeed, in recent
years, journalists rather than psychoanalysts have frequently displayed
the greater sophistication, sense of humor, and sense of proportion
when discussing the human failings of analysts in relation to their
scientific contributions, another potential *effet de retour* of the culture
onto the movement.[13] In Great Britain, too, this effect is in some
evidence.

In 1988, a play adapted from Phyllis Grosskurth's biography of Melanie Klein opened on the London stage (Wright 1988). *Mrs. Klein* shows psychoanalysis as a calling that can excite damaging passions. Melanie Klein, like Sigmund Freud, analyzed her children. The play explores the tragic dimensions of this undertaking: to feed the theory, its most creative minds had a form of intercourse with their children that the theory itself would dismiss as impossible, and as destructive in its impossibility. In the play, the analyst, Klein, is at war with herself and her offspring. She does not seem to know who her true offspring are. Are they in the theory, her analytic candidates, or her biological children? Her daughter, Melitta Schmideberg, and her "analytic daughter," Paula Heinemann, are locked in battle for her allegiance. Incredibly and cruelly, as the last act of the play unfolds, the daughter by blood does not win. We are far from a Hollywood popularization of psychoanalysis where a rich and beautiful analytic patient (in American films, Ginger Rogers was the actress most likely to play this role) tells all to an omniscient, silent, and bearded analyst. We are in the rag and bone shop of the psychoanalytic life. It is a world that Jacques Lacan and Jacques-Alain Miller, joined to each other through marriage, ambition, and a fusional intellectual relationship, would surely understand.

Many British analysts, especially Kleinians, did not like the play *Mrs. Klein*, thinking it disrespectful of their beloved mentor and friend. That British analysts are troubled by the story of Melanie Klein and her children reflects their fear that telling it undermines the legitimacy of the Kleinian enterprise—it was after all, the same fear that caused the story of Anna Freud's analysis by her father to remain, until recently, cloaked in taboo. But to my mind, *Mrs. Klein* responds to a critical current challenge to the psychoanalytic culture, or rather, a challenge that the psychoanalytic culture poses to the psychoanalytic movement.

If you accept the myth of the well-analyzed analyst, materials that cast doubt on the psychological state of the theorist cast in doubt the status of the theory. Lacan's theory of the analyst rejecting the place of the *sujet supposé savoir* would be called into question if he insisted on taking that place himself,[14] just as the status of Melanie Klein's work on reparation to a mother would be called into question if she never made peace with her own.[15] But this point of view is too simple.

Deep truths about the issues that psychoanalysis touches are very often best understood and communicated by individuals who have experienced them in a raw form. During his visit to MIT in 1976, Lacan held a conversation with an American analyst who claimed she had chosen her profession out of her sense of being the sort of strong person to whom others could turn for help; Lacan admitted that he had come to analysis in "just the opposite way," drawn to Freud for the emphasis he had put not on human strength, but on human vulnerability. Lacan spoke of the analyst as someone deeply in touch with the sense of being at risk and deeply in touch with the knowledge that it is possible "for each of us to go mad." In the case of psychoanalysis, a science of self-reflection, theories embody the personalities of their theorists; elements of character etch themselves in theory, leaving traces of both strength and limitation.[16] The limitations of each theorist and each theory mean that psychoanalysis is best seen as an art form in which theorist and patient, theory and symptom, need to be delicately matched. The construction of theory is a social process; theorists with different personality structures must collaborate on the edifice.

The passions of *Mrs. Klein* and the excesses of the Lacanian saga illuminate but do not necessarily undermine the power of their contributions. Only when psychoanalysis faces all aspects of its history can it fully address the question of the relationship between psychoanalytic theory and the psychological vulnerability of its theorists. For me, confronting this question stands between where we are today and a mature psychoanalytic culture.

*Notes*

1. My narrative draws on my archives of correspondence among Lacanians during the period of the dissolution of the Freudian School (L'Ecole Freudienne) from 1979 to 1981, and in the years following. In their translation I wish to acknowledge the able assistance of Dr. Martin Roberts of the Department of French of Harvard University, who helped me puzzle over the possibilities of meaning in their ambiguities, word plays, and puns. I, of course, am responsible for any errors in the final results of these labors. When possible, I give a reference from a widely available published source. Much of the correspondence relevant to the dissolution and formulation of the Freudian Cause (La Cause Freudienne) and the School of the Freudian Cause (L'Ecole de la Cause Freudienne) from the point of view of those hostile to the dissolution is anthologized in Claude Dorgeuille's 1981 work *La Seconde Mort de Jacques Lacan*. Documents that trace the history of the dissolution from the perspective of its partisans appeared in *L'Ane* 1 ( April–May 1981) and were republished in *Almanach de la dissolution*. Texts signed by Lacan during the dissolution, the founding of the Freudian Cause, and the founding of the School of the Freudian Cause were first collected in the School's 1982 mem-

bership directory and are reprinted in its 1985 publication *Actes de fondation et autres textes*. Letters and documents pertaining to the actions taken by the School of the Freudian Cause against Gérard Pommier beginning in October 1989 were distributed to School members in a three-part collection entitled *Annexe aux Pré-Rapports*. Letters pertaining to the political crisis at the School of the Freudian Cause beginning with Jacques-Alain Miller's December 1989 declaration of crisis were distributed to school members in a three-part collection, *A Ciel ouvert*.

This history of the dissolution of the Freudian School has been admirably chronicled in Elisabeth Roudinesco's *Lacan and Co.: A History of Psychoanalysis in France 1925–1985*. This second volume of Roudinesco's history is of the greatest interest to all students of the period. Carefully researched, using archival and interview material never previously reported on, *Lacan and Co.* recounts the Lacanian saga from a unique, insider's point of view. Roudinesco and I were often working from the same primary sources, in particular, the circulars and letters that constituted the correspondence among Lacanians, but I owe a special debt to her work. Embroidered with finely drawn portraits and personal reminiscences, her account provides a rich context for written source material.

2. Personal communication, interview with Jacques-Alain Miller, 20 June 1989.

3. For a recent explication and critique of the link between Lacanianism and feminism, see Macey (1988).

4. I have a copy of this letter in my personal archives. I do not know of its being available in any published source.

5. Leclaire was joined by Jacques Sédat, Danièle Lévy, Lucien Israël, and Philippe Girard. The proposal was published in *Le Monde* on 15 December 1989, accompanied by a news story and a set of commentaries by analysts both for and against the plan, a good example of what from an American perspective seems like an extraordinary level of coverage for matters psychoanalytic in French media.

6. This estimate was made by analyst Gérard Mendel and cited in *L'Express* (19–27 May 1989, 72). Danièle Lévy estimates the number of French analysts as considerably lower, between forty-five hundred and five thousand (*Le Nouvel Observateur* 4–10 January 1990, 6).

7. Where psychoanalytic discourse has entered the broader intellectual culture—for example, in the area of film and feminist criticism as seen in the journals *Screen* and *m/f*—it is significant that these publications are influenced by Lacanian analysis rather than indigenous Freudian and object-relations perspectives.

8. For an example of an information-processing perspective on the Freudian, see Norman (1979, 1980, 1981).

9. The notion of programs as agents is well represented in computer science. Among the most explicit of the "social" metaphors is Minsky (1986).

10. The notion of objects carrying theory is one of the central issues in Mary Douglas's classic *Purity and Danger* (1966). Her analysis of the Jewish

dietary code for example, depends on an explication in which food from forbidden animals embodies the rules of classification and the danger of ambiguous categories.

11. For example, Russell Jacoby deals with the "forgetting of psychoanalysis" and the emergence of a primarily American "conformist psychology" (1975); Barry Richards analyzes the normalization of psychoanalysis in America and elsewhere in terms of its assimilation into doctrines of utilitarianism and romanticism (1989).

12. A recent example of this textual approach in relation to a Lacanian political position is David Macey's work, which called into question Lacan's feminism (Macey 1988).

13. Elisabeth Roudinesco makes this point in reviewing the way the media and psychoanalytic community responded to Lacan's death:

> In 1939, on the eve of the war, Freud's death was celebrated in the French press with an assortment of nonsense. Only Marie Bonaparte, the official representative of psychoanalysis for public opinion, defended the memory of the Jewish and Austrian scientist persecuted by the Nazis. By the time of Lacan's death, forty-two years later, the situation had reversed itself. . . . Generally, speaking, the journalists did their job properly. On the other hand, and with only a few exceptions, the testimony of intellectuals and therapists was painful in the extreme. [1991, 682]

14. François Roustang testifies on this point: "In adopting the position of master and producing pupils who were supposed to remain such indefinitely, Lacan was no longer merely *supposed* to know, he *knew*, and even saw himself as the only one who knew. Indeed, did he not repeatedly tell us that, on any given question, we could not go beyond the stage he had reached himself, and that to make further progress, we would just have to wait until he was ready to take another step?" (1990, 9).

15. Klein's biographer, Phyllis Grosskurth, had access to Klein's unpublished autobiography. In it, Klein did not seem able to separate fact from fiction. She presented her mother and brother as near-saints while documents reveal them to be jealous and intrusive. Her sickly brother worked hard to make Klein feel guilty for her vitality and for the fact that she would outlive him. Her mother actively worked to promote her depressions and undermine her marriage (Grosskurth 1986).

16. Didier Anzieu has investigated psychoanalytic theory in terms of the personalities of its theorists. Anzieu sees Freud as a man who could only see the world through the prism of depressive anxiety and who was dominated by the desire to protect an idealized image of the maternal. Because Freud was "hysterophobic," the maternal dimension of psychoanalysis had to be added by others, most notably by Melanie Klein. But of course, there were things that Freud could see that Klein was not able to. "Just as Freudian psychoanalysis is the fruit of the formation of the depressive position," says Anzieu, "Kleinian psychoanalysis is the fruit of the formation of the schizo-paranoid position" (1975, 742).

Anzieu speculates that if psychoanalysis had been invented by a hysteric such as Fliess, it would have been too taken up with the physical experience of fantasy, and if by an obsessional such as either Breuer or Charcot, it would have been made too systematic. Prepsychotics such as Tausk or Reich would have alternated between making the theory too subjective and making it too abstract.

*References*

Althusser, Louis. "Freud et Lacan." *La Nouvelle Critique*, nos. 161–62 (December-January 1964–65): 88–108.

Anonymous. *Séductions sur le divan ou le malentendu amoureux*. Paris: La Découverte, 1989.

Anzieu, Didier. *L'Auto-analyse de Freud et la découverte de la psychanalyse*. Paris: Presses Universitaires de France, 1975.

———. *Un Peau pour les pensées*. Paris: Clancier-Guenaud, 1986.

Augerolles, Joelle. *Mon analyst et moi*. Paris: Editions Lieu Commun, 1989.

Berger, Peter. "Towards a Sociological Understanding of Psychoanalysis." *Social Research* 32 (Spring 1965): 26–41.

Cardinale, Marie. *The Words to Say It*. Cambridge: Van Vactor and Goodheart, 1983.

Clastres, Guy, et al. "Communiqué du conseil: Une Issue pour la crise." Ecole de la Cause Freudienne, 2 April 1990.

Dorgeuille, Claude. *La Seconde Morte de Jacques Lacan*. Paris: Actualité Freudienne, 1981.

Douglas, Mary. *Purity and Danger*. London: Routledge and Kegan Paul, 1966.

Ecole de la Cause Freudienne. "Acte de fondation et autres textes." [Excerpts from the 1982 membership directory of the School of the Freudian Cause]. 1985.

———. *Almanach de la dissolution*. Paris: Navarin, 1986.

———. "Reflections sur l'Ecole/1." *La Lettre Mensuelle*, no. 69, May 1988.

Ferry, Luc, and Renaut, Alain. *French Philosophy of the Sixties: An Essay on Antihumanism*. Amherst: University of Massachusetts Press, 1990.

Fish, Stanley. *Is There a Text in This Class? The Authority of Interpretive Communities*. Cambridge: Harvard University Press, 1980.

Forrester, John. *The Seductions of Psychoanalysis: Freud, Lacan, and Derrida*. New York: Cambridge University Press, 1990.

Freud, Sigmund. *The Standard Edition of the Complete Psychological Works of Sigmund Freud*. Edited and translated by James Strachey. 24 vols. London: Hogarth Press, 1953–74.

*The Psychopathology of Everyday Life* (1901), vol. 6.

*On the History of the Psycho-Analytic Movement* (1914), vol. 14.

Granoff, Wladimir. *Filiations: L'Avenir du complexe d'Oedipe*. Paris: Editions du Minuit, 1975.

Grosskurth, Phyllis. *Melanie Klein: Her World and Her Work*. New York: Alfred A. Knopf, 1986.

Hall, G. Stanley. Letter to Sigmund Freud of 7 October 1909. Worcester, Mass.: Clark University Papers.

Jacoby, Russell. *Social Amnesia*. Boston: Beacon Press, 1975.

Kurzweil, Edith. *The Freudians: A Comparative Perspective*. New Haven: Yale University Press, 1989.

Lacan, Jacques. "Founding Act." In *Television: A Challenge to the Psychoanalytic Establishment*, edited by Joan Copjec. New York: Norton, 1990.

LaCapra, Dominick. "History and Psychoanalysis." In *The Trial(s) of Psychoanalysis*, edited by Françoise Meltzer. *Critical Inquiry* 13 (1987): 222–51.

Lévi-Strauss, Claude. *Structural Anthropology*. New York: Basic Books, 1963.

———. *The Savage Mind*. Chicago: University of Chicago Press, 1968.

Macey, David. *Lacan in Contexts*. London: Verso, 1988.

Miller, Jacques-Alain with François Ansermet. *Entretien sur le seminaire*. Paris: Navarin, 1985.

———. "Position de Jacques-Alain Miller à l'Assemblée du 2 decembre." In *Annexe au Pré-Rapports II*. Ecole de la Cause Freudienne, 1989: 25–9.

———. Letter of 11 December 1989, "Acier l'ouvert." In *La Lettre Mensuelle*. Ecole de la Cause Freudienne, no. 85, January 1990: 1–6.

Minsky, Marvin. *The Society of Mind*. New York: Simon and Schuster, 1986.

Norman, Donald. *Slips of the Mind and an Outline of a Theory of Action*. San Diego: Center for Human Information Processing, University of California, November 1979.

———. "Post-Freudian Slips." *Psychology Today*, April 1980, pp. 41–44ff.

———. "Categorization of Action Slips." *Psychological Review* 88 (1981): 1–15.

Oliner, Marion Michel. *Cultivating Freud's Garden in France*. Northvale, N.J.: Jason Aronson, 1988.

Pommier, Gérard. *La Névrose infantile de la psychanalyse*. Paris: Point Hors Ligne, 1989a.

———. "Letter of 22 November 1989." In *Annexe Aux Pré- Rapports II*. Ecole de la Cause Freudienne, 30 November 1989b: 3–7.

Richards, Barry. *Images of Freud: Cultural Responses to Psychoanalysis*. London: J. M. Dent, 1989.

Rieff, Philip. *The Triumph of the Therapeutic: The Uses of Faith after Freud*. New York: Harper and Row, 1966.

Roazen, Paul. "Freud and America." *Social Research* 29 (1972): 720–32.

———. *Encountering Psychoanalysis: The Politics and Histories of Psychoanalysis*. New Brunswich, N.J.: Transaction, 1990.

Roudinesco, Elizabeth. *Lacan and Co.: A History of Psychoanalysis in France 1925–1985*. University of Chicago Press, 1991.

Roustang, François. *Un Destin si funeste*. Paris: Editions de Minuit, 1976.

———. *The Lacanian Delusion*. New York: Oxford University Press, 1990.

Silvestre, Daniele. "Rapport de la Directrice devant l'Assemblée du 23 Juin

1990." In "Information sur l'Assemblée du 23 juin." Ecole de la Cause Freudienne, 1990: 2–6.

Suleiman, Susan Rubin. *Subversive Intent: Gender, Politics, and the Avant Garde*. Cambridge: Harvard University Press, 1990.

Turkle, Sherry. *Psychoanalytic Politics: Freud's French Revolution*. New York: Basic Books, 1978.

———. *The Second Self: Computers and the Human Spirit*. New York: Simon and Schuster, 1984.

Turner, Victor. *The Ritual Process*. Chicago: Aldine, 1966.

———. *The Forest of Symbols*. Ithaca: Cornell University Press, 1967.

Wright, Nicholas. *Mrs. Klein*. London: Nick Hern, 1988.

# 11 Ricoeur, Freud, and the Conflict of Interpretations

## Thelma Z. Lavine

Where in the historical currents of twentieth-century intellectual culture can Freud and Paul Ricoeur, his influential interpreter, be located? Freud was a carrier of both of the great traditions of Modernity, the Enlightenment tradition of the truths of natural science and classical liberalism, and the Romantic Counter-Enlightenment tradition of the dialectical dynamics of the inner life, culture, and history. Ricoeur derives from the Romantic Counter-Enlightenment tradition as it had evolved in the gathering darkness of World War II into the phenomenology of Edmund Husserl and the hermeneutic phenomenology of Martin Heidegger. As a hermeneutic phenomenologist, Ricoeur closes off the scientific tradition and focuses on the interpretation of meaning in the "texts" in which human existence objectifies itself. What are the implications of Ricoeur's undertaking to interpret Freud's naturalistic drive theory and his theory of meaning from the standpoint of an antinaturalistic hermeneutics? How, then, is Ricoeur's defense of the naturalism and realism of Freud's metapsychology possible? And what is the significance of the older and deeper tradition of religious faith for Ricoeur's *Freud and Philosophy* and *Time and Narrative*?

### Modernity and the Hermeneutic Conflict

The magisterial scope and analyticity of Paul Ricoeur's phenomenological studies over a vast range of twentieth-century philosophic concerns is approached on the American scene, if at all, by the naturalistic pragmatism of John Dewey in *Experience and Nature* (1925), *The*

264

*Quest for Certainty* (1929), *Art as Experience* (1934), and *Logic: The Theory of Inquiry* (1938). Although Dewey engaged in strenuous philosophic criticism of Viennese logical positivism upon its appearance in America before World War II, and expressed foreboding concerning the linguistic analytic philosophy that was to sweep across American universities after World War II, he did not live to confront and debate the countertradition of phenomenology, which did not become known here until the 1960s.

It is intellectually striking that although Ricoeur's philosophic formation was strongly influenced by Husserl's phenomenology, which struggled against naturalism and positivism, and by Dilthey's formulation of the concept of *Verstehen* in order to provide for the rising *Geisteswissenschaften*, a method and objectivity parallel to that of the *Naturwissenschaften*, nevertheless Ricoeur has not undertaken directly to address the great philosophic conflicts of Modernity that these historic developments exemplify. Yet Ricoeur presents an important and sustained aspect of his thought as the *Conflict of Interpretations*; moreover, the idea of dialectical conflict is his own characteristic mode of interpretation, and aporetic conflict is his constant mode of criticism. But the conflict between the great historical traditions of Modernity, the Enlightenment and the Romantic Counter-Enlightenment, fails to come into focus. What does Ricoeur understand by the "conflict of interpretations," and how does his understanding relate to the conflict of interpretations engendered by the cognitive and cultural structures of Modernity?

It is only in the last decades of the twentieth century that the intellectual culture has gained sufficient reflective distance from these philosophic vicissitudes to begin to frame a conception of Modernity and of its conflicting philosophic traditions and modes of interpretation.[1] The conceptual structure of Modernity may be seen to be a framework that exists in the form of historically evolved counterframeworks that constitute it and that provide the horizon of our time. Modernity is the conflict and confluence of the Enlightenment and the Romantic Counter-Enlightenment cognitive styles, each subverting and delegitimatizing the other's conception of human nature, truth, morality, and politics and the appropriate method for knowing them. Here is what has been identified as the "great divide" in contemporary philosophy. On one side of the divide are the eighteenth-century Enlightenment pursuers of rationally grounded objective, universal, and realistic truth and the analytic philosophers who are their twentieth-century descendants, deploying Enlightenment-style empirical, logical, and linguistic modes of argumentation that attack the Enlightenment intuitions of objective and realistic truth and of a rational foundation for knowledge.

On the other side are the counterintuitions of the nineteenth-century Romantic displacers of reason by subjectivity, the ground and projections of consciousness, and personal and collective will, as these constitute history and culture. Their twentieth-century descendants among phenomenologists, hermeneuticists, textualists, and deconstructionists are interpretivists (see Lavine 1989), affirming a Derridean interpretational dimension ("everything is always already interpreted") in all conceptual structures and in the webs of meaning that mediate everyday life, social institutions, culture, and philosophy; thus they undermine Enlightenment views old and new—the old Enlightenment's ahistorical, unmediated rational foundations for knowledge and the new analytic philosophy's ahistorical, unmediated empiricism of language games, ordinary language usage, and speech-acts.

In a recycling of the bitter conflict between nineteenth-century Romantics and the institutionalized Enlightenment, twentieth-century phenomenologists and hermeneuticists, from Husserl and Heidegger to Gadamer and Ricoeur, do battle with current modes of Enlightenment philosophy—positivism, pragmatism, naturalism, empiricism, "analytic" philosophy, objectivism, verificationism, geneticism, normativism, realism. With Heidegger, followed by Gadamer and Ricoeur, a phenomenological hermeneutics emerged in which the text became the exclusive object of philosophic interpretation; the result is a monologic mode of discourse in which (following Husserl) the natural attitude, the objects of the natural world, and the natural sciences are "bracketed out." Beginning with Heidegger, whose hermeneutics draws upon the early religious mode of textual interpretation, hermeneutics designates an antirationalist, antiscientific, antimethodological mode of interpretation.

How did the hermeneutic mode of the interpretive turn in twentieth-century philosophy come into being? No one has surpassed Paul Ricoeur's understanding of the emergence of hermeneutics and the clarity of his perception that hermeneutics, as a theory of interpretation, is revolutionary in its philosophic significance. The question that had been raised from Descartes to Hume, Husserl, and Dilthey is: How can a knowing subject apprehend the objects of nature or human culture with certainty? Ricoeur shows clearly that Heidegger's philosophic significance lies in his breaking with this epistemological and methodological question and asking instead an ontological question: What kind of being is it whose being consists in understanding? What kind of being exists through understanding?

Ricoeur notes in "Existence and Hermeneutics" that this changing of the question constitutes "a revolution in thought," according to which understanding is no longer regarded "as a mode of knowledge, but rather as a mode of being" (1974, 6–7). But the costs are high for a monologic purism that pursues a single philosophic style or method to the exclusion of elements from other approaches that would supply its philosophic deficiencies. Insofar as hermeneutics divorces itself from the empirical contexts of interpretation, it cuts itself off from relating interpretive structures to the actual conditions of the world in which interpretations arise; insofar as hermeneutics divorces itself from the epistemological and methodological problems of interpretation, it cuts itself off from the possibility of objectivity, validity, and normativity for the human sciences. Thus the shadow of the Enlightenment falls upon the monologic defenses of Romantic, Counter-Enlightenment hermeneutics.

But the subtle strengths of Ricoeur's overdetermined dialectical and thematic complexities resist any simple categorization of him as a Heideggerian hermeneut. In a crucial break with Heidegger, Ricoeur dissociates himself from an aporia within Heidegger's philosophy: "Why not stop here and simply proclaim ourselves Heideggerian? Where is the famous *aporia* previously announced? Have we not eliminated the Diltheyan *aporia* of a theory of understanding, condemned in turn to oppose naturalistic explanation and to rival it in objectivity and scientificity? Have we not overcome it by subordinating epistemology to ontology?" (Thompson 1981, 59). Ricoeur's answer is that the aporia persists. It is no longer *within* epistemology, between explanation and understanding, "but it is *between* ontology and epistemology taken as a whole." "With Heidegger's philosophy, we are always engaged in going back to the foundations, but we are left incapable of beginning the movement of return . . . to the properly epistemological question of the status of the human sciences." Ricoeur concludes with the caustic rebuke: "Now a philosophy which breaks the dialogue with the sciences is no longer addressed to anything but itself."

Ricoeur's subsequent line of philosophic development, as he sees it, is a deliberate, far-reaching, and continuous effort to open the dialogue with the social sciences, to connect truth with the method of the exegetical sciences, and in this way to avoid Heidegger's failure, in which, having broken the dialogue with the human sciences, he was left alone with his philosophy. And so began Ricoeur's famous "detours" through psychoanalysis, symbolism, metaphor, structural linguistics, texts, time, history, narrative, literature, political philosophy, and cultural anthropology. In these human sciences are to be found the "documents" of human life, the "objectifications" of human existence. Expressed symbolically, these are the meanings that it is the task of hermeneutics to interpret and to appropriate from the "multiple modalities" of symbolic expression (Ricoeur 1974a, 18, 24).

The irony of Ricoeur's prodigious effort to avoid Heidegger's failure to provide recourse from ontology to the human sciences is that Ricoeur faces an opposite failure of his own. Whereas for Heidegger, there is no way back from the ground of being to the human sciences, for Ricoeur there appears to be no way back to his ontology from his laborious quarrying of the human sciences. Hence Ricoeur's own repeated references to the "paradise lost" of Husserl's *Lebenswelt*, to his own "fractured ontology," and to ontology as the "promised land" for the reflective philosopher, whose fate is like that of Moses, who "can only glimpse this land before dying" (1974a, 24). Hence also the long-awaited, long-postponed *Poetics of the Will*, the projected third volume of *The Voluntary and the Involuntary*.

In a second departure from Heidegger Ricoeur reflects the important influence of Gabriel Marcel[2] upon the formation of his early religious and existentialist views and confirms that his project among the symbolic objectifications of human existence is to discern signs of transcendence, signs of the being to which our being belongs, and of an opening to the sacred. But a hermeneutic that seeks and understands such signs as "the manifestation or restoration of a meaning addressed to me" as a "message" or "proclamation" or "kerygma" finds itself opposed by arguments aimed at demystification of these claims as illusory. It is this phenomenon, this "extreme polarity, . . . the truest expression of our modernity," which Ricoeur construes as the "conflict of interpretations" in his celebrated concept of the conflict between the "hermeneutics of faith" and the "hermeneutics of suspicion." We have here discovered why Ricoeur writes of the conflict of interpretations without reference to the great conflicts of Enlightenment and Romantic Counter-Enlightenment Modernity that agitated Husserl, Dilthey, and Weber and brought forth Heidegger's hermeneutics as a "revolution in thought." Ricoeur recasts the conflict of interpretations as occurring within the problematic of hermeneutics itself; the conflict is presented as centered upon the defense of religious faith from skeptical attack. A further difficulty with Ricoeur's conflict of hermeneutics lies in his misreading of Marx, Nietzsche, and Freud as "the masters of suspicion" and thus as hermeneuts. But monologic hermeneutics cannot claim Marx, Nietzsche, and Freud as hermeneuts. They are representatives of contextual interpretation theory, explaining interpretive structures in relation to their empirical conditions, precisely the empirical reality closed off by phenomenology.[3] Thus we have reached the crucial and unsurpassable difficulty confronting Ricoeur's hermeneutical conflict: *the conflict between the hermeneutics of suspicion and of faith is intelligible only as the conflict between Enlightenment scientific explanation and Counter-Enlightenment interpretive understanding—as the conflict of Modernity.*

A further departure from Heidegger emerges in Ricoeur's complex theory of reference, which appears, in the case of psychoanalytic theory, to commit the great aporia of affirming an accommodation within phenomenological hermeneutics to empirical reality. Despite these differences from Heidegger, Ricoeur acknowledges that his hermeneutics is "grafted" to the phenomenology of Heidegger and significantly to his "desire for an ontology." The first chapters of *Freud and Philosophy* disclose that its driving force is to find a path to ontology from the interpretation of human existence as desire.

## Objectifications of Human Existence: Freud and Philosophy

*Freud and Philosophy* is Paul Ricoeur's masterwork and one of the classics of philosophic interpretation produced in the modern era. Nowhere else than in the work of Freud—with the possible exception of the texts of Hegel or Weber or Dewey—has the archeology of Western culture and the vicissitudes of its teleology been presented with such a "surplus of meaning." Psychoanalysis serves Ricoeur as the ultimate text.[4] Not only does it reflect and critique Western personal and cultural desire, arche and telos, but it is an inexhaustible source of double meanings, symbols of good and evil, metaphors, lost or abandoned objects, and the quest for fullness of meaning.

Ricoeur's deciphering of the text of psychoanalysis may be seen to employ a hermeneutic paradigm for textual deciphering of multiple meanings. His interpretive materials are culled from the text in the form of symbols and countersymbols, metaphors, idealizations, and redescriptions of reality, and from relevant thematizations in the human sciences. His interpretive critique draws upon the philosophical analyticity of aporia and dialectic, the problematics of Descartes, Spinoza, Hegel, Husserl, and Heidegger, and biblical critical exegesis. Ricoeur's hermeneutic paradigm deploys this battery of interpretive and critical structures by using a strategy of stages: the text is first subjected to aporetics and dialectical critique; it is then recast ("hermeneuticized") by the prioritizing of its ideational ("hidden") language; and, finally, the exposed doubleness, inconsistencies, gaps, ambiguities, and equivocations are probed for meanings that are openings to the transcendent, or that offer redescriptions of reality or linkages of arche, telos, and eschaton.

This is the hermeneutic paradigm by which Riccoeur's massive study of Freud is organized, from the "Problematic," in which psychoanalysis is dialectically destabilized by being placed within the modern crisis of the conflict of interpretations; to the mounting tensions of the "Analytic," with its minute, detailed tracking of the aporias of two languages and double meanings, and in which the unbridgeable gap of "force" and"meaning," "reality" and "ideality," is bridged dialectically; and to the "Dialectic," in which Freudian desire as arche is dialectically linked to Hegelian desire as telos and both are sublimated in a veiled eschatological unity. This is the paradigm that, in outline, directs Ricoeur's analyses and critiques in his various detours among the objectifications of human existence.[5]

In Ricoeur's hermeneutic conflict of interpretations, psychoanalysis is a principal influence and Freud is its principal protagonist. What is the philosophic frame of reference that Ricoeur imputes to Freud? Ricoeur presents a Helmholtzian Freud, a product of a physicalistic scientific environment under the influence of the Helmholtz school in biology, which promulgated a "physico-physiological theory based on the ideas of force, attraction and repulsion, all three being governed by the principle of the conservation of energy" (1970, 72). This portrait of a wooden, deterministic Freud is supported by the example of Freud's 1895 "Project" and its quantitative mechanisms of the charge and discharge of energy, and by Ricoeur's citations from earlier scholarly studies of the development of Freud's views. Ricoeur himself not only insists that Freud "will never disavow" the scientism of his environment as reflected in the "Project," but underscores the persistent influence of Helmholtzian physicalistic mechanics upon Freud's thought by characterizing psychoanalysis as an "energetics" in which meaning must be discerned.

But if Freud's dominating philosophical frame of reference is Helmholtzian, how is it possible to account for the Ricoeurian Freud who "restores the problematic of existence as desire"? Or the Ricoeurian Freud whose concepts of "sublimation" and "identification" find their "philosophic truth" in the "Hegelian *Aufhebung*"? Or the Ricoeurian Freud whose "genius ... is to have unmasked the strategy of the pleasure principle ... its rationalizations, its idealizations, its sublimations ... [as] actually a revival of the old: substitute satisfaction, restoration of the lost archaic object" (461ff, 466)? The philosophic profundities that Ricoeur's hermeneutics discovers in the Freudian texts have no possibility of derivation from the mechanics of a physicalistic physiology. Ricoeur has failed to identify the Romantic Counter-Enlightenment frame of reference that, along with the scientific Enlightenment frame, pervaded turn-of-the-century Vienna, and from which Freud gained primary and secondary access to the Romantic poets, and to Hegel, Schopenhauer, and Nietzsche.[6] Reflected even within the passages cited here from Ricoeur's study of Freud are Hegel's idea of the dialectical development of the sublimations of desire and his conception of the great cycle of spirit that returns to itself from its objectifications in finite existence; Schopenhauer's ideas of the primal urges of the will as self-preservation and sexual desire, the unconscious, repression, projection, sublimation, reaction formation, and the quiescence of Nirvana; and Nietzsche's ideas of the "death of God," substitute satisfaction, rationalization, and relativistic perspectivism.

Misled by scientist studies of Freud and by cultural and philosophical insularities, Ricoeur fails to bridge the intellectual gap between the Helmholtzian Freud, which he has assumed, and the Romantic Freud, which he has deciphered. His recourse is to speculate briefly about the possible influence of Goethe's *Naturphilosophie* upon the young Freud and to trace the philosophic problematic of the hermeneutic conflict of interpretations and thus of Freud to the cogito of the early Enlightenment. Ricoeur fails in each case to recognize the conflict of Enlightenment and Counter-Enlightenment Romantic Modernity. He does not see that a Helmholtzian Freud would be strongly opposed to *Naturphilosophie* as Romantic antiscientism. Nor does he see that the Cartesian cogito, at the dawn of Enlightenment Modernity, cannot provide a philosophic ground for the Freud who derives from Hegel, Schopenhauer, and Nietzsche.

Despite the great achievement of *Freud and Philosophy*, it must then be acknowledged that Ricoeur has erased a crucial phase in modern intellectual history: the interrelationship between Enlightenment and Romantic cognitive frameworks. In this interrelationship, the Romantic philosophy of will, which had arisen in opposition to Enlightenment natural scientific determinism, became naturalized in a developmental line leading from Hegel through Schopenhauer and Nietzsche to Freud. Ricoeur has erased the idea of synthesis between the frameworks of Modernity (since he operates within the conflict between faith and demystification) as well as the perception of Freud's genius as that of synthesizer of these cognitive modes.[7] Yet theory construction in the human sciences from elements derived from and satisfying the intuitions and methodological concerns of both frameworks of Modernity have been undertaken by such notable theorists as Marx, Weber, Mannheim, Dewey, and Habermas, as well as by Freud. Although their synthesizing efforts have varied in clarity of theoretical design, and their products have in various degrees been flawed, their integrating contributions to social and psychological theory, social philosophy, and intellectual history have in large part defined these fields for the intellectual culture.

Failing to perceive Freud as boldly venturing a synthesis of the cognitive structures and methods of Modernity, Ricoeur perceives psychoanalysis as a "hybrid" language, a mixed discourse of energetics and hermeneutics, which opened a path to the phenomenology of human existence as desire. But if Ricoeur's hermeneutic paradigm recasts Freudian psychoanalysis by prioritizing its ideational meaning, what significance can be assigned to energetics? The question of empirical reality haunts *Freud and Philosophy*, and Ricoeur confronts it in a major departure from the monologic phenomenology of Heidegger and Gadamer.

The issue of reality is most familiar to readers and interpreters of Freud in the form of the reality principle. By contrast to the dangerous pleasure principle, Ricoeur presents the reality principle in terms of utility, as representing that which is useful to "the organism's true and proper interests." Reality is "the opposite of fantasy—it is facts, such as the normal man sees them" (324). The reality principle implies adaptation to time and society, to what is possible and reasonable; reality is the correlate of consciousness and the ego. On the one hand, in pointing to "facts," "adaptation," and "interests," the reality principle suggests the naive realism of the "natural attitude," which Ricoeur's phenomenology, following Husserl, brackets off; on the other hand, after the theory of the death instinct, the reality principle points to Ananke, the harsh view of the world without illusion, "shorn of God" (327). But what is the epistemological status of psychoanalytic reality?

Ricoeur confronts the epistemological issue of realism in relation to the metapsychology by defending the "empirical reality" of the metapsychological concepts: the instincts, the topographic theory, and the id. "Freudianism," he says, "aims at being a realism of the unconscious" (431). Ricoeur defends also the empirical reality of the mechanistic laws governing the unconscious system, the naturalistic economy of instincts, the psychoanalytic method, and the typical psychical diagnostic configurations ("a kind of dictionary of preconstituted types"), all of which are implied and validated by the realism of the metapsychology.

Ricoeur draws back, however, from this remarkable introduction of empirical reality into phenomenological discourse and soon questions it: "But in accepting the realism, one must also ask the question, What sort of reality? Reality of what?" (434). Ricoeur's first answer is Kantian (375, 432–33). As Kant's transcendental logic establishes the constitutive elements of a type of experience and a corresponding type of reality, with a resultant complex of concepts, principles, and laws, so, Ricoeur argues, psychoanalytic metapsychology establishes the constitutive elements of its own type of experience and corresponding reality and complex of concepts and laws.

But there are obvious difficulties with Ricoeur's invoking Kant's transcendental logic in order to show that the metapsychological concepts are analogous to Kant's transcendental categories. Kant's constitutive elements, the formal categories of the understanding are necessary conditions of the possibility of experience and knowledge, whereas the metapsychological concepts are not formal conditions of experience and knowledge, but products of such conditions; the Kantian categories, as conditions of experience, do not appear as such in experience, whereas "instinctual representatives" do appear in experience; the formal categories have no empirical reality, whereas the metapsychological concepts are specifically claimed to have empirical reality; the Kantian categories are "deduced" from perceptual experience and the existing science of physics, whereas the metapsychological concepts can claim no perceptual or scientific deduction.

Thus Ricoeur's effort to establish the empirical reality of the metapsychological concepts as a Kantian transcendental foundation for psychoanalysis fails: it is an upside-down, inverted transcendentalism, an attempt to install empirical concepts as a transcendental foundation for psychoanalysis, in place of the formal categorical structures that transcendental logic requires as the necessary conditions of the possibility of all empirical concepts.

How, then, to understand Ricoeur's insistence upon securing for these empirical concepts a transcendentally necessary status? "The metapsychology is not an optional, advantageous construction; it is not an ideology, a speculation; it has to do with what Kant called the determining judgments of experience; it determines the field of interpretation" (433).[8] Ricoeur appears to perceive the empirical realism of the topography, the instincts, and the id as comparable to the Kantian categories in their necessary and far-reaching power to determine "the field of interpretation," to define what is real, and to regulate the ensemble of the mechanisms of the unconscious, the naturalistic economy of instincts, and the types of method and of psychological diagnostic configurations. It is within this framework of empirical realism and the "naturalistic point of view" required by the "forces and mechanisms" of the economy of instincts that, to Ricoeur, psychoanalysis is alone "feasible."[9]

Ricoeur is specific in finding psychoanalysis to be feasible only upon the realism of three psychoanalytic operations: explanation, discovery, and praxis. Explanation is possible only within the interlocking realistic mechanisms of the unconscious and the economy of the instincts. The possibility of psychoanalytic discovery "stems primarily" from the naturalistic economic model and the "type of intelligibility it confers." "All the power of discovery ... stems from this model" (434). Psychoanalytic technique, as a "unique and irreducible form of praxis," is possible only within the realism of the unconscious, which is expressed, investigated, and treated in the analytic situation as repression, resistance, repetition, and transference. "No phenomenology of intersubjectivity can parallel this" sequence, he says, which is a function of the realism of psychoanalytic praxis. "Phenomenology is not psychoanalysis" (415, 390).

Ricoeur is especially critical of the "internal" efforts of phenomenologists, ordinary language philosophers, and hermeneuticists to reformulate psychoanalysis. Since these reformulations reduce the "hybrid" energetic and hermeneutic discourse of psychoanalysis to the hermeneutic, they succeed only in paralleling or transcribing psychoanalytic concepts, while failing to offer either explanations or discoveries. Thus the linguistic conception of the unconscious, "instead of replacing the Freudian topographic and economic point of view, ... parallels that point of view in every respect" (395–96).[10] Similarly, Ricoeur protests, "To say that repression is 'metaphor' is not to replace the economic hypothesis but rather to parallel it with a linguistic interpretation" (409). Ricoeur amplifies this critique in his claim that all existing reformulations of psychoanalysis have failed. (In effect, his views pronounce the following efforts as failures: the reformulations of positivism and behaviorism, seeking to improve the status of psychoanalysis by reconstructing it as an observational and verificatory science; the formulations of Anglo-Saxon analytic philosophers, seeking to clarify psychoanalytic discourse by assigning it to the language of motives rather than causes; the formulations of phenomenology, seeking to establish a homology with psychoanalysis by reducing psychoanalytic praxis to reflective discourse.)

Notwithstanding the importance that Ricoeur assigns to the realistic and naturalistic frame in which psychoanalytic explanations, discoveries, and praxis are alone possible, in a complete turnaround, he proceeds to appropriate his Kantian argument to his hermeneutic phenomenology. The empirical realism of psychoanalysis, he cautions, is "a reality of the psychical representations of instincts and not of the instincts themselves" (434), which we never have "access ... to ... as such, but only to their psychical expressions, their representatives in the form of ideas and affects" (174). Moreover, the empirical realism of the metapsychology "is not an absolute reality but is relative to the operations which give it meaning"—the "hermeneutic constellation" of deciphering operations, "together with the analytic method and the explanatory models" (437). The reality of the metapsychology "only exists as a 'diagnosed' reality," he says, repeating his statement of 1950, but now "with a greater concern for justifying Freud's realism and naturalism" (432).

With this turn to a hermeneutic appropriation of the realist frame of psychoanalysis, Ricoeur has followed his own hermeneutic paradigm in prioritizing hermeneutics over the realistic frame of psychoanalysis by showing its relativity to the hermeneutic constellation. The outcome of this tortuous line of argumentation (430–39) is Ricoeur's claim that in "referring the unconscious to the hermeneutic constellation ... we define both the validity and the limits of the reality of the agencies" (439). Outside of the hermeneutic constellation the reality of the metapsychology "is no longer meaningful."

But a formidable aporia appears to be the outcome of Ricoeur's reflections on psychoanalytic theory. He has, in effect, concluded with two theories of psychoanalysis that are fundamentally inconsistent with one another: (1) the theory of psychoanalysis in which the empirical realism of the metapsychology is the ground of psychoanalysis, and (2) the theory of psychoanalysis in which the empirical realism of the metapsychology is a consequence of the theory.

Yet the apparently damaging logical aporia reveals itself to Ricoeur to be a philosophically advantageous dialectic. How is this possible? It can be understood only by noting that, despite Ricoeur's epistemological reflections on the issue of the realism and naturalism of Freudian psychoanalysis, his philosophic mode is not epistemological but exclusively and consistently hermeneutical and dialectial. As a hermeneutic phenomenologist, he does not engage the problematics of epistemology and methodology. "Empirical realism" is nowhere defined in *Freud and Philosophy*, nor is this term distinguished from the realism of the natural attitude or from scientific realism. His unwavering position with regard to psychoanalysis is that it is a mixed discourse, a hybrid of energetic explanation and hermeneutic interpretation. As a mixed discourse, psychoanalysis does not yield successfully to philosophical disjunction or reduction, on Ricoeur's view, but only to dialectic, which can reinterpret its aporias into necessary reciprocities in which the hermeneutic is prioritized. Thus the aporia that appeared between the metapsychology as ground or as consequence of psychoanalytic theory is redescribed and reconstructed by Ricoeur as a dialectically necessary reciprocity in which the realistic ground is prioritized by the hermeneutic consequences.

Thus the enduring and effective significance of Ricoeur's contributions to psychoanalytic theory is his defense of a nonreductive, nondisjunctive understanding of the Freudian texts and of psychoanalysis. It is in this sense that Ricoeur is to be seen as a defender of psychoanalytic realism. His defense of psychoanalytic realism must be seen to be dialectical and to stem from his view of psychoanalysis as a mixed discourse that is integrated by dialectic; it does not rest on epistemological grounds, nor does it offer a methodological critique other than the rejection of reductionism. Hence the sharpness of his criticism of reductive reformulations of psychoanalysis: they reduce psychoanalysis to linguistic or phenomenological discourse, thus denying its "thing" language, its energetics. But the subtle complexities of Ricoeur's presentation should not conceal that his own hermeneutic phenomenology, while insisting that Freud uses two languages, hermeneuticizes both; thus he himself reduces psychoanalysis to phenomenological discourse.

Reflecting in 1977 upon the issues increasingly raised by "reformulations which borrow from phenomenology, from ordinary language analysis, or from linguistics," Ricoeur reaffirms the logical structure of his position of a decade earlier, but with significant changes in his conceptualization and theory of psychoanalysis:

> All these reformulations omit the task of integrating an explanatory stage into the process of [symbolization] ... But if we were to follow the suggestion of the concepts of the text and interpretation ... psychoanalysis would be purely and simply subsumed under the aegis of the historico-hermeneutical sciences, alongside philology and exegesis. [Thompson 1981, 256, 267]

Ricoeur's opposition to the "text and interpretation" reformulations of psychoanalysis is that they erase the dialectical structure of force and interpretation upon which his study of Freud was organized. Whereas the textualists operate with text and interpretation, Ricoeur operates with the mixed discourse of explanatory energetics and interpretive symbolization. But it is once again the case that by encompassing both energetics and symbolization in the "hermeneutic constellation" Ricoeur, like the textualists, has subsumed psychoanalysis under the "historico-hermeneutical sciences."

In his critical observations in 1977 Ricoeur is reflecting the changes brought about in the intellectual culture by the hermeneutics of Gadamer, the Habermas-Gadamer debate on hermeneutics and ideology critique, the structural linguistics of Lévi-Strauss and Lacan, the ordinary language philosophy of Strawson and Flew, and the deconstruction of Derrida. Having detoured through all of these developments, Ricoeur's own conceptual focus has shifted to the interpretation of the text, the investigation of the historical sciences, and the methodological issues of explanation and understanding; he has moved away from the specific concerns of *Freud and Philosophy* with symbolism, the hermeneutics of suspicion and belief, the dialectic of arche and teleology, and the epistemology of the metapsychology.

What do those changes mean, he asks, "for our epistemological inquiry?" What is now called for, he says, is "a theory in which the psyche will be presented as a text to be interpreted and as a system of forces to be manipulated" (Thompson, 250).

That a new theory for psychoanalysis would fail if it were to meet Ricoeur's requirement of the prioritizing of hermeneutic while encompassing force and meaning is clear by his own example. A theoretical reconstruction of psychoanalysis that would incorporate the realism and naturalism of force with meaning cannot be successfully undertaken by a hermeneutic phenomenology that disassociates "force," along with the empirically known natural world, by phenomenological bracketing.

The strength of Ricoeur's theoretical position is its refusal to follow a reductive course with regard to the metapsychology of psychoanalytic theory; its weakness is in the attempt to incorporate Freud's naturalism and his hermeneutic dialectically in a monologic hermeneutic phenomenology.

To follow Ricoeur in this effort is to end, with him, in a dialecticism of force and meaning, archaeology and teleology, that is redeemed only in the language of religious faith.

## The Poetics of the Will

There is a deep irony in the emergence of Paul Ricoeur as a defender of Freudian realism within the current anomalous situation of psychoanalytic theory, in which phenomenologists, hermeneuticists, deconstructionists, structuralists, and ordinary language philosophers oppose his viewpoint. How, indeed, is Ricoeur's defense of the rationalism and realism of the metapsychology comprehensible in view of his long-sustained Counter-Enlightenment phenomenology and its antinaturalistic, antirealist, antiscientific implications? Or in view of his building upon Descartes's cogito but remaining silent with regard to Descartes's realm of material substance? Or in view of his repudiating Dilthey's effort to find a firm methodology for the social sciences? Or in view of his repudiation of Husserl's effort to find an apodictic certainty for science as a bulwark against the rising power of Nazism?

Ricoeur did not come to his study of Freud through involvement with the epistemological and methodological issues within the conflicting traditions of Modernity, as these are reflected in psychoanalysis. Ricoeur himself has told the story (1973, 315; Thompson 1981, 33) on his turning to Freud initially through working on the problem shared by "all existentialist philosophies of the [nineteen-]forties and fifties"—how to introduce into the philosophy of will "some fundamental experiences such as guilt, bondage, alienation, or, to speak in religious terms, sin." From within the frame of this religious existentialism Ricoeur's primary and continuing project evolved as the search for an ontology of understanding, for a self-understanding of human existence. Ricoeur saw the problem as the gap between "the intended meaning of freedom of the will" and the fallen, servile condition of the human will, "prisoner of the passions and prone to evil." Hence the detour, in *The Symbolism of Evil*, through the indirect, symbolic avowals of guilt in the myths of the cultures of the world, which led him to an "amplifying" hermeneutic of double meanings and symbolic spiritual meanings, and to a hermeneutic of "recollection and faith." But against the hermeneutic of faith, psychoanalysis now stood forth to Ricoeur as the paradigm of a demystifying hermeneutics of suspicion. He saw psychoanalytic theory as reducing guilt to the guilt feeling of neurosis or societal coercion; it questioned the primacy of the subject, and it introduced the semantics of desire.

Ricoeur's primary problem, and the telos of *Freud and Philosophy*, is the defense of a hermeneutic of recollection and faith from the demystification of psychoanalysis. But it is evident that within his prioritizing hermeneutic frame, Ricoeur seeks not only to defend a hermeneutics of faith but to turn the hermeneutics of suspicion into a hermeneutics of faith, by showing that suspicion is tied to faith as its dialectically necessary other. "The symbols of evil," Ricoeur affirms, evoking at once familiar biblical rhetoric, Hegelian dialectic, and his own (anti-Heideggerian) phenomenology of hope, "are always the obverse side of a greater ... symbolism of salvation" (*Fallible Man*, 215). The logic of Ricoeur's position is that of the ineluctable dialectical potentialities discoverable within "double" meaning, "multiple" meaning, the "surplus" of meaning, the "fullness" of meaning in human discourse. Hence his expansive exploration and disclosure of dialectical necessity: between the literal and the figurative meanings of the symbol, between energetics and hermeneutics, between explanation and understanding, between the desires of archaeology and those of teleology, between objects lost and regained. This is the logic of the necessary dialectic between the empirical realism of the metapsychology and the ideality of psychoanalytic meaning. And it is the logic of necessary dialectic that connects and supports Ricoeur's two theories of the metapsychology, which he had failed to defend epistemologically: the necessary dialectic between the empirically real concepts of the metapsychology as transcendental ground and as consequence of psychoanalytic deciphering, explanation, and method.

But why has Ricoeur persisted in affirming the realism of the unconscious and the naturalism of the economy of instincts? As a follower of Heidegger's revolutionary turning of philosophy from the problem of knowledge to the problem of being, Ricoeur, like Heidegger, abjures epistemology and its concern with the problems of perception, knowledge, validity, meaning, and truth, as well as methodology and its concern with the problems of the nomological and the historical-hermeneutic sciences—"Enlightenment" issues of importance to philosophers from Descartes to Kant and from Peirce to Dewey and Habermas. Unlike Heidegger, Ricoeur ventured into dialogue with the social sciences, in which epistemic and methodological problems and their implications for phenomenology cannot be ignored. As he has become involved in issues in the social sciences (notably the conflict of realism and hermeneutics in psychoanalysis, explanation and understanding in the historical sciences, and tradition and ideology critique in social theory), Ricoeur's only recourse has been to resolve the conflict in a dialectical logic that prioritizes hermeneutics. Ricoeur has recourse to this logic of overcoming aporia by dialectic in his criticism of Karl Mannheim's *Ideology and Utopia*; in his criticism of Hayden White on the distinction between fictional and historical narrative; and in his adjudication of the Habermas-Gadamer debate.[11] Thus the shadow of the Enlightenment falls upon Ricoeur's efforts at conflict resolution in the human sciences (*After Philosophy*, 378).

And it is Ricoeur's reliance upon the logic of dialectical conflict resolution that makes it possible to identify the unity of his thought and the linkage it reveals between his monumental studies, *Freud and Philosophy* and *Time and Narrative*. Despite the vast, detailed analyticity of both works, the identical logical structure and ontological conclusion may be found to emerge.[12] In *Freud and Philosophy* Ricoeur pursues the dialectic of desire from the arche of instinctual desire to the prioritizing telos of Hegelian ideal figures, and beyond these he moves to the deeper structures of eschatology in which the aporetics within and between arche and telos are redeemed in faith. So in *Time and Narrative* Ricoeur pursues the dialectic of historical narrativity from the chronology of individual events or acts to the long durée and large scale of the Annales school's anonymous historical "forces"; in dialectical opposition to these is the historicity of narrative, encompassing emplotment, the accentuation of the past, and the sense of time as extended between birth and death. Beyond historicity in the hierarchization of temporality, there lies the deep temporality from which historicity is derived and in which there is a reconciliation of the ultimate dialectic of death and eternity, of Augustine's philosophy of time as divine eternity and Heidegger's philosophy of the finitude of death.

As the aporetics of psychoanalysis are resolved by the dialectic of arche and telos and are sublated and reconciled in eschatology, so the aporetics of history are resolved by the dialectic of chronology and historicity and are sublated into the ontology of deep temporality, in which death and eternity are reconciled.

Thus for Ricoeur the deep structure and ontological vision of historical narrative is isomorphic with the deep structure and ontological vision of psychoanalysis. Here is to be found the unity of Ricoeur's thought.

Among his extensive detours, including his recent *Time and Narrative*, Ricoeur's study of Freud remains unsurpassable. Nowhere else was there to be a text as richly rewarding in depth and range for the subtlety and tenacity of his ontological quest, and as homologous with that other great text of human existence in Modernity, *The Phenomenology of Spirit*. It is the genius of Ricoeur to have found in the Freudian texts the meaning of human existence as desire, in its passage from the arche of instincts to the sublimations of the Hegelian telos, and to the sacred symbols of eschatology. In Ricoeur's continued effort to reappropriate the lost objects of human desire and the promised land of ontology, he looks to an originary unity of arche and telos, and to signs of the sacred in the mythicopoetic symbolization of human origins; and he is turning, in the promised *Poetics of the Will*, to the problematic of faith. And already at the end of *Freud and Philosophy*, he proposes a chastened, nonnarcissistic symbol of God,[13] sublated from Freud's father figure into Spinoza's *Deus sive Natura*, and a conception of the love of God as the love of totality, of the all-encompassing whole of a divinized Nature. But Ricoeur as a hermeneutic phenomenologist cannot rightfully aspire to Spinoza's noble love of God, since he has closed off the great world of nature in which we live and have our being. The shadow of the Enlightenment thus falls again upon the exclusionary philosophy of hermeneutic phenomenology. The call to resolve the conflict of Enlightenment and Romantic Modernity may be said to be the "kerygma" to which philosophy must now respond.

## Notes

1. See, e.g., Daniel Bell, Hans Blumenberg, Jurgen Habermas, Irving Howe, David Kolb, T. Z. Lavine, Joseph Margolis, Alisdair MacIntyre, Richard Rorty, Stephen Toulmin.

2. See "From Existentialism to the Philosophy of Language," Appendix, in Ricoeur (1973). Here Ricoeur traces the beginning of his detours to his search for a "symbolic language as an indirect approach to the problem of guilt." Also see "Conversations between Paul Ricoeur and Gabriel Marcel," translated by Stephen Jolin and Peter McCormick, in Marcel (1973).

3. See Lavine on contextual interpretation theory (1989, 45–67). The "doubt" of Marx, Nietzsche, and Freud is not propelled by Cartesian "reflection."

4. *Freud and Philosophy* is in fact the only text that Ricoeur fully explicates and to which he applies his hermeneutic paradigm systematically.

5. It is a significant comment on the fate of hermeneutic phenomenology that whereas Ricoeur finds the presence of symbol or metaphor to indicate a potential expansion or fulfillment of meaning, for Derrida it is evidence of the collapse of logocentric thought into rhetoric and the bottomless relativity of metaphor. See Jacques Derrida, "Structure, Sign, and Play in the Discourse of the Human Sciences" (1978, 279–80).

6. Similar difficulties exist for Roy Schafer in Chapter 1 of this volume. Schafer presents a Freud who "for theory turned to the scientific models of his day: Newton, Helmhotz, Darwin. . . . There were no frameworks anchored in relativistic, contextualistic epistemologies." Yet Schafer credits Freud with the "monumental achievement" of introducing "destabilization, deconstruction, and defamiliarization" into clinical dialogue. How was this achievement possible for a Helmholtzian Freud?

7. The theoretical significance of the naturalization of the Romantic philosophy of will points to a different reading of Freud from Ricoeur's "hybrid," "mixed discourse."

8. See also "Consciousness and the Unconscious" (Ricoeur 1974a, 103–8); "Question of Proof in Freud's Writings" (Thompson 1981, 251).

9. It may be possible to understand Ricoeur's defense of psychoanalytic realism in Kuhnian rather than in the Kantian terms that he proposed. Ricoeur acknowledges (1970, 432) that he had come since 1950 to "a greater concern for justifying Freud's realism and naturalism." Ricoeur may in effect be viewing Freud as achieving a quasi-Kuhnian experimental breakthrough, which eventuated in establishing the paradigm of psychoanalysis as the naturalistic economy of instincts, the mechanisms of the unconscious, the topographic theory, the interpretive method, and the set of diagnostic psychological configurations. These complex elements of the model could then be seen to "govern the field" of psychoanalysis, while avoiding the epistemological difficulties of a Kantian transcendental foundation. But Kuhnian paradigm theory would not accord with Ricoeur's view of psychoanalysis as a mixed discourse of two languages that are connected by the necessity of dialectic.

10. A similar criticism has been made of Roy Schafer (*The Analytic Attitude*, 1983), who proposes eliminating most of the concepts central to the metapsychology but "states that in his own practice he uses 'the storylines that characterize Freudian retellings.'" See Greenberg and Mitchell (1983, 347–48).

11. See Taylor, *Lectures on Ideology and Utopia* (1986, 162–312); Ricoeur, *Time and Narrative*, vol. 1 (161–68), vol. 3 (152ff.); "Hermeneutics and the Critique of Ideology" (in Thompson 1981, 63–100); also "Ethics and Culture: Habermas and Gadamer in Dialogue" (1974b).

12. For an interpretation of Ricoeur's view of history that is consistent with my interpretation, see Hayden White, "The Metaphysics of Narrativity: Time and Symbol in Ricoeur's Philosophy of History" (1987).

13. On the concept of a nondefensive religion see Joseph H. Smith, "On Psychoanalysis and the Question of Nondefensive Religion" (1990).

## References

Dewey, John. *The Later Works of John Dewey*, 1925–53. 17 vols. Carbondale: Southern Illinois University Press, 1981–90.
    *Experience and Nature* (1925), vol. 1.
    *The Quest for Certainty* (1929), vol. 4.
    *Art as Experience* (1934), vol. 10.
    *Logic: The Theory of Inquiry* (1938), vol. 12.
Derrida, Jacques. *Writing and Difference*. Translated by Alan Bass. Chicago: University of Chicago Press, 1978.
Greenberg, Jay R., and Mitchell, Stephen A. *Object Relations in Psychoanalytic Theory*. Cambridge: Harvard University Press, 1983.
Lavine, Thelma Z. "The Interpretive Turn from Kant to Derrida: A Critique." In *History and Anti-History in Philosophy*, edited by T. Z. Lavine and V. Tejera. Nijhoff International Philosophy Series. Dordrecht: Kluwer Academic Publishers, 1989.

Marcel, Gabriel. *Tragic Wisdom and Beyond*. Evanston, Ill.: Northwestern University Press, 1973.

Ricoeur, Paul. *The Voluntary and the Involuntary*. Vol. 1, *Freedom and Nature* (1950). Evanston, Ill.: Northwestern University Press, 1966.

———. *The Voluntary and the Involuntary*. Vol. 2, *Finitude and Guilt: The Symbolism of Evil* (1960). New York: Harper and Row, 1967.

———. *Fallible Man* (1960). Chicago: Regnery, 1965.

———. *Freud and Philosophy: An Essay on Interpretation*. 1960. New Haven: Yale University Press, 1970.

———. "The Task of Hermeneutics." *Philosophy Today* 17 (Summer 1973): 112–28. Reprinted in Thompson (1981).

———. *The Rule of Metaphor*. Translated by Robert Czerny et al. Toronto: University of Toronto Press, 1973.

———. *The Conflict of Interpretations*. Evanston, Ill.: Northwestern University Press, 1974a.

"Existence and Hermeneutics".

"Consciousness and the Unconscious".

———. "Ethnics and Culture: Habermas and Gadamer in Dialogue." In *Political and Social Essays*, edited by David Steward and Joseph Bien. Translated by David Pellauer. Athens: Ohio University Press, 1974b.

———. *Time and Narrative*. Translated by Kathleen McLaughlin and David Pellauer. Chicago: University of Chicago Press. Vol. 1, 1984, vol. 3, 1988.

———. "On Interpretation." In *After Philosophy*, edited by Kenneth Baynes, James Bohman, and Thomas McCarthy. Cambridge: MIT Press, 1987.

Schafer, Roy. *The Analytic Attitude*. New York: Basic Books, 1983.

Smith, Joseph H. "On Psychoanalysis and the Question of Nondefensive Religion." In *Psychoanalysis and Religion*, edited by Joseph H. Smith and Susan Handelman. Psychiatry and the Humanities, vol. 11. Baltimore: Johns Hopkins University Press, 1990.

Taylor, George H., ed. *Lectures on Ideology and Utopia*. New York: Columbia University Press, 1986.

Thompson, John B., ed. and trans. *Paul Ricoeur's Hermeneutics and the Human Sciences*. New York: Cambridge University Press, 1981.

White, Hayden. *The Content of the Form: Narrative Discourse and Historical Representation*. Baltimore: Johns Hopkins University Press, 1987.

# 12    Historiography as Narration

## *Hayden White*

Icontemplated approaching this topic by way of a narrative account. Almost reflexively, I outlined a "history" of the various discussions of "historiography as narration" that have taken place in Europe
and North America since the 1940s. In the anglophone world, the
terms of future discussion were laid down during World War II—by
Popper and Hempel in one way and by Collingwood in another. The
interchange between these two conventions would dominate philosophical discussions of the topic for nearly three decades. In France,
the critique of "narrative history" launched by the Annales group was
carried forward by Braudel in the 1950s, largely in the interest of
uniting historical studies with the social sciences, especially ethnog-
raphy and demography, but also geography and what might be called
the history of "environments," rather than that of human agents and
political institutions. This critique of narrative history was balanced
by a defense of narrative as a kind of explanation, different from though
not inconsistent with the "nomological-deductive" explanatory mode
of the physical sciences, elaborated in different ways by Walsh, Don-
agon, Dray, Gallie, Mink, Danto, Morton White, and Maurice Mandel-
baum in roughly the same period. In the 1960s, Structuralism, no
longer only a movement within linguistics and anthropology, was now
represented as *the* method of the human sciences, characterized by
its disdain for the "historical method" and its analytical approach to
the study of "narrative" representations of reality. Structuralism constituted a threat to history-in-general as much as to "historiography
as narration." But this threat was countered by hermeneutics, revived
in Germany by Gadamer especially, which took "historical conscious-

ness" as one of its bases and "narrativity" as a privileged representational strategy conducing to the "understanding" of human events that could not be "explained" by scientific procedures. At the same time, within literary and linguistic studies a new field of inquiry called "narratology" immensely complicated discussions of "narrative" by submitting it to microanalysis in all its forms, from the humble folk tale and fable all the way up to the most complex of Post-Modernist novels. Structuralist and Post-Structuralist criticism, represented by Barthes, Genette, Greimas, Althusser, Eco, Derrida, Kristeva (see Appendix), and a host of others, soon would bring the very notion of "narrativity" under question, especially insofar as it had been considered an ideologically "innocent" representational strategy or tactic. Not only "historiography as narration," but also "narration" in general, was indicted as the principal instrument of a "realist" ideology, indeed as ideology *tout court*.

It was tempting, therefore, to think of this congeries of discourses, all concerned in one way or another with "historiography as narration," as moments of a sequence that could be conceived or at least represented as phases in a single story, a single history. The sequence could have been conceptualized as a dialectical process through which a single subject, namely, the topic of "historiography as narration," had passed on the way to a clarification (or, to use Hegelian terminology, an "actualization") of the elements of its "concept" (*Begriff*). The relative value of the contributions of the several discourses to this process of clarification could then be assayed. And *we* would then be permitted to regard ourselves as the legatees of the positive aspects of this *agon*. We could think of ourselves as capable of determining (as Croce would have said) "what was living and what was dead" in recent notions of "historiography as narration." For after all, narratives deal in births and deaths, arrivals and departures, and promotions and demotions of the various characters that inhabit the scene of their attention.

But a "narrative account" of the many discussions of "historiography as narration" launched during his period would have been open to charges of distortion, reductionism, and inattention (*disattenzione*, as Moravia might have said) to the diversity of interests and variety of disciplinary concerns that had motivated them. The topic had been addressed by historians, social scientists, philosophers, and theorists of literature and language—from perspectives so different that one could legitimately question whether the phrase "historiography as narration" could be said to designate a single topic common to them all. "Historiography as narration" had been viewed by some as a model of humanistic discourse, alone capable of depicting the variety, vivacity, particularity, and indeterminacy of specifically *human* actions. The "historical method" had been characterized as a *mode* of inquiry especially well suited to guard against the misrepresentation of social processes to which "ideology" and "philosophy of history" (in its totalitarian forms) were especially prone. For some theorists, ideology *was* philosophy of history elaborated as the basis for a politics inevitably totalitarian in nature, while "historiography as narration" was the antidote for this disease. At the same time, "historiography as narration" had been seen as a paradigm of retrograde practices in the human sciences, as a residue of "mythical" thinking in the social sciences, and as an impediment to the creation of a genuinely scientific method of historical analysis itself. Finally, "historiography as narration" had been attacked as the very type of ideological discourse that traded in putatively "realistic" representations of reality while inevitably identifying "reality" with the social status quo.

Obviously, one could have adopted the broad perspective of the cultural historian and made of this cacophony of voices, discourses, arguments, hypotheses, charges, countercharges, and celebrations a symphony of "moments" in a much more general cultural process, aspects of that "crisis of representation" in Western culture of which Post-Impressionist art, Post-Modernist literature, and Post-Newtonian science were all thought to be manifestations. For historiography is— or has been traditionally thought to be—a quintessentially *representational* enterprise, of which narration was the principal *discursive* instrumentality. As Auerbach indicated in his classic account of Western culture's millenial effort to "represent reality realistically," the fate of representation conceived as *mimesis* was intimately linked to, if not identifiable with, the attainment of a specifically "historical consciousness" and a specifically "historical" manner of representing *social* reality, whether in "factual" or in "fictional" prose.

But to have subsumed the story of recent discussions of "historiography as narration" to this more general crisis of representation could have been to suggest that the crucial issue in these debates was historical consciousness, an interest in history, or the possibility of historical knowledge. And this was not the case at all—at least, as I see it now, with the benefit, as it is said, of "historical perspective." On the contrary, it was not "historiography" that was being questioned in these discussions, but rather the *narrative mode* of historiographical representation. Not even Lévi-Strauss, Barthes, Foucault, Derrida, or Kristeva suggested that a knowledge of history (the past, historical processes, events, structures, and so on) was unnecessary, undesirable, or impossible. The point at issue was whether that knowledge was most profitably represented in the form of a narrative discourse.

To be sure, there was substantial disagreement over how the object of study designated by the term "history" should be construed, the "method" that was to be used in the study of it, the kind of "explanation" such study might possibly yield, and the uses to which this kind of explanation might be put in social planning, political theory, educational policy, and so on. But these were issues that could be discussed without having to take a position one way or another on the question of whether historical knowledge was best *conveyed* in a narrative mode of discourse or not. For as Lévi-Strauss himself suggested, insofar as a historical narrative could be conceived as simply a chronologically (or diachronically) organized discourse, there was nothing problematical or intrinsically objectionable about it. Such an organization of the data gathered in any field of inquiry was a necessary moment or stage in their subjection to a properly scientific analysis, which consisted of bringing to light the structural coherency that these data could be shown to display. And in fact most contemporary historians—especially those working in the fields of social and economic history, but also cultural historians and even political historians—were concerned to do just that.

This is why many historians took so little interest in philosophers' discussions of "narrative explanations" and took umbrage at social scientists' identification of "historical studies" with "narrative history." Only a minority of professional historians regarded historiography as a predominantly "literary" art concerned primarily with the composition of a "story"—although, at the same time, many professional historians resisted the wholesale importation of the methodologies of the "behavioral sciences" into historical studies on grounds of their inutility to the analysis of the kinds of "evidence" that historians had to deal with. For most historians, narrative was a representational mode that they could use or not, depending upon whether they wished to provide a *description* of a form of life, an *analysis* of it, or a *story* about it. Historians thought of themselves as interested especially in the study of processes of change, transformation, variations over the course of time in their objects of study, and so on; but this interest did not necessarily commit them to the kind of "storytelling" that had characterized what the lore of the profession held to be the main line of nineteenth-century historiographical practices—and certainly not to the "dramatic" accounts of social processes that the proponents of "analytical" or "structuralist" social sciences accused them of dealing in.

Braudel's own criticism of "narrative history" was connected with his interest in shifting attention from the study of *political* events and processes alone to the study of larger-scale, relatively *impersonal* processes that, in his view, constituted a different order of causality and correlation than that prevailing on the relatively superficial level of quotidian political maneuverings among nations, states, regions, and prominent political figures studied by traditional historians. "Narrative" accounts of processes and conflicts on the political level could be viewed as legitimate and even necessary because, on this level of analysis, the "data" did not yield to the techniques of statistical correlation in the way that the "series" of the "longue durée" seemed to do. And indeed, as Raymond Aron suggested in his summary of a conference held at Venice in 1971, perhaps a kind of historiography that was *only* narrativistic in its mode of representing events was both necessary and desirable for pointing attention to certain areas of human experience *not yet* brought under the control of scientific techniques of analysis—of which the area of political experience was surely one.

In any case, the question of the best way to study "history" could be distinguished from the question of representing historical processes in a narrative mode of discourse. Moreover, this question could be separated as well from the question of whether such processes were "explained" or not by the telling of a "story" about them. In other words, three problems were being discussed under the rubric of "historiography as narrative": the problem of how to study the past and its processes; the problem of the discursive mode in which to speak about historical processes; and the problem of the explanatory force of representations of historical processes as "stories."

It was the third of these problems that was being addressed by philosophers, social scientists, and historians concerned to reform historical studies in a more scientific direction. Everyone could agree that a variety of methods might be used in the study of the past and its processes. Lines might be drawn at the point at which methodology became identifiable as ideology, but within the lines thus drawn, eclecticism was not only tolerated but also recommended. But there was a general tendency to confuse the second problem (that of the discursive mode in which to speak about historical processes) and the third problem (that of the explanatory force of representations of historical processes as "stories"), and to conclude that one had resolved the latter when one had resolved the former, or vice versa.

This confusion, I think, resulted from an ambiguity in the notion of "narrative," which indicates both a manner of speaking or address and a structure of a discourse. In this respect, the term "narrative" is not unlike the term "history," which may indicate both an *account* of an object (the past, its processes, and component events, and so on) and the *object* itself. But as contemporary narratological theory *seems* to demonstrate, it is virtually impossible to avoid the narrative manner of speaking, on at least some level of discourse, when one wishes to designate a potential object of study as belonging to "the past" rather than to "a present." Considered as a manner of speaking or mode of address, narrative is distinguishable from other modes of discourse by identifiable lexical, grammatical, and rhetorical features. It is characterized by a favoring of the third (rather than the first) person, various forms of the past tense (rather than the present or future), the indicative (rather than the imperative, interrogative, or optative) mode, and the avoidance of certain kinds of deictics or adverbial indicators featured prominently in direct discursive address (such as "here," "now," "yesterday," "tomorrow," and so on). Not even Braudel could dispense with a narrative *manner of speaking*, for it is unavoidable in any discourse wishing to speak *impersonally*, about *past* events, considered as objects of (possible) perception with discernible patterns of *development*. Classical rhetoric distinguished among a number of such modes of discursive address, of which the narrative was only one—the dissertative, the dialogistic, the lyric, the deliberative, and so on, being others.

Most historical accounts, even the most ancient, use a number of these modes of speaking and, in fact, are rather more "polyglossial" (the notion is Bakhtin's) than the phrase "historiography *as* narration" would suggest. The question at issue, then, is a spurious one if the topic indicated by the phrase "historiography as narration" is supposed to turn on the analysis of actual historical discourses cast in a *uniformly* "narrational" or "nonnarrational" manner of speaking. For no such thing exists or could ever exist—and still be considered a "historical" discourse.

A specifically "historical" discourse must contain narrational elements simply in order to *indicate* its object of study as belonging to the past rather than to some putative present and to *designate* features of the object that make it apprehensible as an element of a discernible *process*. It is only if the process of which the object is construed to be an element is *then* represented as displaying the kind of formal coherency met with otherwise *only* in the plot structures of recognizable story forms (or genres) that the question of the *epistemic* status of "historiography *as* narration" can arise.

Sets of events originally ordered only as a sequence are given a secondary meaning by their redescription as elements and functions of recognizable story types. This redescription is usually what is meant by the "narrativization" of the events (or facts) registered in the "chronicle," whence the distinction between historiography as *mere* chronicle, on the one side, and historiography as narrative, on the other. But the distinction is spurious insofar as it suggests that the "story" extracted from the chronicle and "told" in the narrative is more adequate to the veracious representation of the "events" registered in the chronicle than is the chronicle itself.

In fact, it is the chronicle, considered as a sequence of singular existential statements (predications), that can alone be submitted to the test of a correspondence criterion of truthfulness. Historical stories, the products of "narrativizations," cannot be said to correspond to anything other than the generic story types of which they are instantiations. Historical stories necessarily deviate from both the order and the contents of the literal descriptions of events given in the chronicle. The process of deviation itself is governed by procedures more "tropical" than "logical" in kind. By tropological encoding, the "facts" registered in the chronicle are given a secondary, figurative meaning. This meaning is more in the nature of an allegory than an explanation. As thus envisaged, the meaning that is supposed to be provided by the telling of the "true" *story* that lies embedded in the "facts" registered in the chronicle may no doubt consist in part in the truth that is claimed for the account, but it also consists of the claim that the events described possess the *form* of a story. The story told is an allegory of how real events can be said to replicate the structural patterns of generic story types: fable, epic, romance, tragedy, comedy, farce, etc.

Viewed from this perspective, Marx's apothegm about certain kinds of historical events occurring "as it were, twice, the first time as tragedy, the second time as farce," can be amended to say: any sequence of events can be *allegorized* as *either* tragedy *or* farce without threatening the accuracy with which the "facts" are represented in the story actually told in one way more than the other. In fact, there would be no impulse to distinguish a putatively "real" (or "true") story from the chronicle account if there were not at least *two* ways of plausibly emplotting the facts as stories of different kinds. On the level of historical interpretation represented by the narrativization, it is not a question of "truthful" *versus* "false" accounts, but rather which of a number of possible emplotments of the "facts" is to be deemed "appropriate" to their representation as a "story." And this depends, in turn, upon the perspective (what used to be called the "mode") adopted by the narrator vis-à-vis the events represented, particularly the *moral* perspective from which they are viewed (as superior, inferior, or on the same plane, as Aristotle said). Historical stories are *always* moral allegories, even if the morality reflected therein is the amorality of the merely ironic observer of a "human comedy."

This allegorical aspect of historical storytelling is often lost sight of by those who would defend "narrative history"—for a number of reasons. Since allegorization is conventionally thought of as a technique for producing a distinctively mystical (or anagogical) meaning, the historian's commitment to factual truth would make of him the natural enemy of the allegorist and suspicious of the figurative techniques used to produce allegories. Historical accounts are considered defective in the extent to which they depart from literalness of statement and indulge in the kind of figurations that poets and rhetoricians practice as a matter of course. The "real" story is opposed to a "fictitious" or "mythical" story as an account (of anything whatsoever) intended to be taken literally is opposed to an account intended to be taken allegorically. But this opposition obscures the fact that a factual story can be apprehended *as a story* only to the extent that it can be read as an allegory of the processes involved in the endowment of "imaginary" events with the coherency of fictional plot types.

This notion is recognized by historians and theorists who condemn "philosophies of history" (such as those of Hegel, Marx, Comte, etc.) that pretend to have *discovered* the "plot" of world history when in reality, the critic has it, the philosophers of history have *invented* this plot and *imposed* it on the motley of events that the world chronicle displays to view. And indeed, the defense of "narrative history" is often launched on the grounds that rather than imposing a plot on the events, it merely tells the story of "what happened," thereby saving the human agents of the events from a determinism that is merely authorial in nature. In reality, philosophies of history may well be, as critics of them maintain, "conceptually overdetermined" and inattentive to concrete, factual detail, and they are all *allegorical* to the extent that they tell their stories in such a way as to produce a figurative meaning for what is supposed to be a literal account of "what is really happening" in world history. But this does not distinguish them from those histories or aspects of histories cast in the story form of representation. For a story is not recognizable as such unless it be emplotted; the notion of a plotless story is an anomaly. It is only that in the philosophy of history the plot is given more prominence than the chronicle of which it is a narrativization.

Much of what many historians perceive as the irrelevance of recent

philosophers' attempts to identify the "logic" of "historical explanations" cast in the form of "stories" derives from a failure to apprehend
the difference between constructing a story and compiling a chronicle.
As a result, in their efforts to identify the criteria by which to assess
the truth claims and coherency of historical stories, philosophers have
often provided analyses of the logical structures and relationships
between statements and referents that are characteristic only of chronicles, and not of stories at all. As one philosopher who has contributed
much to the discussion of narrative histories, Louis O. Mink, puts it:

> One can regard any text in direct discourse as a logical conjunction of
> assertions. The truth-value of the text is then simply a logical function
> of the truth or falsity of the individual assertions taken separately: the
> conjunction is true if and only if each of the propositions is true. Nar-
> rative has in fact been analyzed, especially by philosophers intent on
> comparing the form of the narrative with the form of theories, as if it
> were nothing but a logical-conjunction of past-referring statements; and
> on such an analysis there is no problem of *narrative truth*. The difficulty
> with the model of logical conjunction, however, is that it is not a model
> of narrative at all. It is rather a model of a chronicle. Logical conjunction
> serves well enough as a representation of the only ordering relation of
> chronicles, which is ". . . and then . . . and then . . . and then . . . and then
> . . ." Narratives, however, contain indefinitely many ordering relations,
> and indefinitely many ways of *combining* these relations. It is such a
> combination that we mean when we speak of the coherence of a nar-
> rative, or lack of it. It is an unsolved task of literary theory to classify
> the ordering relations of narrative form; but whatever the classification,
> it should be clear that a historical narrative claims truth not merely for
> each of its individual statements taken distributively, but for the complex
> form of the narrative itself. [Mink 1987, 197–98]

There may or may not be a "logic" of storytelling; but there are
certainly "formulas" of storytelling, which are classifiable as the poetic
or rhetorical tropes, figures, and commonplaces, generic codes, and
narrative modalities used in the composition of any fiction. And while
it may be possible to contrive a model of the logic informing any
given arrangement of such formulas in a specific narrative, narratives
gain their effects as "interesting" stories as much by the violation of
normal readerly expectations regarding how these formulas ought to
be used as they gain an effect of being "plausible" stories by fulfilling
these expectations. The historical "story" gains in plausibility as much
by its "bending" of the chronicle to the exigencies of generic emplotment as it does by the veracity of its statements of fact, on the
one side, and the logical consistency of whatever formal arguments it

may offer in its nonnarrative, more purely dissertative passages, on the other.

Mink's observations point to the difficulties inherent in any analysis of the historical "story" based solely on a *communication model* of discourse. This model directs attention to the "story" in its aspects as a *message* about an extrinsic *referent* (the events) transmitted by an *addresser* (the historian) to an *addressee* (the reader). From this perspective, the "story" told is to be regarded as the *form* of the message, as against the *contents* thereof (conceived as "information" on the one side, and as "explanations" on the other). But such an approach will inevitably tend to ignore or dismiss as irrelevant the *performative* aspects of storytelling, the manipulation by the narrator of the narrative *codes* by which to endow sets of events with the attributes of story elements and plot functions. This performative aspect of storytelling is often regarded, quite correctly, as rhetoric, but rhetoric understood as mere ornament rather than as a technique of structuration that produces a "content" of the discourse quite other than the "facts" reported in the chronicle and the "explanations" offered in whatever arguments are set forth in dissertation. The story told, or rather constructed by rhetorical figuration, is not merely a medium of a message, but part of the message itself—though, of course, in any narrative pretending to represent reality "realistically" it is necessary to mask the story's status *as* message. If historical processes are to be represented as displaying the kind of patterns that permit their representation in a "story" that is also to be considered as "truthful" or "real," the tropes and figures used in them must be made to appear to have a purely *descriptive* function, rather than the *translational* function they actually fulfill.

The translation alluded to is that between the facts registered in the chronicle and the generic plot structures available in any culture for endowing events with a meaning *other than* their status as elements of explanations, whether of the commonsensical or the scientific kind. As thus conceived, the "story" produced by the narrativization of the facts registered in the chronicle has two *referents*: the facts themselves, on the one side, and the generic plot structure chosen to serve as the model for encoding the facts as a story, on the other. In other words, the historical story splits the reader's attention and points it in two directions simultaneously: toward the facts, which it treats as a *manifest* referent, on the one side; and toward the generic plot structure, which serves as an "icon" of the structure of the facts and as a *latent* referent, on the other. This process of translation as thus conceived can be said to use all of the principal tropological transfers that classical rhetoric classified as metaphor, metonymy, synecdoche, and irony (or catachresis) and that Freud, in his discussions of the mechanisms of the "dreamwork" called "condensation, displacement, symbolization, and secondary revision." Such a process of translation was what Barthes had in mind in "The Discourse of History" when he characterized the historical narrative as a surreptitious substitution of signifieds (conceptual or ideational contents) for signifiers (the putative referents, the facts, of the discourse). This transfer has the effect of making the story told appear to be a *mimetic* reproduction of the events characterized as facts in the chronicle. But in reality whatever resemblance the story has to the facts contained in the chronicle is a function of the process of *symbolization* produced in the fusion of a generic plot structure with the facts of the chronicle. It is precisely such a fusion that is indicated by the term *allegorization*. And this is why it is more appropriate to consider historical stories less as explanations of the events of which they speak than as allegories cast in the *modes* of the story types of which they are instantiations in discourses.

Permit me to remind you that what I have been saying does not apply to the *whole* of any given historical discourse, but only to that aspect of it which I have called narrativization or storytelling. One could imagine a historical discourse that contained very little "storytelling" but consisted primarily of the levels of chronicle and dissertation (or formal argument) alone. Burckhardt's *Die Kultur der Renaissance*, Tocqueville's *La Démocratie en Amérique*, and Huizinga's "Waning of the Middle Ages" would be examples of such discourses. Whatever "stories" they contain appear *within* the structure of their texts and serve primarily as examples or illustrations of dissertative general principles, rather than as frameworks for the texts taken as wholes. Huizinga is supposed to have said that he did not provide a detailed account of Jeanne d'Arc in his great study of the religious sensibility of the late Middle Ages because his book could not afford the luxury of a heroine. There are stories aplenty in "The Waning of the Middle Ages," but they are more in the nature of anecdotes and illustrations of organizing concepts than of frameworks for the discourse as a whole. The narrational mode of address is used to designate the object of study and its various parts and to characterize the structure of the whole process of which the metaphor of the "autumnal hour" is a figurative indicator. But if Huizinga's account has a "plot," it is the nonplot of the *satura*; and if it has a "story," it is the nonstory of dessication and demise that only anticipates a story-emerging-and-forming-in-order-to-be-told at another time, the story of the Renaissance itself.

My remarks are intended only to address the question of historiography as storytelling. If they seem to suggest that, insofar as a historical discourse is cast *as a story*, it is indistinguishable from such literary "fictions" as epics, romances, novels, novellas, and so on, or even "myths," I must confess that this is the way I see the matter. The art of the great historical narrators, from Herodotus to Gibbon to Mommsen and beyond, is often praised as worthy of contemplation and even emulation long after their "data" have been augmented by modern research far beyond anything of which they were even aware and their "explanations" have been consigned to the status of prejudices of the age in which they wrote.

## Appendix: Illustrative Quotations

The following quotations might well have been inserted into my discourse at the appropriate places, as illustrations of the views I have attributed to the discussants of the problem of "historiography as narration." But in the gnomic form that quotation imposes on every utterance, what kind of authority could I have claimed for them? They are given in the alphabetical order of their authors' surnames.

ARON: How can one narrate the development of a single sector or a complete entity ... without a schema or theory for that sector or entity? ... Is the representation of a unilinear development *ipso facto* erroneous? ... Or should we remember that the aligning along a single thread of the successive states of a historical entity is not the same thing as an explanation and does not lead to scientific knowledge? [1973, 250]

BARTHES: Does the narration of past events, which, in our culture from the time of the Greeks onwards, has generally been subject to the sanction of historical "science," bound to the unending standard of the "real," and justified by the principles of "rational" exposition— does this form of narration really differ, in some specific trait, in some indubitably distinctive feature, from imaginary narration, as we find it in the epic, the novel, and the drama? ... As we can see, simply from looking at this structure and without having to invoke the substance of its content, historical discourse is in its essence a form of ideological elaboration, or to put it more precisely, an *imaginary* elaboration if we can take the imaginary to be the language through which the utterer of the discourse (a purely linguistic entity) "fills out" the place of the subject of the utterance (a psychological or ideological entity). ... In other words, in "objective" history, the "real" is never more than an unformulated signified, sheltering behind the apparently all-powerful referent. This situation characterizes what we might call the *realistic effect*. [1981, 17]

Claims concerning the "realism" of narrative are therefore to be discounted.... The function of narrative is not to "represent," it is to constitute a spectacle.... Narrative does not show, does not imitate. [1977, 124]

BRAUDEL: The narrative history so dear to the heart of Ranke offer[s] us [a] gleam but no illumination; facts but no humanity. Note that this narrative history always claims to relate "things just as they really happened." ... In fact, though, in its own covert way, narrative history consists of an interpretation, an authentic philosophy of history. To the narrative historians, the life of men is dominated by dramatic accidents, by the actions of those exceptional beings who occasionally emerge, and who often are the masters of their own fate and even more of ours. And when they speak of "general history," what they are really speaking of is the intercrossing of such exceptional destinies, for obviously each hero must be matched against another. A delusive fallacy, as we all know. [1980, 11]

CROCE: *La storia narra.* [1951, 19]

ELTON: Historical works belong to one of three categories: description, analysis, and narrative.... Narrative tells the story, and it is not material how long the time span may be.... Description and narrative ... have two guises, one of them is higher than the other. Their lower forms are antiquarianism and chronicle: their higher the meaningful description of the past ... and narrative history properly so-called. [1967, 119]

FOUCAULT: The more [history] accepts its relativity, and the more deeply it sinks into the movement it shares with what it is recounting, then the more it tends to the slenderness of the narrative, and all the positive content it obtained for itself through the human sciences is dissipated. [1970, 371]

GADAMER: Yet, the true intuition of historical knowledge is not to explain a concrete phenomenon as a particular case of a general rule.... [I]ts true goal ... is to understand an historical phenomenon in its singularity, in its uniqueness. [1970, 116]

GAY: Truth and rhetoric are bad bedfellows. . . . Historical narration without analysis is trivial, historical analysis without narration is incomplete. [1974, 189]

KRISTEVA: In the narrative, the speaking subject constitutes itself as the subject of a family, a clan, or state group; it has been shown that the syntactically normative sentence develops within the context of prosaic and, later, historic narration. The simultaneous appearance of *narrative* genre and *sentence* limits the signifying process to an attitude of request and communication. On the other hand, since poetry works on the bar between signifier and signified and tends to erase it, it would be an anarchic outcry against the thetic and socializing position of syntactic language. [1980, 174]

LE GOFF: Ethnology leads to a sweeping rejection of the event, and thus to the ideal of a non-narrative history. [1973, 206–7]
    The Annales school loathed the trio formed by political history, narrative history, and chronicle or episodic (*evenementielle*) history. All this, for them, was mere pseudo-history, history on the cheap, a superficial affair which preferred the shadow to the substance. [1972, 340]

LÉVI-STRAUSS: We need only recognize that history is a method with no distinct object corresponding to it to reject the equivalence between the notion of history and the notion of humanity. . . . In fact, history is tied neither to man nor to any particular object. It consists wholly in its method. . . . The progress of knowledge and the creation of new sciences take place through the generation of anti-histories which show that a certain order which is possible only on one (chronological) plane ceases to be so on another. [1962, 261–62]

MUNZ: It must be clear by now that there is no absolute distinction between myth, fiction, and history and that all stories be they mythical, fictional, or historical can be assessed by looking at other stories. They cannot be assessed—and this is as true of history as of fiction—by looking at reality or res gestae. [1977, 220–21]

POPPER: I wish to defend the view, so often attacked as old-fashioned by historicists, that *history* is characterized by its interest in actual, singular, or specific events, rather than in laws or generalizations. . . . In the sense of this analysis, *all* causal explanation of a singular event can be said to be historical insofar as the "cause" is always described by singular initial conditions. And this agrees entirely with the popular idea that to explain a thing causally is to explain how and why it happened, that is to say, to tell its "story." [1961, 143–44]

RICOEUR: My first working hypothesis is that narrativity and temporality are closely related—as closely as, in Wittgenstein's terms, a language game and a form of life. Indeed, I take temporality to be that structure of existence that reaches language in narrativity and narrativity to be the language structure that has temporality as its ultimate referent. Their relationship is therefore reciprocal. [1981, 165]

## References

Aron, Raymond. "Postface." In *The Historian between the Ethnologist and the Futurologist*, edited by Jerome Dumoulin and Dominique Moisi. Paris: Mouton, 1973.

Barthes, Roland. "Introduction to the Structural Analysis of Narratives." In *Image, Music, Text*, translated by Stephen Heath. New York: Hill and Wang, 1977.

———. "The Discourse of History." Translated by Stephen Bann. In *Comparative Criticism: A Yearbook*, vol. 3, edited by Elinor Schaeffer. 1981.

Braudel, Fernand. "The Situation of History in 1950." In *On History*, translated by Sarah Matthews. Chicago: University of Chicago Press, 1980.

Croce, Benedetto. "La storia ridotta sotto il conetto generale dell'arte." In *Primi saggi*. Bari: Laterza, 1951.

Elton, Geoffrey. *The Practice of History*. New York: Thomas Y. Crowell, 1967.

Foucault, Michel. *The Order of Things: An Archeology of the Human Sciences*. New York: Pantheon Books, 1970.

Gadamer, Hans-Georg. "The Problem of Historical Consciousness." In *Interpretive Social Science: A Reader*, edited by Paul Rabinow and William M. Sullivan. Berkeley: University of California Press, 1970.

Gay, Peter. *Style in History*. New York: Basic Books, 1974.

Kristeva, Julia. "The Novel as Polylogue." In *Desire in Language*, edited by Leon S. Roudiez. Translated by Thomas Gora, Alice Jardine, and Leon S. Roudiez. New York: Columbia University Press, 1980.

Le Goff, Jacques. "Is Politics Still the Backbone of History?" In *Historical Studies Today*, edited by Felix Gilbert and Stephen R. Graubard. New York: Norton, 1972.

———. "The Historian and the Common Man." In *The Historian between the Ethnologist and the Futurologist*, edited by Jerome Dumoulin and Dominique Moisi. Paris: Mouton, 1973.

Lévi-Strauss, Claude. *The Savage Mind*. London: Weidenfeld and Nicolson, 1962.

Mink, Louis O. "Narrative Form as a Cognitive Instrument." In *Historical Understanding*, edited by Brian Fay, Eugene O. Golob, and Richard T. Vann. Ithaca: Cornell University Press, 1987.

Munz, Peter. *The Shapes of Time: A New Look at the Philosophy of History.* Middletown, Conn.: Wesleyan University Press, 1977.

Popper, Karl R. *The Poverty of Historicism.* London: Routledge and Kegan Paul, 1961.

Ricoeur, Paul. "Narrative Time." In *On Narrative*, edited by W. J. T. Mitchell. Chicago: University of Chicago Press, 1981.

# Index

Abraham, Nicolas, 106, 108–13, 116, 121, 123, 123–24n.2, 124nn. 3, 7, 157n.4
Adler, Alfred, 157n.3, 203
Aesthetic, 125n.10
"The Aetiology of Hysteria" (Freud), 166, 167, 173, 174
Akchuran, Marat, 242
Allegory: defined, 93–94n.1; path as, 56–67; and relationship of psychoanalysis and history, 49–53; river as, 67–77; as structuring principle, 94n.2
America. *See* United States
"Analysis Terminable and Interminable" (Freud), 105, 154
*Anti-Semite and Jew* (Sartre), 207
Anzieu, Didier, 256, 260–61n.16
Arendt, Hannah, 205, 206
Aron, Raymond, 288, 295
Art: and sublimation, 134–38
*Aufschreibsysteme 1800/1900* (Kittler), 21
*Aus der Geschichte einer infantilen Neurose* (Freud). *See* "Wolf Man"
Austin, J. L., 84, 124n.4
*An Autobiographical Study* (Freud), 57–58
Autobiography: as psychoanalytical theory, 83–91
Ayer, A. J., 143

Barthes, Roland, 51, 75–76, 295–96
Baudelaire, Charles, 116–19, 123, 125nn. 9, 10

Beardslee, William, 216–17
*Bemerkungen über einen Fall von Zwangsneurose* (Freud). *See* "Rat Man"
Benjamin, Walter, 114, 115, 116–20, 125n.9
Benveniste, Emile, 51
Berger, Peter, 240
Berkhofer, Robert, 40
*Beyond the Pleasure Principle* (Freud), 57, 116, 119, 130
Biography: as narrative, 26–28, 66–67
*Black Skin, White Masks* (Fanon), 207, 208–9, 213
Blum, Harold, 150–51
Bonaparte, Marie, 255, 260n.13
Braudel, Fernand, 284, 288, 296
Breuer, Josef, 161, 164
Bricolage, 246
*The Broken Connection: On Death and the Continuity of Life* (Lifton), 119
Brooks, Peter, 21, 23, 38, 39, 147
Brown, John, 211
*Bruchstück einer Hysterie-Analyse* (Freud). *See* "Dora"
Brunswick, Ruth Mack, 106, 108, 111, 154

*Cahiers pour l'analyse*, 225
Cantona, Eric, 238
Carby, Hazel, 188, 195–96
Cardinal, Marie, 239
Caruth, Cathy, 123n.1
Case history: as literary genre, 21–25
Case reports: validity of, 145–47

301

Cause Freudienne. *See* Freudian Cause
Cercle d'Epistémologie de l'Ecole Nor-
   male Supérieure, 225
Charcot, Jean-Martin, 29, 43n.11, 173
Cohn, Dorrit, 66–67, 147
Cohn-Bendit, Daniel, 222
Coleridge, Samuel Taylor, 93n.1
*The Complete Letters of Sigmund Freud
   to Wilhelm Fliess, 1887–1904* (Freud).
   *See* Fliess, Wilhelm: Freud's letters to
*The Conflict of Interpretations* (Ri-
   coeur), 265
Consciousness: Freud's concept of, 119–
   20; and perception, 61–65, 96–97n.17
"Constructions in Analysis" (Freud), 52,
   80, 81, 82–83, 85–87, 89–91, 97n.17,
   108, 117, 120–21
"Contributions to the Psychology of Love"
   (Freud), 31
Croce, Benedetto, 296
"Cross" (Hughes), 185
*Cryptonomie: Le Verbier de l'homme aux
   loups* (Abraham and Torok), 106, 108–
   13, 116, 121, 123, 123–24n.2, 124nn.
   3, 7
Cuddihy, John M., 204
Culler, Jonathan, 44n.20, 95n.10, 124n.4,
   147

Danger: Freud's concept of, 130–31
Dearborn, Mary, 197
de Certeau, Michel, 21, 29
Deconstruction. *See* Psychoanalytic deconstruction
Defenses: Freud's concept of, 164–65; as
   interpreted in psychoanalytic dialogue,
   11–12, 13–14
Delusions: as element of Freudian theory,
   80–81, 83, 84, 85, 120–21
de Man, Paul, 93–94n.1, 96n.16, 114–15,
   124n.6
Denial, 92, 98n.29
Depression. *See* Melancholia
Depressive: as compared with artist, 135–
   36
Derrida, Jacques, 42n.1, 113, 122–23, 123–
   24n.2, 124n.4, 281n.5
Dewey, John, 264–65
*Die Philosophie des Als Ob* (Vaihinger),
   23, 42n.2

Difference: as signaled by lack, 128–29
Dilthey, Wilhelm, 265
Disavowal: Freud's concept of, 86–87, 91–
   92, 98n.26, 103–4, 107, 121; and sex-
   ual difference, 87–88
Doctorow, E. L., 24
Dolto, Françoise, 237
"Dora" ("Fragment of an Analysis of a Case
   of Hysteria" [Freud]), 21, 24, 31, 36, 37,
   43–44n.17, 52, 147, 148; narrative
   process in, 53–67; river metaphor in,
   68–77
Dorgeuille, Claude, 258n.1
Douglas, Mary, 259–60n.10
Douglass, Frederick, 211
Dreams: Freud's interpretation of, 53–54,
   57–58, 61, 63–64, 68
Du Bois, W. E. B., 184, 199n.2
"The Dynamics of the Transference"
   (Freud), 114

Eckstein, Emma, 163
Ecole de la Cause Freudienne. *See* School
   of the Freudian Cause
Ecole Freudienne de Paris. *See* Freudian
   School
Ego, 124n.3; splitting of, 103–8
Eissler, Kurt, 149–50
Elkins, Stanley, 213
Elton, Geoffrey, 296
Empiricism, 143–44
England. *See* Great Britain
Erikson, Erik, 204, 213, 216, 248
"Existence and Hermeneutics" (Ricoeur),
   267
Existentialism: appeal of, 251

Faladé, Solange, 227
Fanon, Frantz, 201; and therapeutic effects
   of violence, 207–16
Feminism: Freud's contribution to, 16–17
Fenichel, Otto, 202
Ferenczi, Sandor, 181n.8
Fetishism: Freud's concept of, 86, 108
Fiction: Freud's case histories as, 21–25,
   28–38, 67; meanings of, 22–25, 42n.2;
   as nonreferential narrative, 25–26, 42nn.
   6, 7. *See also* Narrative; *Quicksand* (Lar-
   sen)

"Fictions of the Wolf Man" (Brooks), 21, 23–24, 38
Fineman, Joel, 94n.2
*Finitude and Guilt: The Symbolism of Evil* (Ricoeur), 278
Fish, Stanley, 42n.6, 146, 148–49, 221
Fliess, Wilhelm: Freud's letters to, 48, 50, 95n.13, 161, 164, 165, 167, 171, 172, 181n.2
Forrester, John, 222
Foucault, Michel, 296
Foundation of the Freudian Field, 232
"Fragment of an Analysis of a Case of Hysteria" (Freud). *See* "Dora"
France: psychoanalytic culture in, 220–25, 238–40, 248–50, 254. *See also* Lacan, Jacques
"Fräulein Elisabeth von R." (Freud's case history), 28–29, 35–36, 72
Free association, 11, 113–14
Freud, Anna, 97–98n.26, 161, 175, 181n.2, 255
Freud, Mathilde, 176, 181n.6
Freud, Sigmund: case histories considered as fiction, 21–25, 28–38, 67; case histories as act of narration, 53–67, 148–49; contribution of to clinical dialogue, 11–14; concept of danger of, 130–31; concept of defense of, 164–65; concept of delusion of, 80–81, 83, 84, 85, 120–21; concept of disavowal of, 86–87, 91–92, 98n.26, 103-4, 107, 121; discursive context of, 2–6; contribution of to feminism, 16–17; concept of fetishism of, 86, 108; figurative language of, 51, 94n.5; historical truth and, 77–83; historicity of case histories of, 38–41; enactment of history in, 49–53; legacies of, 6–10, 17–19; theory of memory of, 48, 113–14; 122–23, 125n.10, 141–43; as a novelist, 21–22, 44n.17; path metaphor in, 56–67; personality of, 260n.16; and politics, 201–3; and concept of psychic reality, 15–16; concept of repression of, 55, 66, 68, 72–73, 79, 86; rhetoric of, 6, 148–49; Ricoeur's interpretation of, 269–81; river metaphor in, 67–77; seduction theories of, 160–81; and splitting of the ego, 103–8; and concept of transference, 111–14; trauma theory of,

70–71, 78–79, 103–5, 161–62; varying approaches to, 7–10. *See also* "Wolf Man"
"Freud and Dora" (Marcus), 21
*Freud and Philosophy* (Ricoeur), 264, 269–81, 281n.4
Freudian Cause, 229–31, 258–59n.1
"The Freudian Novel" (de Certeau), 21
Freudian School (Paris): leadership crisis of, 225–38, 258–59n.1
Freudian slips, 243–46
Friedman, Lawrence, 211
"From the History of an Infantile Neurosis" (Freud). *See* "Wolf Man"
Frye, Northrop, xiii, 24, 50, 51, 94n.1
"Further Remarks on the Neuro-Psychoses of Defence" (Freud), 166
*The Future of an Illusion* (Freud), 42n.2

Gadamer, Hans-Georg, 284, 297
Gandhi, Mahatma, 215–16
Gardiner, Muriel, 149
Gay, Peter, 32, 297
Genette, Gérard, 95n.10
Girard, Philippe, 259n.5
Goethe, Johann Wolfgang von, 271
Great Britain: psychoanalytic movement in, 240–41
Grosskurth, Phyllis, 257, 260n.15
Grubrich-Simitis, Ilse, 79
Guys, Constantin, 117–18, 123

Hall, G. Stanley, 239
Hallucinations: as element of Freudian theory, 84, 85, 121
Harlem Renaissance, 184
*The Harlem Renaissance* (Huggins), 184
Hegel, Georg Wilhelm Friedrich, 125n.10, 271
Heidegger, Martin, 264, 266, 267, 268, 269, 279
Henninger, Peter, 32
"Heredity and the Aetiology of the Neuroses" (Freud), 166, 174
Herman, Judith L., 162
Hermeneutic conflict. *See* Ricoeur, Paul
Hertz, Neil, 36
Hillman, James, 142, 143–44
Historical truth: in psychoanalysis, 77–83
Historicity, 127–28

Historiography: as narration, 284–98
History: and psychoanalysis, ix–xiv, 49–53
Huggins, Nathan, 184
Hughes, Langston, 185
Huizinga, Johan, 294
Husserl, Edmund, 264, 265

Ibsen, Henrik, 25
Ideas: transmission of, 10–11
*Ideology and Utopia* (Mannheim), 279
Imaging, 127–30, 136–38. *See also* Art
Incest. *See* Seduction
Information processing: errors in, 243–46
International Psychoanalytic Association, 233, 237–38
*The Interpretation of Dreams* (Freud), 42nn. 1, 2, 45n.22, 53, 57–58, 61, 63–64, 68, 70
*Introductory Lectures on Psycho-Analysis* (Freud), 40–41
Israël, Lucien, 259n.5
Iterability, 113

Jacobsen, Paul, 143
Jacoby, Russell, 202, 260n.11
Janet, Pierre, 29
Jones, Ernest, 149, 157n.4, 161
Jung, Carl, 33, 157n.3, 203

Kant, Immanuel, 273
Kaye-Smith, Sheila, 197
King, Martin Luther, 215–16
Kittler, Friedrich, 21
Klein, Melanie, 257, 260nn. 15, 16
Kohut, Heinz, 146, 248; theory of narcissism of, 188–98
Kojeve, Alexandre, 207
Krafft-Ebing, Richard, 181n.1
Kris, Ernst, 161, 164, 175, 181n.2
Kristeva, Julia, 297
Kurzweil, Edith, 247

Lacan, Jacques, 107, 128, 189, 208; as an analyst, 255–56, 257–58; and dissolution of Freudian School, 225–38; impact of on psychoanalytic theory, 245–53; as leader of Lacanian movement, 222–24

Lacan, Judith. *See* Miller, Judith Lacan
*Lacan and Co.: A History of Psychoanalysis in France 1925–1985* (Roudinesco), 259n.1
LaCapra, Dominick, xiv
Langs, Robert, 145
Language: appropriation of, 252; changing perspectives on, 3–6
Laplanche, Jean, 107
Larsen, Nella, 184–98
Leclaire, Serge, 237, 259n.5
Left-Existentialism, 207–8
Le Goff, Jacques, 297
Lewis, John, 215
Lévi-Strauss, Claude, 246, 287, 297
Lévy, Danièle, 259nn. 5, 6
Libido: Freud's concept of, 73–75
Lifton, Robert Jay, 119, 204
Literature. *See* Fiction
Loewald, Hans, 141
Loewenstein, Rudolf, 255–56
Loss, 130–31, 138n.3

McDowell, Deborah, 186, 199n.1
Macey, David, 260n.12
MacIntyre, Alasdair, 205
Malcolm, Janet, 43–44n.17, 147, 148, 151
Mannheim, Karl, 279
Marcel, Gabriel, 268
Marcus, Steven, 21, 24–25, 29, 32, 42n.3
Marx, Karl, 290
Masson, Jeffrey, 162, 181n.2
Mathis, Paul, 238
Melancholia, 115–16
Melman, Charles, 226, 230–31
Memory, 157n.1; Freud's theory of, 48, 113–14, 122–23, 125n.10, 141–43
Mendel, Gérard, 259n.6
*Metahistory: The Historical Imagination in Nineteenth-Century Europe* (White), 50–51
Metaphor, 128, 136–37
Metonymy, 128, 136–37
M. G. *See* Guys, Constantin
Miller, Alice, 162
Miller, Jacques-Alain, 223; role of in dissolution of Freudian School, 225–38
Miller, Judith Lacan, 225, 232, 234
Mink, Louis O., 292, 293
*Mise en abyme*, 97n.24

Modernity, 265–66, 268, 271–72
*Moses and Monotheism* (Freud), 48–49, 82, 91, 105
Mourning: aspects of, 133–34, 138
*Mrs. Klein* (Wright), 257
Mulatto image: as literary device, 184–86
Munz, Peter, 297
*My Analyst and Me* (Augerolles), 239

Narcissism: Kohut's concept of, 188–98
Narration: historiography as, 284–98
Narrative: case histories as, 147–48; collective and individual, 203–6; "Dora" as, 53–56; Freud's case histories as, 42n.4, 44n.18; truth of, xii; types of, 25–28, 95n.10. *See also* Fiction; Freud, Sigmund: case histories as act of narration
"The Neuro-Psychoses of Defence" (Freud), 71, 164
*La Névrose infantile de la psychanalyse* (Pommier), 234
*A New Language for Psychoanalysis* (Schafer), 204
Nietzsche, Friedrich, 18, 271
"A Note upon the 'Mystic Writing Pad'" (Freud), 119
"Notes on an Alternative Model—Neither/Nor" (Spillers), 185
"Notes upon a Case of Obsessional Neurosis" (Freud). *See* "Rat Man"

Obholzer, Karin, 149, 151, 152
Oedipus complex, 50, 132–33; and seduction theory, 175–78
*The Old Regime and the French Revolution* (Tocqueville), 200–201
"On Some Motifs in Baudelaire" (Benjamin), 116–19
*On the History of the Psycho-Analytic Movement* (Freud), 173
"On the Sexual Theories of Children" (Freud), 87–88
*An Outline of Psycho-Analysis* (Freud), 104, 181n.4

Pankeiev, Sergei. *See* "Wolf Man"
*Passing* (Larsen), 186–87
Path: as metaphor in Freud, 56–67
Patterson, Orlando, 213

*"Le peintre de la vie moderne"* (Baudelaire), 118
Perception: and consciousness, 61–65, 96–97n.17. *See also* Disavowal
Phenomenology, 264–69
*Pocahontas's Daughters* (Dearborn), 197
Politics: and psychoanalysis, 200–217
"The Politics of Historical Interpretation: Discipline and De-Sublimation" (White), 211
Pommier, Gérard, 233–36, 259n.1
Pontalis, J.-B., 107
Popper, Karl, 297–98
Post-Structuralism, 285
Power: as factor in history of psychoanalysis, 7–9
"Project for a Scientific Psychology" (Freud), 166. 270
Proust, Marcel, 122
Psychic reality, 15–16, 142. *See also* Reality principle
Psychoanalysis: role of allegory in, 49–53; case reports in, 145–47; cultural appropriation of, 238–58; dialogic nature of, 4–5; diverse meanings of, 9–10; in France, 220–23; historical truth in, 77–83; and history, ix–xiv, 49–53; humanistic existentialist approach to, 1–2, 17; as interpretation, 142–45; language of, 3–6; Marxist view of, 249–50; and the myth of the well-analyzed analyst, 254–58; and politics, 200–217; Ricoeur's examination of, 269–81; tension between past and present in, 140–43. *See also* Freud, Sigmund; Psychoanalytic dialogue
Psychoanalysts: as distinguished from novelists, 30–31; licensing of, 236–38
Psychoanalytic culture, 221–25; in France, 238–40, 248–50, 254; in the United States, 240, 247–48, 254. *See also* Lacan, Jacques
Psychoanalytic deconstruction, 12–13
Psychoanalytic dialogue, 11–14, 144; multitude of voices involved in, 14–15; self-reflexive nature of, 16
Psychoanalytic language: rhetorical perspective on, 5–6
Psychoanalytic theory: appropriability of,

Psychoanalytic theory (*cont'd*)
221–24, 246–54. *See also* Freud, Sigmund; Lacan, Jacques
"The Psychoanalytic Vision of Reality" (Schafer), 1, 50–51
*Purity and Danger* (Douglas), 259–60n.10
*The Purloined Letter* (Poe), 227
*The Pursuit of Signs: Semiotics, Literature and Deconstruction* (Culler), 44n.20

*Quicksand* (Larsen), 184–98; psychoanalytic approach to, 186–98

Rank, Otto, 157n.4
"Rat Man" ("Notes upon a Case of Obsessional Neurosis" [Freud]), 21, 32–33, 42n.3, 44n.21
Rawls, John, 200
*Reading for the Plot* (Brooks), 21
Reality principle, 272–76, 277–78, 282n.9. *See also* Psychic reality
Reich, Wilhelm, 202, 204, 252
"Remembering, Repeating, and Working-Through" (Freud), 92, 113–14, 141
*Representations: Essays on Literature and Society* (Marcus), 21
Repression: Freud's concept of, 55, 66, 68, 72–73, 79, 86, 169
Revolution. *See* Politics
Richards, Barry, 240, 250, 252, 260
Ricoeur, Paul, 41, 42n.5, 134, 202, 298; and twentieth-century hermeneutic conflict, 264–69; study of Freud and psychoanalysis, 269–81, 281n.4, 282n.9
Rieff, Philip, 202, 203, 206, 239
River: as metaphor in Freud, 67–77
Rorty, Richard, 200, 203, 215, 217, 218n.2
Roudinesco, Elisabeth, 222, 259n.1, 260n.13
Roustang, François, 260n.14
Russell, Diana E. H., 162
Russia. *See* Soviet Union

"Sanctuary" (Larsen), 197–98
Sartre, Jean-Paul, 207, 213
Sato, Hiroko, 186
Schafer, Roy, xi–xiii, xiv, 35, 44n.18, 50–51, 94–95n.6, 127, 142, 144, 146, 147, 204–6, 214, 281n.6, 282n.9
Schimek, Jean G., 174

Schnitzler, Arthur, 30
School of the Freudian Cause, 231, 233–36, 258–59n.1
Schopenhauer, Arthur, 271
Schorske, Carl, 201
"Screen Memories" (Freud), 66, 71
Searle, John, 42nn. 6, 7
Searles, Harold, 145
*La Second Mort de Jacques Lacan* (Dorgeuille), 258n.1
Seduction: Freud's theories on, 160–81, 202
*Seductions on the Couch* (anonymous), 239
Self: Kohut's concept of, 189–90; as shown in Larsen novel, 192–98; transformation of, 201, 212–17
Sexual difference: Freud's theories on, 56, 87–89
Sédat, Jacques, 259n.5
Sharpe, R. A., 143
Sleep: and experience of loss, 132
Smith, Joseph, 206
"Some Psychical Consequences of the Anatomical Distinction between the Sexes" (Freud), 56, 88–89
*The Souls of Black Folk* (Du Bois), 199
Soviet Union: psychoanalysis in, 241–43, 253
Spence, Donald, 77–78, 81, 146–47
Spillers, Hortense, 185
Spinoza, Benedict de, 280–81
"The Splitting of the Ego in the Process of Defence" (Freud), 103–8
Steele, Robert, 143
*Strom. See* River
Structuralism, 284–85
Structure: current applications of, 4–5
*Studies on Hysteria* (Freud), 28–29, 164, 165
Sublimation: art and, 134–38
Sullivan, Harry Stack, 146
"A Supplement to Freud's 'History of Infantile Neurosis'" (Brunswick), 106

*Three Essays on the Theory of Sexuality* (Freud), 73–74, 172, 242
*Time and Narrative* (Ricoeur), 264, 279–80
Tocqueville, Alexis de, 201

Torok, Maria, 106, 108–13, 116, 121, 123, 123–24n.2, 124nn. 3, 7, 157n.4
*Totem and Taboo* (Freud), 49
Transference: as enactment of past experience, xiv, 141–43; of Wolf Man to Freud, 111–14, 154–56
Translation: analyst's task as, 114–17
Trauma: Freud's concept of, 70–71, 78–79, 92, 93, 103–5, 106, 116, 161, 162. *See also* Seduction
Trauma and defense: theory of, 164–65
*The Trial(s) of Psychoanalysis* (Meltzer), xiii
Truth. *See* Historical truth

*Umweg. See* Path
"The Unconscious" (Freud), 53–54, 96n.17, 110
Union of Soviet Socialist Republics. *See* Soviet Union
United Kingdom. *See* Great Britain
United States: psychoanalytic culture in, 240, 247–48, 254

Vaihinger, Hans, 22, 23, 42n.2
Vasse, Denis, 226–27, 236
Violence: therapeutic effects of, 207–16

Wall, Cheryl, 186–87
Washington, Mary Helen, 187–88
*Weg. See* Path
Weigert, Edith, 1
Wetzler, Scott, 157n.1
White, Hayden, xi, xii, xiv, 24, 49, 50–51, 78, 202, 211, 218n.4, 279
Winnicott, Donald, 153
Wish: image as, 128, 138n.1
Wittman, Blanche, 29
"Wolf Man" ("From the History of an Infantile Neurosis" [Freud]), 21, 23–24, 33, 36–41, 44n.21, 45n.22, 50, 106–16, 121, 124n.7; other analysts' views of, 149–56
*The Wolf Man's Magic Word: A Cryptonomy. See Cryptonomie: Le Verbier de l'homme aux loups* (Abraham and Torok)
Woolf, Virginia, 39
*The Words to Say It* (Cardinal), 239
*The Wretched of the Earth* (Fanon), 207, 210, 213, 214

Yerushalmi, Josef Hayim, 43n.14